The encyclopedia of GREEN WOODWORKING

Ray Tabor

eco-logic books

First Published in 2000
by eco-logic books

ISBN 1 899233 07 5

Illustrations	Ray Tabor
Design & Typesetting	HMD 0117 914 5536
Printing & Binding	Russell Press Ltd.

Further copies of this book can be purchased from:
eco-logic books
10-12 Picton Street, Bristol BS6 5QA, England
Telephone: 0117 942 0165
Fax: 0117 942 0164
email: books@eco-logic.demon.co.uk

Acknowledgements

Most of the detail described in this book has come from watching, listening to and talking with innumerable people over the last 25 years, all of whom either work green wood, or produce tools for those who do. Many are from my native East Anglia and Kent, for Kent is a county where woodlands still have meaning. It is not possible to acknowledge each contribution individually, but I must thank the following for advice and friendship so freely given: Simon Leatherdale on growing trees; Fred Hams and the late Cyril Mummery on coppicing, tools and the wisdom of Kent; Andrew Breese, Alec Morris and Bryony Driver for making superb tools I could no longer find anywhere; Noel Cullum, Suffolk rake and scythe stick maker; Sidney Lukehurst, Kent gate hurdle maker; the late Frank Bird, Suffolk hurdle and rake maker; the late Charles West, Dorset wattle hurdle maker; Malcolm Lee, traditional woodwright and expert bodger; Hugh Spencer on pole lathe design; Janet Spencer for introducing me to spoons; Jon Warnes on stick furniture; Will Wall on charcoal making.

Some of the research could not be done face to face: some crafts have ceased, their practitioners often passed on. This gap was largely filled by study in the archives and collections at the Institute of Agricultural History under Dr. T. Collins. Their help was invaluable.

My thanks go to the Essex Wildlife Trust in whose Shadwell Wood reserve I have worked for all my time as a woodman, and particularly to the volunteer workers Tony Morton, Mark Hinton, Sue Birnage and Richard Tabor who have helped so much in preparing products and looking for new markets for our wood.

Lastly thank you to my family who have endured another year of not going out much because Dad is working on his book. And a special thank you to my wife, Judith, for typing the manuscript and putting up with part-finished spoons in the fridge and shavings on the floor.

Ray Tabor
Hundon, West Suffolk, 2000

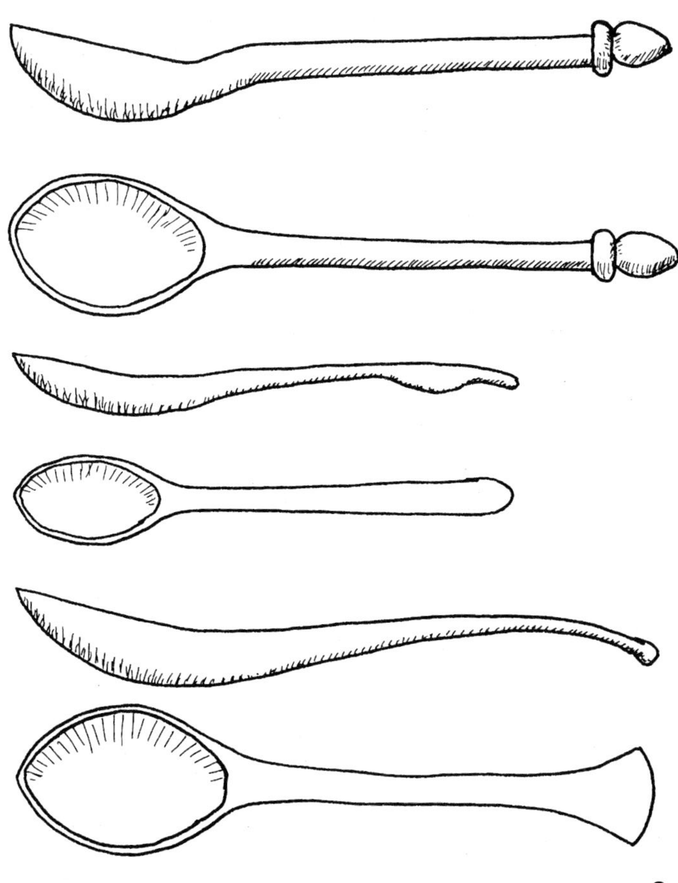

Contents

Preface

It is appropriate at the dawn of a new millennium to publish a new book on one of the oldest of all crafts – woodmanship. Man has been working green wood for over 5000 years, producing most of his everyday needs from tools to utensils, providing a roof over his head and warmth in his hearth. And wood itself is the most remarkable raw material on this planet. When properly managed it is infinitely renewable as testified by our ancient woodlands. Every tree species has some unique property of use to man – and who knows what still remains to be discovered about it.

This book is intended to start you on a journey of discovery. In it you will first explore the remarkable properties of wood and how it varies from species to species; then learn the millennia-old skills of woodmanship; next, understand how simple tools together with subtle devices help make elegant products; and finally discover the range of products, functional, durable and uniquely beautiful, that can be made from green wood. I hope that by the end of your journey through green woodworking you are as passionate about it as I am.

The interest in caring for our ancient woodlands and in green woodworking increases year by year. This is hardly surprising since working with wood requires a unique balance of mental challenge, aesthetic appreciation and steady physical work that result in great satisfaction for the worker. Thus it is not only those seeking a hobby sufficiently different from their day to day work who take it up, but also increasingly young craftsmen seeking a satisfying career. The importance of this is reflected in the National Vocational Qualifications (N.V.Q.) now being developed for the green wood trades, and which will confer a qualification on those able to demonstrate the appropriate skills.

Within the covers of this volume I have tried to outline the core skills of the green woodcrafts. Although basket making is included, this is for baskets derived from coppice wood and not the skills of the craftsmen in willow. The joy of green woodworking is in doing it, so this is a very practical book describing 'how'. It is a book for the coppice, workshop or wherever you do your woodwork. It gives sufficient detail to get you going. To become proficient join craft associations, go to demonstrations and talk to real craftsmen; this way and by reading the books recommended at the end of each chapter you will come to understand the subtleties that will make your products good. This book will enable newcomers to get started, it will widen the horizons of those that have already started, and it will provide some of the underpinning knowledge for those seeking a N.V.Q. qualification.

Some truths never change and this is the case in your approach to green woodwork: take it step by step, understand wood and then the tools before you start making products. Every piece of wood you work will be unique. Notice the grain and its individual properties and work with them or you will forever be a botcher (not a bodger!)

I have worked in one East Anglian woodland making a range of simple products for over 25 years. I have been lucky to meet and receive the advice of many craftsmen in that time. What I have written in this book is based on that advice; any errors are mine.

Finally, all who work green wood should remember they are the custodians of an ancient craft. With our help it will continue as long as our world remains habitable. I hope those who use this book will share my delight in seeing wood well worked.

Chapter 1

The Nature of Wood

What is wood?

Wood is the tough, lignified, fibrous substance between the pith and cambium of trees and shrubs. Its dense cellular structure provides the mechanical support that allows trees to grow to considerable heights. So say the dictionaries.

Table 1.1
The Specific Gravities (Densities) of Common Woods

Species	S.G	Species	S.G
Box	1.00	Cherry	0.70
Oak	0.80	Elm	0.65
Beech	0.80	Alder	0.64
Yew	0.80	Hazel	0.62
Maple	0.80	Chestnut	0.62
Holly	0.76	Sycamore	0.60
Hornbeam	0.75	Lime	0.52
Apple	0.75	Poplar	0.50
Birch	0.72	Willow	0.40
Ash	0.70	Aspen	0.34

This is the stuff of green woodworking. Wood is an incredible material that is both easy to work and has wide-ranging properties that make it useful throughout every facet of our daily lives. Over 5000 timbers have been identified worldwide, although only about 300 are in common use. In England we have about 50 indigenous broadleaved woods, and most of these are discussed in chapter two. The most common are listed in **Table 1.1**.
In this chapter we shall explore the nature of wood so that you can understand better how best to use it.

The chemical composition of wood: Wood in its living form is over 50 percent water, which is present in both the contents and the walls of the cells that provide the structure. The cell walls are rigid, mainly consisting of celluloses that are long chains of glucose. Cellulose is the principal structural material of all plants, and as such is the most abundant organic compound in our world. In older cells, particularly heartwood, other compounds are laid down in their walls. Two are particularly important to us. Firstly lignin, a complex polymer, whose function appears to be to cement the cellulose fibres and stiffen the cell wall. It reduces infection, rot and decay, whilst its inert nature is such that it has been identified in fossil remains. Secondly tannins, complex compounds containing phenols and glycosides that make the plant less palatable to browsing animals.

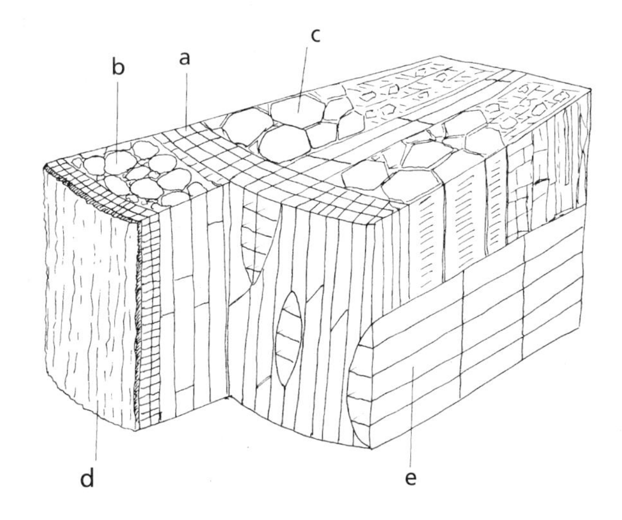

Fig 1.1
Segment of a tree trunk showing: a. cambium; b. phloem or bast; c. xylem; d. bark; e. wood rays.

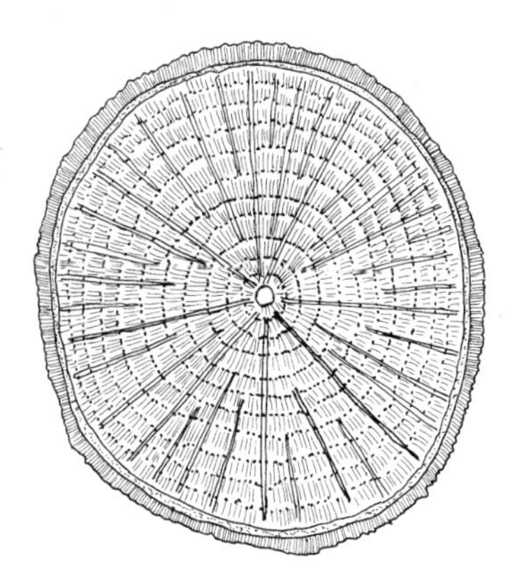

Fig. 1.2 Cross section of a tree trunk showing rays, annual rings and bark.

The structure and growth of wood

Structure: If you look at the cross-section of a typical tree stem (**figs. 1.1 and 1.2**), you will see that it is made up from a range of different types of cells, all of which have a particular, unique purpose.

The cambium is perhaps the most important group of cells, for this is the seat of growth. Cambium cells are small, soft, and divide rapidly during growth. They produce the water and sugar transporting cells of the tree, which results in its steadily increasing girth. Being very close under the bark, the cambium is easily damaged by impact, heat, or gnawing; any of these can result in the death of all or part of the stem. In deciduous trees the cambium grows fastest in the spring, which makes it very easy to remove the bark in large sheets

Between the cambium and bark is the bast or phloem. These cells are for transporting sugars and other materials within the plant. They are not thickened and hard, but can be very tough as in the bast of lime or hickory. The bark itself is the outermost layer of the tree. That which we see is mainly dead cells penetrated by corky layers that render it waterproof, and the smooth, scaly or fissured texture we recognise is determined by those layers, together with the phloem.

From its inner surface, the cambium layer produces the water conducting vessels of the tree, the xylem, and the wood fibres that provide strength. The walls of these cells are considerably thickened and they form the main strengthening tissue of the stem. Each spring, when growth is rapid, the vessels are large and often visible to the naked eye; in the summer they are smaller and the wood denser and darker. These areas are known as spring and summer wood; the latter is stronger, hence fast growing trees that have a higher proportion of summer wood produce stronger material. In deciduous trees the visible difference in the size of spring and summer wood vessels creates the annual rings that we see in the end grain and that measure the tree's annual growth. As most tropical trees of course grow continuously they have no annual rings. Very visible large pored wood (such as ash and oak) is often called 'ring porous'; that which is not (such as maple and cherry) is called 'diffuse porous'. As trees age it is into these vessels that oils, resins, tannins and other organic compounds are deposited, often creating a darker heartwood.

Travelling radially across the stem from pith to bark are a series of vertical sheets of cells – the medullary or wood rays. Secondary rays, produced later in life, do not reach all the way to the pith. These cells aid the transfer of sap and sugars within the stem, as well as adding cohesion to the whole. In many woods you will need a lens o see them; in others such as oak they are very visible. Wood sawn to follow these rays, often results in a beautiful figure such as 'silver grain'. Medullary rays also contribute to the impermeability of radial clefts from trees such as oak, hence the reason barrel staves and shingles are always made from such clefts. Rays are also lines along which the wood will cleave easily.

The growth of wood: All through the spring and summer water and minerals are transported up the wood vessels to the leaves. Here, as a result of photosynthesis, organic compounds are produced that return down the phloem to be converted into wood, a process recorded by the annual rings.

How fast a tree grows is dependant on many factors. Available water may be a limiting factor. In very dry summers it is difficult for the tree to extract sufficient water from the soil to match the amount it loses through its leaves. At worst, and more commonly with shallow rooted trees such as beech, the tree can die. In a wood, shade will also slow a tree's growth. Coppice grown under too many standards often displays this problem. Some species are less shade tolerant than others, and again they may succumb. Severe infestations of caterpillars, an intermittent problem with oaks for example, will severely reduce the growth of any trees that are heavily defoliated by them.

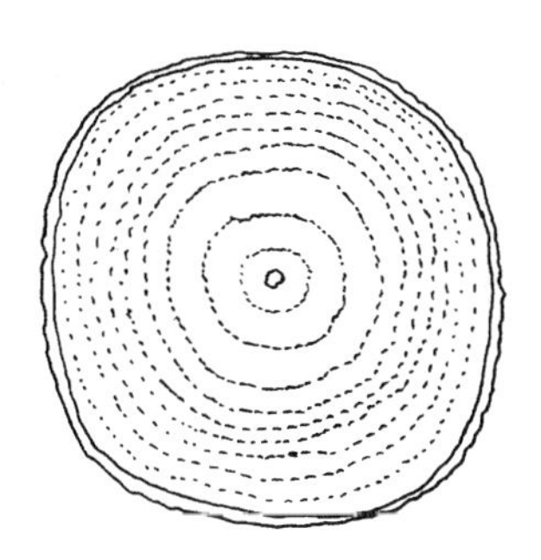

Fig. 1.3 Cross section of a coppice pole showing wide annual rings in early years growth.

Similarly elm that is infected with elm disease will grow more slowly as its leaf area, and thus its ability to produce sugars, is reduced.

Coppice shoots grow incredibly quickly in their first years after cutting. Because there are no large stems, and the stool has a massive root system, all of the plant's energy goes into the production of new stems. Coppice poles are easily recognised by the very wide annual rings laid down during their early years (**fig. 1.3**).

Wind also affects the growth of exposed trees. In a wind trees do not thrash backwards and forwards, their tops actually rotate. Continuous rotation such as this invariably results in a twisted grain – a particular problem if you are going to cleave the trunk. A similar effect if often quoted by woodmen for coppice on the south face of a wood where, they claim the poles twist as they follow the sun.

Lastly, the growth of stems is controlled by their leading shoots. The growing points produce hormones which promote growth, ensure a stem is growing vertically or towards light, suppress lateral bud growth, and control leaf drop. Thus if a hard frost destroys the leading buds, those behind it are stimulated to grow and produce new leading shoots that in time will look normal. If suddenly shade is removed from the side of a tree, perhaps by felling its neighbours, lateral shoots may be stimulated to grow, producing large knots. And should a young stem be forced over, it will grow differentially on either side to correct the problem (great for natural walking sticks!).

Properties and Drying of Wood

Properties: Wood is possibly the most versatile raw material on our planet. It is infinitely renewable, non-polluting, and has many distinctive properties that explain its importance in our crafts, mythology and history. Some of these properties that we value so much are:

Appearance: wood is incredibly beautiful. It comes in a wide range of colours to suit all tastes. The patterns in its grains are endless, natural and uniquely attractive. Even as wood decays, fungal colonies create their 'spalted' patterns so coveted by turners.

Resonance: no one can duplicate the magical sounds of stringed or woodwind instruments in anything other than wood.

Elasticity/resilience: it can be bent repeatedly without fracturing, and absorb violent shocks as tool handles, wheels and carts without breaking.

Strength/weight: for its weight wood is remarkably strong. Along the grain it is strong in compression and unbreakable in tension. Its end grain is ideal for mallets.

Conduction: it does not conduct heat well, making perfect tool handles that even absorb sweat – for seasoned wood is hygroscopic.

Hygiene: it is scientifically proven that wooden cutting boards harbour less bacteria than do scored synthetic ones!

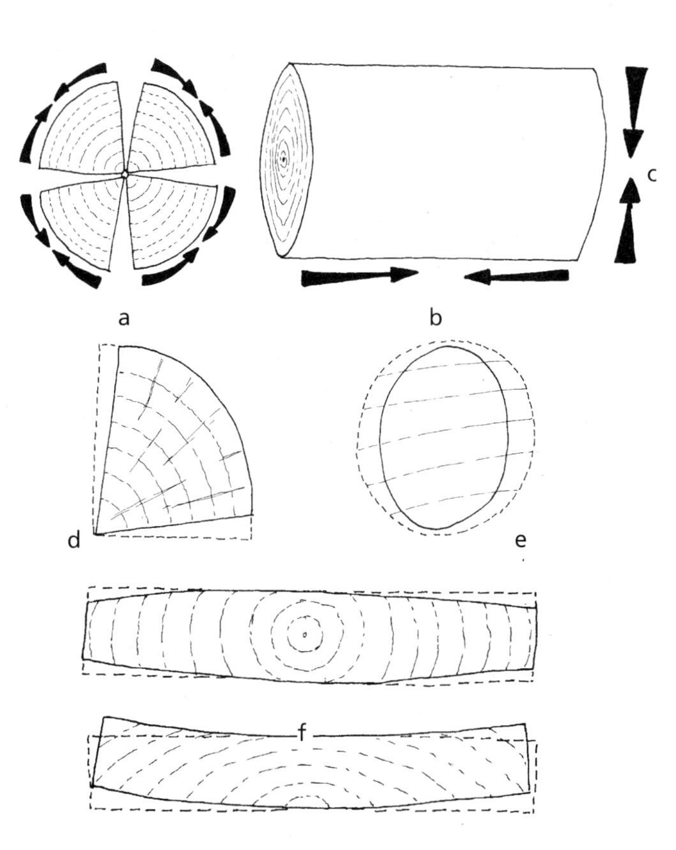

Fig. 1.4 How wood shrinks: a. tangentially, b. longitudinally, c. radially; d, e and f. show how clefts and poles shrink as a result.

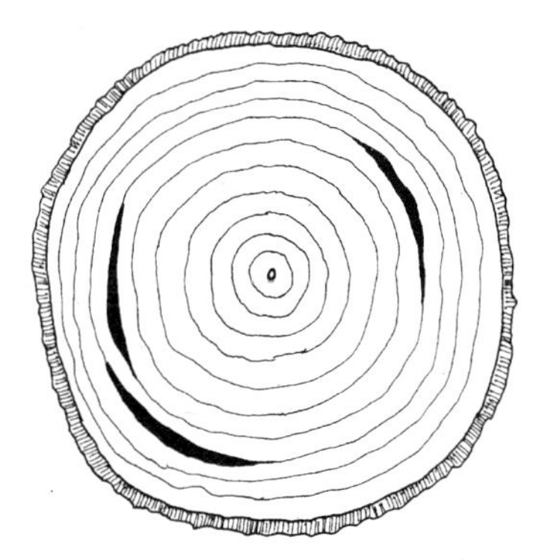

Fig. 1.5 Ring shakes.

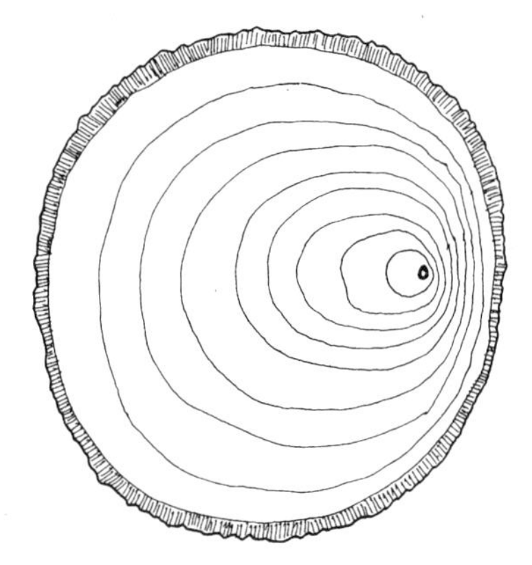

Fig. 1.6 Eccentric pith.

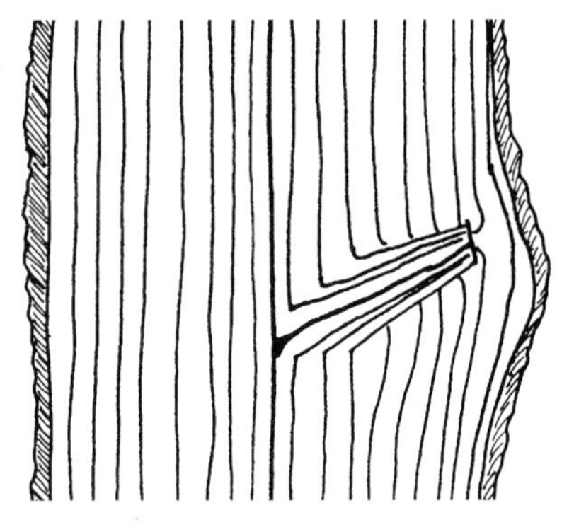

Fig. 1.7 Hidden knot.

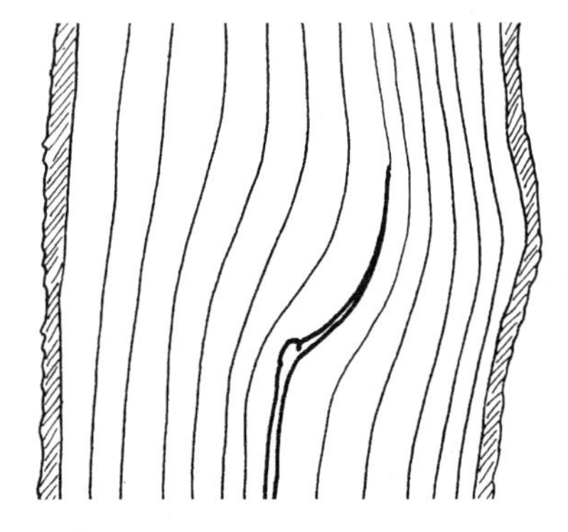

Fig. 1.8 Effect of leading shoot/bud dying.

Water barrier: radially cleft wood is very waterproof – there are enough wooden boats and barrels to confirm that fact.

What happens as wood dries: At the time of felling wood contains anywhere between 40 and 200 percent water depending on the species, site, time of year and which part of the tree you sample. This moisture occurs as 'free' water in the cell contents, and as 'bound' water in the cell walls. Free water is lost quickly after felling, but the wood remains green until the bound water in the cell walls is progressively lost. This is the process of seasoning, and as the bound water reduces so the wood hardens and toughens. The final moisture content of seasoned wood will be that of the atmosphere in which it is stored. Since wood is hygroscopic, this moisture content will fluctuate with the weather, but will be around 15%, below the 20% moisture needed by most fungi for growth.

Water is lost from all surfaces of the wood, but far more quickly from the cross cut face of the log where the open ends of the water containing vessels are exposed. Moisture loss is greater here than from the exposed surface of a cleft log (**fig. 1.4**). As moisture is lost from wood, so it shrinks in size. This shrinkage is greater in some directions than others: longitudinal shrinkage is about 1%; radial is about 5%; and tangential is greatest at 10 to 15%, causing the splits that occur in cross cut faces. Dense woods shrink more than light woods. Once you understand this process of shrinkage, you can plan for it in your work:

- keep wood, particularly small rods, in the shade to slow their drying, and if necessary soak wood to retain its suppleness (this is used by hurdle makers and chair makers)
- work wood while it is still green and easy to handle
- once wood is cleft into small pieces, use it quickly, or store in water
- when cutting poles leave an extra few inches to allow you to cut off any split ends that arise later
- for turnery always try to turn clefts, for whole poles will split radially
- allow for oval shapes and shrinkage – for example always try to put very dry tenons into green mortices so the joints tighten afterwards
- paint the faces of important butts with a moisture-proof material to avoid splits.

Reading wood

Every tree or pole is like a book. It has a story to tell! A story that records that tree's competition with others, the weather, what has been eating its bark or its leaves, and the nature of the site on which it grows. You must learn to read the signs and to make the most of your wood.

The 'covers' can tell you a lot before you split your 'book' open. You know that ash usually rives well, that hazel will wind a withe, that oak has dark heartwood. You can see the visible damage and rot on some trees – like a book with a damaged spine, is it valuable or worthless? You can read the branching, the curves and conformation that may offer fascinating and unforeseen opportunities to produce products or designs only lurking at the back of your mind. The bumps, scars and twists may tell of hidden knots or scars from frost or animal damage that has left an unworkable grain. You must plan to cut and use your tree accordingly.

But you have to open the book to savour its contents: how close is the grain; how tough the wood; is it fast grown; is there wet rot, or black heart at its core; are these fascinating colours and patterns or rot beyond use; does the grain wind or is it sweet and true. Only when you discover these can you finally decide how best to use each piece.

What you may find in your wood: Here are the more common qualities you may reveal on opening a log.

Shakes: these are splits around the annual rings in large logs of particularly chestnut – split out clefts that avoid them (**fig. 1.5**).

Eccentric pith: common where any poles curve significantly – useless for cleft work, but good for beetle heads (**fig. 1.6**).

Hidden knots: common where lateral branches die and are grown over, sometimes leaving a tell-tale bump – result is areas of grain unworkable for quality product such as turnery, furniture, tent pegs etc. (**fig. 1.7**).

Death of leading shoot: this usually results in a lateral shoot taking over, and although the tree straightens in time, a slight kink may still show – result is unworkable grain as for hidden knot (**fig. 1.8**).

Wavy grain: this can be caused by small knots, burrs or canker – wood fine for rough clefts but not quality products (**fig. 1.9**).

Wound grain: wind or sun are usual causes, sometimes obvious from twisted bark or twist in

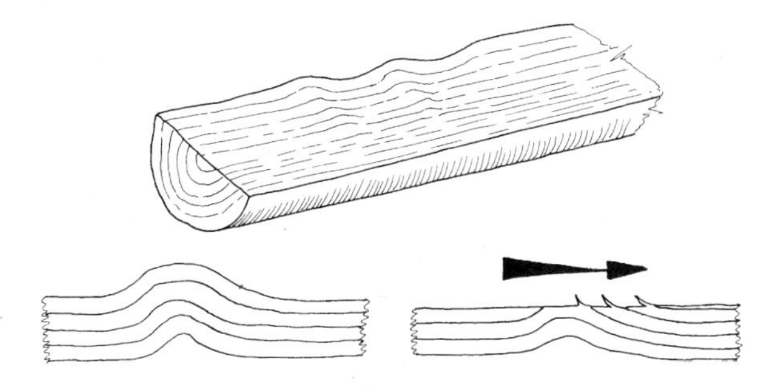

Fig. 1.9 Wavy grain, which leaves a rough finish when shaved.

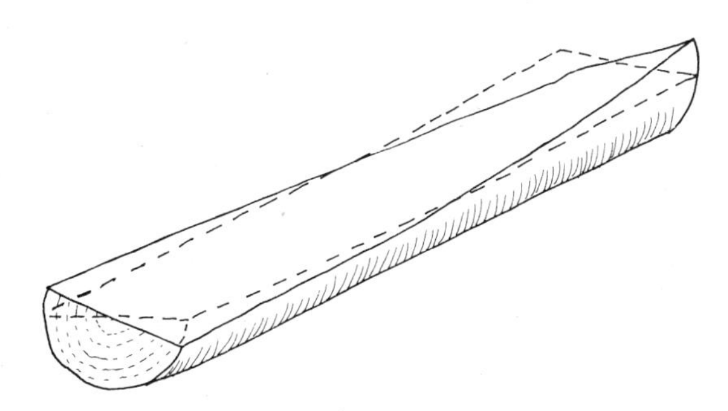

Fig. 1.10 Wound grain resulting in a twisted cleft.

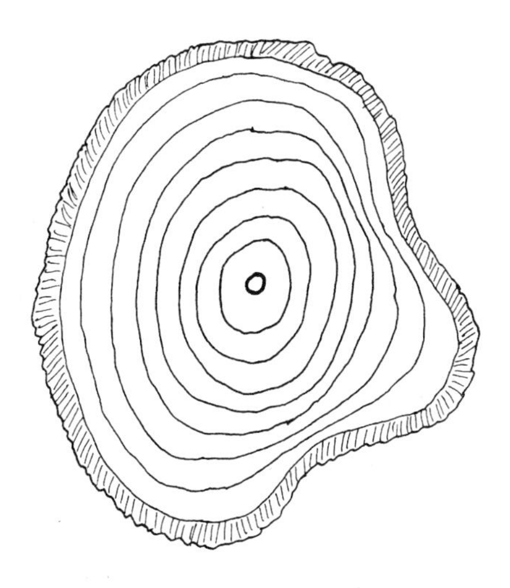

Fig. 1.11 Fluted stem, resulting in a grain which cannot easily be split.

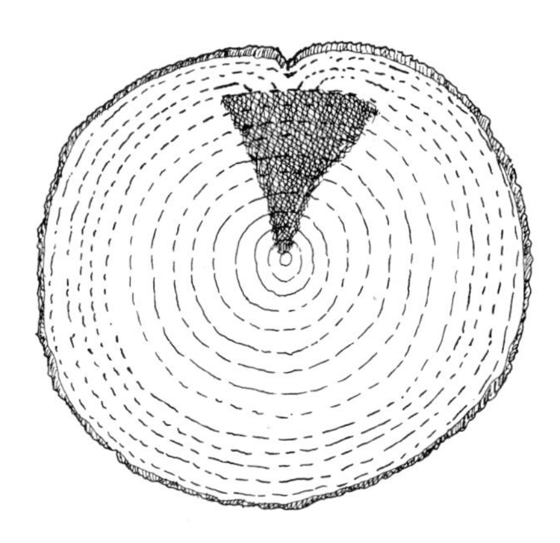

Fig. 1.12 The effect of losing bark: the hatched area is dead wood which can often be recognised from the groove on the outside.

position of buds along the stem - use for short products if cleft, but better left round (**fig. 1.10**).

Fluted stems: usually genetic, or the result of two stems growing very close together, and readily visible - what you cannot see is the very dense grain in the troughs, making wood difficult to rive or turn (**fig. 1.11**).

Discolouration: most common are black heart in ash, which is prized for turnery; wet rot in elm which can be used for any purpose if still hard; and beefsteak fungus in oak, again prized for turnery.

Loss of bark: usually result of rabbits or deer barking part of young stems - commonly part of the stem is dead, and therefore unusable (**fig. 1.12**).

Dead wood: once infected by fungi interesting patterns may occur (spalting) that are favoured by turners. Difficulty is to catch the wood before the rot progresses too far.

Stringy grain: sometimes the sweetest of woods produce a tough stringy grain; it appears to be mainly a genetic influence - use this material anywhere where you don't want your wood to split.

Further reading:

Abbott, M, ***Green Woodwork***,
Guild of Master Craftsmen Publications, 1989
Alexander, J.D. ***Make a Chair from a Tree***,
Astragal Press, 1994
Corkhill, T. ***A Glossary of Wood***, Stobart, 1970

Chapter 2

The Right Wood for the Job

Every tree species growing in this country has more or less individual properties. Some species even differ markedly from site to site. One of the great things about woodmanship is that over the centuries craftsmen have developed a lore that matches these properties to the products they make. Developed without the aid of science, tried and tested by endless use, this wisdom has stood the test of time. Understanding the resilience of ash, the durability of chestnut or the readiness to cleave of hazel explains why products made from them work so well.

Remember, green wood working is a living craft; understand the wisdom of previous craftsmen, but experiment and develop it further to provide what we need in a new millennium.

The major native trees

Oak: This most English of trees has a great variety of uses in addition to the beams, planks and furniture produced from timber trees. Smaller oaks provide a versatile raw material.

Recognition: There are two main types of native oak in Britain; pedunculate and sessile. They are easily distinguished by their leaves and acorn cups (**fig. 2.1**). Everyone is familiar with the lobed leaves of oak and its fruits. In winter the complex twigs with their cluster of buds and the frequent change in direction of the branches are quite characteristic. Likewise the deep furrowed bark of older trees is well known, although the smooth grey bark of young poles is not.

Silviculture and properties: Standard oaks have been most commonly grown in coppices and felled when demand arose. Short rotation coppice encouraged short boled oaks with many branches. Long rotation coppice on rich soils produces magnificent tall oaks with clean trunks. Oak grows easily from seed, but oaklings are not common in woods, so some planting for timber has occurred. Oak coppice, most common in the valleys of the west and north of England is best spaced at 2.4m (8ft) and cut at a rotation up to 30 years.

Oak has a dark heartwood and a lot of pale sapwood: the heartwood is hard, heavy, strong and durable. It has prominent rays that produce a lovely silver grain and provide a unique waterproof barrier. Sapwood is not durable, but when cleft is used for swills. Clean poles rive well, usually being cut at 150mm (6in) to 300mm (12in) diameter. Clefts from this wood bend easily after steaming and small rods can be wound like withes. The blue colour that appears when oak is split with iron metal wedges results from tannic acid reacting with the metal; this accounts for its durability and also its habit of corroding iron. 'Brown oak', a colouration caused by the beefsteak fungus, is prized for veneers and by turners.

Best uses for oak:

Age	Products
7-12 years	heathers for baskets; flower stakes; sticks
12-20 years	gate hurdles; hedge stakes; lathes; wedges; ladder rungs; trenails; fence rails; paling; bark for tanning; turnery; spelk baskets; screens/pergolas
20-30 years	bark for tanning; fencing; furniture; wheel spokes; shingles; firewood /charcoal; turnery; gates
30 years	cooperage; boats; carving; veneers; furniture; flooring; structural timber; weather boarding; planking; firewood and charcoal

Alder: Traditionally this is the wood for wooden clogs and gunpowder, both uses that have seriously declined: Alder is a lovely wood in search of a new role.

Recognition: you cannot mistake an alder: its winter buds are stalked, and the branches still bear the small false cones of previous summer's fruiting (**fig. 2.2**). In spring male flowers are borne in catkins, and the leaves have a unique notch at their tip. Poles soon develop a scaly black bark, which if blazed reveals a bright orange colour.

Silviculture and properties: alder seed needs damp mud on which to germinate, and grows best on moist soils. You will get the best results in its native habitat of boggy ground and beside streams where nitrogen fixing bacteria grow symbiotically on its roots. It can be grown from cuttings. Although capable of making a large tree at c.80 years, it coppices vigorously, producing a good number of fast growing poles. It is best coppiced at either 9-12 years, or about 25 years.

Alder wood is brown when seasoned, and poles should be blazed to help the process. It is a light, soft wood that is easy to work, but which shrinks up to 12% as it dries. It lasts well if kept either dry or continuously wet; otherwise it will rot in 12 months. Products made from alder hold their shape well in the damp.

Best uses for alder:

Age	Products
9-12 years	faggots; scythe snaiths; small turnery; river revetments
20-40 years	broom heads; clogs; charcoal

Ash: Since primitive man first made his spears with ash plants and found they did not readily break, ash has been considered the best wood for almost any type of handle. And it also makes fine furniture and turnery.

Recognition: ash can be found as coppice or as standard trees. Ash stools can be large in both diameter and height (Dr. Rackham estimates that a particular stool in Suffolk could be 1000 years old) and it is not uncommon to find 50-60 year old stems. Young ash poles have a thin, light grey bark, which in older trees becomes thicker and furrowed. The twigs are very stout and bear distinctive coal-black buds that produce compound leaves in May (**fig. 2.3**). Winged seeds, or keys, often overwinter on the tree.

Silviculture and Properties: ash stools are best cut low to reduce curvature in the butts, and often grow 1.8m (6ft) in their first summer. Coppice is best grown on a 10-12 years rotation for small work, and spaced at c.3.4m (11ft). It prefers the best soils, growing well over chalk. Timber size ash mature at around100 years. It is light demanding and since ring porous, is best grown fast to produce stronger wood. Ash grows easily from seed.

Ash wood is a lovely pale cream colour. There is no distinctive heartwood, so the entire pole can be used. Old coppice is prone to 'black heart', which is not a problem for turnery, but may be for furniture. The wood is very tough, elastic and straight grained. It rives superbly in any plane, and can produce very fine clefts for bonds. It is excellent for steam bending, but not durable outdoors. Un-barked poles are prone to attack by ash bark beetle which burrows into the wood.

Best uses for ash:

Age	Products
7-12 years	rake stails; scythe snaiths; gate hurdles; bean rods; flower stakes; morris staves; truss hoops; wattle rods for houses; scout staves; barrel hoops; walking sticks; besom handles; besom bonds; rick pegs; hay cribs; hay forks
12-25 years	cleft handles; tent pegs; hop poles; furniture; crate heads; turnery; rake heads and teeth; fence rails/ pales; wedges; firewood; charcoal; milk stools; wooden wheels; vehicle body frames and carts; cricket stumps; oars

Beech: To most of us beech conjures the sight of bodgers turning chair legs on their pole lathes. Their rude shelters thatched with shavings and surrounded by the long clean stems of beech trees as yet uncut is an unforgettable part of our woodland heritage; the wood they worked is a superb raw material for green wood workers.

Recognition: the hairy twigs bear long, slender, pointed buds alternately, giving a zig-zag appearance (**fig. 2.4**). In spring they produce glossy bright green leaves, which in young trees may remain through the winter after turning golden brown. In autumn nuts are formed in hairy cupules, often found carpeting the ground. Beech bark is smooth and a pale metallic grey, features retained whatever age the tree.

Silviculture and properties: beech is easily raised from seed, and planting in existing woodlands is rarely needed. When planting new woods, space whips at 1.5m (5ft) and thin at 15 years. Beech is very tolerant of shade; this allows selective felling of trees which are then replaced naturally by seedlings, so that the woodland is never clear felled. It coppices less well, so it is long clean trunks 70 or more years that most craftsmen use. Beech pollards well, but the poles produced are frequently poor quality. It tolerates a wide range of soils, but not frost.

Beech wood is a light reddish-brown with a straight, fine, close grain of even texture. It is hard and heavy, but not difficult to work and its medullary rays give the wood an attractive appearance. After steaming it bends as well as ash, and straight logs cleave well. It is not durable exposed to weather.

Best uses for beech:

Age	Products
>70 years	furniture; chair legs; turnery; woodware; butchers' blocks; bowls; platters; spoons; plane blocks; mallet heads; brush backs; simple hand tools; wedges; tent pegs; trailer/body frames; shoe lasts; firewood and charcoal

Birch: This beautiful tree, tolerant of poor soils and seeding prolifically, is underrated in England. Well seasoned birch wood can resemble oak in its strength, and it is Scandinavian craftsmen who have shown what you can really do with this tree.

Recognition: most of us will recognise the white, papery bark of the silver birch. It has double-toothed triangular leaves, tiny buds, and bears catkins in spring (**fig. 2.5**). Brown birch is distinguished by its brown papery bark and hairy twigs.

Silviculture and properties: birch grows plentifully (sometimes too much so!) from seed. It will form a standard tree, but matures at c.70 years, and is not tolerant of shade. If grown spaced at 3.4m (11ft), it makes nice clean straight trunks. In England woodland birch was coppiced, to which it responds quite well, producing three or four straight poles on a stool if spaced at 2.4m (8ft).

The whitish, light brown wood, which has no separate heart wood is fairly hard, strong and tough. It has a lovely fine even grain that stains and polishes well. It does not last well out of doors. Up to seven years its spray is tough, resilient and straight making it perfect for besoms or horse jumps. Birch bark is very waterproof (to the extent that North American Indians could make canoes with it!). Young rods wind as well as hazel.

Best uses for birch:

Age	Products
5-10 years	besom heads; swales; horse jumps; faggots; withes; hoops
>10 years	besom handles; rake and broom heads and handles; small turnery (cotton reels, darning mushrooms etc.); bowls; spoons; dishes; ladles; butterprints; furniture; carving; toys; wooden shoes; firewood

Sweet Chestnut: Chestnut is the most durable wood that grows in our islands. Brought here by the Romans, probably for the nutritious nuts which gave a taste of home, it has become the material for fencing - paling being the only woodland product with a British Standard to its name.

Recognition: chestnut is more commonly found as coppice, with a cluster of straight, grey-barked poles arising from a low stool. Standard trees can grow to an enormous size and age, and characteristically have a deeply furrowed bark that twists around the tree. Chestnut has long deep green leaves with a saw-like edge that appear in April, and long pale 'candles' of flowers in July (**fig. 2.6**). Everyone recognises the nuts in autumn, borne in that spiky green casing which defies easy entry.

Silviculture and Properties: standard chestnut trees are prone to 'ring shakes', cracks that follow the annual rings and reduce its value as sawn timber. As a result most chestnut is grown as coppice for large poles on a 14-20 year rotation. Stools should be placed app. 2.4m (8ft) apart to suppress side shoots, and should be cut low. Chestnut grows best on warm, light soils, not liking chalk or peat. It grows readily from seed, and young rods can be plashed.

Chestnut wood is hard, heavy, strong and durable, being easy to work whilst green. It is a ring porous wood like oak, but can be distinguished from it by the absence of medullary rays. Chestnut has very little sapwood, meaning even small poles and clefts are very durable. It cleaves beautifully in all planes, hence its role in all forms of fencing.

Best uses for sweet chestnut:

Age	Products
2-3 years	walking sticks
12-20 years	hop poles; bean rods; pea sticks; spiles; posts; pale and wire; gates; gate hurdles; palings; shingles; lathes; trugs; fruit props; charcoal; timber framing

Elm: Dutch elm disease may have taken from us the great elm trees that characterised so many of our hedgerows, but look carefully and you will find in many coppices young elmwood poles growing. And this young elm is versatile and easy to work in ways that their massive predecessors were not.

Recognition: there are several species and varieties of elm native to England. One feature they have in common is an asymetric base to their leaves (**fig 2.7**). Wych elm has prominent alternate buds and coppices when cut; English and Smooth-leaved elms have tiny twigs and buds, and more often sucker than coppice. Young poles are grey and usually covered in tiny twigs, whilst older trees have a deeply furrowed bark.

Silviculture and properties: no-one grows standard elm trees at present, for elm disease remains a major problem. If you have large trees that are still alive, leave them for they may be resistant. Treasure any large useable elm you do fell - ensure it is not wasted. At present elm is best coppiced on a 7/8 year cycle which seems to avoid the worst of the disease, and provides some useable material, although 20 years would be far better. Elm produces the best flat spray for pea sticks. Elm seed is usually infertile, so propagation is by suckers or plashing.

Elm wood is rich, red-brown with a thin layer of yellowy sap wood. It is hard, heavy and tough, and when old is difficult to split. It is very durable across the whole log, particularly when in water continuously. Young poles, which have a yellowy-white wood rive quite well, and small rods can be wound to make withes. The irregular growth and frequent epicormic growths make the wood of older trees difficult to work. A fungal infection called wet rot frequently stains areas of the wood, but does not seriously detract from its usefulness. Elm bast makes good chair seats.

Best uses for elm:

Age	Produce
7-12 years	tree stakes; hedge stakes; gate hurdles; bean rods, pea sticks; withes
12-25 years	turnery; cleft stakes; firewood and charcoal; pulleys; paint brush handles; small beetles/mauls; piles; chair seats
>25 years	planking; chopping blocks and boards; chair seats; beetles; wheel hubs; weather boarding; wheel barrows; bellows backs; dough troughs

Hazel: The humble nut-stub has played a greater role in the development of our civilisation than almost any other plant species. We have evidence from the Somerset Levels of its use in wattle fencing for over 5000 years, and its small rods and poles are a delight to cut and use; it is the supreme coppice wood.

Recognition: usually found as coppice, with a dense cluster of rods growing from a mainly underground stool. Older stools self-coppice, resulting in rods and poles of different ages. Old stems can grow to 30cm (12in) diameter. Young rods are olive green, older rods chestnut brown, usually smooth and shiny. Felty pale brown twigs with alternate buds bear 'lamb's tail' catkins in early spring. The toothed leaves emerge in late April (**fig. 2.8**). Autumn brings the added bonus of a rich crop of nuts - if you can get them before the squirrels!

Silviculture and Properties: hazel coppices very well, often growing to 1.5m (5ft) in its first year, but is intolerant of shade, which can kill it. Stools are best cut very low, and spaced at 2m (7ft) to draw the rods up and suppress growth of lateral shoots. It can be propagated either from seed or by plashing young rods. Hazel produces lovely flat spray for pea sticks up to 12 years old. Its pale wood is soft, elastic and straight grained, riving very easily and cleanly either radially or tangentially. The wood fibres separate easily on twisting, so that small rods can be wound or knotted. When it is green hazel wood bends easily, although the grain has a tendency to wind, particularly when growing in hedges and woodland edge. When older than 15 years, the wood becomes increasingly less pliant, knotty and twisted, and is only usable as firewood since it is not durable as posts.

Best uses for hazel:

Age	Products
6-12 years	pea sticks; flower and tomato stakes; bean rods; bonds; thatching wood; wattle fencing; fascines/faggots; barrel hoops; wattle rods for houses; sticks; ethering rods; clothes props; pheasant traps; sheep feeders; rick pegs, crate rods; stick furniture; scout staves
12-15 years	gate hurdles; rake handles; rustic poles; hedging stakes; morris staves; crate heads; small turnery
>15 years	firewood; charcoal

Lime: Small leaved lime, or prye, is an increasingly uncommon tree, having only a few special uses for the craftsman. But lime woods in early summer with their pale green leaves and droning bees are as beautiful as the carvings of Grinling Gibbons that were fashioned in their wood.

Recognition: the alternate, two scaled buds on winter twigs are quite distinctive, as are the heart shaped leaves. A cluster of flowers hangs on a long stalk with a thin bract – unique to lime (**fig. 2.9**). Poles have a smooth grey bark, but older trees, often develop a bushy outgrowth of twigs at their base.

Silviculture and properties: lime is rarely grown as timber, more often seen open grown in parks. It coppices vigorously, producing a dense crop of straight poles. Stools can be cut low or high, and are ideally spaced at 2.4m (8ft). Lime seed is rarely fertile, so propagation is usually by cuttings.

Lime is a yellowish cream soft, light wood with a fine close grain. It is easily worked and stable. It is not durable out of doors. The bast, or inner layers of the bark, are remarkably tough and fibrous, hence its use in making rope.

Best uses for lime:

Age	Products
10-25 years	pea sticks; bean rods; besom handles; bast; hop poles; turnery; firewood and charcoal
>25 years	carving; piano keys; shoe lasts; hat blocks

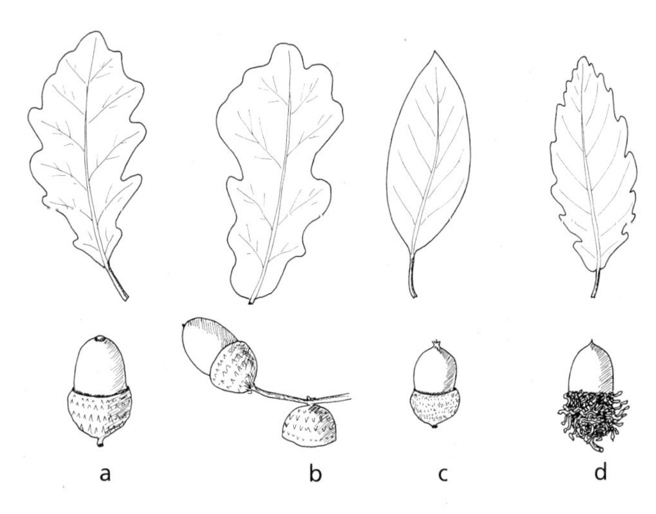

Fig. 2.1 Oak - leaves and acorns from: a. Sessile oak, *Quercus petraea*, b. English oak, *Q. robur*, c. Holm oak, *Q. ilex*, d. Turkey oak, *Q. cerris*

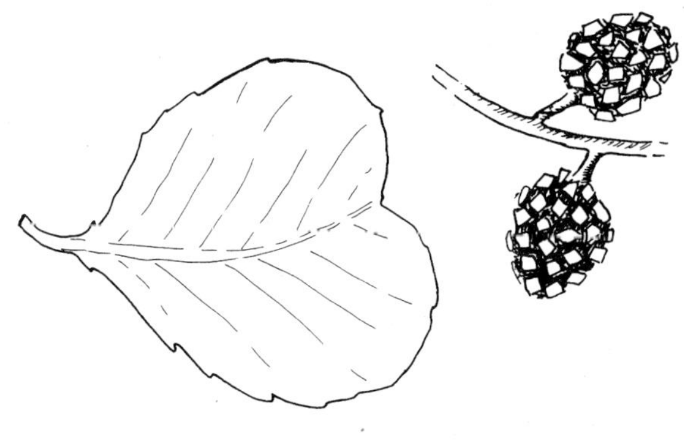

Fig. 2.2 Alder, *Alnus glutinosa*, leaf and cone

Fig. 2.3 Ash, *Fraxinus excelsior*, twig, leaf and keys

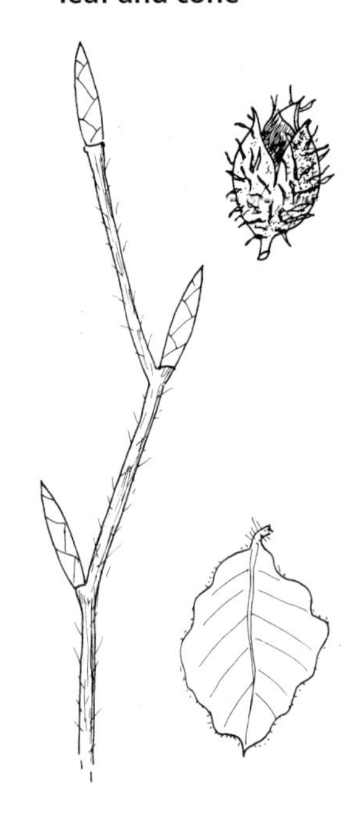

Fig. 2.4 Beech, *Fagus sylvatica*, twig, leaf and nut

Fig. 2.5 Birch, *Betula pendula*, twig and leaf

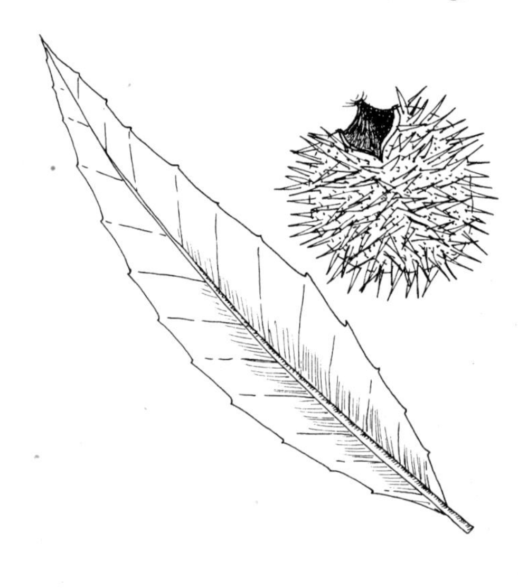

Fig. 2.6 Sweet Chestnut, *Castana sativa*, leaf and nut in its casing

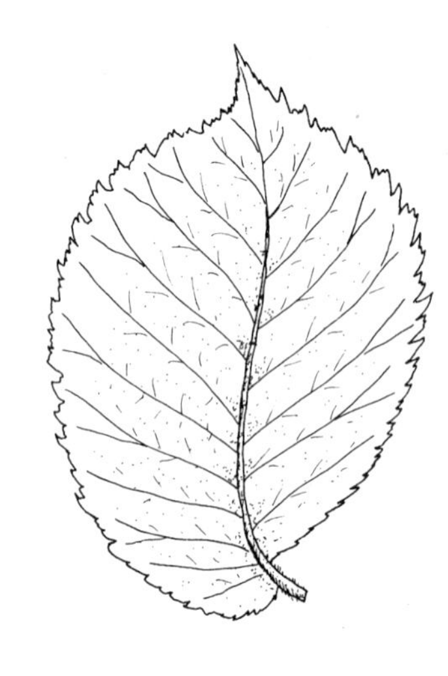

Fig. 2.7 Elm, *Ulmus spp.*, leaf

Fig. 2.8 Hazel, *Corylus avellana*, twig with catkin, leaf and nuts

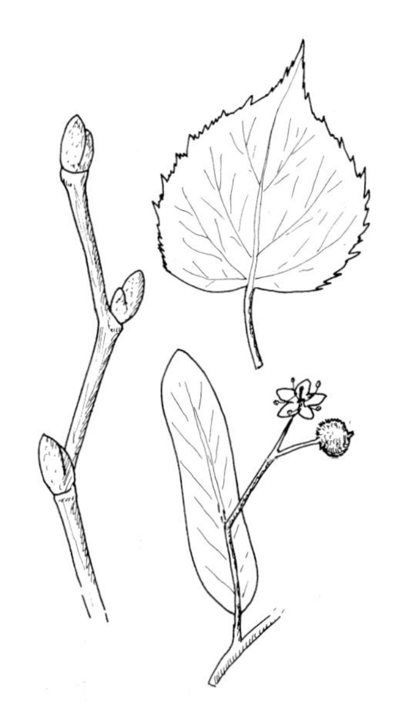

Fig. 2.9 Lime, *Tilia cordata*, twig, leaf and flower with maturing seed

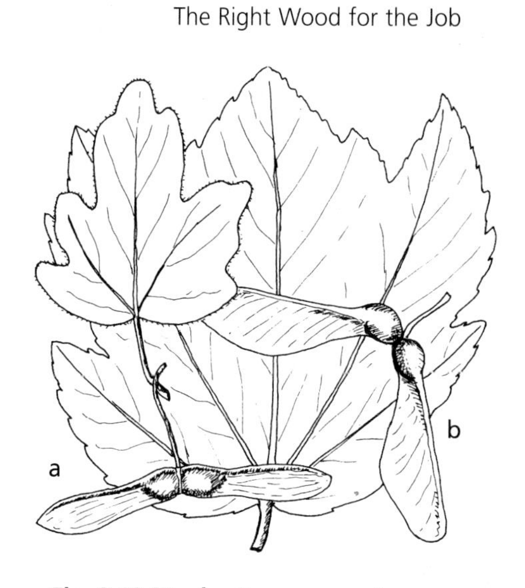

Fig. 2.10 Maple, *Acer campestre* (a), and Sycamore, *A. platanus* (b), leaves and winged seeds

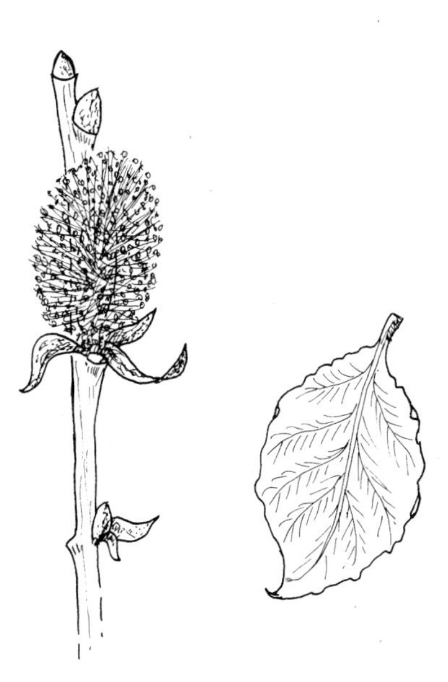

Fig. 2.11 Sallow, *Salix caprea*, twig with female catkin and leaf

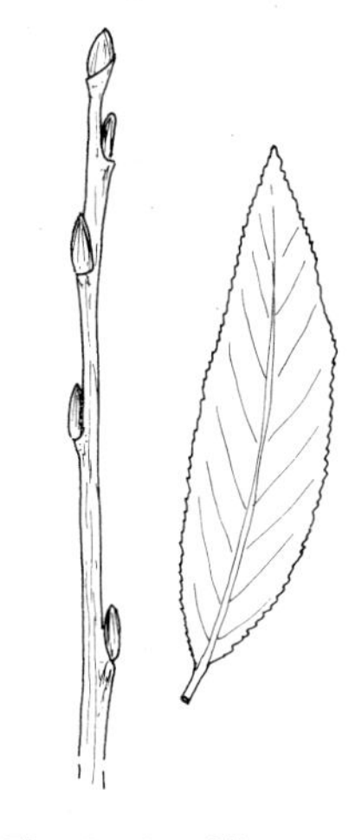

Fig. 2.12 Willow, *Salix spp.*, twig and leaf

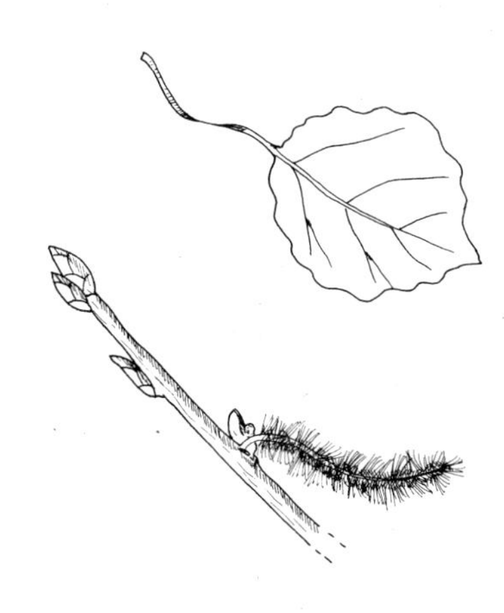

Fig. 2.13 Aspen, *Populus tremula*, twig with male catkin and leaf

Fig. 2.14 Box, *Buxus sempervivens*, leaves and flower

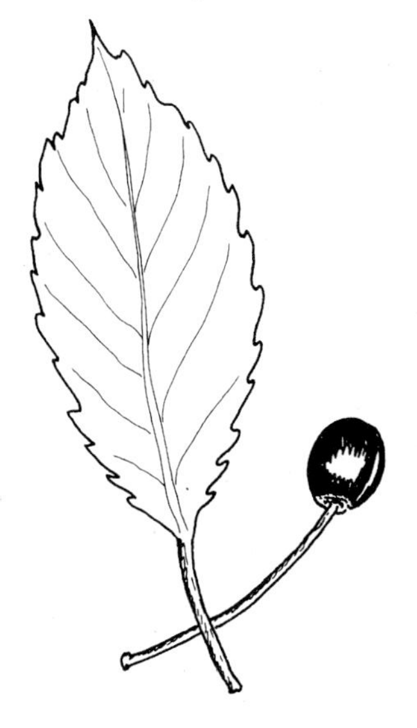

Fig. 2.15 Cherry, *Prunus avium*, leaf and fruit

Fig. 2.16 Guelder rose, *Vibernum opulus*, leaf and flowers

Maple and Sycamore: Every year field maple announces autumn with its beautiful yellow and red foliage, brightening hedge and copse before the dark of winter. Sycamore, its close cousin, arrived here in Tudor times, and remains a rather gloomy green all year; the beauty of sycamore lies under the bark.

Recognition: both maple and sycamore have twigs with paired opposite buds that produce five pointed leaves. Maple twigs are soon furrowed and slightly corky, a feature that stays through to mature trees. It coppices freely, and can form an elegant but small standard tree. Sycamore buds are green, and the bark of twigs and poles is blue grey; this flakes off in older trees, which can also be standard or coppice. Both trees produce the winged seeds with which we have all played 'helicopters' (**fig. 2.10**).

Silviculture and properties: both trees grow well from seed (sycamore too well at times!) and can be selected as standard timber in the coppice. Large trees are mature at c.80 years. If cut as coppice keep at c.3.4m (11ft) spacing, and cut fairly low as chestnut.

Both produce a pale, almost white wood, with no obvious sap wood. It is hard, compact, straight and close grained. Although moderately heavy it is not durable outdoors, and maple in particular fractures easily. Sycamore is easy to work, but maple can suffer from hidden knots and does not rive well.

Best uses for maple and sycamore:

Age	Products
7-12 years	bean rods; hedge stakes
12-25 years	turnery; furniture; small carved objects; spoons; firewood and charcoal
>25 years	wood ware (bread boards; bowls; ladles; spoons; pastry boards; rolling pins; pales; butter moulds); furniture; weavers' shuttles; butchers' tables; beetles; musical instruments

Sallow: Sallow is the fastest growing tree in the coppice: in the height of summer it can put on 50mm (2in) in one day. It is a good standby for ash and hazel.

Recognition: In the early spring sallow is the 'pussy willow' or 'palm' that jewels the leafless coppice (**fig. 2.11**). It has broad, curly edged leaves and a grey smooth bark that is marked with lenticels in older trees. Invariably it will be coppice, but you may find small maiden trees.

Silviculture and properties: Sallow is best treated as coppice: cut low and spaced at 2.4m (8ft) it grows beautiful straight poles. It spreads quite well by seed, but cuttings of young wood root easily. Sallows are not destined for large trees – whenever I have let them grow on they have come down in winter gales.

The wood is yellowish or pale brown. It is light, soft, resilient and tough, denting easily. It rives beautifully and can be wound to make a bond.

Best use for sallow:

Age	Products
6-12 years	withes; bean rods; rick pegs; thatching wood; gate hurdles; scythe snaiths; clothes pegs; barrel hoops; hedge stakes; ethers; fascines; tool handles; rake stails and heads
12-25 years	firewood; charcoal

Willows: There are a wide variety of willows in addition to sallow. They range from the large riverside pollards to fine osier rods, and go to make cricket bats and baskets.

Recognition: All of these willows have long, lanceolate leaves (**fig. 2.12**). Crack willow has bright, smooth, orange-brown twigs that bear stalked catkins in the spring. Young poles are smooth-barked, but older trees are deeply furrowed. White willow is distinguished from crack willow by its white silky leaves and sessile catkins. Cricket bat willow is a variety of white willow, that loses its white hairs very early in the season and has a conical growth shape. Osiers have very long, narrow leaves and a wide variety of bark colours.

Silviculture and properties: Crack and white willows grow well in very moist, but not waterlogged soils; they are frequently to be found beside rivers and ditches. Pollarding is a common way to manage them – this avoids them becoming top heavy and coming over. They grow easily from setts, are frost hardy and light demanding.

Osiers are grown in special beds or 'holts'. Soil requirements are high moisture, high quality and low weed growth. The species used are Salix triandra, viminalis and purpurea. Cuttings are set 150mm (6in) into ground 350mm (14in) apart in rows 700mm (28in) apart. The rods are cut each autumn except a few that may be left for up to three years to form 'sticks'. It takes three years before a bed produces good rods, and weed control is needed from time to time.

Willow wood is a pale fawn colour. It is light, soft, resilient, tough and flexible. It will dent, but is difficult to fracture. It is easily worked. Osier rods are tough and very supple. They come in a wide range of varieties, but some of the more important are:

- Belgian reds – very fine rods used for tying vines
- Black maul – excellent for baskets
- Brittany greens – good for baskets
- S. purpurea – probably the most beautiful

Best uses for willow:

Age	Products
Osiers 1-3 years	basket making; biomass; garden sculptures; wattle fencing
Others >3 years	gate hurdles; stakes; ethering rods; scythe snaiths; fascines; thatching wood; cricket bats; hoops; clothes pegs

Less common native and exotic trees

Alder buckthorn: Very hard, close-grained wood. Like blackthorn without the thorns and with orange-red sapwood. Coppices well. Use for: walking sticks and the best charcoal for gunpowder.

Apple: Close-grained, heavy, hard wood that resists wear. Brittle in small sizes, but easy to work. Usually individual trees. Use for: turnery, mallet heads, carving spoons. Apple is harder than pear.

Aspen: Known as 'the tree of the woman's tongue' because aspen leaves never stop moving due to their flattened stalks (**fig. 2.13**). Rarely seeds, mainly grows from suckers. Prefers wet places. Wood is light, soft, weak and not durable, but easy to split. Use for: withes, besom handles, clog soles, matches and charcoal.

Blackthorn: Variety of plum with horrendous spines. Black-barked trunk and deep brown wood. Very difficult to split. Use for: cudgels and walking sticks.

Box: Evergreen with small, flat, oval leaves (**fig. 2.14**). The densest British wood which is very hard and close grained. Not easy to split, but tendency to crack on drying, which may be overcome by steaming. Use for: chisel handles and cleaves (the very best!), high class turnery, mallets, rulers, chess men, wood engraving, spoons.

Cherry: (**fig. 2.15**) Typical papery bark that peels around the stem. Lovely yellowish brown wood that is fairly hard, heavy, tough and strong. Has a fine, even texture, but not durable outside. Not always straight grained and can be difficult to work. Use for: turnery, pipe stems, musical instruments, spoons.

Dogwood: Small size and lovely red twigs. Yellow-brown wood that is very hard, tough and durable. Use for: small turnery, skewers, arrows, walking sticks, small mallet heads; sticks for baskets.

Elder: Shrub whose flowers and berries make better wine than its wood makes artefacts! Yellowish wood of medium density and a hard even texture with a large pith. Use for: blowpipes, whistles, small turnery.

Gorse: A very contorted shrub, rarely with usable lengths of wood. Quite close grained wood. Use for: small turnery (pieces at base of stem), fancy walking sticks.

Guelder rose: Small shrubs whose umbel of white flowers is unique in having an outer ring of much larger, sterile blooms (**fig. 2.16**). It has a hard, compact wood in small rods. Use for: small turnery, walking sticks.

Hawthorn: A shrub or small tree. Yellow-white wood that is hard, fairly heavy, tough and smooth. Has a close grain. It is difficult to split, and often has a fluted stem that creates much waste. Use for: stakes; faggots; firewood; walking sticks; mallet heads; tool handles (chisels).

Holly: Often not cut in woods and hedges because woodmen believe it may bring bad luck. Underneath a smooth, grey bark is a white wood that is hard, heavy and close grained with distinct rays. Has a tendency to warp, but takes dyes well. Use for: carving; all sorts of small woodware; turnery; small handles and cleaves; whip stocks; engraving blocks; spoons.

Holm oak: An evergreen oak with bark fissured into small oblong blocks. Stems often fluted, causing waste in conversion. The wood is hard and similar to English oak, and in large sizes should be used for similar products.

Hornbeam: Notoriously difficult to work, but makes marvellous charcoal. Can be coppice, standard or pollard tree. Its smooth barked stems are strongly fluted, and the fruit has a distinctive three-lobed wing (**fig 2.17**). Seeds well and is tolerant of poorer soils. The wood is creamy-white with no clear heart and is hard, heavy, strong and tough. It is hard to cleave and shrinks considerably on seasoning. It is durable outside. Its fluted stem makes it difficult to get large pieces to work on. Use it for: gear teeth; pulleys; small tool handles; chopping blocks; piano keys; mallets; skittles; shoe lasts; plane stocks; turnery; firewood and charcoal.

Horse chestnut: The conker tree. Its wood is yellowish in colour, fairly light, soft and not durable. It has a close even grain, with some ripple marks (fiddle back). Use for: bobbins and other turnery; brush backs; cutting boards (they don't last long, but do not blunt your knife!).

Ivy: Forms stout, woody, but contorted stems. Pale creamy wood that is only moderately hard and can be brittle. Use it for: spoons; small turnery; fancy walking sticks.

Juniper: A small evergreen shrub that often produces rather contorted stems. The wood is smooth, fragrant and fairly durable. It polishes well. Use it for: fine turnery; small carvings; paper knives.

Laburnum: The tree with lovely pendulous inflorescences of yellow pea-flowers. Its wood is dark brown with yellow sapwood and is hard and

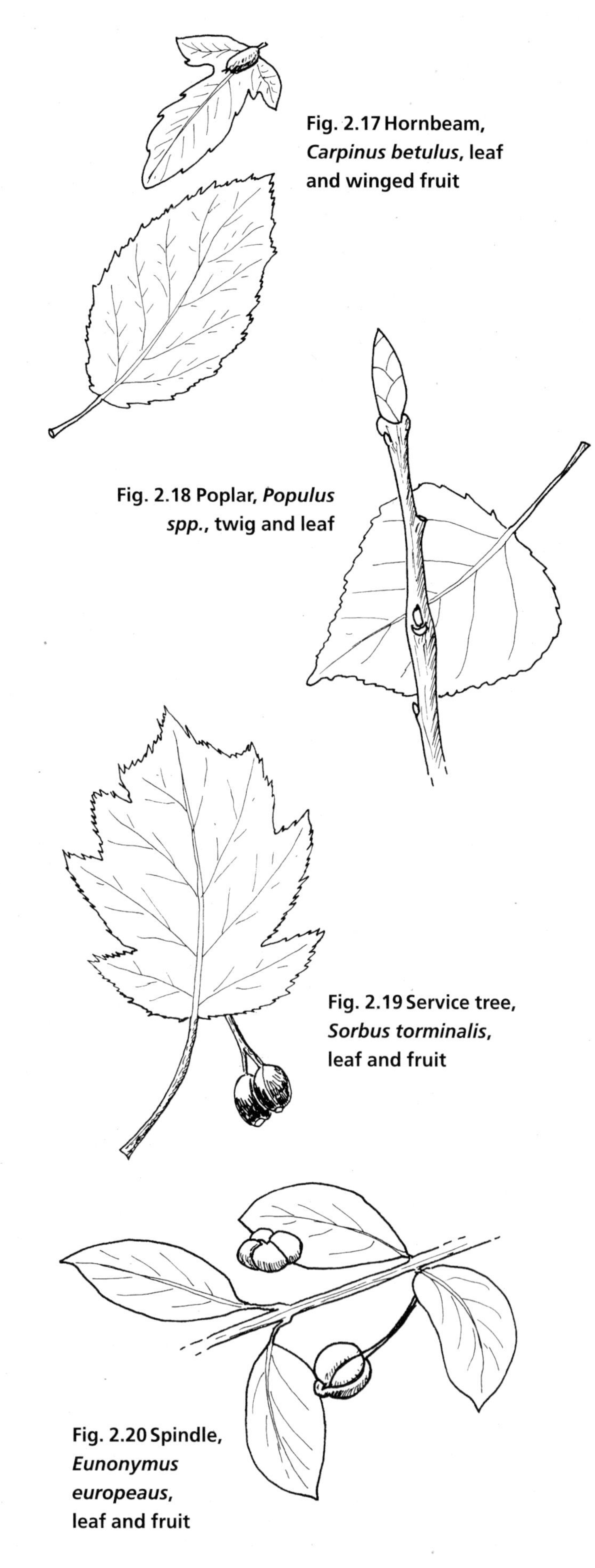

Fig. 2.17 Hornbeam, *Carpinus betulus*, leaf and winged fruit

Fig. 2.18 Poplar, *Populus spp.*, twig and leaf

Fig. 2.19 Service tree, *Sorbus torminalis*, leaf and fruit

Fig. 2.20 Spindle, *Eunonymus europeaus*, leaf and fruit

heavy with a good straight grain. It is quite difficult to work. Use for: cups; ladles; high quality turnery and small woodwork; musical instruments.

Poplar: (**fig. 2.18**) Black poplar is our rarest native tree, so you will get little of that to work. But hybrid and white poplar (Abele) you may find. Poplar wood is very white, light and soft, although it is very resistant to splitting. It is not durable and shrinks a lot during seasoning. Use it for: turnery; toys; clogs; matches; lorry/cart floors.

Privet: Only produces small stems. The wood is hard, heavy, tough and strong. It is pale in colour, and small rods can be wound for withes. Use for: rough baskets; walking sticks; small handles; spoons.

Rowan: Another small tree with white flowers and ash-like leaves. It grows as a small standard or coppice. Its wood is reddish-brown with darker summer wood, and is moderately hard, heavy and elastic. It has a close grain, sometimes with a lovely figure in it. Use it for: crates; hoops; rough baskets; small tool handles; mallet heads and turnery (large stems).

Service tree: (**fig. 2.19**) Another very rare native. Can be a reasonably sized tree with a moderately hard, heavy wood with a close grain. Use for: turnery; mallet heads (if no apple!).

Spindle: Shrub with distinctive greenish bark and four-lobed blushing pink fruits (**fig. 2.20**). Its wood is very white, hard, heavy, tough and difficult to split. It has an even grain and is easy to work. Use it for: turnery; woodware; spindles; spoons; skewers; toothpicks; charcoal for gunpowder!

Turkey oak: Distinguished by its acorn cups that are covered in contorted growths – almost moss-like. An occasional tree of parks. The wood is not as hard, heavy and strong as English oak. It is easier to work and is very similar to American red and white oak. Use as oak.

Walnut: In addition to delicious nuts, mature walnut trees produce possibly the most beautiful wood for fine furniture. It ranges from light to very dark brown, is hard, moderately heavy, strong and tough. The sapwood is not durable. Once seasoned the wood is very stable and absorbs shocks well. All parts are valued for veneers. Use for: gun stocks; bent work; high class joinery.

Wayfaring tree: A very small tree with umbels of white flowers that mature to black berries, and oval leaves that are silky-white underneath. Its pale wood is quite tough, and the young twigs are very pliant, making perfect withes. Use for: withes; rough basket making.

Yew: Last, but by no means least! It is one of the most beautiful woods that you can work with. Large old trees are often heavily fluted and branched, needing careful thought before conversion. The contrast between the orange-brown heartwood and white sapwood is dramatic. Yew wood is hard, heavy, strong, immensely durable, tough and uniquely elastic. It has a close, even fine textured grain that turns well and acquires a natural polish. Use it for: brushes; woodware; turning; gate posts; bows; small tool handles; furniture; spoons.

Further reading:

Corkhill, T ***A Glossary of Wood***, Stobart, 1979

Edlin, H L ***British Woodland Trees***, Batsford, 1944

Edlin, H L ***Woodland Crafts in Britain***, David & Charles, 1974

Forestry Commission Bulletin No. 17 - ***Cultivation of the Cricket Bat Willow***, HMSO, 1968

Forestry Commission Booklet No. 20 - ***Know your Broadleaves***, HMSO, 1971

Mitchell & Wilkinson Collins Pocket ***Guide to Trees,*** Harper Collins, 2000

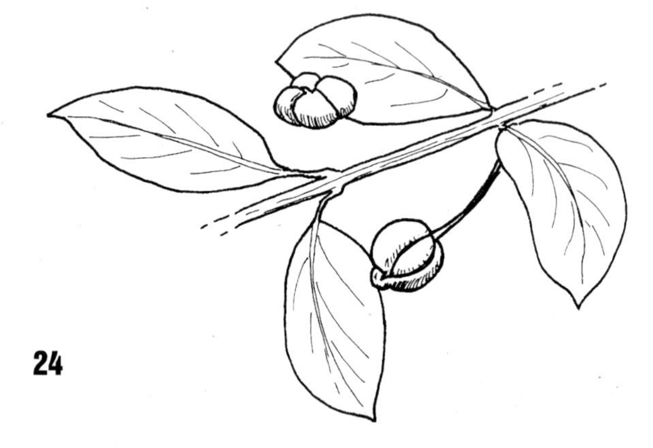

Chapter 3

Growing Your Own Wood

The options and implications

Think hard about this! Growing trees from scratch involves a lot of work and a long term commitment; but if you can wait and have access to suitable land, then creating your own coppice will provide a legacy for future generations as well as satisfaction for yourself.

Options: If you have a small field bounded by hedges of ash, oak and hazel to seed it, you could just leave it to nature, and in 30 to 40 years you will have a young woodland; one third of my woodland developed from a disused meadow this way. A more positive route, however, is to consider:

Hedges: Most native species will grow and coppice in a hedge as well as they will in a woodland. The disadvantages are that the wood often has a twisted grain, making riving difficult, and there are more side branches due to the available light. If your final use is unaffected by these, then go ahead.

Pollards: If firewood or round stakes are your main need, create pollards in your hedge; ash, willow, sycamore oak and beech are all superb for this. Grow maiden trees, then cut them off 2.5m (8ft) above ground when the stem is 130-150mm (5-6in) diameter; new shoots will sprout from the top, and you should repeat the cutting every 10-15 years – long cycles are less likely to succeed. Pollarding necessitates getting into the crown and using a handsaw to drop the poles below the feller.

New woodland: Prepare the ground and plant those species you require. You can mix species as you would find them in a natural woodland, or plant a monoculture as was sometimes done with hazel and chestnut. Choose species that grow well in the wild in your locality: however much you want to grow chestnut, if your ground is wet, chalky clay, you will never succeed.

Provenance: Not only should your choice of trees fit your locality, it should also be for native species, and preferably local stock. The provenance of trees can affect frost tolerance, rate of growth, tree form and the properties of the wood itself. The gene pool held by our native trees is unique; we should treasure it. If you are buying trees, insist on knowing their provenance and that it fits what you have taken the time to find out about your site. And if, as a result of European Union rules, you can only buy German oak and beech selected for their teutonic straightness, do as I do every autumn – grow your own.

Your site: Where possible talk to the previous owners or local people who have used the site – they often have valuable information. Also try to observe your site for a year before undertaking a serious planting schedule. By doing this you could avoid costly mistakes.

To get the best results, make sure you check:

- Its wetness in all seasons: this will affect your choice of trees.
- Avoid frost hollows: frost can kill the leading buds of young hazel, ash and oak, giving dog-legged poles.
- Try to get a symmetrical block, not a long strip; it will be cheaper to fence and manage.
- Plan for adequate access in order to extract your products.

Methods of Propagation

If you are not to buy nursery stock, there are four ways of obtaining new trees; the best method for each species is in **table 3.1**.

Table 3.1 The Propagation of Native Trees

Species	Method [2]	Timing [1]	Notes
Alder	seed (2-3)	Sept/Oct	Pick cones just before ripening; dry to release seed
Ash	seed (3-5)	Aug/Oct	August to sow immediately; Oct to store for 18 months
Aspen	sucker	Oct/Feb	Seed very difficult to collect and germinate
Beech	seed (5-10)	Sept/Nov	Seed may need water in Jan to remain plum
Birch	seed(1-2)	July/Aug	Pick catkins just before they ripen
Box	seed	Aug/Oct	Pick fully ripe fruit
Chestnut	seed (3-4)	Oct/Nov	Best seed in warm summer
Elm	sucker/layer	Oct/Feb	Fertile seed is rare
Hazel	seed (1)	Sept/Feb	Collect seeds as they loosen in husk and before squirrels eat them
Holly	seed (2-4)	Nov/Jan	Collect fully ripe berries; best stored approx. 18 months
Hornbeam	seed (2-4)	Sept/Oct	Seed best stratified for 18 months
Lime	seed (3-5)	Oct	Needs a hot summer to produce fertile seed; store 18 months
Maple	seed (2-3)	Sept/Oct	Seed best stratified 18 months
Oak	seed (3-4)	Sept/Nov	Ripe seed loose in cup and chocolate brown
Poplar	cutting	Oct/Feb	Take hard wood cutting
Rose Family:			
• Apple	seed (2-4)	Aug/Oct	Pick fully ripe fruit
• Hawthorn	seed (1-2)	Sept/Nov	Pick fully ripe berries; best stratified 18 months
• Service tree	seed (2-4) /sucker	Sept/Nov	Pick fully ripe fruit Suckers grow well
Sallow	cutting	Oct/Feb	Take hardwood cutting
Sycamore	seed (2-3)	Sept/Oct	Avoid planting if possible
Willow	cutting	Oct/Feb	See text for osiers
Cherry	seed (1-3)	July/Sept	Pick ripe berries before birds and sow immediately

[1] = Timing defines the best time to collect seed or take cuttings etc.
[2] = The number in brackets denotes the appropriate frequency of good seed years, i.e. 3 means every third year.

Suckers: Some species, particularly aspen and some elms, produce vigorous suckers, which if cut from the root that supports them will grow on as separate trees (**Fig 3.1**). Never remove suckers from a hedge or woodland without permission.

Layers: This process was described in the previous chapter. It is the only way to obtain specimens of varieties that produce neither fertile seed nor suckers; it was the favoured by Victorian foresters for propagating elms (**Fig 3.2**). Follow the method described, but then after two growing seasons, transfer the young tree to its new site.

Cuttings: For willows, osiers and poplars, this is undoubtedly the simplest and easiest means of producing new trees. Follow these steps, which have produced many native black poplar trees for me:

- When the sap is down (October to February), take approx. 200mm (8in) cuttings of hard wood pencil thick and with 3-4 good buds.
- Cut top back to approx. 300mm (1in) above topmost good bud
- Insert cutting in ground so topmost bud app. level with soil
- After 12 months lift the rooted cutting, and cut new growth back to a basal bud; replant this "rooted stump" (**fig 3.3**)
- After a further 12 months you will have a "rooted set" with a sturdy stem. Lift this and plant in its final position.

Osiers (Salix triandra, viminalis and purpurea) are treated slightly differently. Cut 'sets', from one year old rods, approx. 350mm (14in) long, and insert them straight into their final position

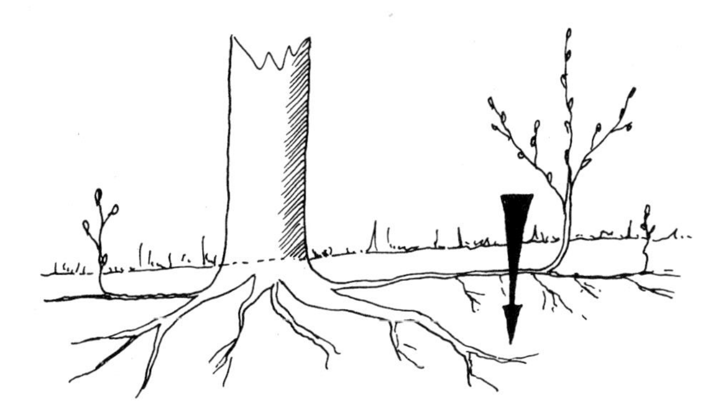

Fig. 3.1 **Root suckers showing where to separate them from the parent tree.**

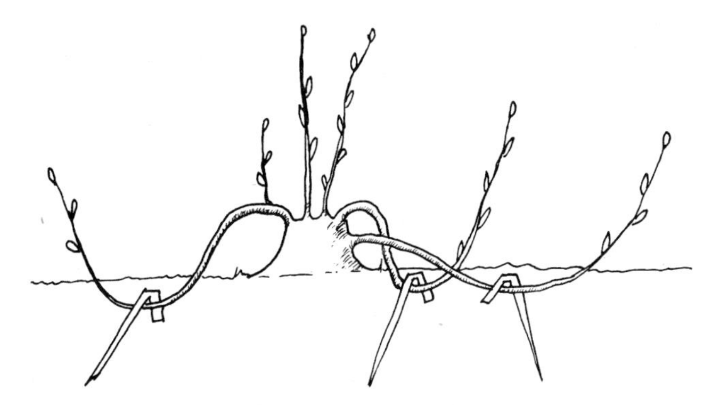

Fig. 3.2 Elm shoots being layered to produce new trees (after Brown, 1882).

with approx. 200mm (8in) above the ground. Site the rows 700mm apart, and the sets 350mm apart in each row (16,500 sets/acre). You will get your first usable rods in year three, and be in full production in year seven after planting.

Seed: A majority of native trees reproduce perfectly well from seed (**see Table 3.1**) provided you follow certain basic rules for their collection, storage and sowing. I have collected seed of ash, maple, oak, hazel and hawthorn, and successfully grown young trees from them. Collect seed from the immediate vicinity of your planting site to be sure the soil chemistry and moisture are suitable.

There are three limitations you may face: firstly for some species simply getting at the seed is difficult, and a very long hooked stick is invaluable for pulling down branches, and safer than a ladder. Secondly not all species have good seed production every year, and although a guide to the frequency is given in **Table 3.1**, nothing beats careful inspection each year; and lastly, not all seed is biologically ready to germinate as it falls from the tree – **Table 3.1** indicates the problem species.

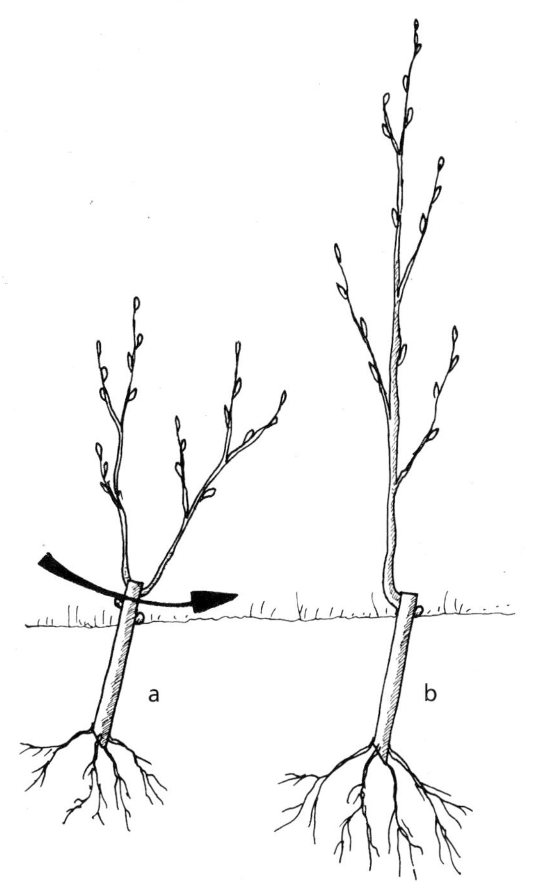

Fig. 3.3 Cuttings: a. the initial cutting, its first year growth and how to cut it back; b. the next year's growth.

Collection and storage: To collect and store seed, follow these steps:

- Collect at the right time (**see Table 3.1**) for seed maturity and to beat the squirrels!
- Check the quality as you go; aim for plump, firm seed
- Don't pick more than you need: 1kg of acorns will raise at least 100 trees, whereas the same weight of birch seed will raise 100,000!
- Plant quickly, where possible, into a prepared seed bed or containers, which can be trays or pots, covering the seed to the same depth as its own size (i.e. 3mm cover for a 3mm seed)
- If not planted straight away, store dried seed in airtight containers in a cool, dry place
- Dry your cones and catkins in a warm room till they open and shed their seed, which is then stored as above
- To 'stratify' seeds that are not mature enough to germinate the first spring after collection, mix with an equal volume of damp sand (enough to keep the seeds separate), pack into

Table 3.2 Weight, Germination Rate and Sowing Density of Native Seeds

Species	App. number of seeds/kg	App. % germination rate	Sowing density. sq. metres/kg	Probable trees/ kg of seed
Ash	13,200	50	20	6,100
Birch	550,000	20	55	110,000
Beech	4,400	50	5	2,200
Chestnut	240	45	1	110
Cherry	5,500	20	8	1,100
Oak	280	40	2	110
Maple/Sycamore	13,200	35	20	4,600
Hazel	300	75	10	225

a pot protected by 6mm (1/4in) wire mesh, and bury in the ground in more damp sand (**fig. 3.4**)

- Stored seed should be sown in March/April, using the same method already described for fresh seed, and if into a bed, using the densities shown in **Table 3.2**

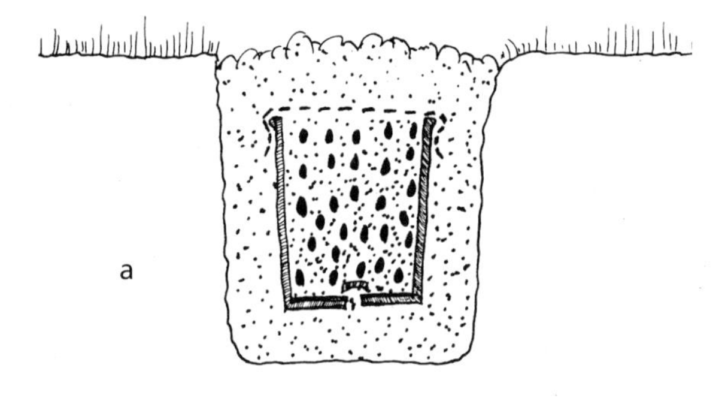

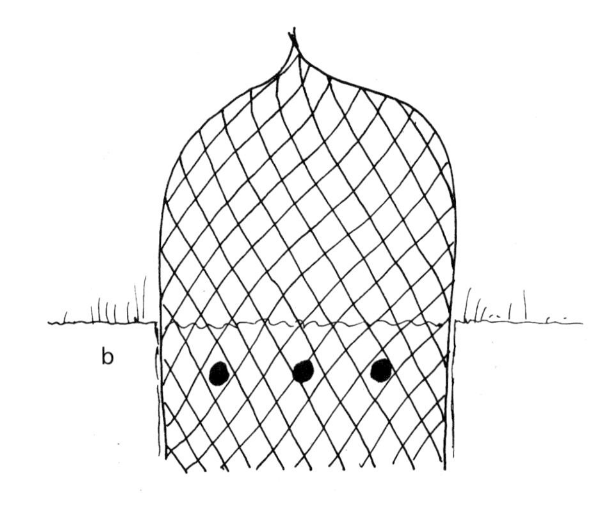

Fig. 3.4 a. Storing seeds in damp sand; b. seeds planted direct into the soil and protected by wire mesh.

Growing your seedlings: The golden rule is weed, weed and weed again in order to give young seedlings any chance. Ensure the young plants do not dry out so much that they wilt; check that the soil under the surface is moist. Another problem for seedlings in open beds may be birds or cats; layers of pea sticks laid flat across the seed bed will protect them, as will wire mesh over your containers.

Young plants should be left in the seed bed until they are 0.6-0.9m (2-3ft) tall whips. Depending on the species they will reach this stage in two to five years. Young trees should not be kept in beds for more than two years without being moved, and 'undercutting' them (**see fig. 3.5**) in order to stimulate a strong, bushy root system which will increase their growth rate when finally planted out. Likewise containers must be large enough to allow good root development, and after two years in their seedling container, they must be transferred to 150mm (6in) pots or similar.

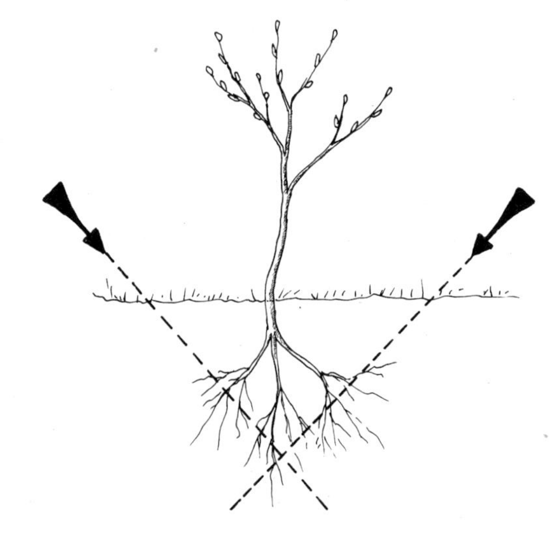

Fig. 3.5 Undercutting a young tree to move it and stimulate stronger root growth.

Planting out

This is best done between November and February, but not when the ground is frosted or snow covered.

Preparation: Land just cleared of trees will require no preparation, and planting should begin immediately to ensure the young trees get a head start against any weeds.

Some preparation may be needed for bare land. If it is grassy, mow the grass down hard, and with spade or mattock, 'screef' a bare patch app. half a metre in diameter at each planting point. Bracken, if not burned, is best crushed when green

Finally the whips themselves should be carefully lifted from their bed as follows:

- Insert a garden fork vertically into ground beside the whip, and lever to 45°; repeat this around the whip to loosen it
- Carefully lift whip from soil, shaking to remove excess soil only
- Trim off roots longer than 180mm(7in) to aid lifting and planting
- Protect the roots of whips from drying out by placing them in buckets or plastic bags until planting with moist moss protected from frost and direct sun.

Planting: Before any trees go into the ground, have a clear plan as to where they will go. What spacing should you be using, and how many trees will you need per acre of new planting?

Table 3.3 shows the distance between trees, and how many per acre will result. How close trees are placed depends on your ultimate goal, but coppice must be close planted to draw the stems up straight with few side branches; timber trees

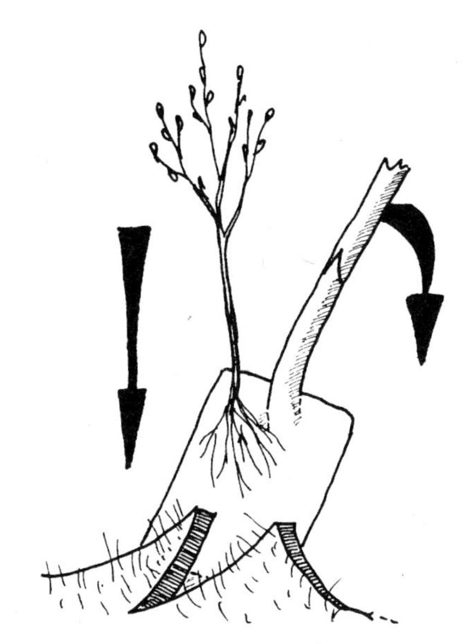

Fig. 3.6 Making a 'T' cut to plant a young whip.

start close to control weeds, but are gradually thinned out to give their crowns space. Some typical examples are:

- hazel coppice – 2m (6.5ft)
- chestnut coppice – 3m (10ft)
- young timber – 2m (6.5ft)
- bat willows – 10m (33ft)
- poplars – 6.5m (21ft)
- oak/beech woodland – 7-8m (23-26ft) at maturity

If you want to grow some timber amongst your coppice, do not exceed 10/12 mature trees per acre, or the shade will hold back the coppice growth

To get whips into the ground make a 'T' or 'L' cut with a spade (**fig. 3.6**); open the soil sufficiently to insert the young tree, and carefully firm the ground back to complete the job. Larger trees

Table 3.3 Trees per hectare at specified spacing

Distance (m)	Trees/hectare	Distance (m)	Trees/hectare
2	2988	6.5	247
2.5	1911	7.5	185
3	1326	8	148
3.25	975	9	118
3.5	745	10	98
4	590	11	86
4.5	476	12	74
5.5	330	13	61

Note: one hectare = 2.47 acres

(1-2m/3-6.5ft) require a hole of sufficient size to take all the roots, which is then back-filled and firmed with the tree in place; do not plant trees any deeper than they were in the nursery bed.

Any whips not planted should be 'heeled in' to a trench (**fig. 3.7**) to keep their roots moist and frost free. I have kept hazel heeled in for four months without damage.

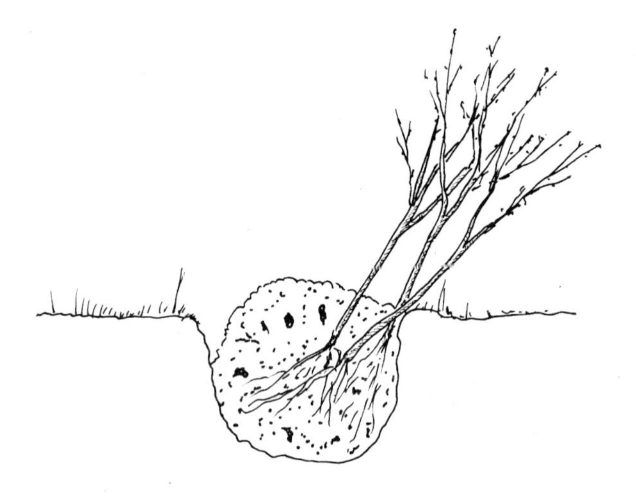

Fig. 3.7 Whips 'heeled in' to protect them from frost and from drying out.

Care: In order to facilitate mowing and weeding, your trees will probably be in serried ranks. Weeds and grass must be kept back to approx. 600mm (23in) around each tree. Use a mower, hook or glyphosate, avoid damaging the bark, and use any cuttings as a mulch to retain precious moisture. You will need to continue this until the young trees are at least 1.5m (5ft).

The battle with your local wildlife also begins now, for rabbits, hares, grey squirrels, mice, voles and deer all find young trees very palatable! It is inevitable that you will have to protect your young woodland.

- ***Rabbit fencing:*** Use 1" mesh wire netting 1.1m wide with the bottom 15cm turned out flat on the ground and ideally covered in turf. Fix fencing to 1.5m (5ft) posts placed approx. 3m (10ft) apart, and preferably to a top wire of 8 gauge material.
- ***Deer fencing:*** Although rabbit fencing will probably keep muntjac deer at bay, fallow protection will require a 1.8m (6ft) high fence. Use 2.4m (8ft) posts placed at 2.4m (8ft) intervals driven in securely 0.5m and high tensile deer netting stapled to them. Electric fencing is difficult to maintain, and not fully effective.
- ***Tree guards and shelters:*** For areas less than five acres check if tree guards and shelters are cheaper than fencing. Spiral guards are ineffective against deer. Use 1.5m (5ft) guards against fallow, or 1.2m (4ft) against muntjac.

Creating coppice: After 5-7 years you must cut the young trees down to virtually ground level. The strong root system they have developed will result in a really rapid growth of young shoots. Protect these from browsing, and in a further 7 years you will at last have your first crop of usable hazel rods; larger ash or chestnut poles will take longer.

Grants

Financial assistance for planting, re-planting and hedge improvement is often available. These grants vary periodically in their source and scale, so you must be prepared to shop around. Also understand that grants usually involve commitments to carry out work over a period of years, to wildlife, and to public access.
For advice contact:

- Local Forestry Commission Office for details of Woodland Grant Schemes
- Local Authority - via the county tree or woodland officer that most authorities now employ – for direct aid
- Local Farming and Wildlife Advisory Group (FWAG)representative for advice on sources, which may include: Ministry of Agriculture; Tree Council; Countryside Agency; National Park Authorities; and any European Union schemes.

Further reading:

Blyth, J. et al., ***Farm Woodland Management***, Farming Press Ltd., 1991
Brooks, A. ***Woodlands – A Practical Conservation Handbook***, British Trust for Conservation Volunteers (BTCV) Ltd., 1980
Edlin, H. ***Collins Guide to Tree Planting and Cultivation***, Collins, 1975
Rodwell, J. + Patterson, G. ***Creating New Native Woodlands***, Forestry Commission Bulletin 112, H.M.S.O. 1994
Mutch W. ***Tall Trees and Small Woods***
Broad K.***Caring for Small Woods***

Chapter 4

Obtaining Your Wood

Sources

There are many sources from which you can obtain wood. Some may be expensive, but many will require little more than your time and effort and the goodwill of the owner. Even if you are lucky enough to have your own woodland, there may be occasions when you want to acquire some special wood.

Standing trees: Buying standing trees is probably the best way to get exactly what you need. This way you can cut when you want (within limits); you control how long the wood is felled before use; you can paint special butts to reduce splits as you fell; you can cut and trim the trees to exactly the sizes and shapes that you want; lastly you probably get all the firewood as bunce.

Don't overlook your own back yard: I have hazel, ash and hawthorn hedges around my garden that supply poles, bean rods, pea sticks, walking sticks, handles and firewood.

Never ever cut someone else's tree without permission; every tree is owned by someone.

Community woodlands: in a number of areas Local Authorities or charitable trusts have set up 'community woodlands'. Purchased to encourage local communities to become involved in caring for woodlands, it is often the case that the trustees are more than happy for trees to be felled as a part of their programme for the wood. All you have to do is ask.

Conservation coppicing: one of the most useful sources of wood is the cutting of trees on nature reserves. This can be coppicing ancient or secondary woodlands, or the removal of unwanted trees from heathland or grassland. Most of these sites are owned or leased by charitable trusts such as The Woodland Trust, County Wildlife Trusts, English Nature or The National Trust. Much of this work is carried out by volunteers, so you will always be welcome and it often possible to take wood free or at a minimal charge. This is how I started. If you get serious, you can offer to cut an area under contract.

Farm woodlands: a majority of small woodlands remain as important features of farms. Whilst many farmers manage their own woodlands, particularly those to whom shooting is important, there are a few who would welcome help. Your best approach is through the local FWAG offices (see useful addresses).

Hedgerows: despite the publicity of recent years, there are still hedgerows that have to be managed. Those that are coppiced can provide some useful poles, so if you know the farmer or contractor and he is going to burn it, have a chat. A word of caution on hedgerow wood, however: it very frequently has a twisted grain resulting from the trees rotational movement to wind and sun, and older trees invariably have nails or staples embedded in them.

Pylon sites: in their march across the landscape electricity pylons frequently pass through areas of scrub and wood. The trees must be kept a specified distance from the power lines, meaning the responsible body has to go round cutting down the trees every few years. I have found them more than happy to let someone else do it, and pay you as well! It might also be worth contacting the Environment Agency about fellings of riverside trees.

Woodlots: this magazine is a splendid Forestry Commission publication in which standing wood is advertised. If you are serious, you can advertise free in Woodlots for the wood you want to cut (see appendix for address), but must pay for a copy of the magazine.

Coppice sales: these are for the serious practitioner. Advertised in local papers or at the roadside, these sales will be of high class wood for professional craftsmen. The 'cants' for sale are usually marked with white 'wash marks' on the trees or lines of cut stools, and craftsmen will walk the whole cant to be sure of its quality before the sale, which is usually in the local hostelry. Payment is normally 10% down with the balance due before the next sale.

Timber sales: these are advertised in appropriate journals or papers. I recommend talking to your local F.C. Woodland Officer or Forest Enterprise office who often know of small lots for sale.

Felled wood: This is often a very good means of obtaining less common woods, or getting small amounts of wood to experiment with. Expect to pay for the wood though, for it has cost someone time and resource to fell and cord it.

Firewood/timber merchants: Both of these groups produce a lot of cordwood during their work. If you know what you want, tell them, and if you are prepared to sort it out from their stock, you will probably obtain some good wood. You will need to have an eye for the particular wood you want so that you can sort it out. And make sure you are getting freshly felled wood; firewood is often left to season for two or three years, by which time it is no longer green wood and unsuitable for many of the methods in this book.

Conservation coppicing: We have already discussed how you could work with conservation volunteers to fell wood. If you do not have the time to fell the wood, you will find most organisations very ready to sell it felled. Again you may have to select your own, and you will have to collect it from the site.

Tree surgeons: this is another source of green wood, and is often a good way of obtaining more exotic species since much surgery is done in peoples' gardens. If this is the case, expect to pay a reasonable price for tree surgeons usually have good contacts and know how to dispose of their wood.

Wood fayres: these are an increasing part of the rural scene today. They are events at which in addition to craft demonstrations, wood of all sorts is frequently sold. If the fayre is held on a large estate, much of the wood can be exotic species. At some of the larger fayres it is also possible to have wood cut to your requirements. Do not expect cheap deals at these events, but you may be able to get small branch wood of rare species at a reasonable price.

Woodlots magazine: this magazine contains adverts for parcels of felled wood, but you must subscribe to obtain it.

Other peoples' waste: incredible as it may seem, to many people the trees that they fell are not a resource but a nuisance. There is always the opportunity to obtain wood that people just don't want and is destined for the bonfire. Hedgerows I have mentioned, but also consider:

Garden trees: people often plant trees without realising how large they grow, and the shade they cast. I have several times been asked to remove cherries and willows from gardens. This can again give you some unusual wood. But never take down large trees unless you are fully insured.

Clearances: Local Authorities are frequently responsible for the management of by-ways, old railway lines and footpaths that are continuously encroached upon by trees. As with hedges, most of this material is burned, so ask if you can take some.

Also keep your eye open for agricultural clearances. Some years ago several apple orchards close by our house were grubbed out, providing me with the perfect material for beetle heads.

Harvesting trees yourself

There is something special about felling and cutting up the tree whose wood you are to work with. There can be opportunities to cut wood yourself either on contract, or as part of a conservation group even if you do not have your own woodland. As with everything in green woodworking though, there is a right way to do it.

Coppice: Before you put billhook or saw to any trees, take the time to consider and plan what you are going to do.

Rotation: the age or rotation at which you cut coppice is ideally determined by the products you are making. Assuming good coppice of predominantly one species is available then the ages described in Chapter 2 would be the time to cut. Thus for good wattle hurdles cut at seven to ten years; for chestnut fencing cut at 16 years; for firewood cut at 25 years etc. If you have a range of ages to choose from, select the oldest from which

Table 4.1 Yields per acre of coppice

Species	Stools/acre	Rods or poles/acre	Main use
Good hazel @ 9 years	600	11,000	Hurdles and thatching wood
Poor hazel @ 19 years	400	4,500	Stakes, thatching and firewood
Good chestnut @ 16 years	590	2,350	Stakes, palings and firewood
Mixed coppice @ 17 years	440	3,600	Stakes; thatching; rakes; firewood
Mixed coppice @ 50 years	320	2,600	Firewood plus a few stakes; tent pegs; rakes; furniture

your target product can be made, for the younger wood will not spoil for a year or two.

Due to the neglect of many woodlands, it is much more likely that you will be cutting rather old mixed coppice. In this case you must adapt the traditional process by adjusting what you make to the material available, and develop markets for a range of products. Or you can sell on what you cannot use to another craftsman for whom it is ideal.

Measuring: Measure out what you are going to cut. Remember that with coppice all the stools will be felled; you cannot thin or select coppice or you will kill it. So you must mark out the area that will be clear felled (excepting timber trees). The basic measure of area is now the hectare, which is 2.47 acres. An acre is 4840 square yards, and an easy approximation of this in the wood is 70 paces (70 yards or 64 metres) by 70 paces. Half an acre is 70 x 35 paces and so on.

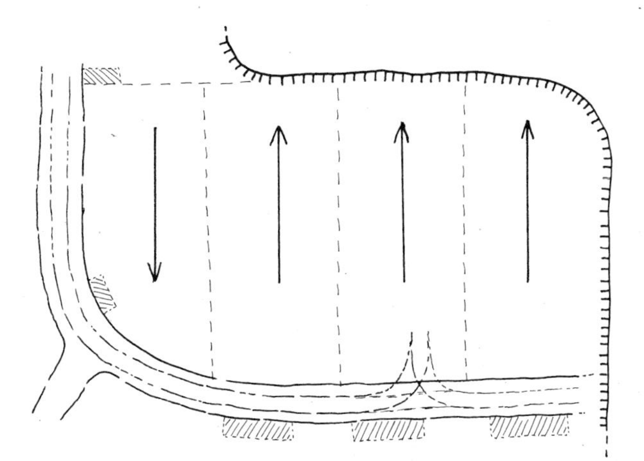

Fig. 4.1 Plan for cutting coppice and extracting product; the hatched areas are for storage.

Planning your cut: There are several points to consider.

- When – the traditional wisdom is to cut only when the sap is down, which is from September (when the hazelnuts are loose in their cup) until Lady Day, the 25th March. It is believed that this winter cut wood lasts longer when used outdoors, and that regeneration of the stools is better through having a full growing season. I believe that wisdom is right. If you need lime bast you are best to cut in April/May.
- How much – the most common failing is to under estimate how long it will take to select and clear up what you have felled. A professional hurdle maker would take nearly six weeks to utilise all he could fell in one week. Obviously a lot of wood can and should be held and worked up through the summer, but remember it will get progressively drier and more difficult to work. **Table 4.1** shows how many rods and poles you will get from one acre.
- Access and cutting plan – take a good look at the site and decide how you are going to fell your cant. Plan your means of extracting the cut wood, preferably down hill, and arrange

for storage adjacent to your route (**fig. 4.1**). Allow for tractor access if necessary. Plan how you will cut, where to start, and the width of the strip you will cut. Remember, always cut to a line, and try to arrange it so that however or whenever you finish you do not leave inaccessible blocks of uncut coppice. The felling of any standard trees should also be planned, and inevitably today when so many deer roam the countryside, fencing your regenerating stools to protect them from browsing. Remember that in everything you do with trees you must be planning ahead – think of the quality of the wood you will want to cut in 10 years time. And if you don't react to a serious deer problem you will have no wood to cut!

Cutting: Now you can start cutting! Good woodmen only do a job once: they 'think about it thrice, measure it twice and do it once – properly'.

- Hazel coppice less than 12 years old is best cut in a strip 10m (11yds) wide if you are working alone.
- Fell the rods and lay them at each side of the strip in drifts, butts to the middle but with a good gap between (**fig. 4.2**). Fan out the stems so they are easier to separate when working up. Continue cutting the strip until you reach the end of your cant. Now come back through the drifts working up the wood. Pile the different grades of rod separately ready for bundling, and put the rubbish to one side for faggotting or onto a small controlled fire. Bundle and stack your wood off the ground and in shade before you move on to another strip. If you are making wattle screens in the wood, you will not want to cut more than an acre before stopping to make up some product.
- Mixed coppice or chestnut is cut older than hazel so that many of the poles are larger. Still work by cutting a strip, but sort and clear the poles as you go. Cord up any firewood, bundle and stack the different material against your planned use or sales, put pea sticks to one side in a 'ringe' to be bundled later, and burn the waste material as you go. Keep your work area clear, with everything put away in its right place.
- Most importantly when you are working up, look closely at the wood in your hand before you put the saw or hook to it. You must develop an eye for what you can use and remember it is always possible to trim wood down later, but you can never put it back together again. Look for those crotches that make a thumbstick or a prop; look for the curve that will make a good spoon; look for the branch that will make a good walking stick handle. You may be under pressure to get on and complete the cut, but don't let that blind you to the opportunities in front of you.
- It is very important to cut stools properly. Your objectives are to maximise the usable product you harvest, and equally important, to ensure a good quality crop of poles next time. The advice of John Evelyn, written in 1786, still cannot be bettered: 'The cutting, slanting, smooth and close is of great importance cut not above half a foot from the ground, nay the closer the better'. The most common failing is to cut too high (**fig. 4.3**). Not only does this waste wood, but the re-growth from high

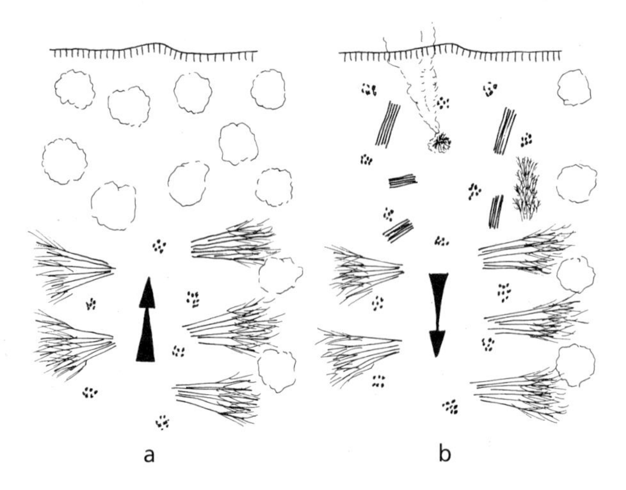

Fig. 4.2 Hazel coppice: a. cutting into drifts; b. working up.

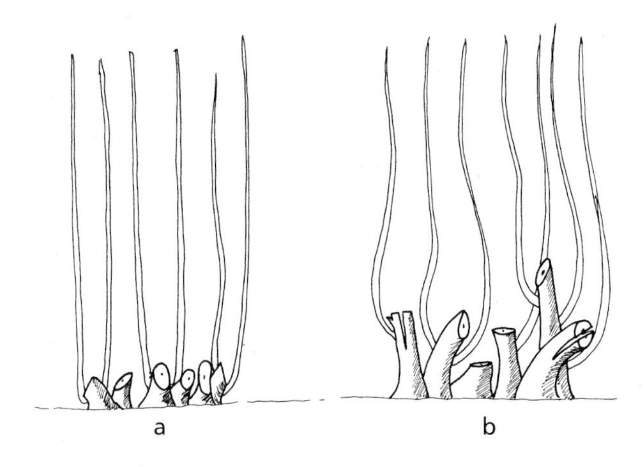

Fig. 4.3 The advantages of cutting low is shown in a; the disadvantages in b.

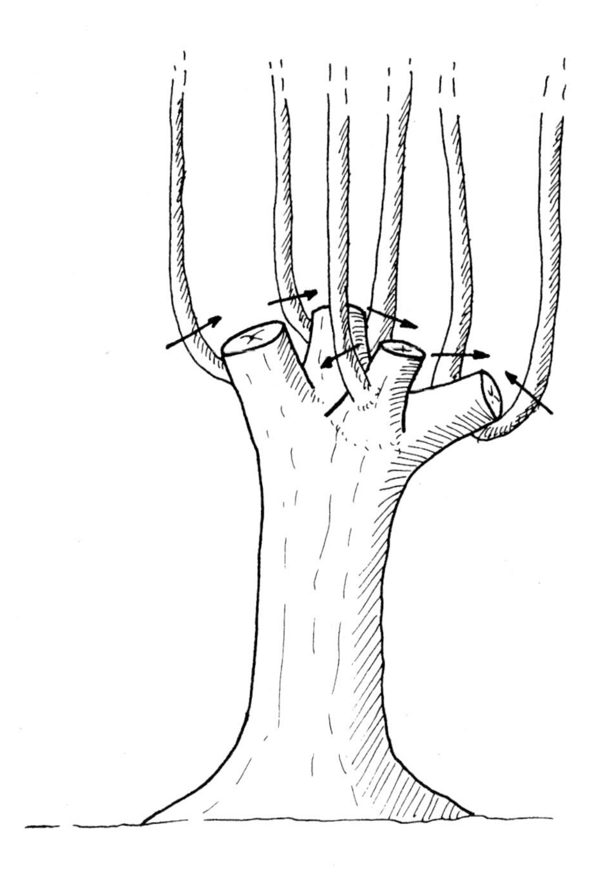

Fig. 4.4 Pollarding: leave reasonable stubs to ensure good regeneration.

stools is always more curved and more like a branch than a stem, resulting in a poorer crop next time. Cut with care so that the butts left on the stool are not split and ragged, with the bark pulled away, and angled so that the cut faces slope away from the centre of the stool. These points will all help to slow the rotting process and put back the time when you have to replace the stool.

Pollards: Pollards are, in effect, coppice cut 2.4m (8ft) above the ground (**fig. 4.4**). They are a compromise to allow wood to be grown whilst animals graze the surrounding vegetation, for the regenerating shoots are beyond their reach. Most trees will pollard successfully if the process is started when the stem is 15 to 20cm (6 to 8in) diameter. Beyond this size the risk of failure increases. In most cases the re-growth is that of a branch – frequently curved and twisted with many lateral shoots, normally rendering the product suitable for firewood and not much more.
The exceptions in my experience are willow, ash and occasionally beech, which can produce long straight poles; in the case of willow these are good enough to make cleft gate hurdles.

Fig. 4.5 Using a 'prog' to guide a stem; hold the prog to the side of the body.

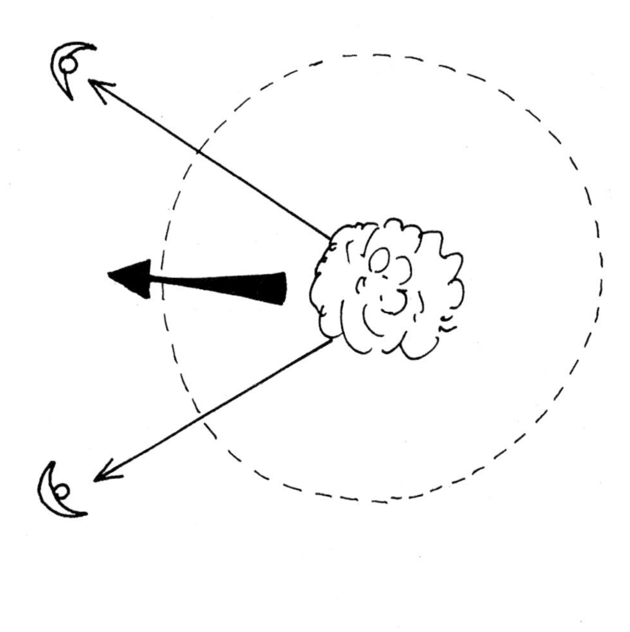

Fig. 4.6 When using ropes stay outside the danger zone defined by the height of the tree.

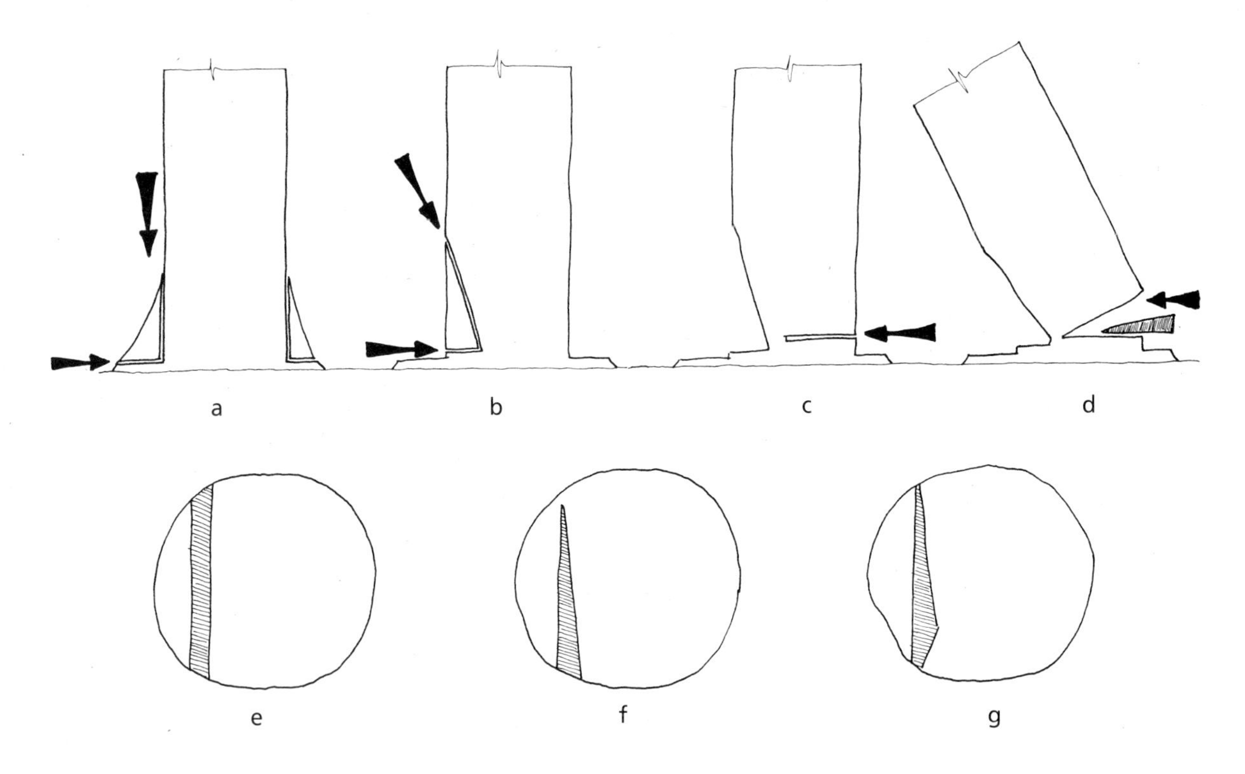

Fig. 4.7 Felling: a. removing buttresses; b. cutting a sink; c. the felling cut; d. using a wedge to fell the tree; e. a good hinge; f. and g. unsafe hinges.

Cutting pollards means working in the crown of the tree. Use a hand saw. Undercut a sink (see next section) on the side you want the pole to fall, and then cut through from the back, letting the pole fall away from you. Leave c.15cm (6in) of butt so there are buds to produce re-growth, for as we have seen progressively older stems are less likely to regenerate. Indeed on trees not cut for a very long time it is good practice for the first season to leave one or two stems uncut.

Larger standard trees: I shall assume in this section that you are not felling timber, which is the job of specialists, but rather maiden trees perhaps 60 years old and 30cm (12in) or so diameter at breast height. The best way of sustaining a supply of trees of this size is not to clear fell, but to either fell small groups or selected trees and allow natural regeneration to replace them. This produces mixed age woodland in which some trees are always ready to fell. You will have to bite the bullet and fell some poor quality trees each year or you will end up with no good ones!

Before felling trees, carefully read the Forestry Commission's free safety guides. In a confined area decide very carefully where you want to drop the tree in order to avoid damaging others, or even worse getting it hung up – a problem which will waste a lot of valuable time. Look at the crown of the tree and assess where its natural weight lies (the head of thick-twigged trees such as ash is very heavy – never under estimate it), and also the effect of any wind. You may need to consider the use of progs or ropes to assist you (**see figs. 4.5 & 4.6**). Once you have decided where the tree is to fall, the procedure is:

- Remove all the buttresses from the butt of the tree, making your horizontal cut about 2.5cm (1in) above the ground.
- Cut a sink on the side the tree is to fall (**fig. 4.7**). The position and accuracy of this is critical. Make the angled down cut first. To get the position of this right I find it best to stand behind the trunk facing the point I want the top of the tree to hit, and make the cut from this position. It is essential that the second, horizontal, cut does not go beyond the first cut and into the hinge, for it is this that controls the direction in which the tree will fall.
- Make the felling cut from the back, about 25mm (1in) above the sink. Go slowly and make sure you keep the hinge even at all times. If the tree rocks back, put two wooden gluts into the kerf behind the saw.

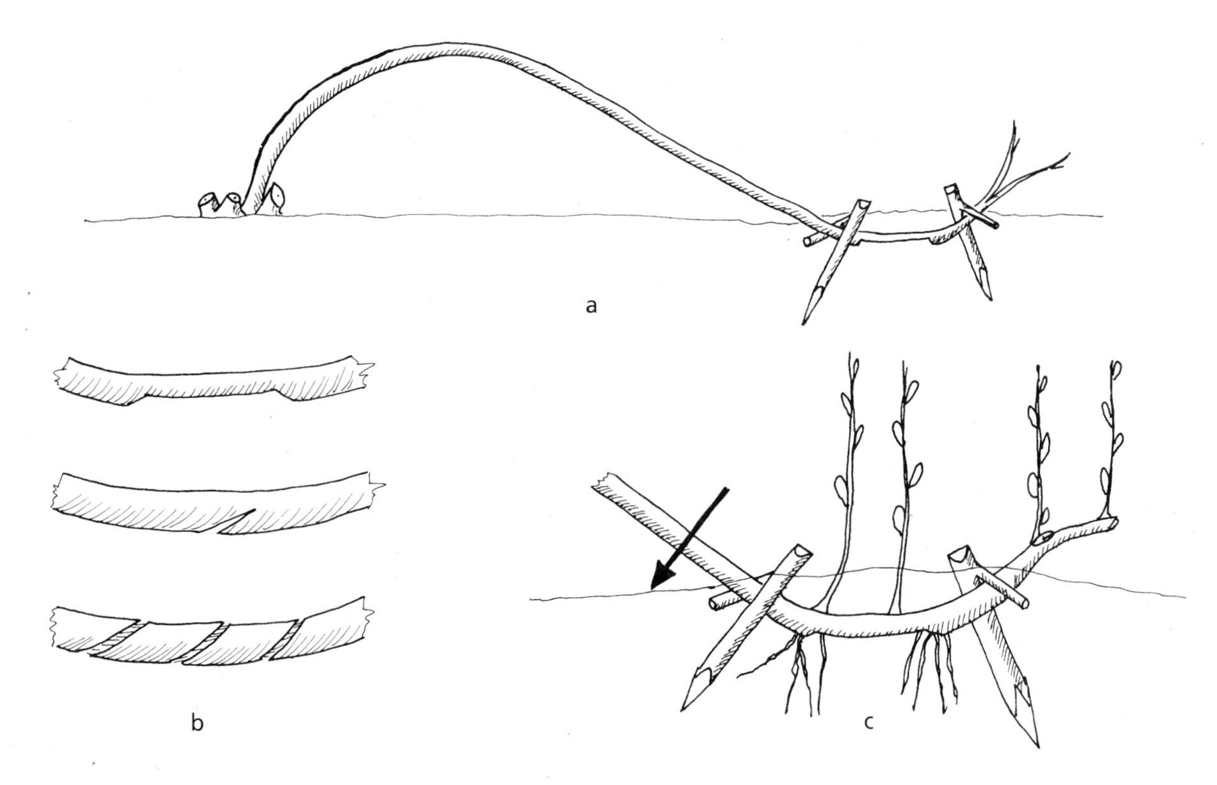

Fig. 4.8 Plashing: a. laying the stem over and c. cutting it free after one year. b. three ways of stimulating root growth – removing a sliver; a single cut; and twisting the stem to open the wood fibres.

- If the tree does not fall naturally under its weight, leave a 25mm (1in) hinge and drive the gluts in to topple the tree. Stand back clear of the butt, which might kick as the tree falls.
- You can now sned the tree and cut the bole as required.

Replacing dead trees: inevitably and however well a wood is managed, trees die, and whilst natural regeneration is ideal, nature sometimes needs a helping hand. The first golden rule, however, is that if you are managing an old woodland site do not bring outside stock in; maintain the unique biodiversity that already exists. The best ways of doing this are:

- In the autumn carry a pocketful of acorns and hazel nuts with you as you walk around the wood, and heel a few in where gaps exist.
- Take some seed home, germinate them in pots, and plant out after two or three years (see Chapter 3).
- Plashing. This was widely used by woodmen to fill gaps in the coppice. It requires thin young coppice stems at least 2.7m (9ft) long. Dig a short trench about 10cm (4in) deep where the new stool is to be. Carefully bend your selected stem over and where it will lay in your trench remove a strip of wood 7.5cm (3in) long and peg the stem into the trough (**fig. 4.8**). Cover the pegged stem with earth, and cut back the top of the stem to five or six buds. In 12 months, when the stem has rooted from the cut area and developed shoots, you can sever the plashed stem and you have a new tree.
  This works very well for hazel, chestnut and ash. Alternate ways to stimulate the plashed stem to root are shown in **fig. 4.8**.

Further reading:

Anon. ***Utilisation of Hazel Coppice***,
Forestry Commission Bulletin No. 27, 1956
Begley, C.D. ***Growth and Yield of Sweet Chestnut Coppice***, Forestry Commission Forest
Record No.30, 1955
Brooks, A. ***Woodlands***,
British Trust for Conservation Volunteers Ltd., 1980
Evelyn, J. ***Sylva, or a discourse on forest trees***,
London, 1786
Tabor, R. ***Traditional Woodland Crafts***,
Batsford, 1994

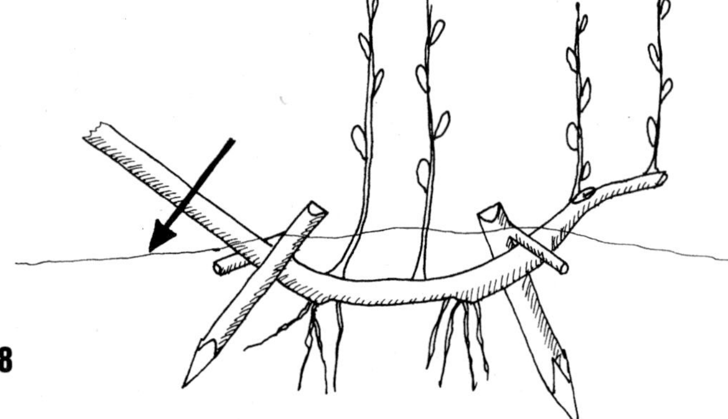

Chapter 5

Safety

Planning safety into your work

Safety at work is something that we all, quite rightly, have to take more seriously today as a result of changes in legislation. But irrespective of the law it makes good common sense to work safely: apart from the physical discomfort resulting from an accident, the potential for loss of income may be considerable. If you are working on someone else's site, you will have to comply with the Health and Safety at Work Act 1974, and probably have sufficient public liability insurance.

You must ***plan*** safety into what you do: avoid clutter both overhead and under your feet; exclude small children and animals from the working area; maintain a safe working space whether you are alone or in a group; concentrate on what you are doing and avoid distractions; and avoid taking shortcuts for they rarely pay off. Craftsmen had a long apprenticeship that gave them time to learn the safest methods, they worked alone with little distraction, and because they spent long periods repeating the same task they spent a lot of time setting up their work place. All of this contributed to minimising the risks, but in truth I have not met a woodman without a scar or two that marks a moment's indiscretion.

Obtain and read the relevant Safety Guides from the Forestry Commission – they are good, and free. Most of this chapter is common sense: take the time to stop and think. And don't work when you are too tired – take a rest.

First aid kit: You should always have an individual first aid kit with you wherever you are working. It should be in a clean, damp-proof container, and should typically contain:

- First aid guidance
- One large wound dressing
- Airstrip plasters
- 2 Triangular bandages + safety pins
- 6 Cleansing wipes
- 1 pair plastic gloves
- 1 pair blunt ended scissors
- 1 resuscitation mouthpiece
- 1 thermal blanket

Clothing: Sartorial elegance is secondary to safety and practicality in clothing. You want to be warm and comfortable whether indoors or out, for the day you are not concentrating on the job is the day you have an accident. Avoid clothing that snags easily, has dangling ties on it, or flapping scarves. When working outside, water or shower-proof clothing is sensible given English weather.

Understand when to wear and when not to wear your protective clothing – for example, in the coppice gloves are essential when handling bramble or thorn, but should never be worn for holding a billhook, which is likely to slip as a result. Footwear in the coppice or workshop should be non-slip, and where heavy butts of wood are being handled protective toecaps are a good idea. Clothing should also be appropriate to the tools you are using: never use a chain saw without full protective clothing (see below) and if using a draw knife or sharpening broches, protect your midriff or thigh respectively with a leather pad or several layers of sacking.

Health risks: Green woodworking usually requires quite a lot of work in the coppice. Now I firmly believe that a coppice is the most beautiful and spiritually satisfying place in which anyone could work. But that said, when you are working there, just take the following precautions:

- make sure you have an up to date tetanus injection
- watch out for ticks; they are carried by deer and harbour Lyme disease
- avoid working in stale water due to the risk of Weil's disease.

The tetanus injection is, of course, just as important if you are in the workshop.

Safety with tools

Hand tools: Do not use any tool until you have been trained, or you understand how to use it properly. All edge tools should be sharp – they are much safer that way than when you have to use extra effort to force a blunt tool to do a poor job. When you understand how to use your tools, use them with conviction to complete the job quickly, simply and neatly with minimum effort. Always give yourself a safe working space, and never cut towards yourself with an edge tool (**figs. 5.1 & 5.2**) - excepting shaves. With any tool that requires a swing make sure your footing is secure, that you are balanced and that there is nothing to impede or deflect your swing. With axe, billhook or mattock don't overreach; work in the way that is most effective for both the tool and yourself. Select the tool that matches your ability; for example if you use felling or side axes, select one of a weight you can use and control for most of the day – if you don't you will lose control with the inevitable result. Carry tools by your side with the cutting edge facing downwards or backwards.

Look after your tools. Inspect them regularly for faults that may lead to a failure and possible accident – chipped blades, broken handles, loose heads, rusty surfaces through putting them away wet – all items that a good workman will automatically keep on top of. Whether out in the coppice or at home in the workshop, tools should always have a place and be kept there. Edge tools hidden under leaves or shavings are a hazard; tools left with their cutting edge uppermost are even more so and these risks are doubled if you are working as a group instead of alone.

You will find details of how to use edge tools safely in Chapter 6.

Chain Saws: I am told that a sharp chain saw will cut through a 12 inch log in about 10 seconds; any part of the human body it will manage rather more quickly. In trained hands a chain saw is a tremendous aid to the green woodworker, saving much sweat and tears. In untrained hands it is potentially lethal. No one who has not been professionally trained and has not passed an NPTC training course should use one.

Never use a saw without full protective clothing, which is:

- Safety helmet with eye and ear protection to BS 5240 and replaced every 4 years if not damaged before that time
- All round leg protection (casual users) or full leg and front protection; any damage to the long woven fibres and they must be replaced
- Gloves with protective pad on back of left hand
- Chain saw boots.

The BTCV's book 'The Power Chain Saw' is an excellent guide to the safe use of this tool, and I

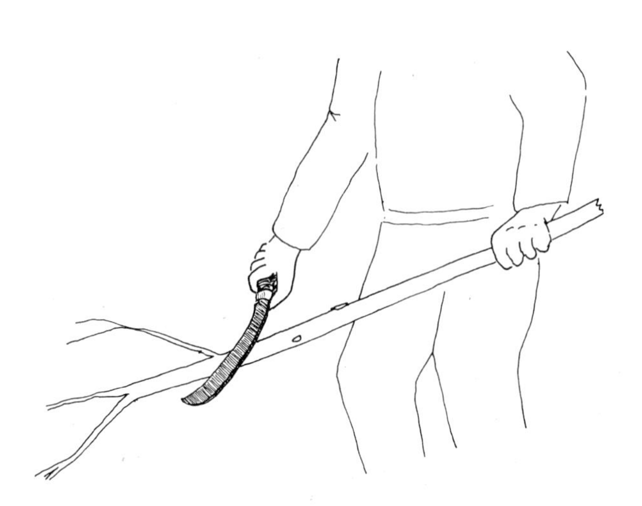

Fig. 5.1 Cut away from yourself with a billhook.

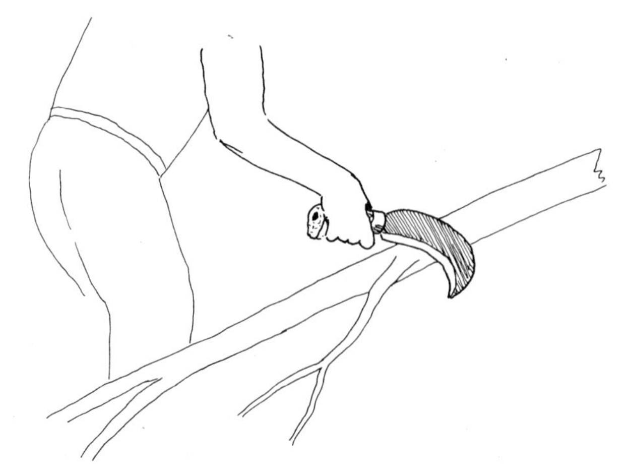

Fig. 5.2 Where possible keep a trunk between yourself and the branch being removed.

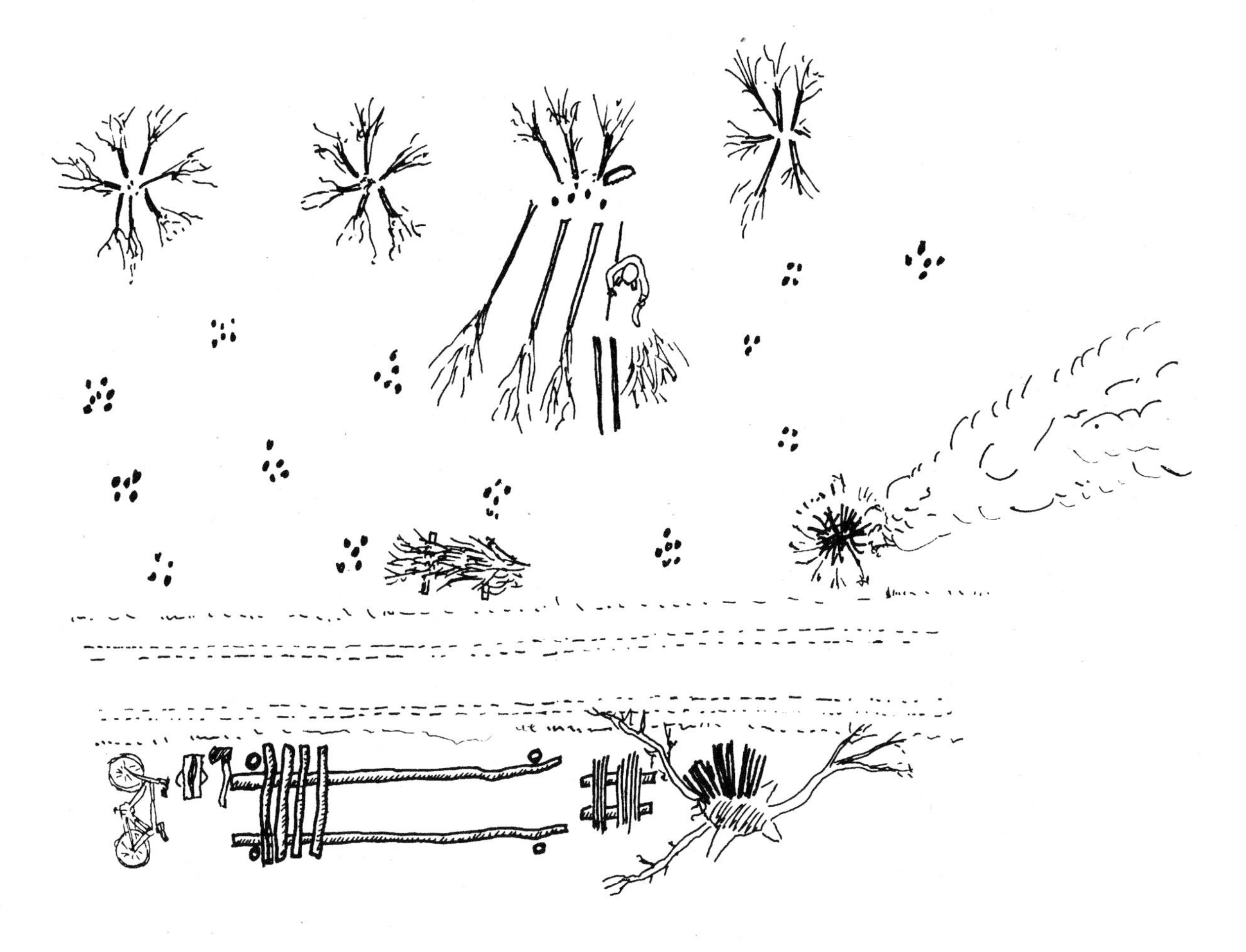

Fig. 5.3 Plan your worksite: fell into a clear area; keep the fire at a safe distance; keep worksite clear – stack product as you go; keep tools in a safe place.

recommend serious users refer to it. When I am using a chain saw I always: carry an extra large wound dressing in my pocket; check the chain brake at full engine revs; keep more that 5m away from other workers; never use it if I am alone; have an agreed sign language with my colleague; and take frequent rests.

Safe Working Methods

Coppicing: When harvesting coppice plan your work safely (**fig. 5.3**). Select a site for tools and personal belongings (and fuel if using a chain saw), a site for a fire, where wood will be stored and a safe route to it, and in what direction the trees will be felled. When working with others, make sure they know your plan as well!

Clear undergrowth that will impede your work. Carefully consider where the weight of a tree lies, the effect of the wind, the risks from any dead branches (called 'widow makers' in America), and that you have a clear fall so that the tree will not hang up. Fortunately most green woodworking relies on small round wood less than 20 years old, so that these risks can be minimised. If coppice poles do get hung up, then walk the butt away on your shoulder until the top falls safely behind you (**fig. 5.4**). Cut stumps low to avoid tripping hazards. Any stems under tension must be cut on

Fig. 5.4 When coppice poles get hung up, walk the pole away on your shoulder.

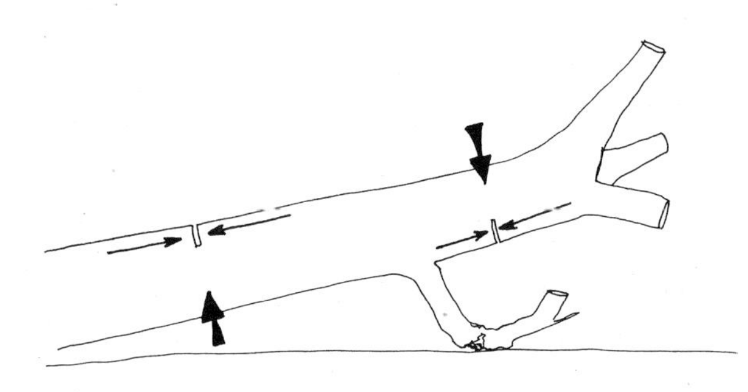

Fig. 5.5 Those parts of a trunk in compression are shown by the facing arrows; make the first cut here, followed by the main cut (heavy arrow).

the compression side first (**fig. 5.5**), and when making the final cut be prepared for sudden movement of the stem.

Fires: Fires in a wood should be few, small and carefully sited. Unfortunately when coppicing today they are a wasteful necessity since most of the twiggy top cannot be sold. Site your fire so that it is clear of the felling area, so that you are not working in smoke, and at least 3 metres (10ft) away from standard trees so that their bark is not lifted by the heat (Ash are particularly prone). Cut your waste wood to c.1 metre (3ft) long so the fire is not too large, and keep a prog or bale fork to hand to turn in the straggly ends and stop the fire from spreading.

Understand the nature of the woodland in which you are working and the effect of the time of year when planning a fire: some woods are like damp blotting paper and present little risk; others may be tinder dry and much more dangerous.

Keep the fire burning hot, never stand on it, never drop a tree across a fire, and avoid inhaling smoke – use a plastic sack as a temporary bellows if it needs a blow to get it going (**fig. 5.6**). When making charcoal in an oil drum, make sure it is stable on its brick supports, beware of smoke and twigs flaring up when leaning in to light it, and use gloves when sealing down at the end of the burn for the drum is very hot indeed.

Green woodworking sometimes requires the use of a steamer. Always ensure this is properly vented, it is not a pressure vessel, and wear gloves when unloading to avoid the risk of scalding.

Lifting and Carrying: These activities now warrant a regulation of their own (the Manual Handling Operations Regulations 1992), reflecting the very high number of injuries sustained whilst performing these apparently simple tasks. The main risk is the handling of large butts of wood, particularly on slippery ground or in a congested workshop.

You must remember that injury can result from: lifting weights that are too great; not bending the legs when lifting; overreaching; lifting a weight too high; twisting the body with a load; lifting with arms instead of legs; pulling heavy objects when off balance.

As with everything, there is a best way. You should remember it:

- Get as close as possible to the item
- Do not bend the back or lean forward from the hip (**fig. 5.7a**)
- Keep the feet apart, one slightly in front of the other and lower the body by bending legs (**fig. 5.7b**)
- Get a good grip of the item and straighten the legs
- Pull the load into the body keeping the elbows in (**fig. 5.8**)
- Lower the load by bending the legs

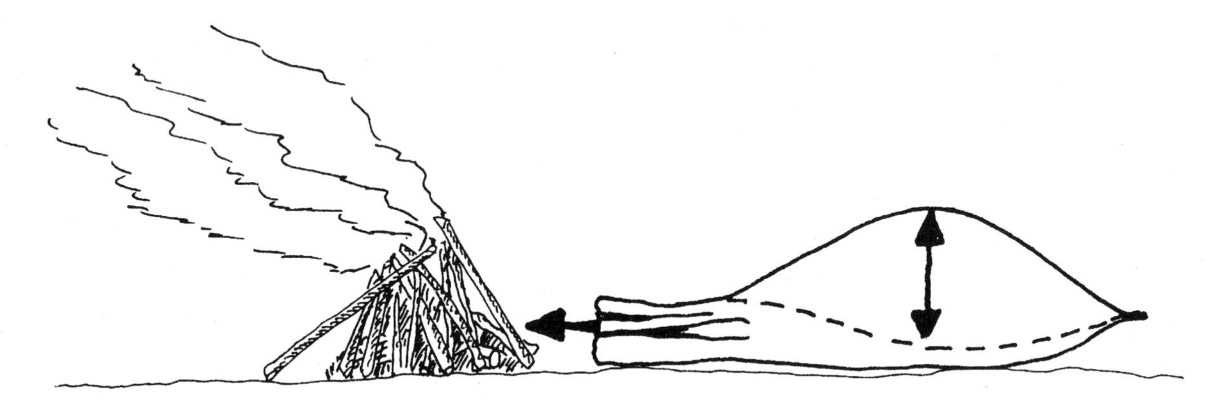

Fig. 5.6 Using a plastic sack as a temporary bellows.

Make sure you have a clear route when carrying a heavy object. Use your brain to do your lifting and moving: use simple trolleys where possible; use levers to lift and move heavy butts **(fig. 5.9)**; cut down large pieces to the smallest usable size before moving them.

Fig. 5.7 Do not bend your back when lifting.

Fig. 5.8 Carry heavy weights close to the body.

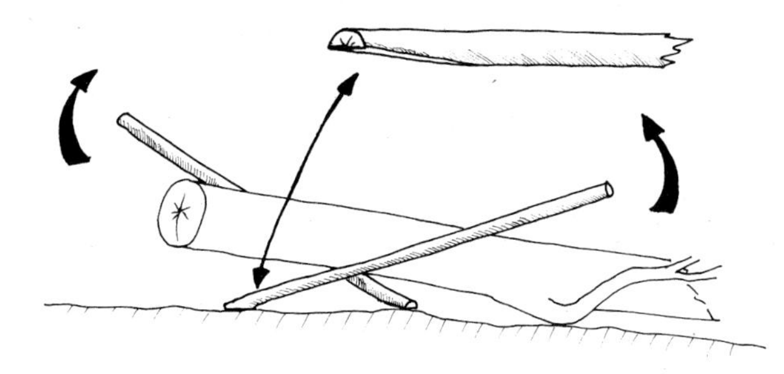

Fig. 5.9 Using flat-tipped levers to move a heavy trunk.

Further reading:

Anon. ***Forestry and Arboriculture Safety & Training Council Safety Guides***, Forestry Commission

Anon. ***Codes of Good Practice***, Essex Wildlife Trust 1998

Brooks, A., ***Woodlands – A Practical Conservation Handbook***, British Trust for Conservation Volunteers 1980

Brooks, A. ***The Power Chain Saw***, British Trust for Conservation Volunteers, 1974

Chapter 6
Edge Tools

The types of edge tools

Edge tools is the generic title woodmen and toolmakers use to describe those tools with a sharpened edge or blade. It includes all of the most important tools for the woodworker, with the exception of the saw. Axes, billhooks and knives are tools of great antiquity and the flints mined from Grimes Graves in Norfolk around 4000 years ago were a valuable commodity from which primitive edge tools were made.

Many edge tools such as billhooks are deceptively simple in appearance. This belies their efficiency, resulting from patterns honed by generations of woodmen and blacksmiths. In this section we will explore the range of edge tools and understand what they are used for. The right tool for the job, working well, will give you immense satisfaction.

Billhook or Handbill: Billhooks are the single most important tool for the coppice worker, performing a wide range of tasks. Wattle hurdles can be made with no other tool, although in fairness a hurdle maker may use two or three patterns of hook for different tasks.

Patterns and uses: Look in any of the major tool makers (Nash, Gilpin, Brades, Swift or Elwell)

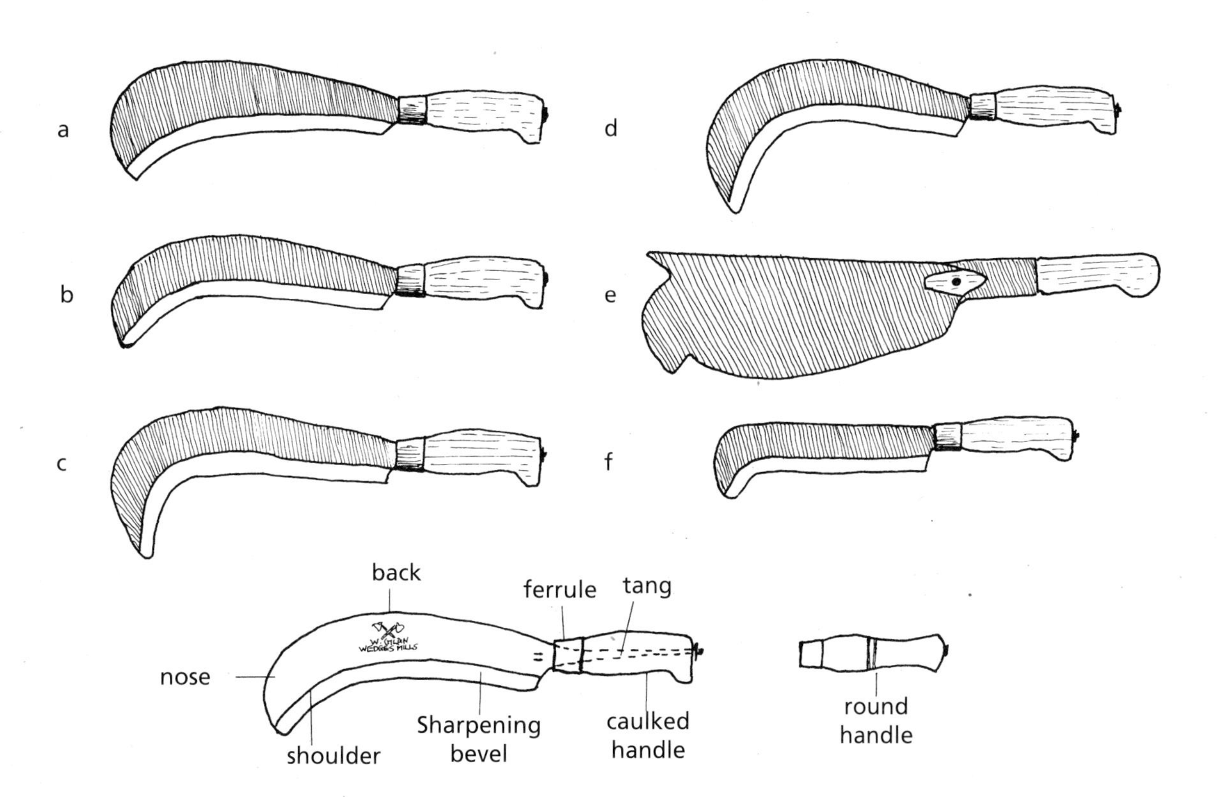

Fig. 6.1 Billhooks: a. Cutting/felling; b. Tenterden; c. Hurdle makers; d. Faggoting; e. Suffolk; f. Spar

catalogues from the beginning of this century and you will find over 100 patterns of billhook. Although this range appears bewildering, there are a few key factors that determine the performance of a billhook; a range of billhooks illustrates these. (**fig. 6.1**).

- a convex cutting edge ***(Suffolk)*** is better for cutting through large poles, and chopping material on a block; a concave edge ***(Faggotting)*** is best for work on twiggy branches which are gathered and cut by the blade's curve
- a short nose ***(Suffolk)*** is best for cutting downwards close to the ground (laying a hedge) or chopping on a block for there is nothing to drive into the ground or snag into the block
- a long nose ***(Hampshire hurdling/Tenterden)*** is ideal for riving small rods, where the tool is used to lever the clefts apart rather than to cut them, and it is ideal for hooking rods up from the floor and saving your back
- a single sharpening bevel ***(Suffolk/Kent)*** is best for sharpening small poles (it bites into the wood) or removing knots very flush to the pole. Remember these hooks are left or right handed.
- Weight and size needs to match the task: splitting spars needs little weight ***(Spar hook)***; cutting larger poles needs more weight and a socketed handle ***(Suffolk)***, the extra length of which gives a more powerful stroke
- caulked handles of ash, willow or alder, unvarnished are best: they absorb moisture and do not easily slip from the hand
- a good hook should have a minimum of shoulder behind the cutting edge so that it cuts ***through*** the wood – it should not be like a chisel. Older hooks are better since they were hammered from a billet, not pressed – you will see the thickness tapers from tang to nose and from back to edge, resulting in a superb balance that is never tiring in use.

Using a billhook: Use the hook with conviction, matching the stroke to the thickness of the material to be cut. Always cut away from yourself, and when snedding try to keep a stem between you and the branch being cut (**figs. 5.1 & 5.2**). When threading rods of their twigs keep your hand ahead of the hook to maintain the strength of your stroke, and pull the rod backwards with your other hand. Trim and cut towards the top of la branch, and keep the blade flat on the rod to remove twigs.

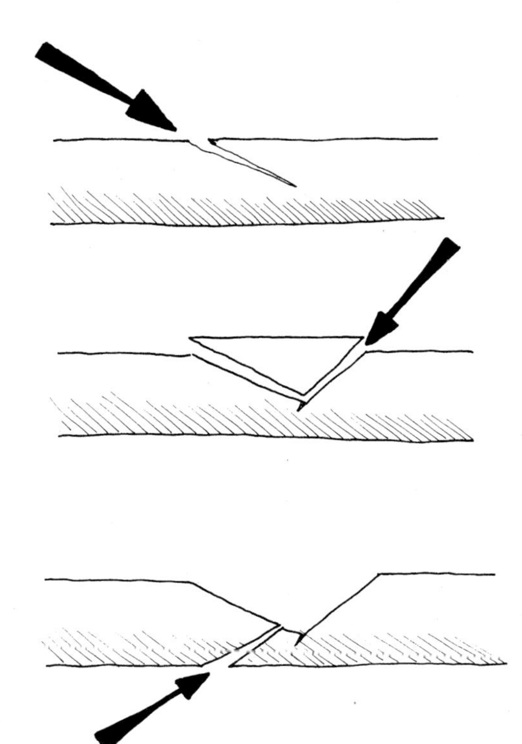

Fig. 6.2 Cutting a thick stem with three cuts.

Thicker rods may need three or four cuts – remove a 'v' of wood from one side, and then sever the rod from the other (**fig. 6.2**). When cutting poles from a stool try to cut upward with a curving cut to avoid splitting the remaining stub (**fig. 6.3**). Using the hook to rive rods is described in Chapter 11.

Always store your billhook safely – edge down, and wrapped in a rag when in your bag.

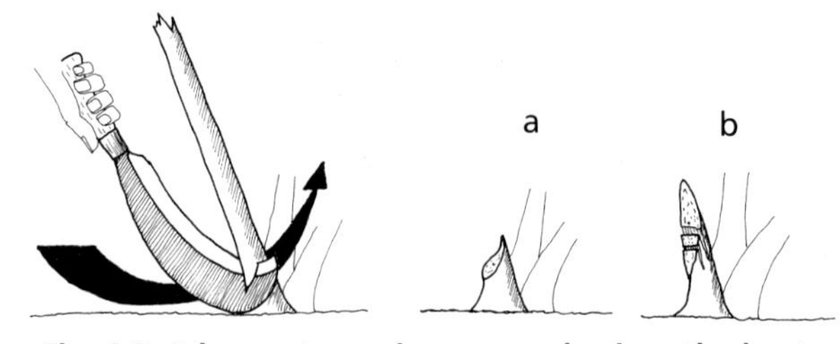

Fig. 6.3 A low cut, curving upwards gives the best finish (a); cutting downwards splits the stub (b).

Axes: Over the last 25 years we have seen the axe completely supplanted as the tool for felling trees by the chain saw. Green woodworking, however, still provides a number of tasks for which an axe, the oldest of all edge tools, is still essential.

Patterns and uses: Axes are almost as bewildering as billhooks in their types and patterns, but the key types are (**fig. 6.4**):

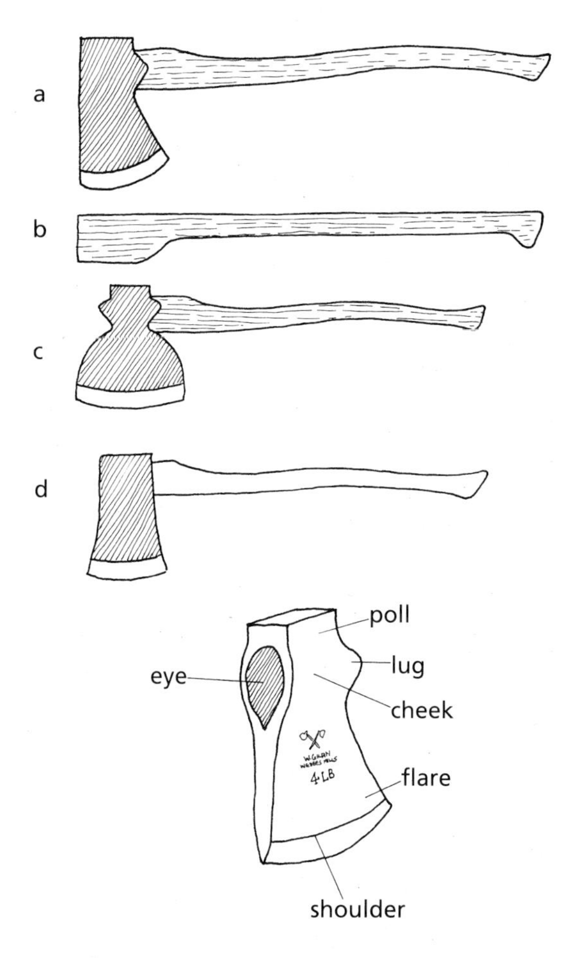

Fig. 6.4 Axes: a. English felling axe with fawn foot handle; b. English straight handle; c. Kent pattern snedding axe; d. US style wedge axe.

- ***Felling axes*** are only of use today if you are felling large old coppice, for there are occasions with very awkward trees in which axe is safer than chain saw. An English pattern flared head is best, for when thrown the centre of the blade cuts first. Only use a weight you can handle; 1.8 – 2.3kg (4 or 5lbs) is usually adequate, and the shoulders should not be too thick. American pattern fawn foot handles in ash or hickory are more secure in the hands than the traditional English straight handle. They should be secured with an oak wedge, and 0.9m (36inches) is the normal length (**fig. 6.5**).
- ***Snedding axes*** remain a faster and safer tool than the chain saw for removing branches from a large stem. I find that a Kentish pattern head with its wide cutting face, weighing c.1.4kg (3lbs) and fitted to a 0.76 (30in) fawn foot handle is very effective. When snedding, cut towards the crown of the felled tree, cut flush to the stem, and keep the trunk between axe and legs.

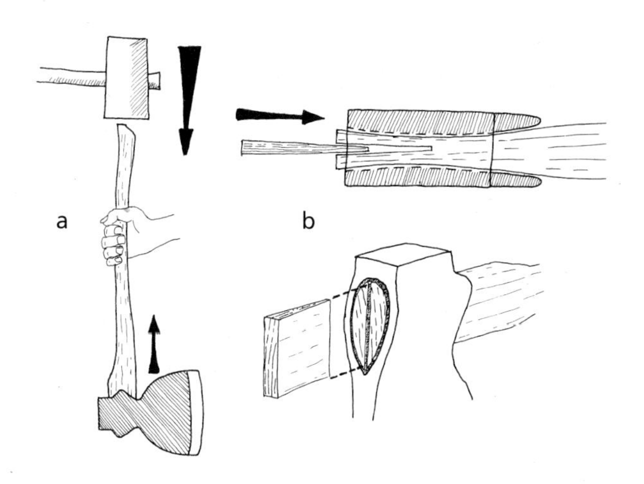

Fig. 6.5 Fitting an axe handle: a. hit the end of the handle to force head onto helve; b. wedging the handle into the socket.

- ***Wedge or splitting axes*** are intended for splitting logs or starting clefts in large poles. A Yankee pattern is probably the best, and here you do need weight and heavy shoulders to open the wood; fine shouldered axes just jam in the grain. Never hit an axe with a sledge hammer – use a wooden beetle.
- ***Side axes*** are irreplaceable; they perform tasks no other tool can do as well. The key that makes them unique is that they have one sharpening bevel, and the opposite face is dead flat from cutting edge to poll. Because of this the tool is left or right handed, the flat face being that facing the worker. This design

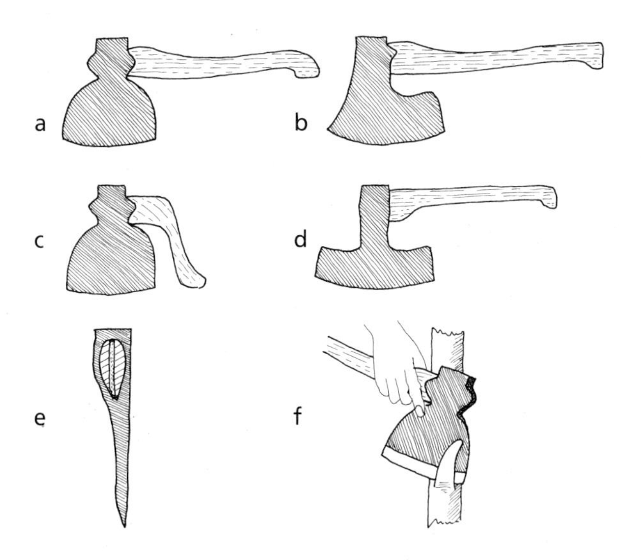

Fig. 6.6 Side axes: a. Kentish pattern; b. Coach maker's; c. Chair bodger's; d. Cooper's; e. profile of blade; f. holding the axe in use.

Fig. 6.7 Using the broad-axe to flatten a log; note the preliminary cuts to help waste fall away and dog to hold the log.

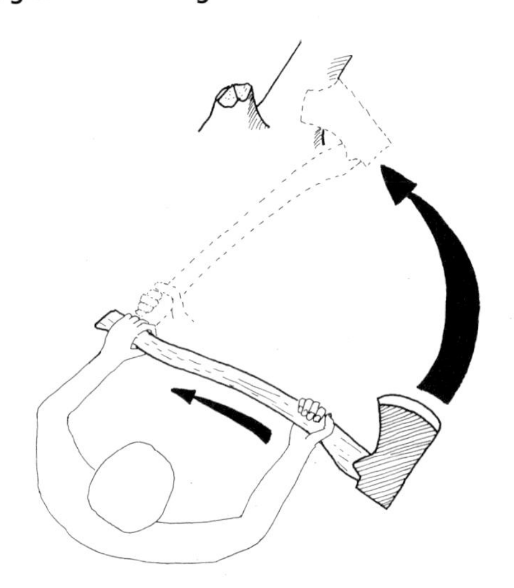

Fig. 6.8 Swinging a felling axe – slide the hand along the shaft.

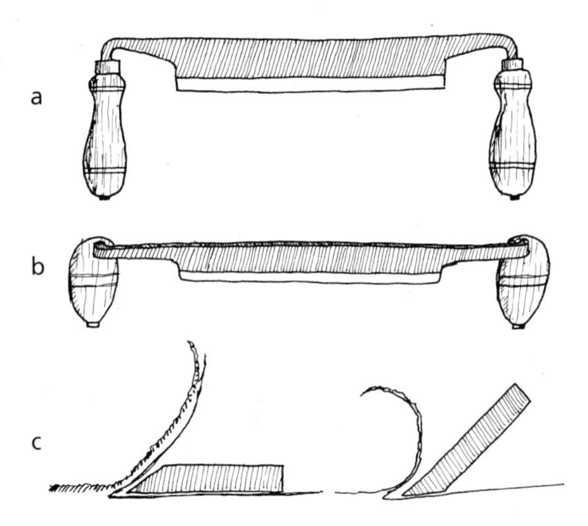

Fig. 6.9 Draw knives: a. standard handle; b. egg shaped handles; c. the draw knife removes a thinner shaving when used bevel down.

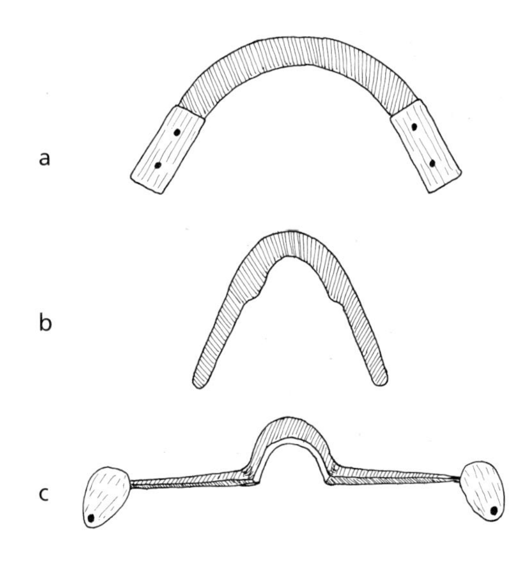

Fig. 6.10 Curved shaves: a. for large poles; b. and c. for rake/scythe handles.

ensures the blade draws into the wood and will cut straight, removing long shavings, rather than leaving a scalloped surface. This is the tool for sharpening posts, flattening battens, sizing wood for turning, or any general shaping. There are many patterns associated with particular trades (**fig. 6.6**), but the Kentish pattern is particularly good since it can be handled to suit left or right handed workers. I use a coach makers axe which is extremely effective. Head weights vary from 0.9kg (2lbs) to 2.3kg (5lbs). Handles are normally only c.350mm (14ins) long, since for most uses the side axe is held with the hand close to the head; indeed many bodgers fitted their axe with a very short down turned handle which precluded any other means of use. Wherever possible the strokes of the axe should be vertically downwards for accuracy, using the weight of the axe. Always keep your legs well apart when sharpening posts to avoid any risk of hitting them with the axe. When squaring logs for timber framing a long handled side axe known as a broad axe was used (broad because it had a wide blade) (**fig.6.7**). The handle was often 'swayed' to keep the users hands clear of the log, and the woodman always stood with the log between him and the axe.

Throwing an axe: Make sure there are no snags in the way of the axe. Stand comfortably, feet apart, and check your distance from the pole to be felled; too close and the handle may hit and break. Hold the axe with your left hand at the foot, the

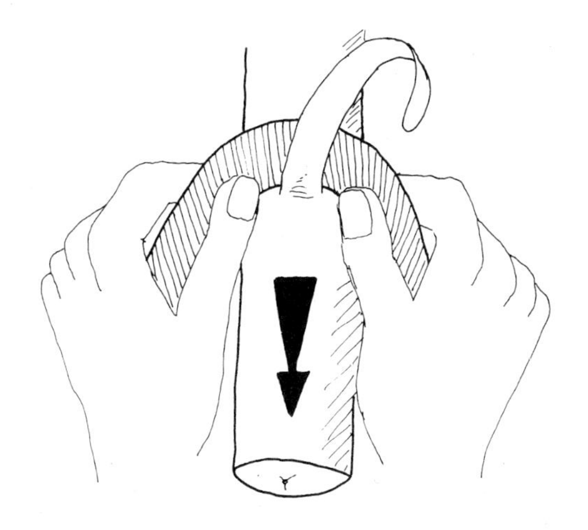

Fig. 6.11 Using the small curved shave.

right under the head; throw the head at your target point, sliding your right hand up the handle from head to foot (**fig. 6.8**). First cut downwards, then horizontally to remove a chip. Bend your back and keep your hands low to make the horizontal cuts parallel to the ground. Make the final felling cut from the back of the pole.

Shaves and Rounders: These are the essential tools for rinding, shaping and smoothing small green wood (**fig. 6.9**).

Draw-knives: Unique amongst edge tools, the draw-knife cuts towards the user, which is why you find serious practitioners wearing a stout leather apron. Draw-knives come in various sizes, but about 280mm (11ins) is a good size for most work. I have never seen the Victorian 'Gentleman's model, only 150mm (6ins) wide, being used by a craftsman! All shaves and rounders need two hands in use, o a device is needed (see Chapter 8) to hold the work piece. Handles are either long and round or short and egg shaped, both working equally well.

Although draw-knives are robust tools, it is best to remove knots and branches from a pole using a side axe or billhook first. The blade has only one sharpening bevel, and is normally used face down, pulled with a firm, smooth stroke. It is ideal for rinding poles, shaping wood, smoothing the faces of clefts, shaping tent pegs or thinning clefts for hoops. The thickness of the shaving can be altered by slightly adjusting the angle of the blade, and thin bark removed without its sapwood by using the tool bevel side down.

Curved draw-shaves: Rarely found in tool makers catalogues, these tools are frequently hand made to perform a very specific job (**fig. 6.10**). But they perform so well, that once used you wonder how you worked without them. All curved shaves

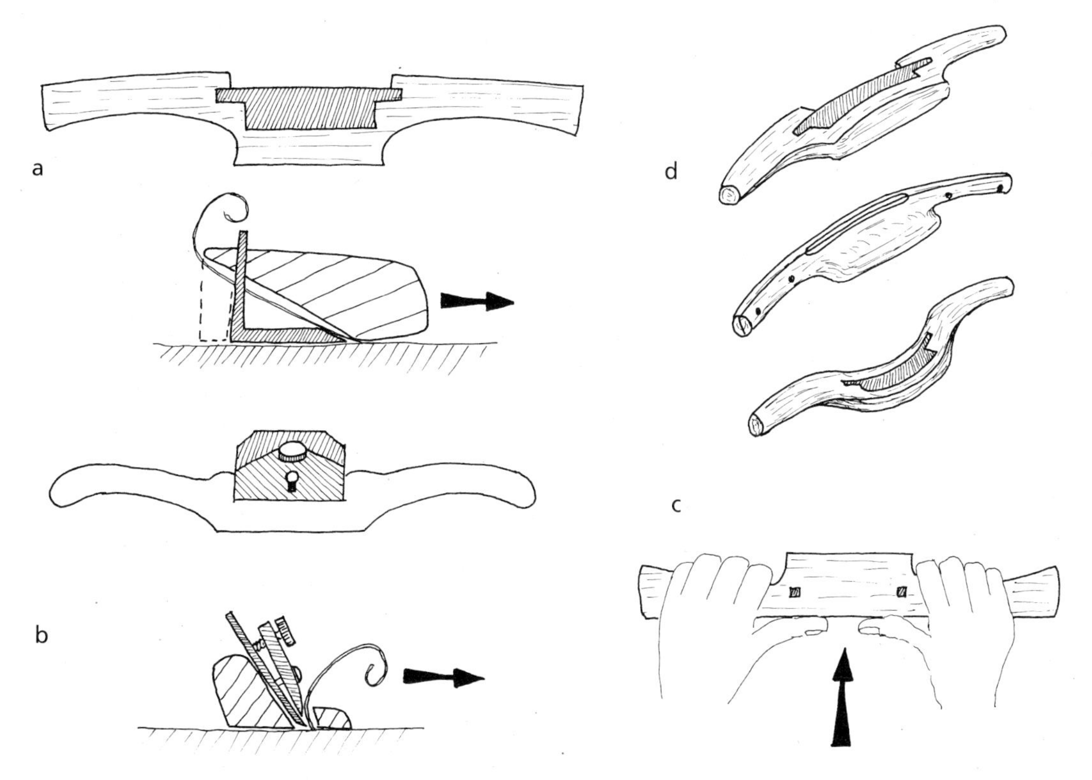

Fig. 6.12 Spokeshaves: a. traditional wooden bodied type; b. more modern type with a plane-type blade; c. holding and using the spokeshave; d. chair makers shaves – from top 'travisher', 'devil' and 'hollow knife'.

work with their sharpening bevel against the piece, removing fine shavings. The simplest shaves, used for rinding chestnut or ash poles, are made from the blade of an old bagging hook with handles rivetted to it at either end; the curve leaves a smoother finish than the draw-knife. Smaller shaves designed for smoothing rake or scythe handles have a tighter curve to match the product.

Shaves are held with the thumbs on the blade to apply pressure, and are drawn forward in a series of short, quick strokes (**fig. 6.11**). Depth of cut is adjusted by the angle of the blade. Being light tools shaves will only work well if knots are removed first. It may be necessary to shave in the opposite direction one side of the knot to avoid raising the grain.

Spoke shaves: This familiar tool is really a very short plane designed to allow the craftsman to follow and smooth the curves of a complicated shape such as an axe helve. In its traditional form the body and handles are shaped from one piece of wood, to which the low-angled blade is attached by two square tangs. More modern metal versions have an adjustable blade with a high angle (**fig. 6.12**).

Set the cutting depth by sighting along the base of the shave and adjusting the blade until

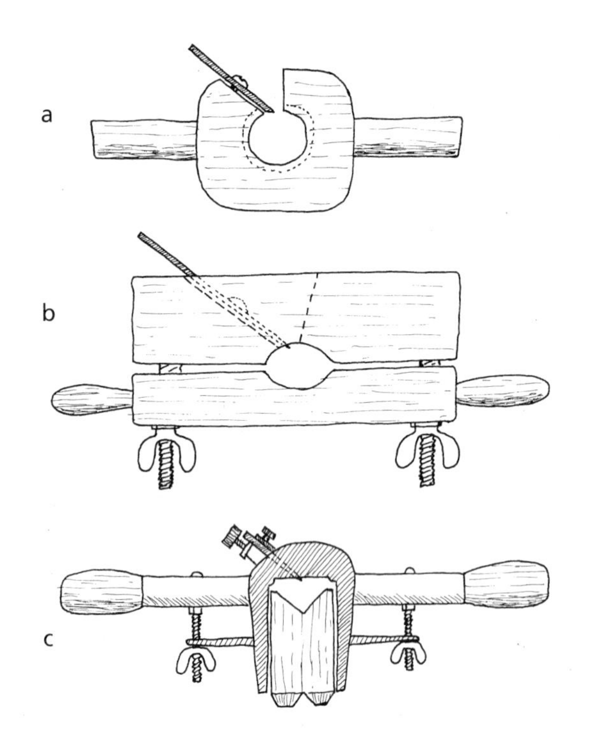

Fig. 6.13 Rounders: a. basic rounder; b. a traditional stail engine; c. a modern version of the stail engine from Ashem Crafts.

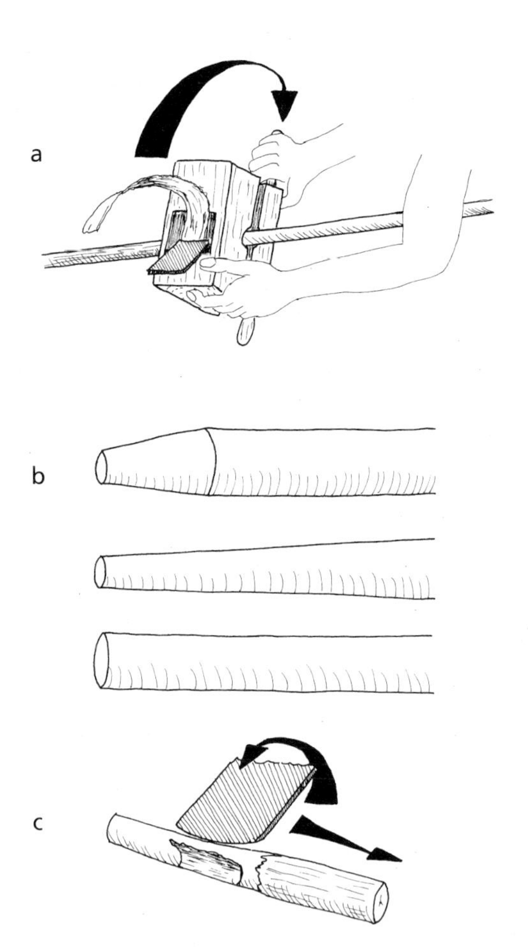

Fig. 6.14 Using rounders: a. using the stail engine; b. shapes top - cone from a rounder; middle-taper from a stail engine; bottom – cylinder from a stail engine; c. how the rounder's blade works.

app. 1mm of blade shows evenly across its width. Once the wooden front of the throat is worn this gap cannot be controlled, and the tool is at the end of its life.

Use the spoke shave by pushing it away from you with steady strokes, keeping it flat on the work and working with or across the grain to avoid tearing it out. It is a good tool for shaping, and chair makers in particular use a range of shaves called 'travishers' and 'cleaning off irons' to complete the work started by the adze.

Rounders: These are rounding planes whose method of operation is akin to a pencil sharpener. They are designed to produce a smooth round rod or pole for handles, furniture, ladder rungs and similar objects (**fig. 6.13**). They comprise a wooden body with a handle at each side and a tapered hole fitted with a plane blade whose cutting edge protrudes along one side of the hole. The tool is placed over the end of the work piece (**fig. 6.14**), and twisted quite rapidly to produce a shaving and reduce the work piece to a fixed diameter. The tapered hole produces a tapered end to a pole, as required for a ladder rung or furniture tenon. More modern metal versions are available.

A more sophisticated version is the stail engine. In this type the diameter of the orifice can be adjusted by two wing nuts, making it the only tool that can produce a long tapered pole as well as accommodating a range of pole sizes. Its name derives from its role in producing rake handles (stails), but it is equally good for any round handle, or parts for chairs.

Success with these tools relies almost entirely on setting the blade correctly. The advice given to me by a Suffolk rake maker was: grind the blade so the edge is slightly convex to avoid it tearing into the wood; set the blade bevel side down; adjust the angle and bite of the blade until it removes a long continuous shaving.

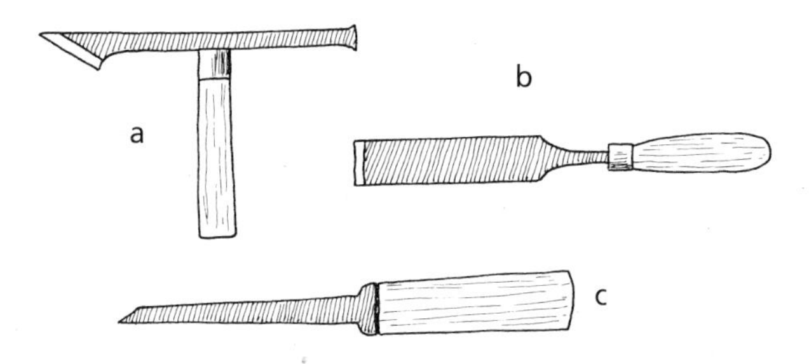

Fig. 6.15 Chisels: a. twybil; b. firmer chisel; c. morticing chisel.

Chisels and Twybils: Normal firmer chisels (**fig. 6.15**) are not tools used extensively in green wood working. Some gate hurdle makers use them to produce mortices (Chapter 13). Proper mortising chisels are far more robust tools with very strong blades and handles; these are essential when morticing fence posts or gates. To make a mortice, cut down vertically with the chisel at either end to sever the wood fibres; then chop and lever out the waste wood – hence the need of the strong blade (**fig. 6.17**).

Twybil: This is a morticing tool well known to medieval carpenters and woodmen (**fig. 6.15**). The smaller tool used by gate hurdle makers to mortice the heads of their hurdles is the most efficient way of producing round ended mortices in green wood. Once the holes at either end of the mortice are drilled the blade of the twybil is used to cut between the holes to make the sides of the

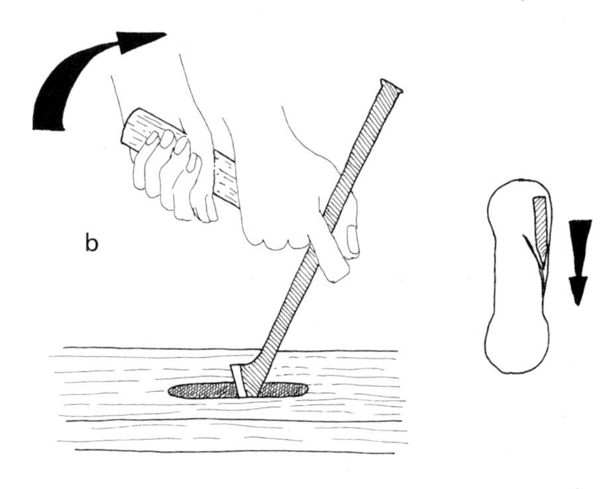

Fig. 6.16 Using the twybil: a. cutting between holes; b. shaving sides of mortice.

mortice (**figs. 6.16 & 6.17**). Reversing the twybil, its tail is used to huck out the waste wood. Finally the sides of the mortice are cleaned and shaped using the blade again; the action is much more that of a knife than a chisel, hence the tool's alternative name – morticing knife.

Turning chisels: Wood turning tools differ from carpentry chisels in having longer blades and tangs. Their long handles are often turned with a swelling at the ferrule to make them easier to control (**fig. 6.18**). The key turning tools are:

- ***Gouge*** – this has a curved blade with one sharpening bevel on the outside of the curve. Available in a variety of sizes from c.38mm (1½in), to small versions at 6mm (¼in), a gouge is designed to cut and remove wood quickly for initial shaping, (roughing out), for smoothing concave curves on spindle work and for hollowing bowls. A 32mm (1¼in) chisel is excellent for roughing out; smaller sizes are needed for delicate shaping.
- **Skew chisel** – this has a slanted cutting edge bevelled on both sides, again available in a

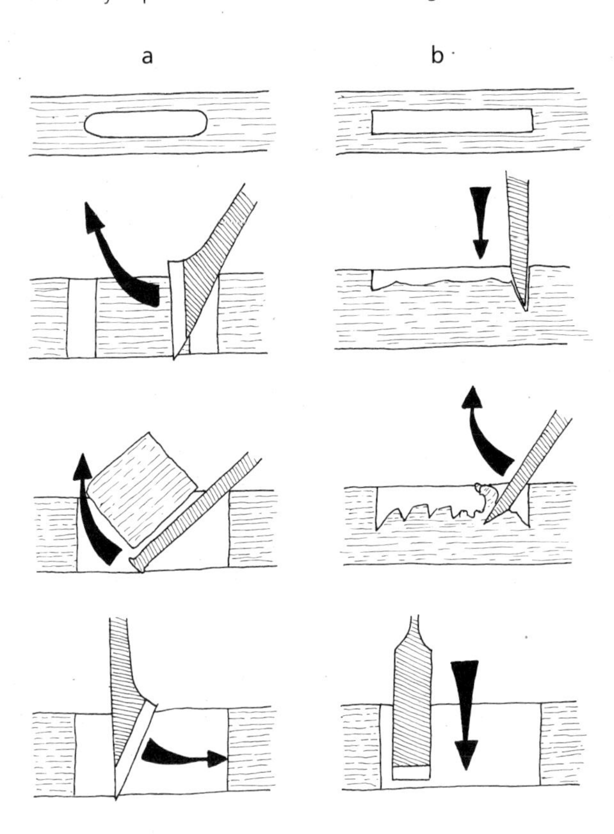

Fig. 6.17 Morticing: a. how the twybil creates a round-ended mortice; b. how to chisel a square-ended mortice.

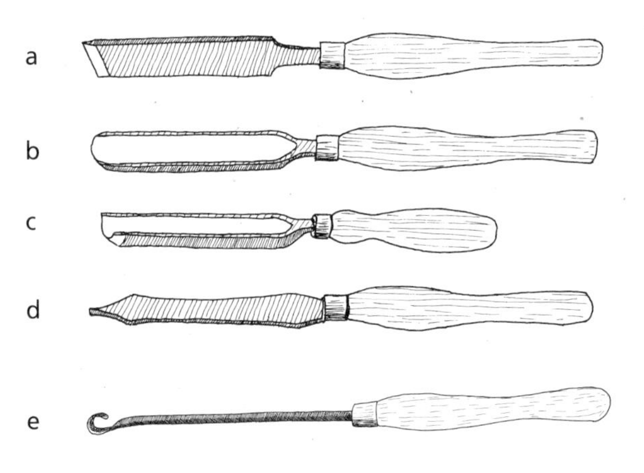

Fig. 6.18 Turning chisels: a. skew; b. bowl gouge; c. roughing gouge; d. parting tool; e. hook tool for bowls.

range of sizes, chosen depending on the size of work piece. A 25mm (1in) chisel is fine for wood of 38mm (1½in) to 76mm (3in). Designed to remove fine shavings to smooth roughed out wood and to create beads. Some turners prefer to use an ordinary carpentry chisel with a square cutting edge, achieving identical results, but I find these tools more difficult to control due to their shorter handles.

- Parting tool – this tool has a sharpened end slightly wider than its main body, and operates by a combination of cutting and scraping. As its name describes, it is used to part the finished work, where appropriate.
- 'V' tool or bruzz – this was a tool favoured by some chair makers. It was devised from a tool with a right angle cutting edge used to tidy up mortices. When sharpened with one bevel on the outside it was used by turners for fine beading. It is difficult to use and no better than a small skew chisel.
- Scrapers – although these are a key part of many turners tool kit, they are designed for working very hard exotic woods, and scraping does not work well with soft, green wood.
- Hook tool – this tool with a hook shaped cutting edge is used for hollowing jobs.

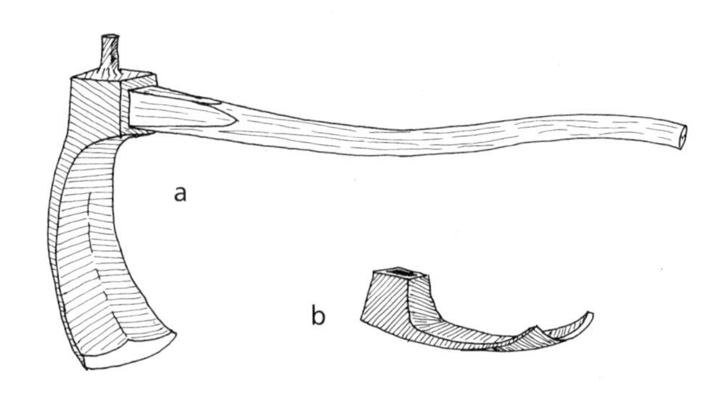

Fig. 6.19 The adze: a. standard type for shaping beams; b. curved blade for chair seats.

Adzes: These ancient edge tools, as old as the axe and without which England's timber framed buildings and boats would not exist, come in numerous patterns. Those important in green wood working are:

Carpenter's adze: The adze differs from the axe in having its blade set at a right angle to the handle (**fig. 6.19**). It has a curved blade, and the carpenter's pattern has a straight cutting edge with only one sharpening bevel. They usually weigh between 1.6 and 2.0kg (3½ to 4½lbs). A 760mm (30ins) handle is held in a tapered eye without wedging so that it can be removed when the blade needs to go onto a grindstone.

It is used for removing waste wood, trimming and shaping surfaces; it is the tool with which to make beams and gate posts. An adze is used in a swinging action with the worker straddling the piece and cutting that area between his legs. This needs extreme care and the expression that 'the adze is the only tool that the Devil is afraid to use' is a sound warning.

When squaring off round wood, fix the piece securely and preferably in a jig so that it is below your feet, offering some protection (**fig. 6.20**). Use the tool with a short, quick, chopping action removing small shavings; don't cut too deep or you will have to lever large chips away, tearing the grain.

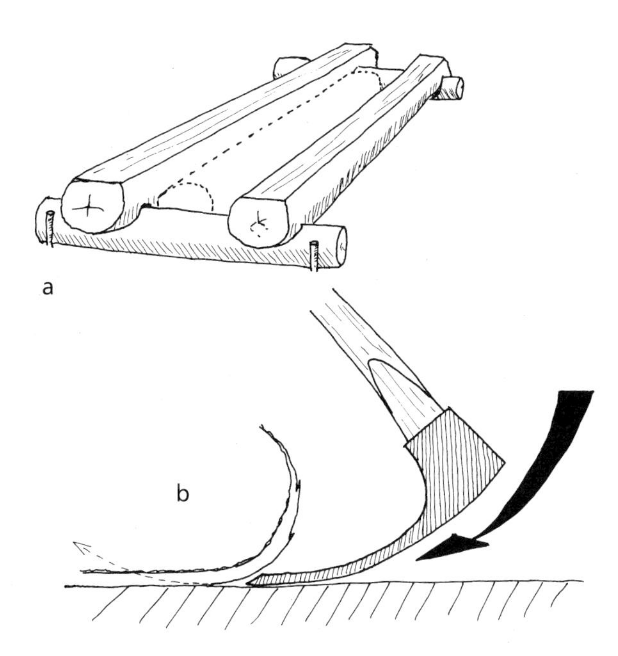

Fig. 6.20 Using the adze: a. jig for shaping beams (stand on the outer two with work piece lower than feet); b. how the adze removes a shaving.

Chair maker's adze: This differs from the carpenter's in having a gouge-shaped blade that is used to hollow chair seats. The seat is gripped by the worker's feet (**fig. 6.21**), and the adze used with short, quick, chopping strokes across the grain to hollow the seat.

Cleaving adze: This has a short, straight edged blade on a 300mm (12in) handle, and is a superb tool for riving small rods for spars, wattle hurdles and hoops.

It is best used in conjunction with a riving post that both supports the clefts and holds them apart (**fig. 6.22**). Chop down into the end of the rod with the adze, and then separate the clefts by levering to and fro with the handle. Since the clefts are levered apart, there is no need for the edges of the adze to be sharpened.

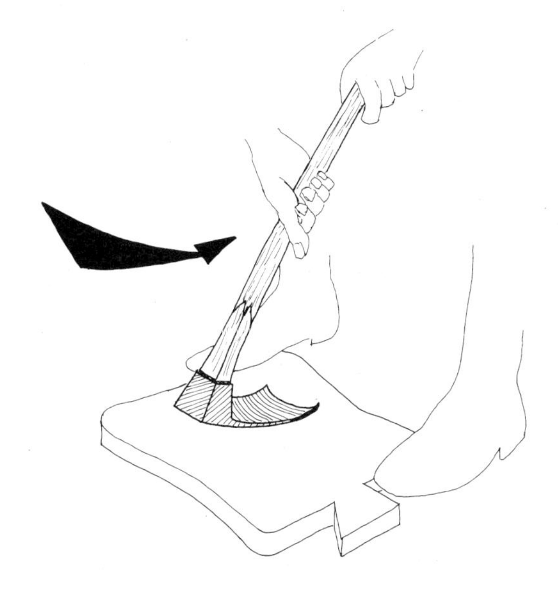

Fig. 6.21 Adzing a chair seat: hold seat with feet and swing the adze between them.

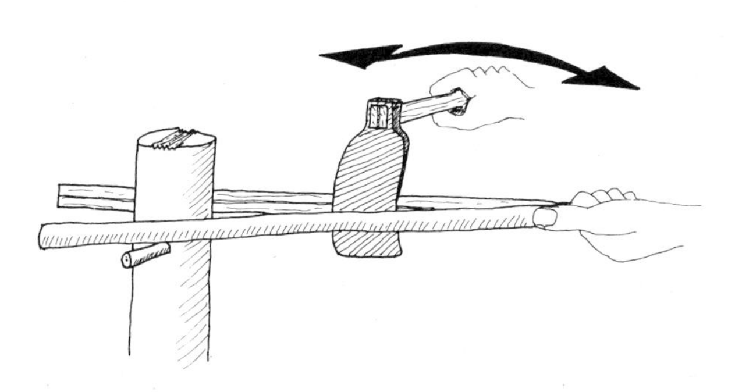

Fig. 6.22 Using a small adze and post to rive hazel rods – simply lever, don't cut.

Knives: An ordinary knife is in the green wood workers pocket at all times, whether to cut string, sharpen a pencil or shape a small piece of wood. It is the perfect tool for splitting and pithing bramble, for thinning small clefts, and some shaving jobs.

Spoon maker's knives (**fig. 6.23**): a simple knife with a short, straight blade is used for much of the finer shaping and smoothing. A curved or hooked knife is used for hollowing out the spoon. These come with different shapes (some are suitable for small bowls), and some forms were fitted with very long handles which whilst grasped close to the blade, could be held between arm and body for better control. The work piece must be held securely in a horse or the hand, whilst the knife is gripped firmly to remove small shavings by cutting with or across the grain; the bowl is made using a twisting and scooping action (Chapter 18).

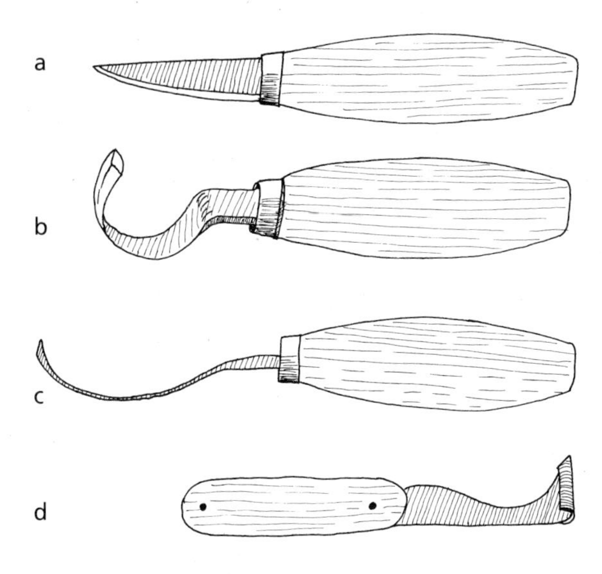

Fig. 6.23 Knives: a.-c. are spoon makers, the curved blades to make the bowl; d. a carpenter's raze.

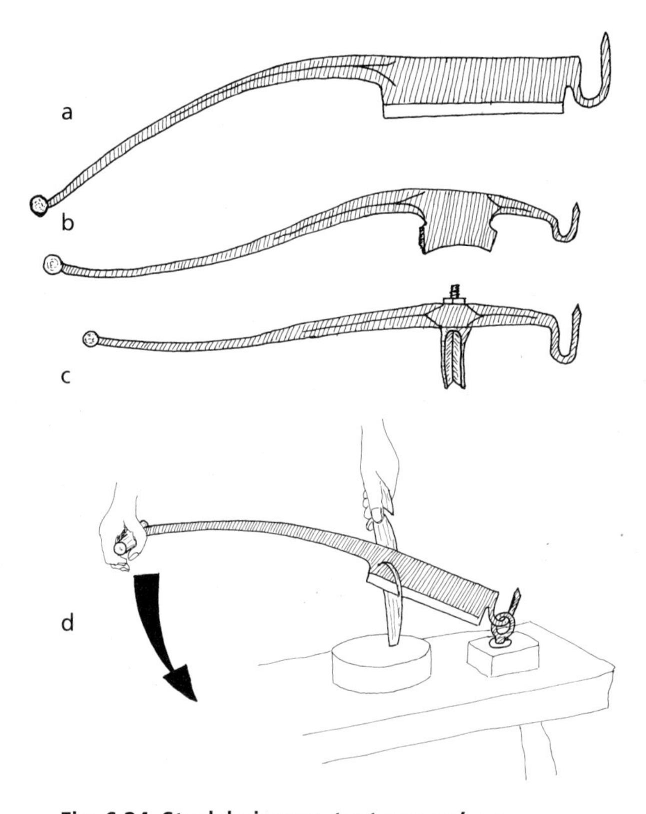

Fig. 6.24 Stock knives: a. tent pegger's or clogger's; b. and c. special shapes used by cloggers to make hollows and grooves; d. using the knife to make tent pegs.

Stock (Bench) Knives: these powerful tools consist of a blade, which may be shaped, forged to an iron bar that may be up to 1.22m (4ft) long. At one end is a hook that locates in an eye fixed to a bench or stool; at the other is a 'T' handle (**fig. 6.24**). They are used by holding the work piece in one hand and operating the knife from the 'T' handle, cutting down towards the bench. The long handle allows considerable force to be applied, but in a controlled manner. Their uses include making clogs, brushes, tent pegs, wooden spoons and shaping rake tines. If you can use a side axe to shape wood, you will find the stock knife better since you can cut in a very controlled manner, but with as much force.

Raze (Scriving) Knife: this knife has a tight curve at the end of its blade which when drawn across the surface of a piece of wood leaves a narrow furrow (**fig. 6.23**). Its purpose it to mark wood. A gatepost in my wood still bears the scribe marks made by the merchant who last removed timber from the wood. And if you look closely at many timber-framed buildings you will see the scribe marks that number the component parts of each joint.

Caring for Edge Tools

Good tools are precious. If well looked after and sharpened they will perform sweetly for more than a lifetime; many a craftsman is still using his father's or even grandfather's tools.

The following simple rules will help care for tools:

- Never drive the tool into the ground and avoid using bill or axe on sere or muddy wood; both will blunt the edge and result in more grinding and a shorter life
- Keep tools wrapped to protect them in transit, and never put them away wet
- Check handles regularly to ensure they are tight and not split. Loose axe handles can often be tightened by soaking in linseed oil or water. If an axe jams don't lever on the end of the handle – hit the head with a billet of wood
- Never burn handles off tools – the chances are you will lose the tools temper and the edge will turn when used
- Never hit edge tools, even the back, with anything steel, use only wood. Likewise, wooden handles should only be hit with wooden mallets.

Where to obtain tools

Unfortunately good edge tools are less common today, so it may take some time to obtain good examples of those you require. Some are still made abroad (e.g.: side axes, spoon carving knives) and these can be obtained from shops or dealers specialising in woodworking tools for particular crafts. These suppliers often produce catalogues, but it is a good idea to ask craftsmen you know where they got their tools, and more to the point, do they work well. Remember as well that some modern tools can be ground to a more traditional profile, and will then work well.

If you are not lucky enough to have a relative who will bequeath you some tools, visiting second-hand shops, sales and markets is still very worthwhile. Look for good makes (W.S., Brades, Gilpin, Nash, Morris, Elwell for example) and be prepared to fit new handles. Don't worry about rust unless it is so pitted you will not be able to get an edge, and if it is ground with one bevel make sure it is the correct hand (right or left) for you.

Some specialist tools you will have to get made. The steel of scrap car springs makes good froes or chisels. Often it is essential to supply an accurate pattern drawing of what you require since the blacksmith will not have made that tool before; I never miss the opportunity to measure good tools being used by craftsmen or in museum collections. Wooden tools (beetles, gauges, cleaves) can be made at home with few basic tools and some care. Some dimensions of less common tools are shown in Appendix 1.

Further reading:

Abbott, M., ***Green Woodwork***,
Guild of Master Craftsmen Publications, 1989
Blandford, P.W., ***Country Craft Tools***,
David & Charles, 1974
Jenkins, J.G., ***Traditional Country Craftsmen***,
Routledge & Kegan Paul, 1978
Salaman, R., ***Dictionary of Woodworking Tools***,
Unwin Hyman, 1989
Smedley, N., ***East Anglian Crafts***, Batsford, 1977
Tabor, R., ***Traditional Woodland Crafts***,
Batsford, 1994
BTCV ***Tool Care*** 1998

Chapter 7

Tools for Sawing, Splitting and Drilling

Saws

Although there is a wide range of saws that woodsmen and green wood workers can use, it is quite possible to produce most of the products described in this book with a good bow saw. We shall look at a range of saws so that you understand what they can do; after that the choice is yours.

Handsaws: Using a sharp, well maintained hand saw which cuts sweetly is a real pleasure, and rarely hard work.

Cross cut saws: Traditionally these are two-handed and used for felling and logging large wood (**fig. 7.1**). They have been superseded by the chainsaw, although I do keep one in the workshop. The best cross cuts for felling have shallow blades to reduce friction and allow a wedge to be put in the kerf behind them, but beware that these blades do not always cut as straight as deeper ones. Handles are usually removable to allow the saw to be withdrawn from the kerf for sharpening after a wedge has been inserted.

I find the peg-toothed blade is fine for hardwoods, but a raker tooth blade is better on softwoods since it cleans the sawdust from the kerf better. Using a cross cut demands a steady rhythm from the two sawyers, and you should only pull the saw, never push. Clog makers and chair bodgers using large diameter alder or beech frequently used this tool.

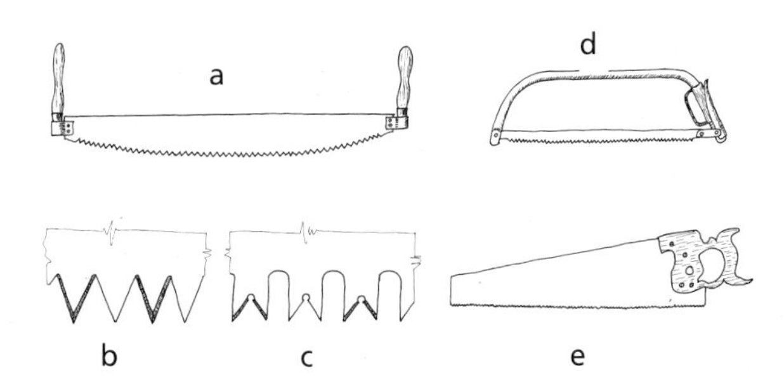

Fig. 7.1 Saws: a. two-handed cross cut saw; b. peg tooth; c. 'M' tooth, better for wet wood; d. steel framed bow saw; e. hand saw – best for dry wood.

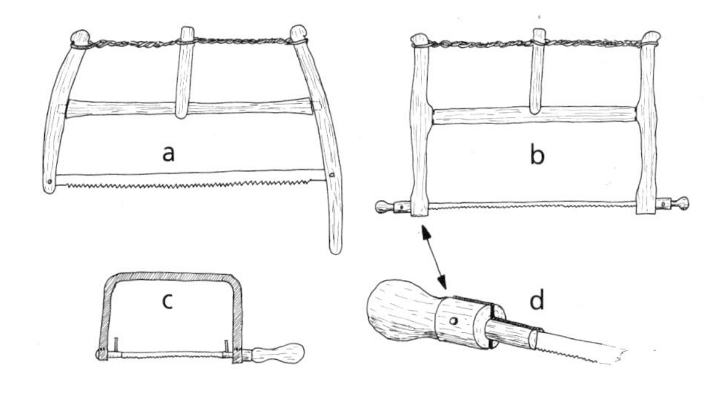

Fig. 7.2 Frame saws: a. wooden framed bow saw or buck saw; b. frame saw with a turning blade for cutting shapes (d. note how blade is fitted to handle); c. coping saw – for cutting fine shapes.

Frame saws: Most cross cutting of small wood today is performed using metal framed bow saws (**fig. 7.1**), the design and technology of which has advanced dramatically in the last 20 years. They come in a range of sizes from 500mm (20in.) to 910mm (36in.) with peg or raker tooth blades. Their blades cannot be resharpened, but last well with care. They are rugged, cut green wood with ease, and are used for felling and sizing small poles of any type.

When using the bow saw, start with slow steady cuts to avoid the tendency of the blade to jump out of the kerf. It is also good practice when felling or cross cutting to make a small cut on the compression side of the material to avoid a strip of bark coming away as the cut finishes. Bow saws will not cut straight over longer cuts due to their very shallow blade.

Buck saws: These are wooden framed variants of the metal bow saw, and tools of great elegance and antiquity (**fig. 7.2**). They are not difficult to make with care, and use modern blades; if properly tensioned with the cord and toggle, they will work well for cross cutting and are easy to use with two hands, but were not designed for felling poles (this was a job for the axe!).

Shaping saws: These come in various forms, but are all designed so that the blade can be rotated in the frame in order that curved cuts can be made to produce a shaped end product (**fig. 7.2**). They can be as large as a buck saw or as small as a coping saw, and are invaluable for complex shapes or fretwork.

Hand saws: The standard hand saw is used by some craftsmen for sizing wood or dressing a finished piece. Their wide blade (**fig. 7.1**) ensures a straighter line over a longer cut, but their smaller teeth blind more easily with very green wood; use one with as coarse a tooth as you can get. Rip saws, designed to cut along the grain are very rarely used in green woodworking – cleaving the wood is more common.

Care of saws: Keep saws hung by the handle and dry to avoid rust. They can be coated with oil to protect them, but if you do get rust forming on the blade, remove it by applying paraffin and rubbing with a very fine emery cloth. Rub a little linseed oil into wooden frames occasionally.

Never force a saw in use, for once a blade is buckled it will never work true, and keep the blade away from contact with stones and metal that will blunt it. As we have seen, only cross cuts and traditional handsaws have blades that can be re-sharpened. You may be best to go to a saw doctor if your saw needs sharpening. Otherwise the procedure is (**fig. 7.3**):

- check all the teeth are the same height; if not file them so that they are, keeping the file absolutely square
- shape the teeth with a triangular file so all teeth are the same, again keeping file at right angles to the blade in both planes
- set the teeth (slightly more for green wood) using a pliers 'saw set'
- sharpen the teeth at an angle of c.70° with two or three steady strokes on each alternate tooth; reverse the saw and repeat with those not sharpened first time.

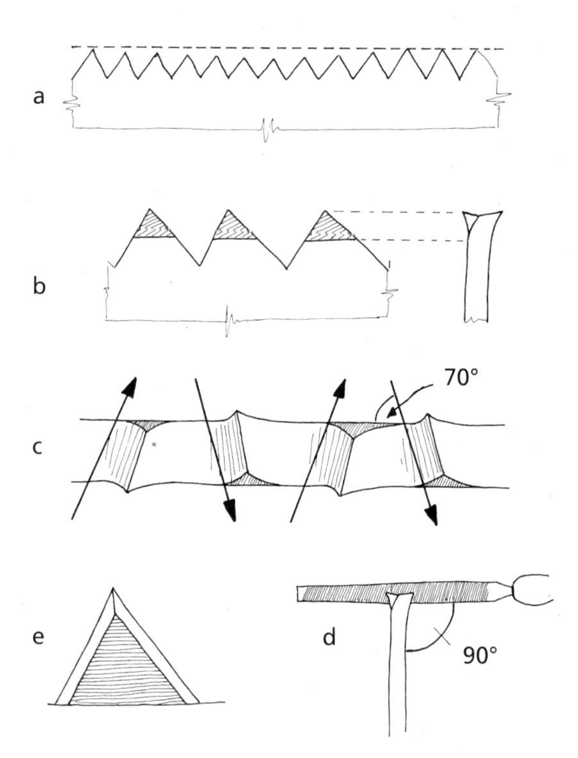

Fig. 7.3 Sharpening saws: a. make sure teeth are same height; b. how saw teeth are 'set' to produce a kerf; c. and d. how to file saw teeth – note the critical angles; e. finished saw tooth.

Chainsaws: There is not space in this book to discuss chainsaws in detail, and readers are strongly advised to read the BTCV book. Some practical tips are, however;

- obtain professional training in the use and maintenance of the saw
- keep your saw regularly maintained; you should clean and check it after every use
- match the tool to the job; chainsaws are quite heavy and tiring to use, so a smaller saw may be better
- if you are felling small coppice, remember a smaller saw will make it easier to get between the poles
- avoid cutting down through the top of the stools, for this is where stones collect; clean stools up at the end of the season using an old chain
- remember to undercut into the compression side of poles before felling or crosscutting
- the most critical feature when felling is maintaining a proper hinge – this controls the direction a pole will fall
- using a chainsaw properly is no more or less damaging to the re-growth from a stool than is the axe.

Tools for splitting

Splitting or riving wood is a fundamental skill to green woodworking. The detail of how it is accomplished for different sizes of wood and for various crafts is explained in Chapter 11. Here we shall just consider the tools used.

Wedges: Wedges can be either of steel or wood, and the first rule is that you should only hit steel with steel and wood with wood. Steel wedges come in various sizes usually between 150mm (6in) and 300mm (12 in). The ends should be chisel-shaped so they can bite into the wood to start a split (**fig. 7.4**). Many have fluting on their flat face, supposedly to relieve the pressure of air that builds up as they are driven into sappy wood; I have never noticed any difference between fluted and non-fluted.

Wooden wedges are frequently longer than metal ones – 300mm (12in) to 450mm (18in), and cut to a less steep profile. The front edge is left c.3mm (1/8in) thick to avoid it turning or splitting, and the back edge is chamfered, again to avoid splitting when hit. Wooden wedges require a split to be started by an axe; they are excellent for producing high quality clefts without bruising or marking in ash and willow for example, but are more easily damaged by oak or elm. Ash is good for making wedges due to its resilience.

Gluts: These are simple wooden wedges made quickly, in the coppice or workshop from round wood. A pole is sharpened on two sides using a side axe, then cut to length, and the top chamfered (**fig. 7.4**). When felling large trees gluts are safer than steel wedges to insert behind the chainsaw to stop it binding and to direct the fall of the tree.

Cleaves: These are essentially wooden wedges carefully designed to produce three or four clefts in one go (**fig. 7.5**). Individually made by the craftsmen, to be effective they must be made from hard wood such as box or holly. Cleaves can split hazel, ash and willow from which fine clefts are frequently used. The cleaving of cane requires a brass edged cleave due to its harder nature.

Cleaves for small rods are the size of a large egg, but rods of 250mm (1in) diameter can be split using much bigger cleaves 230mm (9in) long.

The Froe: Froe, riving iron or doll-axe depending on which county you come from, this is the riving tool par excellence that you cannot be without (**fig. 7.6**). Used on medium sized poles this is the

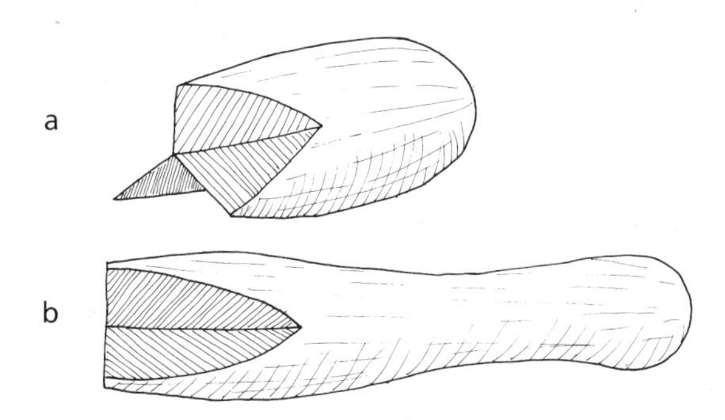

Fig. 7.5 Cleaves: a. small cleave for hazel or willow; b. larger cleave for use on oak.

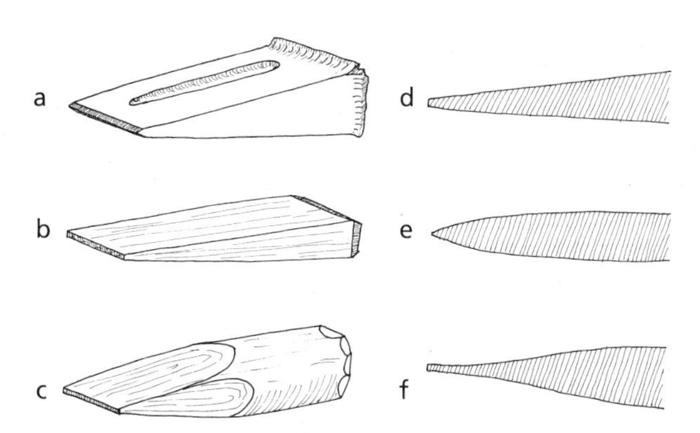

Fig. 7.4 Wedges: a. metal wedge; b. wooden wedge – note champfer and square tip; c. a glut – wooden wedge made from a round pole; d. proper profile for a wedge; e. and f. are respectively too convex and too concave.

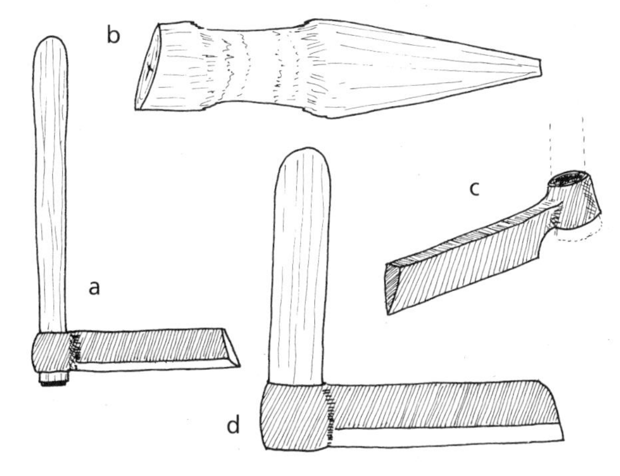

Fig. 7.6 Froes: a. normal pattern; b. beetle to hit froe cut from butt; c. heavy froe blade for big clefts; d. shingle maker's froe.

tool that allows you to make shingles, palings, chair legs, basket rims and so much more. Its blade is sharpened along one edge allowing it to be driven into the end of a pole like a wedge. The handle, at right angles to the blade, allows the latter to be levered to and fro, thus extending the split without cutting the wood. Sharpening profiles, depth of blade and length of handle all vary with the particular use for which the tool is intended

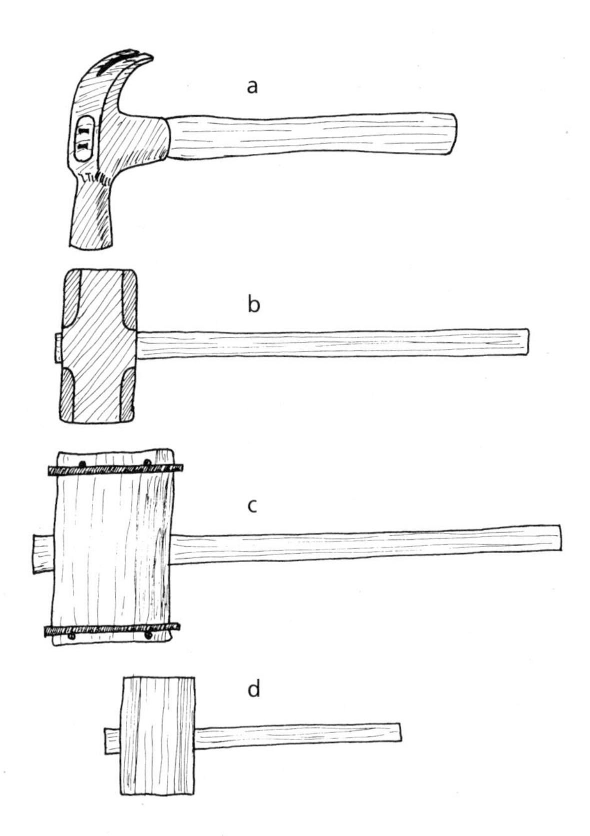

Fig. 7.7 Hammers: a. standard claw hammer; b. steel sledge hammer; c. elm beetle; d. small wooden mallet.

Hammers

Nails, wedges, rake teeth, pegs, stakes, the list of items that need hammering at some stage is endless. The tools you will need are (**fig. 7.7**):

Claw Hammer: A standard claw hammer is fine for any routine nailing. Although soft, green wood can be tough enough to cause wire nails to bend – hence the usefulness of the claw.

Sledge Hammer: For driving posts or metal wedges you will need a sledge hammer with a 0.9m (36in) handle and a head weighing between 1.8kg (4lb) and 3.1kg (7lb), whichever you feel comfortable with. Make sure the handle is safely wedged in place, as you would for an axe.

Commander, Beetle or Maul: This has an apple or elm wood head, usually with forged rings to stop the head splitting in use. The head weighs c.1.8kg (4lb) and is ideal for use with wooden wedges. Beetle handles are usually tapered rather than wedged so automatically tend to tighten in use. Details for making beetles are given in Chapter 14. These can be used with metal wedges instead of a sledgehammer; they avoid metal flakes and 'mushroom' ends on the wedges, but the wooden heads break up very quickly.

Beetle or froe club: Another form of beetle is the basic club fashioned by the woodman. Its most common use is with a froe, where any sort of metal hammer used on the back of the blade would burr it over, not allowing it to pass cleanly between the clefts – in this case you must hit metal with wood.

The best beetles are fashioned from butt ends of ash or chestnut poles, tapered at one end using the side axe so they feel comfortable in the hand. Beetles lose wood and weight in use as the annual rings of wood flake away under constant hammering. When this has gone too far, just make another one.

A square, flat sided beetle is used to force down the weave on a wattle hurdle – the flat surface being less likely to break the rods than a round one.

Making Holes

Drills: These are not novel to green woodworkers (**fig. 7.8**), although there are some useful modifications craftsmen have made in order to perform certain jobs a little better. And the battery powered electric drill has not yet supplanted the gentle growl of the brace!

Hand drill: This is used to make small holes, frequently pilot holes for nails in cleft wood where it is important that the wood does not split.

Brace: One of the commonest non-edge tools of the green woodworker, the brace is used in many crafts. Using a brace, even on green wood and with a sharp bit, is hard work. Making a six bar gate hurdle means drilling 24 holes in quick succession – guaranteed to get you sweating on the coldest day. This is why many Kentish hurdle makers modified their braces with a cast iron ring, this gives the tool a momentum that helps in boring these holes.

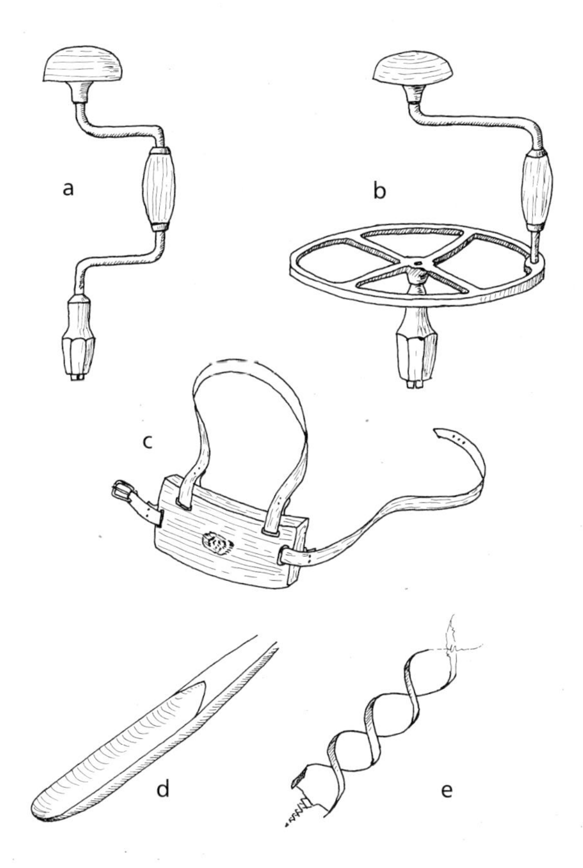

Fig. 7.8 Braces and bits: a. basic brace; b. brace modified with heavy cast ring – gives the tool more momentum; c. breast bib – leaves one hand free; d. chair maker's spoon bit; e. modern twist bit.

Chair framers wore a wooden bib that enabled them to apply pressure to the brace with their chest, leaving one hand free to turn the brace, and one to hold the work piece. These ultra-skilled craftsmen could achieve the correct angle by eye; mere mortals such as we need the assistance of an adjustable bevel.

Bits: Today most of us use modern twist bits with a screw lead at the centre that pulls the drill into the wood (**fig. 7.8**). The twisted shaft keeps the bit straight on longer cuts, and very efficiently removes the waste wood. Smaller centre bits do not do this as well, but are fine for boring clean, relatively shallow holes.

These apparently more sophisticated bits have replaced the more traditional spoon or shell bits. Older chair makers still believe spoon bits are far better since: they can bore to within a fraction of the thickness of a piece of wood without breaking through; a simple line on the back acts as a depth gauge; it will start at any angle; and it always bores a true hole, even when the brace is used on the ratchet. There is wisdom in most of this, but difficulty in obtaining and sharpening spoon bits mean most of us will have to use the modern twist bit.

Further reading:

Abbott, M ***Green Woodwork***,
Guild of Master Craftsmen Publications, 1989
Blandford, P W ***Country Craft Tools***,
David & Charles, 1974
Brooks, A. ***The Power Chain Saw***,
British Trust for Conservation Volunteers, 1974
BTCV ***Tool Care***, 1998
Jenkins, J G ***Traditional Country Craftsmen***,
Routledge & Kegan Paul, 1978
Salaman, R ***Dictionary of Woodworking Tools***,
Unwin Hyman, 1989
Tabor, ***R Traditional Woodland Crafts***,
Batsford, 1994

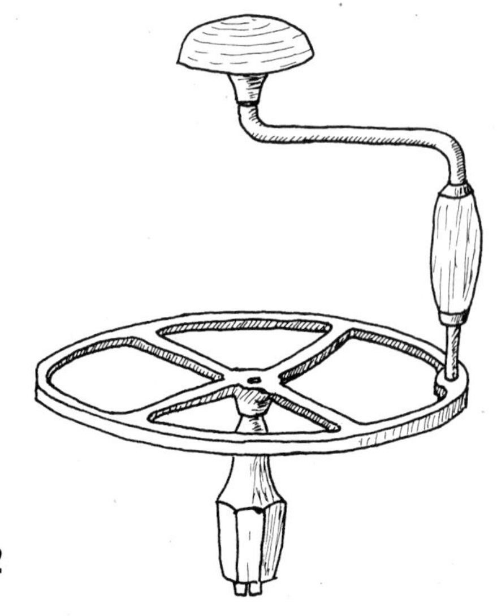

Chapter 8

A Second Pair of Hands

Why you need a horse or brake

When you talk to a craftsman and he uses terms such as 'horses', 'mares', 'dogs' and 'brakes' it is unlikely that he is referring to his pets or the holiday he never gets, but rather to the devices used in making a particular product. Without them a range of tools, particularly those requiring two hands to operate, could not be used effectively. These aids allow you to work safely, fast and effectively producing the right quality product.

Most green woodworking devices are ingenious, and reflect a keen understanding and basic mechanics of the material being processed. In this chapter examples in each of the main generic groups of devices are described. This will give you an understanding of the principles involved, from which you can develop your own designs to meet your specific needs.

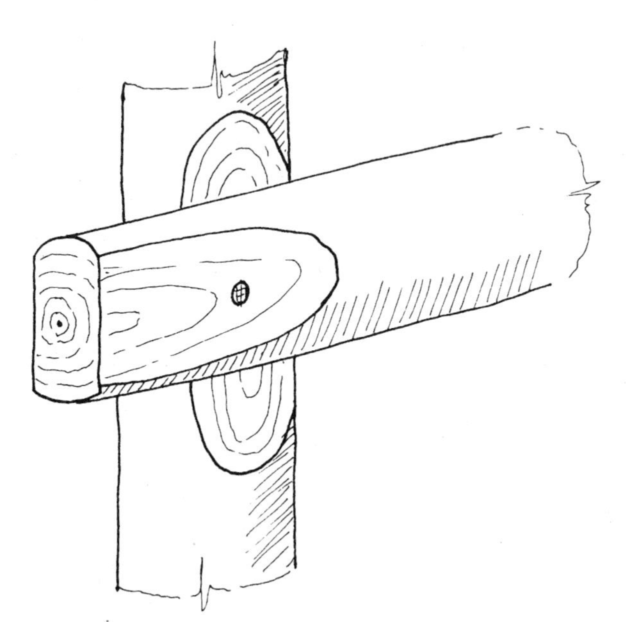

Fig. 8.1 How to flatten round poles to nail them firmly.

Where a particular product requires a unique device, it is described in the section relating to that product.

Planning and making devices: Whether in the workshop or coppice, you should always take time to work out the devices you need and how o site them. In the wood consider being close to your raw material, ease of extracting the finished product, providing shade for summer working, and avoiding sites likely to become mires in wet weather. Likewise in the workshop plan an efficient flow, with space to work and materials easily to hand.

Most devices are relatively easy to make, but remember to size them to suit you. Saw, hammer, drill and side axe will allow you to make most of them. The simpler riving brakes and sawing horse needed for only a year or two are nailed together; more solid devices in the workshop may need coach bolts. When using round wood use the side axe to flatten and shape wood so that you nail flat surfaces together; this avoids the members twisting (**fig. 8.1**).

Different types of device

Supporting work in progress: Devices under this heading are for the most part very simple, designed to hold or support work in use or waiting to be used.

Chopping blocks: Very few workshops will not have one or more blocks. They are best cut from the butt of large diameter trunks (from 300mm/ 12in upward). Oak and elm are particularly good, being resistant to splitting. Make sure you have plenty of weight and a flat base to avoid the block rocking in use. You can drive pegs into the ground around the base and fix them to the block to avoid movement. Height will depend on individual

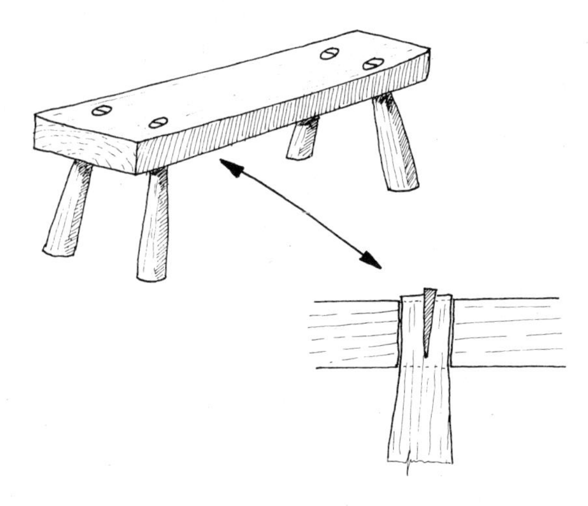

Fig. 8.2 A basic working bench or stool to which endless gadgets can be fitted; note how to wedge the legs into place.

preference and the job you are performing: some craftsmen solve the problem by using a two-level chopping block. To maintain sharp tools always keep the top clean and free from grit.

Bench: The simple low four-legged bench (**fig. 8.2**) finds use for numerous jobs such as drilling, morticing or to sit on when riving rods by hand. When suitably modified it is used for riving broches, making and sharpening rake teeth, and shaping clog soles or tent pegs. To secure the legs, taper their tops so that they tighten when forced into their holes. Take each hole right through the base, and tighten the leg with a wedge driven at right angles to the grain. This way, with a mallet, you can always tighten them up.

Simple frames: Made from forked sticks which support horizontal rods provide a simple means of holding small stuff such as palings or rods awaiting the next process in their conversion. They reduce your bending, make the job quicker, and avoid your materials becoming muddy. The frame used by wattle hurdle makers is known as 'the gallows'(**fig 13.18**).

Sawing horse: A simple portable sawing horse, particularly suitable for larger logs, consists of two separate tripods as illustrated (**fig. 8.3**), the position of which can be adjusted to accommodate a variety of lengths.

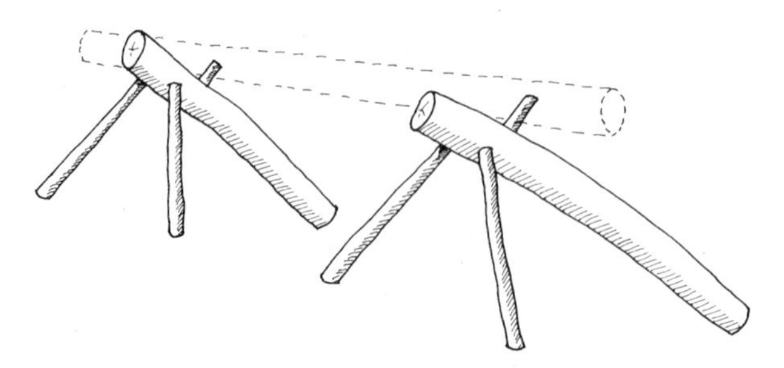

Fig. 8.3 Sawing horse for large logs; the top 'pins' are removable so that logs can be rolled up the long member.

For repetitive sawing of small wood in a fixed working site, however, you cannot beat the six-legged horse (**fig. 8.4**). Its feet are usually driven into the ground, but if fitted with diagonal braces it could be moveable. The centre legs are close to one end to make it easier to cut short pieces of wood, and the horizontal members are not fitted inside the 'V' so that the workpiece fits snugly.

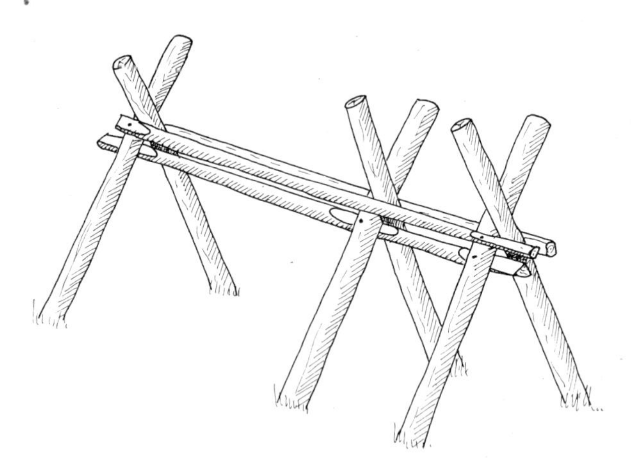

Fig. 8.4 A fixed sawing horse for small wood.

Bundling small wood (**fig. 8.5**): Bundling bean rods or thatching wood on the coppice floor is an awkward and dirty job. The simple solution is to use a couple of crotch sticks, sharpened and driven into the ground to form a cradle in which the rods can lay. A notch on one arm of the crotch may serve as a guide as to how many to put. Cradled this way, you can straddle the rods in order to tie them, and use the 'woodman's grip' to tighten the bundle if required.

In Kent a more refined version, the 'notch', utilises two old galvanised bucket handles to cradle the rods, as shown.

Simple wooden frames are frequently made, like that for collecting broches, for use in wood or workshop.

Shaving brake: Long heavy poles (for hop poles) are best supported on two stout crotches driven into the ground, and shaved in place, their weight stopping them moving. Smaller poles are shaved in a brake which holds them at an angle of

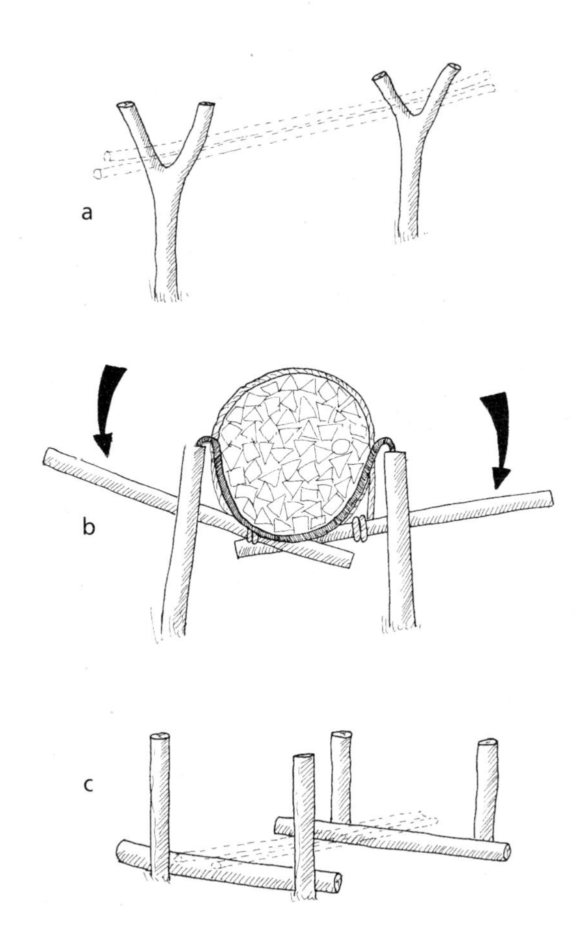

Fig. 8.5 **Devices for bundling product: a. two crotch poles; b. Kentish notch used with a 'woodman's grip' (a rope passing round the stuff, either end of which is tied to a lever, pressure on which tightens the bundle); c. a simple frame.**

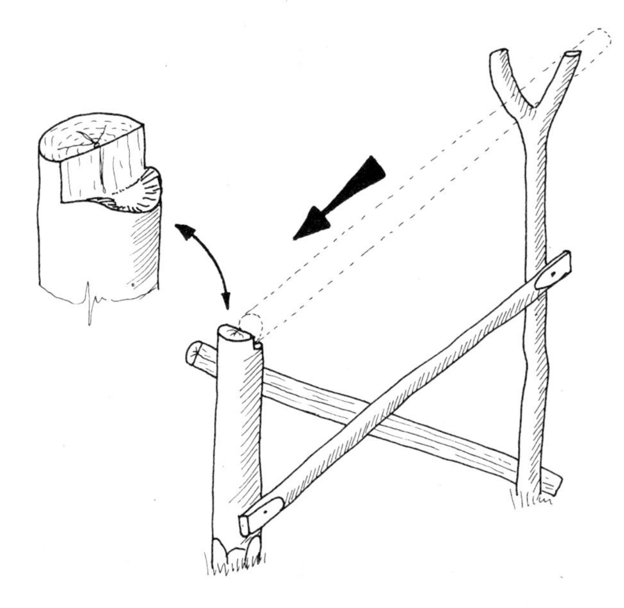

Fig. 8.6 A shaving brake; stand at the shorter post and shave in direction of arrow.

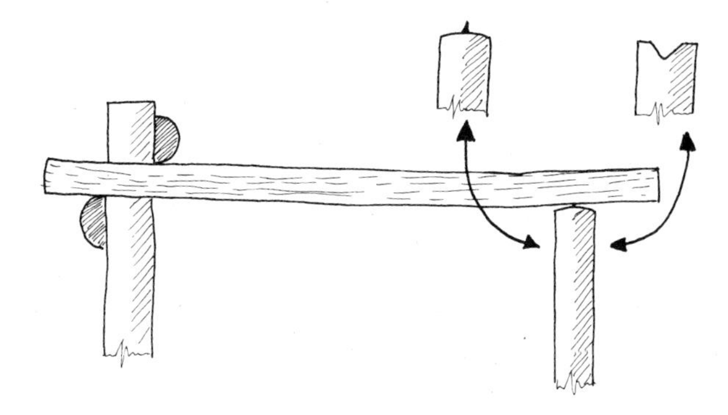

Fig. 8.7 The tension grip: the right end of the workpiece is secured by either a 'V' cut or a short sharpened nail head.

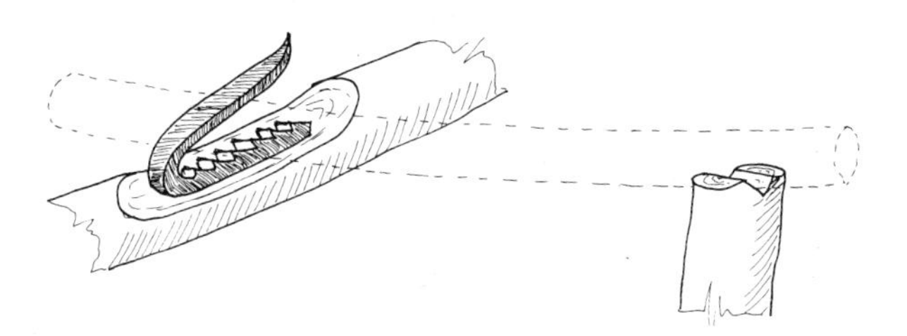

Fig. 8.8 A tension grip using a Kentish hop dog in place of two horizontal bars.

app. 35° which is very comfortable for working (**fig. 8.6**). The poles are held by two posts, the taller of which has a crotch, and the shorter, at about waist height, a stop behind a cup shaped depression to prevent the pole sliding into the worker, or off sideways. This is the fast efficient way to get the bark off green poles.

Devices to grip the workpiece: These devices are designed to firmly grip the material you are working on. This is particularly important when using shaves, draw knives or tying bonds around besoms.

Tension grip: A simple and effective way to hold wood under tension. This is done using two spaced horizontal poles and a post that tensions the piece (**fig. 8.7**). The post has either a notch or a sharpened nail at its top to prevent the workpiece slipping. This is fast to use for shaving poles or clefts, and since the two horizontal poles are a riving brake in reverse, it is common to make a device that performs both jobs.

A neat development of this form used in Kent utilises a hop dog. This toothed metal jaw, designed to grip hop poles and remove them from the ground, replaces the two horizontal poles (**fig. 8.8**). Its teeth hold the workpiece securely, but

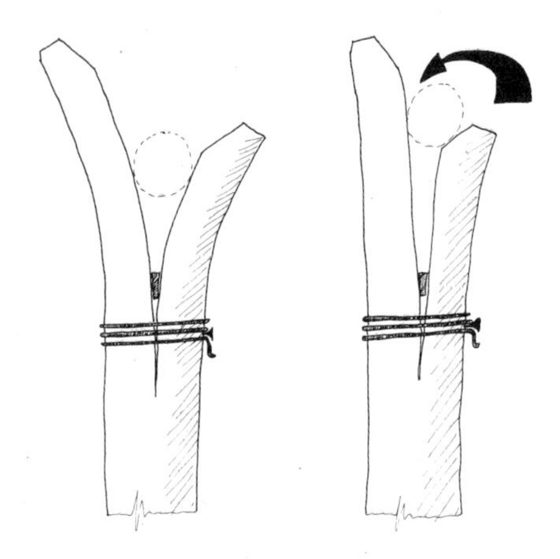

Fig. 8.9 A greenwood vice: note the small wedge, and how round work is 'rolled' into the vice.

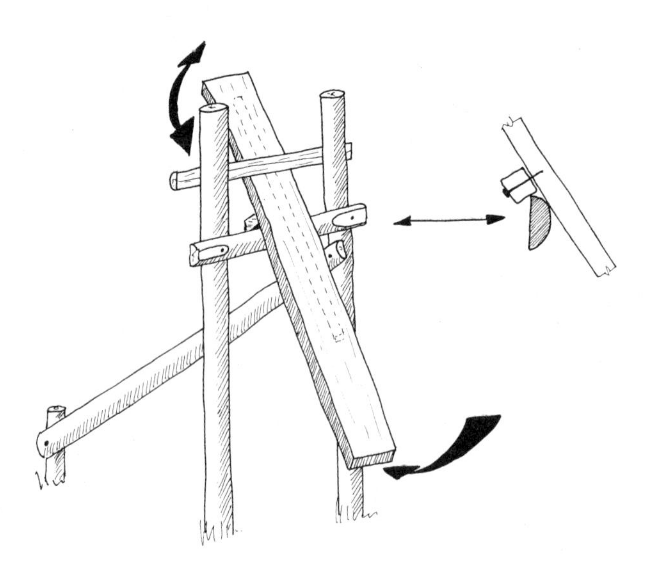

Fig. 8.10 A Suffolk knee operated vice.

you will need to bolt the horizontal to which it is fixed very firmly since nails will pull out with the constant twisting.

Greenwood vice: This vice grips a piece of wood by using the pressure to close together exerted by the two halves of a split green pole. Ash poles c.75mm (3in) diameter are best. Cut one to the length you want, sharpen the butt and drive it into the ground. Then, at about 300mm (12in) below the top tightly wind a wire three or four times around the post and staple it (**fig. 8.9**). This will stop the split you need to make from running too far. Split the post centrally from the top using a froe, and then saw off c.75mm (3in) from one side. Chamfer the top of each cleft as shown, and insert a little wedge just above the wire band so that the 'jaws' of the vice are held slightly open.

To use the vice, put the stuff to be held on the top of the vice: if it is round, twist it towards the longer jaw and down; if it is a cleft, push the longer jaw back pushing down at the same time. Whilst the piece can be popped out of the vice relatively easily, it cannot be moved sideways at all, so that one or two of these vices are capable of holding a piece for shaving or drilling. It will remain effective for 12 months.

Knee vices: The principle of a knee vice is a long, flat-surfaced beam, pivoted towards its top end, and so arranged that when the bottom is pushed by the operator's knee, the top closes against a horizontal bar and securely holds any workpiece on the flat surface. Whilst held on the beam, the work piece is perfectly positioned to be shaved by the operator with a draw knife.

The Suffolk 'ladder' type is the easiest to make, based on two vertical posts as illustrated (**fig. 8.10**). The piece of wood nailed to the back of the beam causes it to pivot on the horizontal cross bar. An advantage of the Sussex shaving horse with its tripod form is that it can easily be moved, although its main beam is more difficult to fashion. In this type the pivoting beam has a groove cut in the back that rocks on a horizontal metal strip, and is frequently weighted at the far end so as soon as the operator releases the pressure of his knee, the vice opens (**fig. 8.11**). With both of these vices you will be amazed how little pressure is required to grip the work piece, a function of the long leverage to the pivoting point.

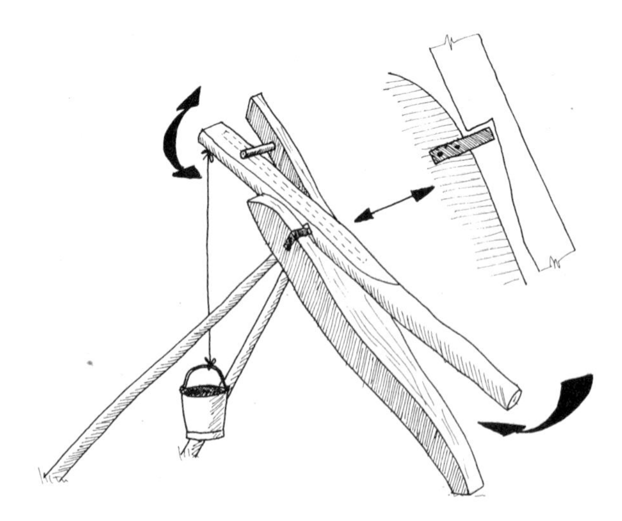

Fig. 8.11 A Sussex knee vice. The weighted bucket automatically opens the jaws; knee pressure closes it.

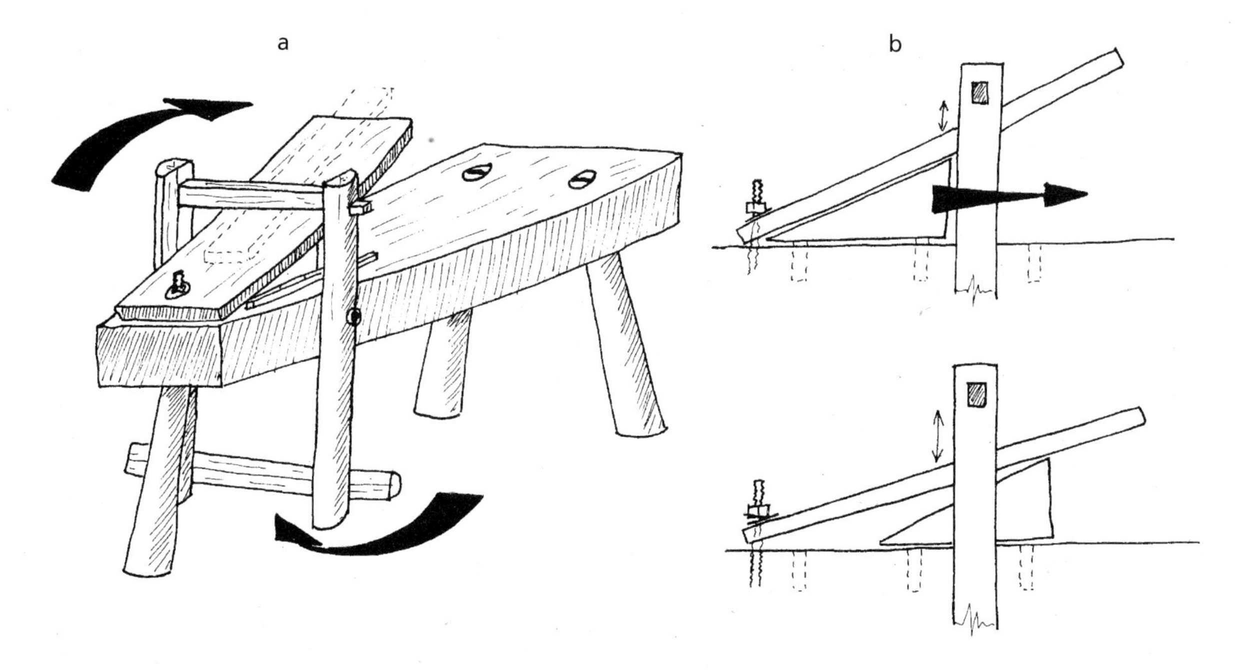

Fig. 8.12 a. foot operated shaving horse; b. shows how a wedge under the main board can adjust the gap for the workpiece.

Foot vices: One of the commonest devices is the small sit on horse with a vice closed by pressure from the operator's feet (**fig. 8.12**). It is used for tent pegs, shaping chair legs, rinding and smoothing handles, tying besoms Once you have used a horse like this, you will wonder how you ever made anything without it. There are two main forms illustrated, one from the southern counties of England, the other from Europe.

For both you need a large baulk of wood which you can obtain sawn or hew from a suitable trunk. Three legs are best (then it will never rock), fitted as described for the bench. For the English horse, the arms of the vice must be made from the mirror clefts of one pole giving as much length below the pivot as possible in order to increase the leverage.

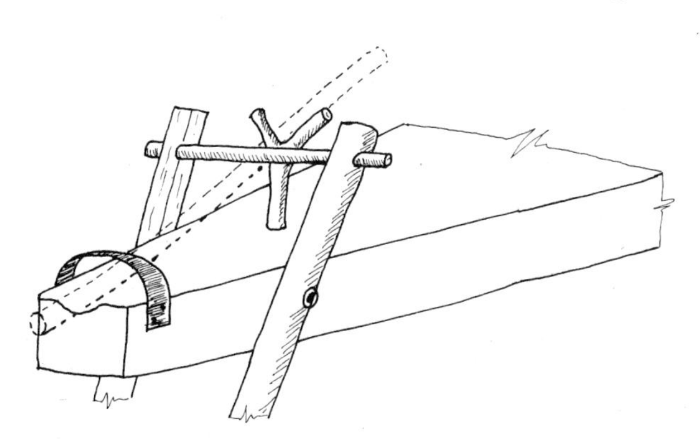

Fig. 8.13 For shaving round poles substitute a crotch stick for the flat bed.

They are usually pivoted on a long coach bolt. The foot bar should project enough to get both feet on, and the top bar should come down flat on the working surface to give a good grip, which can be increased by fixing a metal plate to the top bar. A moveable wedge under the working surface makes the device adjustable for differing sizes of work. Replace the flat plate with a crotch stick (**see fig. 8.13**) and your horse will handle round poles with no problem.

European shaving horses are more complex to build, but do grip very tightly. In this type the vice is operated by one central arm that passes through a hole in the base (**fig. 8.14**) – where it may pivot - then through the horizontal working surface (where on other designs it pivots). The top of the arm is then fitted either with a stout short rod or a block on either side that traps the work piece. This horse can be made to accommodate wood of different thickness by boring a range of pivot points in the central arm and moving it accordingly.

Spindle grips: These simple devices are perfect for shaping tool handles or legs, since not only do they hold a length of wood securely for shaving, they also allow it to be easily rotated to work on any of its surfaces. The construction mimics the bed of a lathe: a bed plate with a central gap that allows one end piece with a fixed centre spindle to be moved to various fixed positions where it is fixed with a dowel, and a fixed end stock with an

Fig. 8.14 An alternative shaving horse: this grips tightly due to the longer leverage. The half-moon block and metal straps at the front retain fresh green clefts in a curved shape if required.

adjustable poppet spindle (**fig. 8.15**). The spindle can be made from studding shaped and sharpened to suit. Both spindles are traditionally angled as shown to reduce the risk of catching them with the draw knife.

Besom vice: Some besom makers simply bundle and tie their heads using a shaving horse (see Chapter 14). Others use a special vice to hold the bundle of twigs tight while they bind it (**fig. 8.16**). All of these devices are blacksmith made. The easiest to use is foot operated and must be bolted to a stout post.

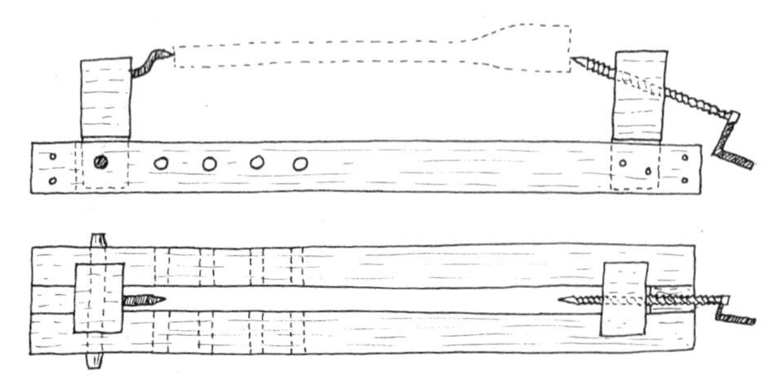

Fig. 8.15 Adjustable spindle grips.

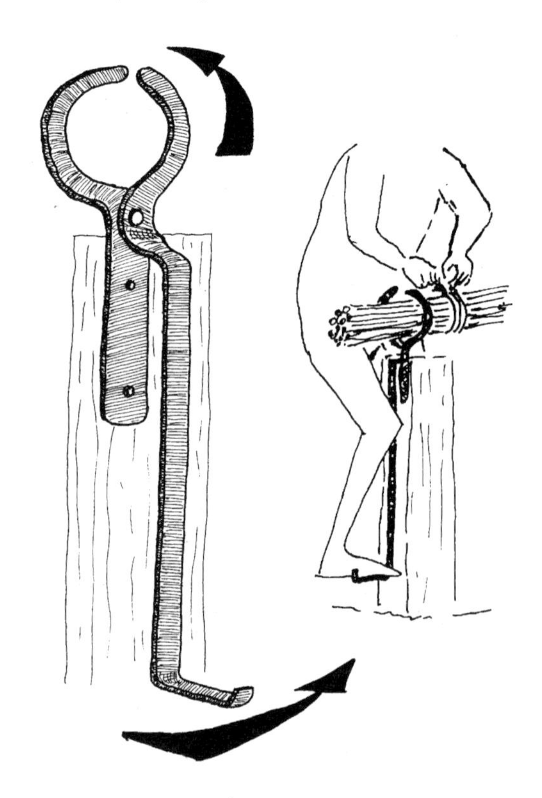

Fig. 8.16 Besom maker's foot operated vice.

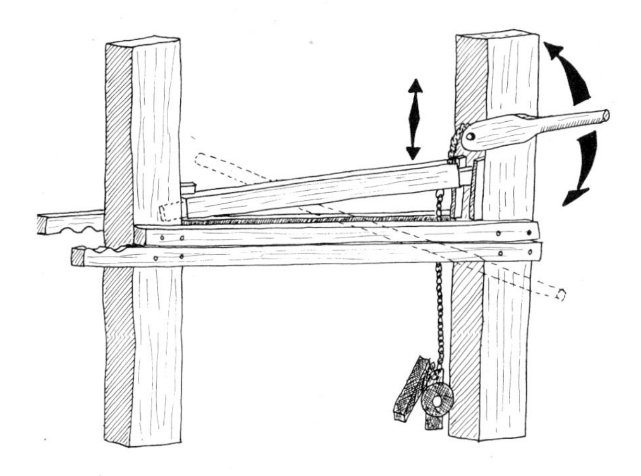

Fig. 8.17 Stail maker's vice: pulling down on the lever opens the vice; the heavy weights close it. Note the setting pins on the left for straightening steamed poles.

Stail vice: I use this title, for this elegant, effective device seems only to be found in rake makers workshops. This vice consists of a horizontal bar, pivoted at one end, of which can be opened or closed against two other fixed bars (**fig. 8.17**). The vice is opened by means of a lever and chain, and is closed automatically by heavy weights tightly enough to allow the craftsman to use his stail engine with both hands. Stout posts are required to support the horizontal bars.

Post and wedge vice: This is often used mounted on a low bench (**fig. 8.18**). It is an excellent way of holding wood for drilling, morticing, marking or shaping.

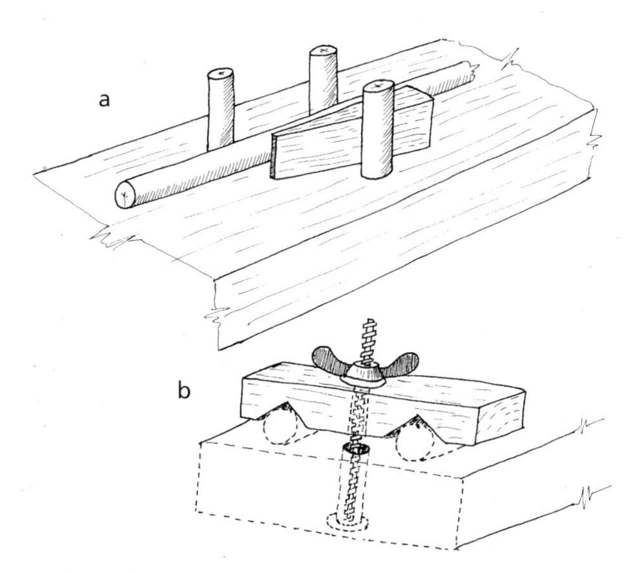

Fig. 8.18 Vices: a. post and wedge vice: a very flexible way of holding workpieces for various operations; b. screw operated vice.

Devices for levering: To be able to split reasonably sized wood effectively you must be able to apply leverage and understand how devices can help you to achieve this.

Riving brakes: The essential element of any riving brake is two horizontal bars with sufficient distance between them horizontally to allow a piece of wood to be put under tension (**fig. 8.19**). That bar nearest the worker is lower than the further one so that tension is applied by pushing down on the workpiece. The minimum distance between the two horizontal is about 100mm (4in) and the simplest brake is made by nailing the two bars to either side of two stout posts. More efficient brakes are triangulated to give a larger spacing over much of the width. It is also essential to vary the spacing between the bars vertically; this allows you to rive material of different sizes efficiently, essential if you are producing small clefts from quite large wood. A spacing of 25mm (1in) at one side and 150mm (6in) at the other works best.

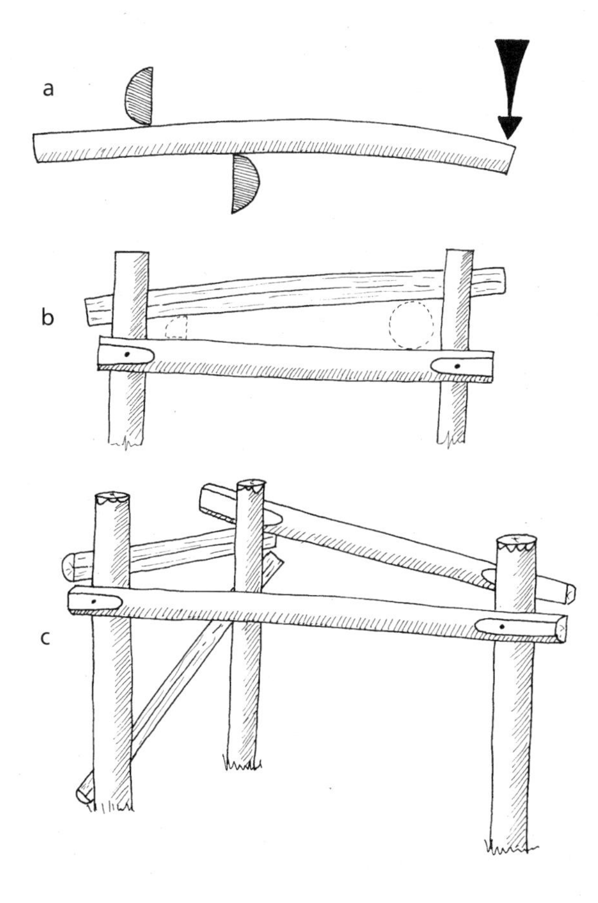

Fig. 8.19 The riving brake: a. using two horizontal bars to lever a pole; b. varying the gap between the horizontals to accommodate differing sizes of work; c. a triangulated brake.

Fig. 8.20 Broche splitter with detail of the wedge post around which the broche is split.

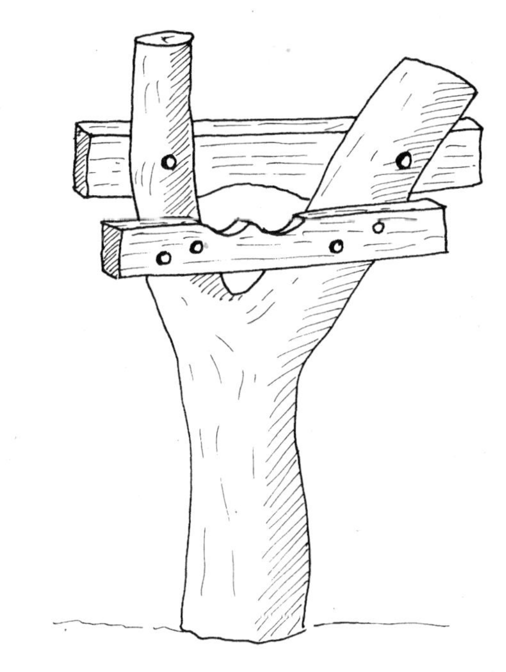

Fig. 8.21 Setting brake for levering softened poles.

Broche splitter: In effect a wedge, this simple device is used to lever apart the fine hazel clefts needed for broches (thatching spars). There are two forms. The simplest is a post c.1.2m (4ft) high with a small 20mm (3/4in) rod passing through it about 100mm (4in) from the top (**fig. 6.22**). The rod supports the clefts whilst the post separates them. A slightly better form has a wedge cut at the top of a short post with horizontal shoulders below the wedge in order to support the clefts. The more gradual levering of the wedge shaped splitter causes less running out than the round post. This form is best used mounted at the front of a stool (**fig. 8.20**); not only can you sit down, but the post is more stable.

Setting pins/brake: These are an inseparable part of the process of making rake handles. Whatever you may think looking at your coppice, there is almost never a truly straight pole. This problem is overcome by steaming them, and then straightening any curves by levering between the setting pins whilst pliable. Two forms are illustrated (**figs. 8.17 & 8.21**).

Devices for shaping: We have just seen how steamed poles can be straightened using simple devices; there is a much wider range of quite complex devices for shaping either steamed or green wood. These are carefully designed and made to produce accurate, consistent shapes.

Form for stable forks: Stable or hay forks require a form or jig to produce their characteristic shape. It is made from two stout side rails with four bars between them that shape the fork. Two of these are fixed and two are removable dowels (**fig. 8.22**). The end member is notched to hold the tines in position. You can change the relative spacing of the members to achieve the shape you require.

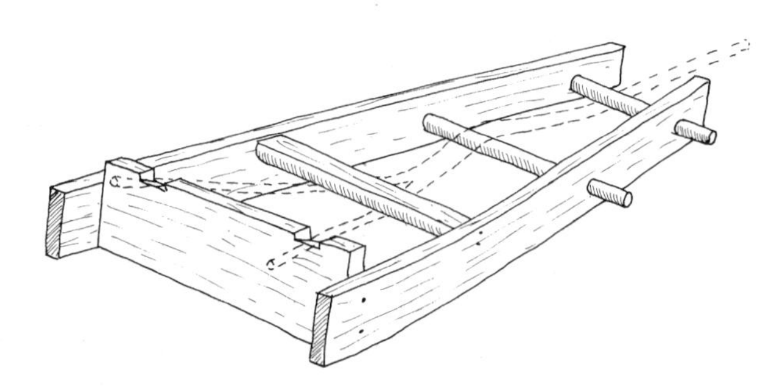

Fig. 8.22 Form for shaping a stable fork. (after Langsner)

To fix a fork in the jig:

- Insert the tines into their slot with them passing under the first bar
- Put a 10cm (4in) block under the end of the fork handle and stand on the form to create the first bend
- Pull the handle sufficiently to insert the first dowel
- Turn the form over, supporting the frame with blocks so that the tines are not on the ground, put a 10cm block under the handle end again, stand on the frame to create the second bend, and insert the second dowel to hold it.

Form for basket rims: To make the rims and handles for trugs a setting frame is used. This comprises a pattern of the exact shape required fixed to a couple of flat boards, and with retaining lugs to keep the bent wood against the pattern (**fig. 8.23**). The rim is steamed to make it pliable for

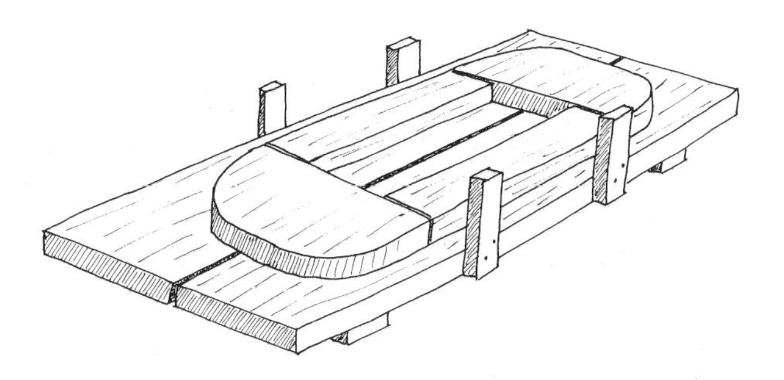

Fig. 8.23 Form for shaping basket rims and handles.

bending, and is overlapped and nailed together at one side. If you get into volume production, you can put a pattern on each side of the boards!

Although the rims for spelk baskets can be shaped by hand, there is an ingenious and fast bending device used by some professional makers. It consists of a rotating pattern exactly the shape required. One end of the steam softened hazel rim is held by a small clip. As the pattern rotates the hazel follows the shape – helped by a weighted roller that holds the hazel against the pattern (**fig. 8.24**). As for trugs, the rim is overlapped and nailed.

Hoop bender: Barrel hoops are very similar to basket rims except they are perfectly round. They are made from cleft hazel which is bent whilst green, without steaming. A simple device is used comprising two wooden rollers so arranged that one can be used to lever the cleft as it is fed between them (**fig. 8.25**). See also Chapter 18.

Bending table for chair backs: A traditional bending table consists of a heavy wooden (or steel) plate 0.6m (2ft) square with a matrix of 13mm (1/2in) holes at 50mm (2in) spacing over its whole surface. This allows both a range of shapes to be made, and the bending to be done progressively. In use this needs to be firmly fixed to the bench or the ground. As for basket rims you need to cut patterns or 'bending forms' from 38mm (1 1/2in) wood to the precise shape required. This is bolted to the bending table. The steamed and softened wood, for the back frame of a chair for example, is then formed around the pattern

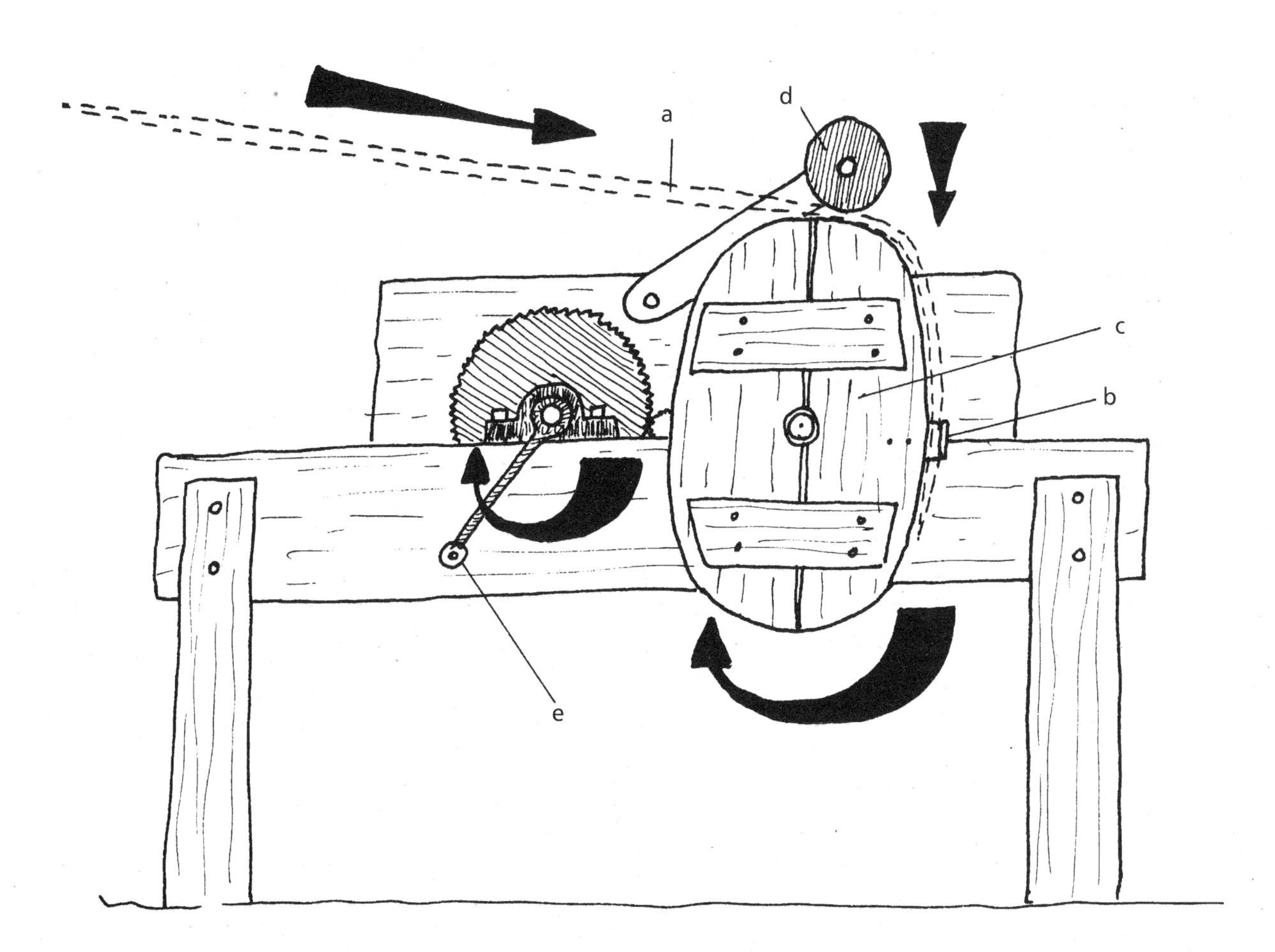

Fig. 8.24 Device for shaping rims for spelk baskets: a. rod for basket rim; b. metal clip; c. form; d. heavy roller; e. winding handle.

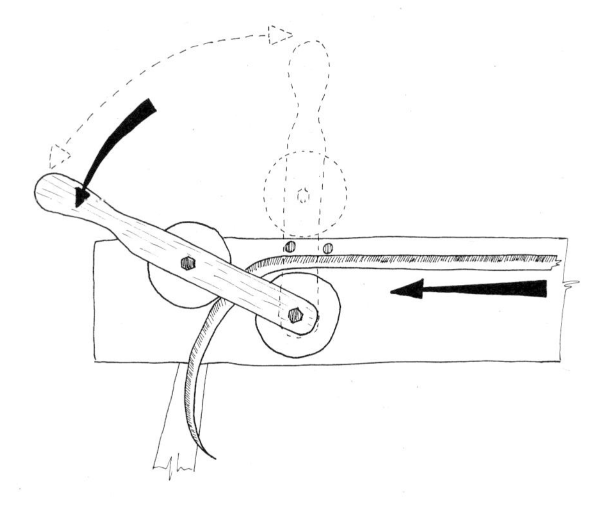

Fig. 8.25 Hoop bender: the lever is worked to and fro to achieve the desired curve as the rod is pushed forward.

using metal pegs or wooden dowels, and wooden wedges (**fig. 8.26**) to hold it in place. Start by wedging the work piece at the top dead centre of the pattern, and then progressively form the sides to the shape required. This is best done using a couple of metal bars one to lever and one to hold the work. This must be done steadily and smoothly; sudden jerky movements are more likely

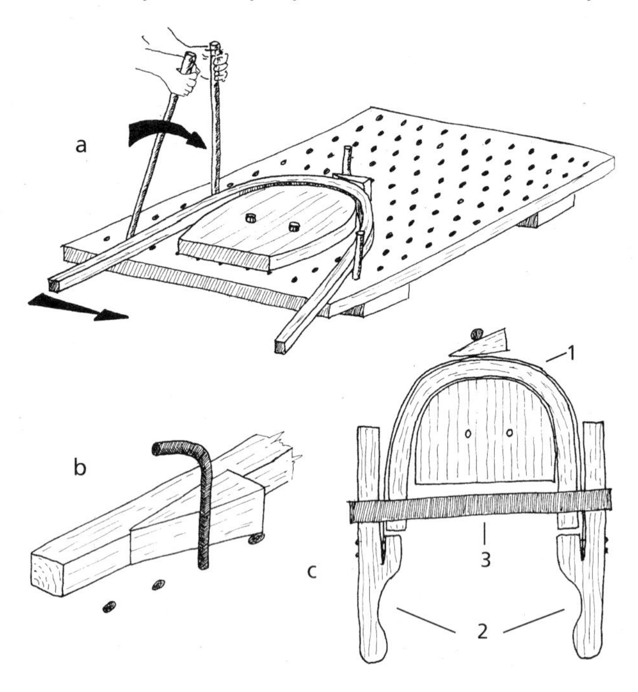

Fig. 8.26 Bending table for chair backs: a. using poles to lever the steamed wood into position; b. using wedges to force the wood against the form; c. a shaping system using a steel band (1); attached to two handles (2); and held in place by a stout bar (3).

to result in the wood fracturing. You must end up with the work piece tightly wedged against the pattern.

Even well steamed wood can fracture under the tension strain of bending. To ease this problem, a steel strap fitted with handles that allows you to bend the wood whilst supporting its outside edge is used (**fig. 8.26**; after Hill).

Stick handle jig: This simple device allows you to form the curved handle of a walking stick. Make a round grooved disk app. 125mm (5in) in diameter (**fig. 8.27**). This has a central hole that loosely fits over a stout peg. A second peg traps the end of the stick while it is bent around the disk and tied. Stick and disk can then be removed from the dowel and left until set; you will therefore need several discs if making more than one walking stick.

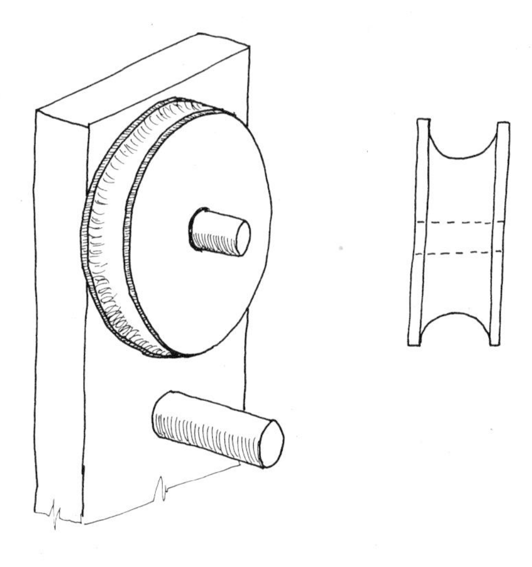

Fig. 8.27 Stick maker's jig.

Scythe snaith setting frame: A scythe snaith is very subtly shaped in order that the nibs (small handles) fall in the right position for the user. It is unusual to find poles with exactly the right combination of curves, so woodmen grow straight poles, steam them, and then form them to shape in a setting frame or rack. In its traditional form this is not a device for the casual woodworker. It comprises a massive hardwood frame with a series of horizontal beams that determine the handle shape (**fig. 8.28**) and to some of which the handle can be held by a metal clip.

The steamed snaiths are fitted under the lowest beam leaving c.200-250mm (8-10in) protruding. They are then bent over the middle beam and clipped with a metal hook to the top

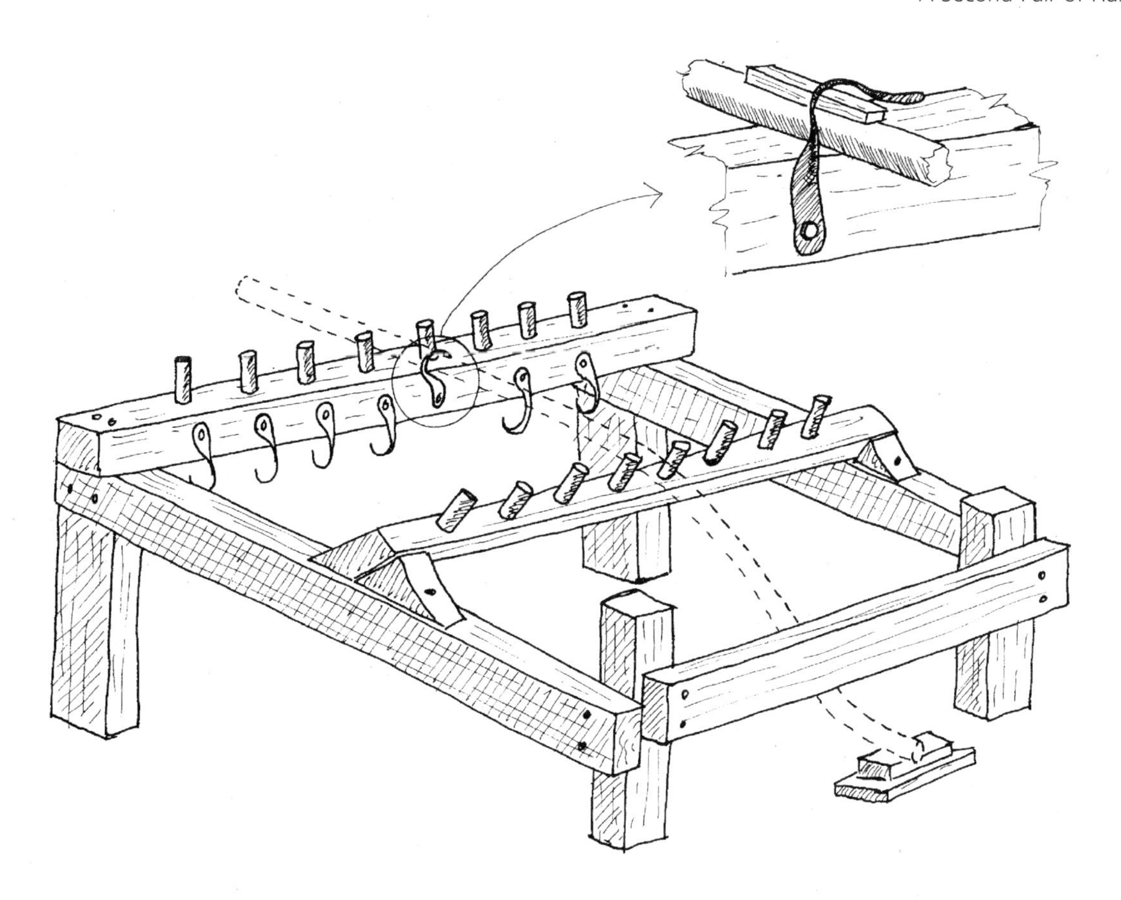

Fig. 8.28 Scythe snaith setting frame: these need to be massive and with their feet securely in the ground in order to withstand the leverage of the bent poles.

beam, using a small piece of waste wood between hook and handle to avoid marking the soft pole. Finally the protruding foot is levered up and a block put beneath it to produce the second curve required at the bottom of the snaith. English pattern handles only require two curves in one plane; American patterns (most commonly used these days) require an additional curve in a second plane, and a correspondingly more complex frame (see Appendix 1).

Further Reading:

Edlin, H.L., ***Woodland Crafts in Britain***, David and Charles, 1973

Hill, J., ***The Complete Practical Book of Country Crafts***, David and Charles, 1979

Lambert, F., ***Tools and Devices for Coppice Crafts,*** Centre for Alternative Technology, 1977

Tabor,R., ***Traditional Woodland Crafts***, Batsford, 1994

Woods, K. S., ***Rural Crafts of England***, Harrap, 1949

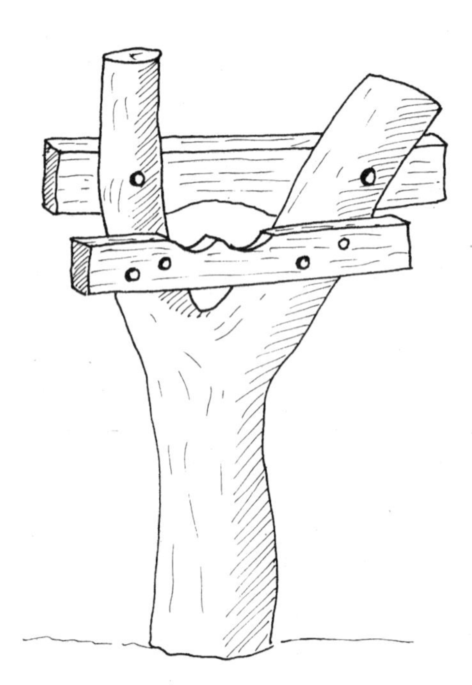

Chapter 9

Measuring, Patterns and Gauges

Some tips on measuring

I don't intend to tell you how to use a ruler, but there are some tips and rules of thumb that I have found useful from time to time.

Area: The acre, a measure still in use, is 4840sq.yards; when in the wood a convenient means to measure it is to pace a 70 x 70 square, assuming your pace is a yard, giving 4900sq.yards. Likewise half an acre is 70 x 35 paces, and a quarter acre is 35 x 35 paces. For contract terms you may want to measure an area accurately with a tape. There are 2.47 acres to a hectare (100m x 100m). To convert acres to hectares, multiply by 0.405.

You may find older woodmen still refer to the chain, which is a length of 19.8m (22yds). A square chain is 1/10acre, and wood was often cut and paid for by the square chain. A chain is still an ideal width for cutting coppice in strips.

Right angles: When marking out a plot it is often useful to be able to ensure the corners are right angles. To do this, use a tape and measure out a triangle with sides three, four and five metres respectively. That peg at the three metre point from zero is at a true right angle (**fig. 9.1**).

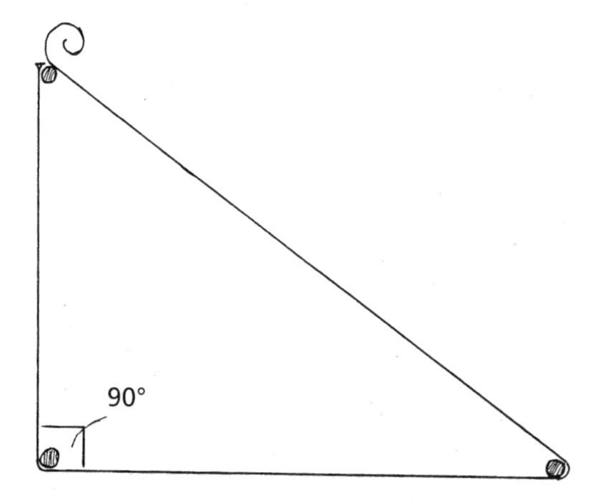

Fig. 9.1 Laying out a true right angle with a tape and three pegs.

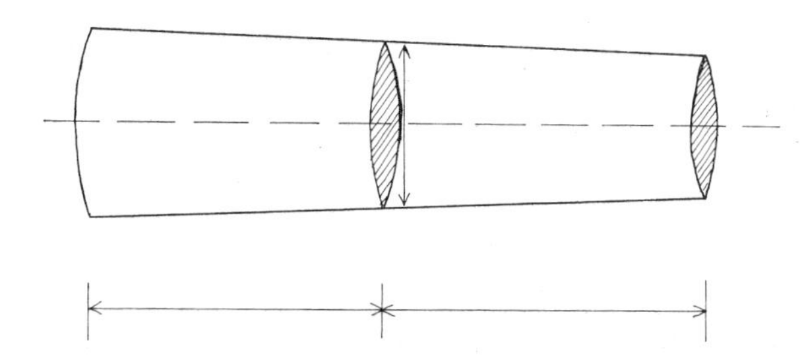

Fig. 9.2 Estimating the volume of a felled trunk by measuring the girth at the mid-point.

Volume: *Cord:* A cord of wood, traditionally fire wood, is 2.4m (8ft) long, 1.2m (4ft) high and 1.2m (4ft) deep, making 3.6 cubic metres (128cu.ft). Roughly half that volume is air space, and the wood will weigh c.2 tons when green, or c.1.25 tons after two years seasoning. The rule of thumb is that seasoned hard woods weigh 19.8kg (43¾lbs) per 0.028cu.m (1cu.ft).

Timber: Hardwoods are still traded using the Hoppus measure, which is a means of determining the volume in cubic feet of the wood in a bark-on log (**fig. 9.2**). It estimates the approximate timber volume after the log has been roughly squared.

$$\text{Hoppus Volume} = \frac{\text{(mid quarter girth)}}{144} \times \text{length in feet}$$

1 Hoppus foot = 1.27 true cubic feet

1 cubic metre = 27.74 Hoppus feet

This is fine for trunks that have been felled since you can easily measure the girth at the mid-point. For standing timber you must measure the

Table 9.1 Square sections possible from a given diameter

Diameter of round Log in mm + (in)	152(6)	228(9)	305(12)	381(15)	457(18)	533(21)
Square section Possible in mm + (in)	133(5¼)	203(8)	266(10½)	343(13½)	406(16)	470(18½)

This table is based on Hoppus' measurer

Table 9.2 Diameter of work possible from quarter clefts of given diameter log

Diameter of round Log in mm + (in)	101(4)	152(6)	203(8)	254(10)	305(12)	355(14)
Diameter possible from a quarter cleft in mm + (in)	38(1½)	63(2½)	82(3¾)	101(4)	120(4¾)	139(5½)

These figures assume a thin bark and a straight log, so treat them as maxima, and be a little generous in the sizing of your wood!

girth at breast height (1.4m-4½ ft above ground) and estimating the length of usable bole, use the tables published by the Forestry Commission to predict the volume. If you are dealing with merchants and discuss price 'per cube', make sure you understand what they mean – it can make quite a difference to your price (or cost).

Usable wood: Although wood grows as a cylinder, we only infrequently use it in that form: large round logs may be hewn to produce square timbers for building, or smaller logs may be cleft for turning into chair legs. So what size tree must you start with? **Table 9.1** shows the size of squared timber you will get from a round log.

Table 9.2 shows the largest diameter object you can achieve from a quarter cleft of a given diameter log.

Height of a tree: You may want to determine this, particularly if you are felling a tree close to buildings, cables or fences. Make yourself a simple hypsometer (**fig. 9.3**). Make sure you are on the same level as the tree you are measuring, and holding the hypsometer at eye level, walk backwards or forwards until the top of the tree coincides with the sighting line. The height of the tree is the distance you are standing from the tree plus the height of your eye above ground.

Metric/imperial conversion: Although we are all now taught in metric measures, I have included both metric and imperial throughout this book. This is not solely for the older amongst us who are imperial trained, but because many of the traditional products and devices were designed in that system. It is not in my gift to change their sizes. **Table 9.3** gives the simple conversion factors you may need.

Table 9.3 Metric/imperial conversion formulae

To convert	Multiply by
Inches to centimetres	2.54
Centimetres to inches	0.39
Feet to metres	0.31
Metres to feet	3.28
Yards to metres	0.91
Metres to yards	1.09
Sq. yards to sq metres	0.84
Sq. metres to sq yards	1.20
Acres to hectares	0.40
Hectares to acres	2.47
Pounds to kilograms	0.45
Kilograms to pounds	2.20
Tons to kilograms	1016.05
Kilograms to tons	0.001
Tons to tonnes	1.02

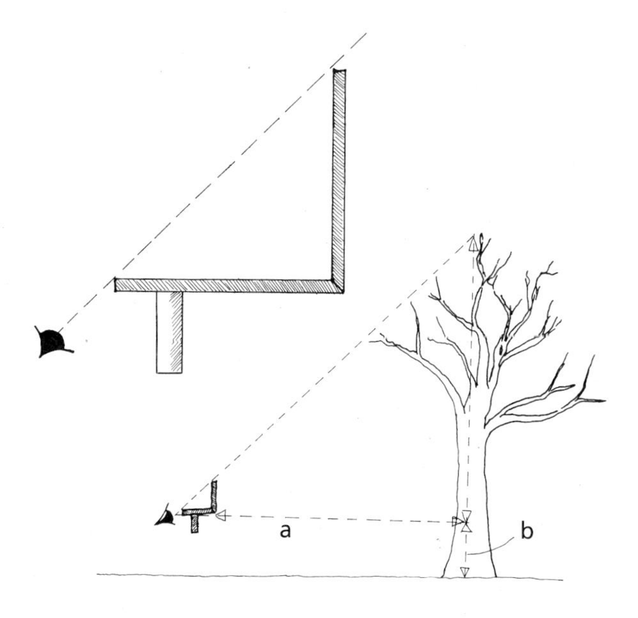

Fig. 9.3 A simple hypsometer and its use: the tree height is a + b.

Using gauges to measure your work

There are endless repetitive jobs for which a simple gauge is useful. When taken from your pattern they help to ensure the finished object is right. But more importantly when you are making numbers of the same object they are a good means of helping to get a consistent appearance. They are items each craftsman develops himself and are well worth the time spent making them. A few examples are described from which you can design your own.

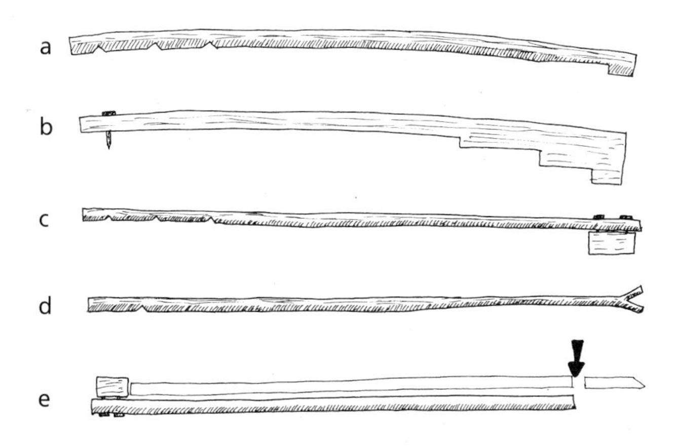

Fig. 9.4 Measuring sticks: a. bent stick; b. stepped gauge; c. an alternative to the curved stick; d. hurdlemaker's width gauge; e. gauge for use on a sawing horse.

Measuring sticks: These are used in a whole range of jobs. They consist of a simple stick with either a block nailed to one end, or a natural curve which can be part cut away (**fig. 9.4**) to allow the stick to be hooked over one end of the work piece. The length of the stick carries one or more marks allowing the work piece to be accurately marked for further processing. Some variations have several steps at one end and a nail at the other which actually marks the work piece.

A different version is that used by hurdle makers which has a crotch at one end and a notch at the other enabling him to measure the width of his hurdle.

Calliper gauges: These are essential when turning or shaving wood for jointing. A simple example is when making gate hurdles, where a test gauge is used to ensure the ends of the rails are a constant size to fit the mortices in the heads (**fig. 9.5**). Similarly round holes in a block of wood can be used to gauge shaved chair rails or round tenons. Beware that these gauges do wear with time and must be replaced.

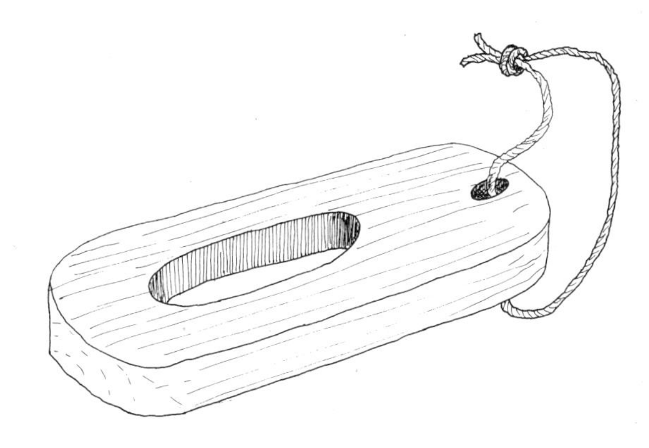

Fig. 9.5 Hurdlemaker's gauge to check the heads will fit their mortices.

When turning or shaving legs or rails for chairs it is very effective to cut a series of gauges from one piece of thin plywood and use that to ensure various parts are the right size **(fig. 9.6)**. You can use a proper metal calliper, but if you have a piece requiring several different diameters, it is a slow job to keep readjusting it.

Gauging the depth of a mortice hole where it is not passing right through the wood can be critical. If you have not got a depth gauge that screws onto a drill bit, use masking tape around the bit to ensure you stop at the right point.

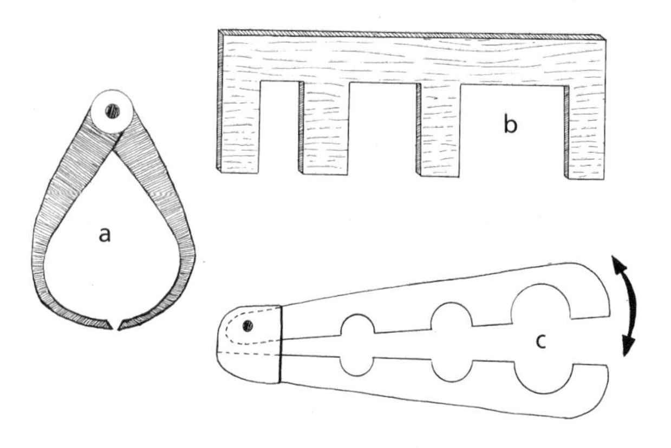

Fig. 9.6 Gauges for turning: a. adjustable metal caliper; b. simple but effective slot gauge; c. more complex two sided gauge.

Collecting and using patterns

There is some overlap between patterns and gauges. A pattern defines all of the parameters for a product, translating what is in the makers mind into hard facts and figures from which the product can be made. Traditionally much of this detail was in craftsman's heads, not committed to paper. When you see a good tool, device or product always make a sketch of it and record as many of the key dimensions as possible. For traditional items that may be hard to find, contact older craftsmen or museums; the latter frequently have collections of artefacts not on display that you may be allowed to inspect.

Some patterns can double as gauges, and a good green wood worker's shop will have an increasing store of these in paper, card or wood. Again some examples are described that outline the principles from which you can develop your own.

For turning: When producing turnery items, it is often critical that repeat items are identical. For an item like a chair leg with beads and tapers in its design, mark these features on a thin board that you can hold against your work piece. This will allow you to actually mark your work-piece if necessary, and you can write diameters on the pattern as well (**fig. 9.7**).

For gate hurdles: When making mini hurdles a pattern can be used for making the heads and marking the mortices (**fig. 9.8**). This cannot be done with full size hurdles because the position of the mortices has to change fractionally to accommodate any bowing in the rails.

However, when it comes to assembling hurdles large or small the use of a pattern or 'mould' on which to nail the parts together, results in consistent square hurdles. The mould defines the position of both heads and top rail by forcing them against stops, whilst the braces are positioned above supports which mark their position.

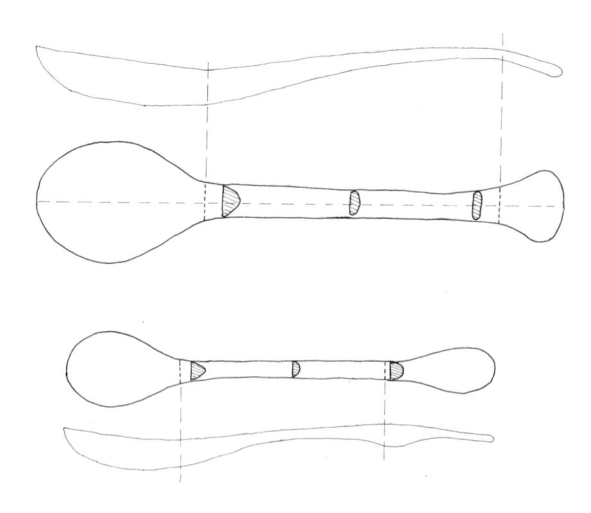

Fig. 9.9 Patterns for spoons; the cross section of the handle is shown hatched in the plan drawing.

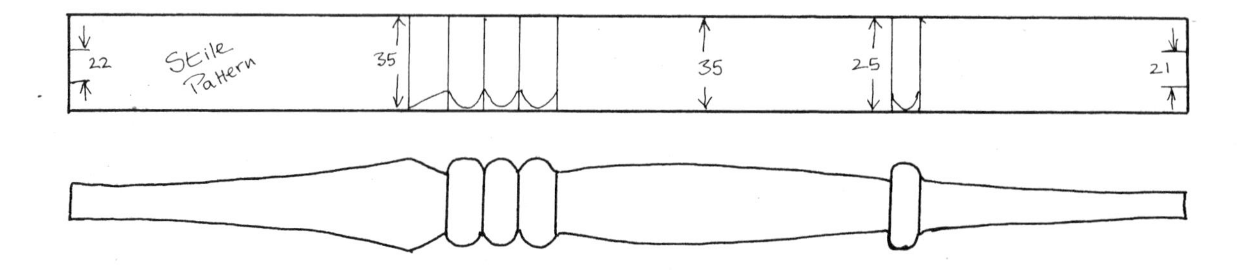

Fig. 9.7 Pattern for a chair stile drawn on a piece of plywood beside the stile itself.

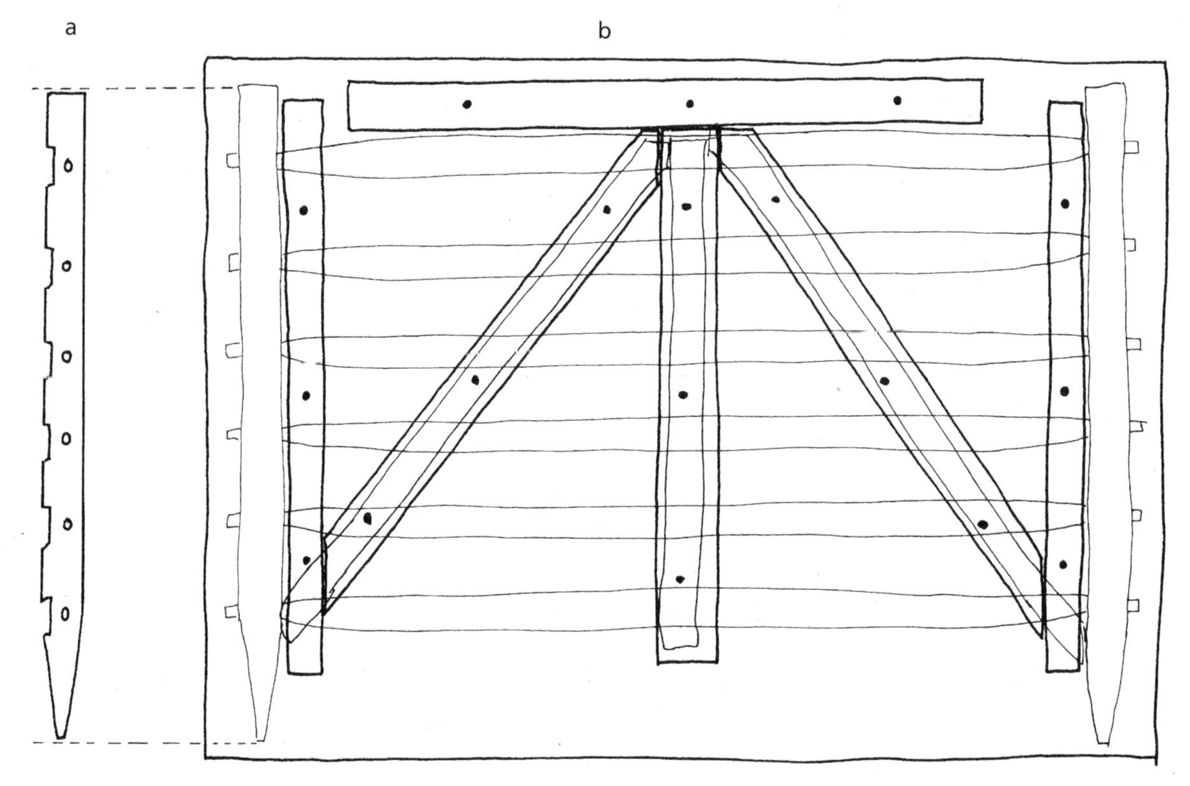

Fig. 9.8 a. the pattern for the head of a mini gate hurdle; b. the pattern or table on which it is assembled.

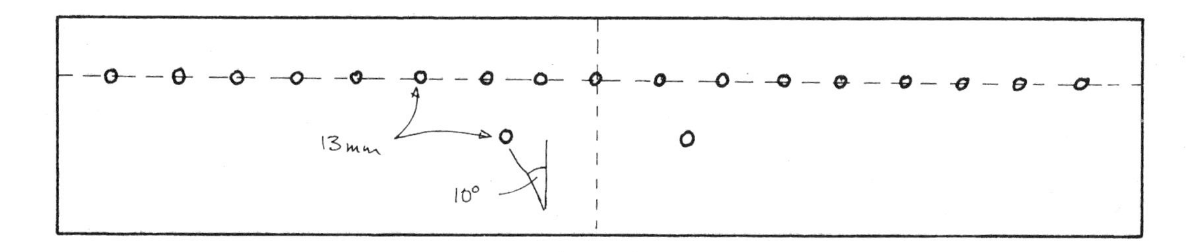

Fig. 9.10 A rake maker's pattern for boring a rake head.

Spoons: As we shall see later, one of the secrets of good spoon making is to mark very clearly the cutting lines. Thin board or thick card is ideal for patterns. When you see a nice spoon put it on a piece of paper and draw round it! Where there is a complicated side profile on a spoon, mark the key changes on your pattern as well (**fig. 9.9**).

Rakes: There are many patterns of rake heads, and the best way to mark out the positions of the teeth is by using a pattern make in plywood or similar (**fig. 9.10**).

Chairs: You can of course keep detailed drawings of chair patterns. However, a very practical and effective way of keeping all the data for a chair on a pattern usable in the workshop is described by John Alexander. This involves marking all the details on a flat board that can be used for marking up the various components.

Further Reading:

Alexander, J., ***Make a chair from a tree***,
Astragal Piers, 1994

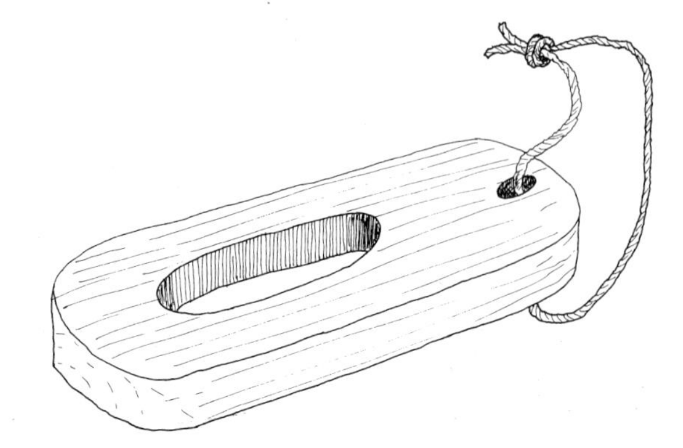

Chapter 10

Lathes, Steamers and Kilns

In this chapter we shall look at some of the more specialised equipment you will need for certain tasks – certainly not the sort you will knock up in half an hour with a side axe and some nails.

Lathes

My encyclopedia says of the lathe: 'Tool that performs turning operation in which unwanted material is removed from a workpiece rotating against a cutting tool'. That is a good description and the key to an effective lathe is its ability to accurately and reliably turn the workpiece whilst providing a system that allows the cutting tool to be held firmly against it. This enables moderate wood workers such as me to produce presentable work, and skilled performers to produce items of great beauty.

Pole lathes are amongst the earliest woodworking tools, turnery being recorded from Greco-Roman times. We shall look at both treadle and pole lathes in this section since they are the main tools of green woodworking. Power lathes are another story.

Principles: There are certain key principles common to any lathe. Firstly there are two centres between which the workpiece rotates. One or both of these are 'dead' (i.e.: do not rotate) centres; these are fixed steel points on which the workpiece rotates and they must be true accurate cones, and very smooth lest any roughness causes them to enlarge the hole in the workpiece, which will then come loose. These centres are held in 'poppets' or 'stocks', one of which is usually fixed and the other is moveable to accommodate work of differing lengths. To allow this, the poppets are supported on a bed, along which one poppet can move. For a lathe to be effective the bed must be true, and the position of the centres in the poppets, and their relation to the bed, must be very accurate.

Lastly the lathe must have a 'rest' to support your chisel whilst cutting. This must be adjustable for different workpieces, and most crucially must be positioned at the line passing between the centres so that the tool it supports always cuts above the centre line of the workpiece. Whatever lathe you make or use, take time to get these key factors right.

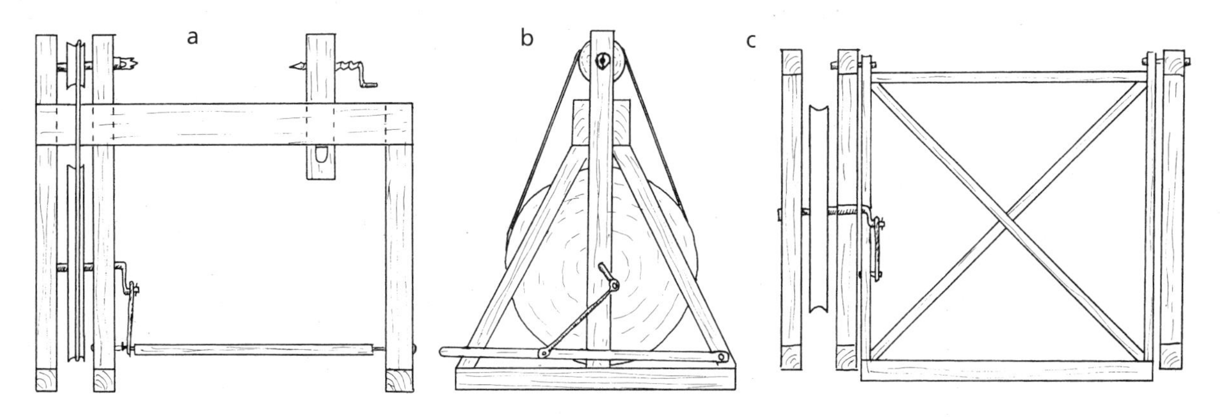

Fig. 10.1 A wooden treadle lathe: a. front; b. side; c. plan.

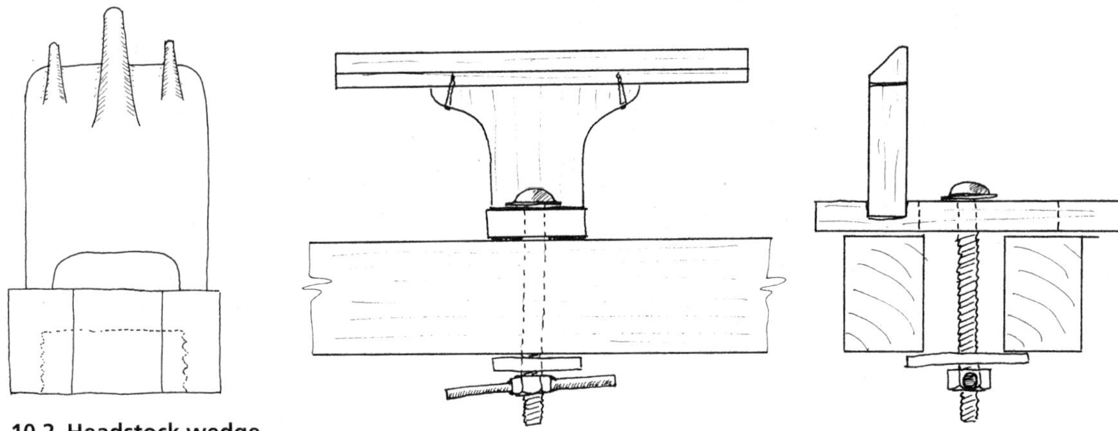

Fig. 10.2 Headstock wedge which jams into the end of the workpiece and drives round.

Fig. 10.3 Adjustable rest for a treadle lathe.

The treadle lathe: The motive power on a treadle lathe is purely the operator's. Pushing on the treadle rotates a crank which drives a large wheel that in turn rotates a 'live' centre in the headstock (**fig.10.1**). The live centre rotates and actually drives the workpiece, and this can either be in the form of a chuck that grips the end of the piece, or more commonly a three pronged steel wedge that bites into the end of the piece (**fig 10.2**). There is a 'dead' centre in the tailstock which can be screwed in or out to give fine adjustment.

Coarse adjustments are made by moving the tailstock along the bed which comprises two parallel beams supported on an 'A' frame through which the tailstock fixing passes. The distance from the centres to the bed of the lathe governs the diameter of workpiece that the lathe can handle.

The rest also fixes through the bed so it can be moved along (**fig 10.3**). It can also be rotated to allow for bowl as well as spindle work. More sophisticated lathes have a speed cone (**fig 10.4**) which allows you to adjust the rotational speed of

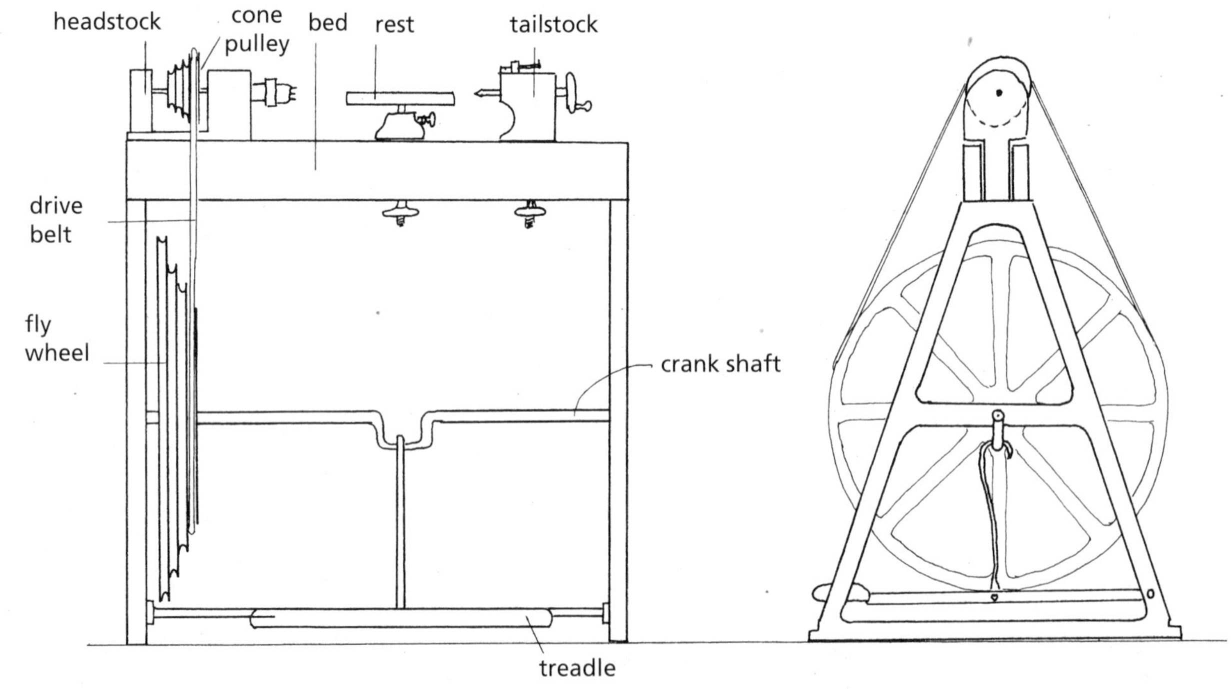

Fig. 10.4 A cast iron treadle lathe with a four speed cone. The hook connection to the crankshaft is a safety feature lest anything, including your foot, is caught under the treadle.

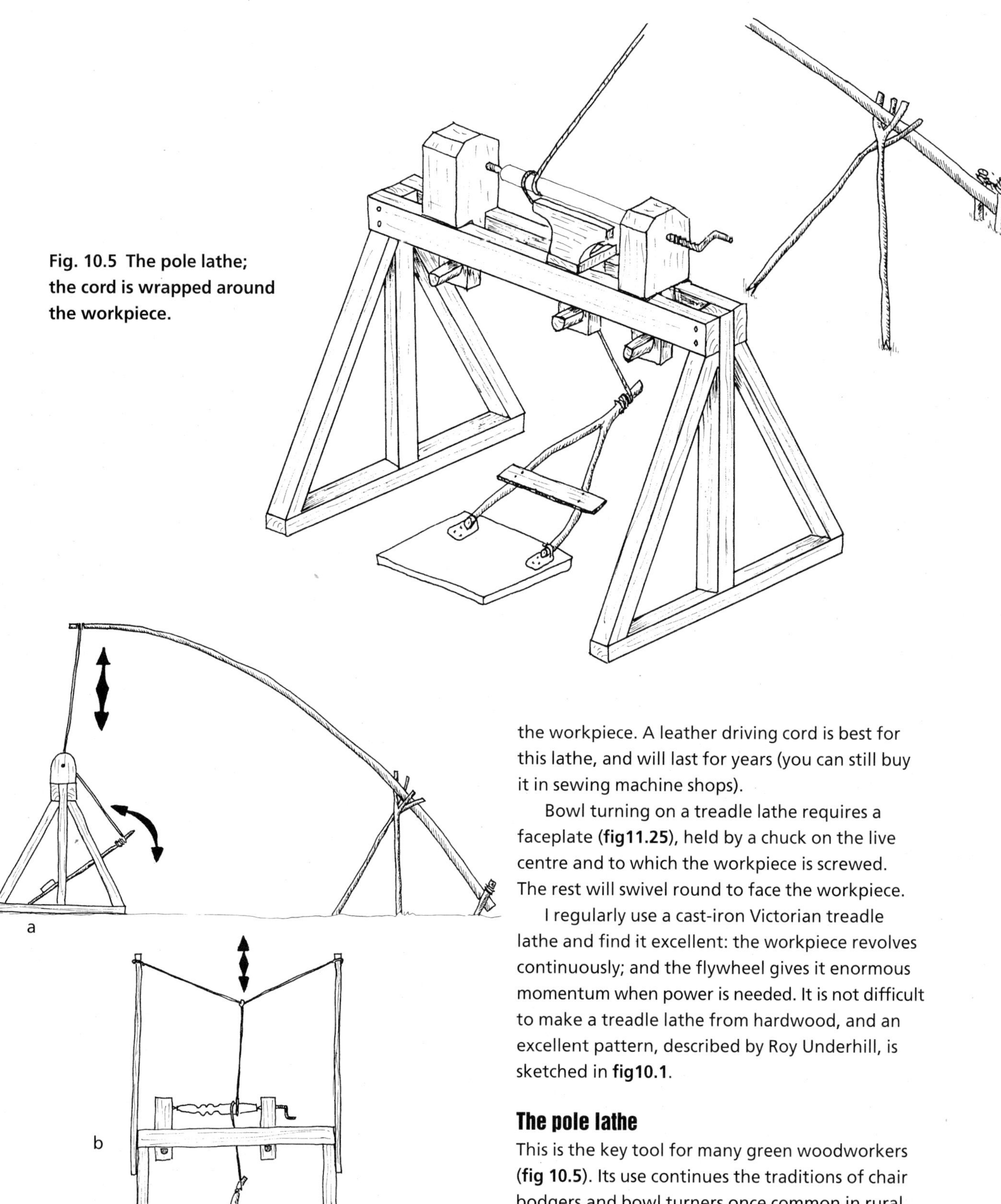

Fig. 10.5 The pole lathe; the cord is wrapped around the workpiece.

Fig. 10.6 a. the spring pole which bends as the treadle is depressed; b. for use in a workshop the cord can be connected to an elastic rope.

the workpiece. A leather driving cord is best for this lathe, and will last for years (you can still buy it in sewing machine shops).

Bowl turning on a treadle lathe requires a faceplate (**fig11.25**), held by a chuck on the live centre and to which the workpiece is screwed. The rest will swivel round to face the workpiece.

I regularly use a cast-iron Victorian treadle lathe and find it excellent: the workpiece revolves continuously; and the flywheel gives it enormous momentum when power is needed. It is not difficult to make a treadle lathe from hardwood, and an excellent pattern, described by Roy Underhill, is sketched in **fig10.1**.

The pole lathe

This is the key tool for many green woodworkers (**fig 10.5**). Its use continues the traditions of chair bodgers and bowl turners once common in rural England. The pole lathe differs from the treadle lathe in that both centres are 'dead' and the workpiece is rotated by a cord that passes around it. This is fixed at one end to a treadle on the floor, and at the other to a flexible green pole; ash and birch are very good. Good quality cord that will grip is essential; baler twine for example will slip on the workpiece. As the operator pushes on the treadle, the cord rotates the workpiece towards the rest (the cutting stroke) and bends the pole; on releasing the treadle the pole straightens, rotating the workpiece away from the rest (the return stroke), during which no cutting takes place. The beauty of the pole lathe is that you can instantly stop and see how the work is progressing, and its speed can be changed instantly.

Fix the spring pole as shown in the drawing (**fig 10.6**), with the butt end firmly fixed to the ground and supported about half way along its length by a couple of crotches. A neat alternative to the spring-pole when using the lathe in a workshop, is to use an elastic rope (bungee straps) fixed to two vertical poles at each end of the bed. The 'feel' is different, but it works fine. Adjust the movement of the treadle by winding more or less of the cord around the end of the treadle. The treadle should be hinged, using two leather flaps, to a flat board on which you stand. Get into the habit of pushing the treadle all the way to the ground – longer strokes give a longer, more even cut.

The bed is similar to the treadle lathe, being supported on two 'A' frames, with the poppets that hold the centres passing through it and being held by wedges underneath. A strip of old leather on the face of wedges stops them vibrating loose. The centres are made from studding which is available in hardware shops, the point being made on a grindstone or with a file. Then screw the centre into a suitably sized hole in the poppet.

The tool rest can either be made as an independent structure that is held in position by a wedge, or it can be supported by the two poppets (**fig.10.7**). The latter works better with longer workpieces which you will also need to support at the middle of their length to avoid

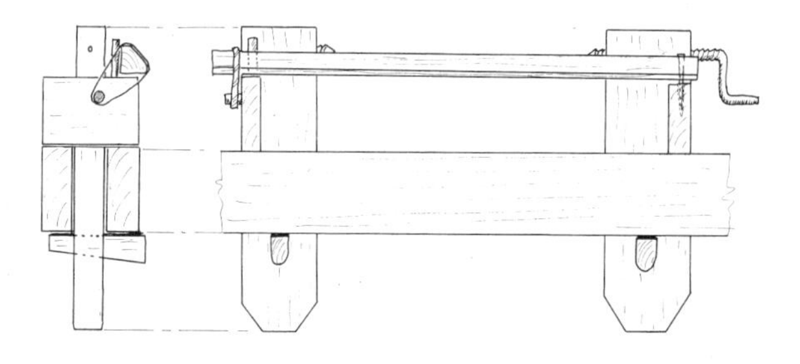

Fig. 10.7 A tool rest supported by the two poppets. It is held by a loose fitting nail at one end and a tie at the other.

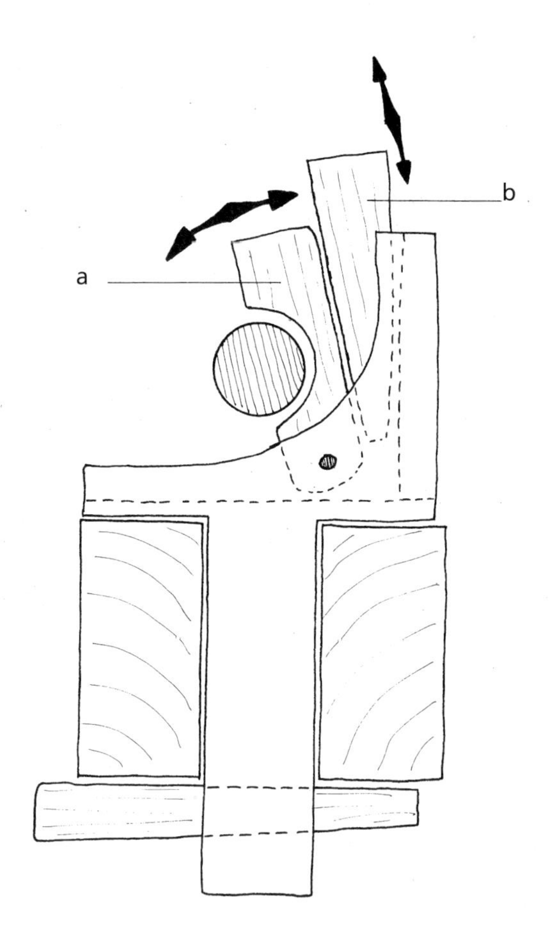

Fig. 10.8 Support for long workpieces: the workpiece is hatched; the supporting member (a) is free to rock and is kept in contact with the workpiece by the loose wedge (b).

flexing; a particularly good support designed by Hugh Spencer, is shown in **fig.10.8**. A short tool rest will be needed for bowl turning.

Bowl turning on a pole lathe requires a mandrel (**fig.11.26**). This should be about 203mm (8in) long by c.64mm (2½in) diameter with three or four sharpened teeth (cut off nails filed to a point) 6-12mm (¼-½ in) long at one end that can be forced into the workpiece. The other end fits onto a centre. This diameter seems to give the right balance of rotational speed and power for a bowl, but you can adjust to suit your preferences (smaller diameter mandrel gives higher rotational speed).

No detailed measurements are given for these lathes, for you should make them and modify them to suit yourself, but a bed height of 0.9m (36in) from the ground is about average. Go to a meeting of the Association of Pole Lathe Turners and you will see a splendid range of ideas based on the key principles outlined here.

Steamers

Wood treated with steam or hot water is rendered pliable so that it can be bent or peeled into fine clefts. Although water plays a key role in softening the fibres, heat is also crucial in making wood pliable. Crate makers always put their fine rods in the chimney above their fire before winding them, and stick makers often heated their walking sticks in only damp sand heated on top of a brick hearth (**fig 10.9**).

Fig. 10.10 A heated tank for soaking/boiling wood.

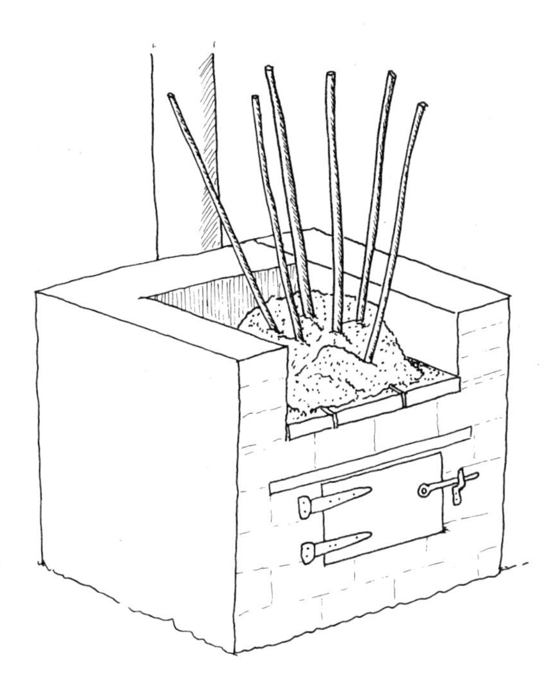

Fig. 10.9 Stick maker's sand steamer – you must keep the sand moist for maximum effectiveness.

A key factor with your steamer is therefore to site it as close as possible to the moulds or frames into which the stuff is to go so that any bending is done whilst the material is hot. Remember that steam and very hot water can scald.

Heat source: In the workshop the cleanest and easiest is electricity, and a 2kw element will effectively heat a bucket or boiler to generate the hot water or steam. A gas heater can be used effectively out of doors, but I hate to use a naked flame in a workshop full of shavings.

However, it seems sacrilege not to use all the shavings and wood chips generated by green woodworking, and if you are going to do quite a lot of steaming build yourself a small brick hearth on which to burn small wood and heat the water.

Hot water: To render oak or ash pliable enough to peel into very fine clefts it must be soaked in very hot water. If you want 1.5m (5ft) lengths, you will need a tank 1.8m (6ft) long (you could use an old bath), heated from underneath, and with a lid to prevent excessive evaporation (**fig 10.10**). Use a hooked rod to remove hot wood from the water.

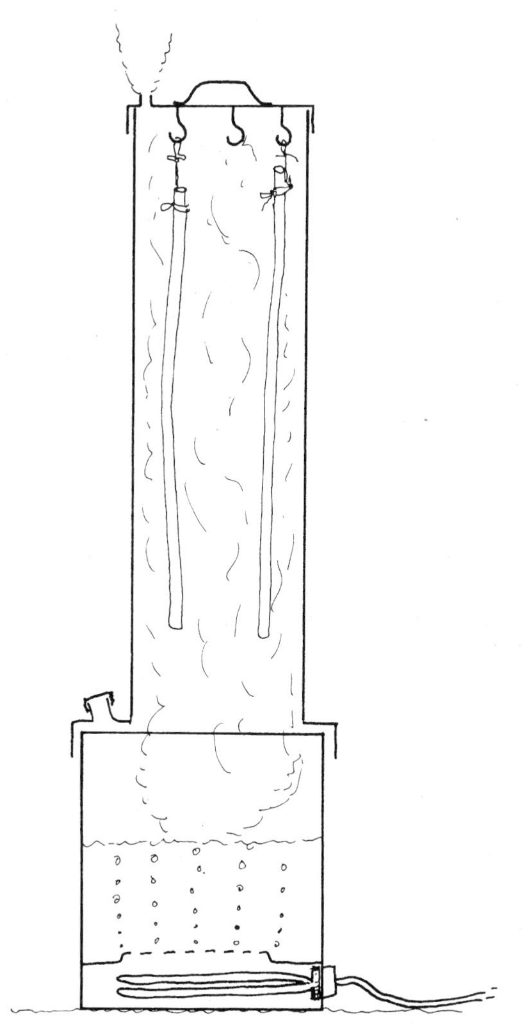

Fig. 10.11 A basic steamer in which product can be hung; this is adapted from an old washing boiler.

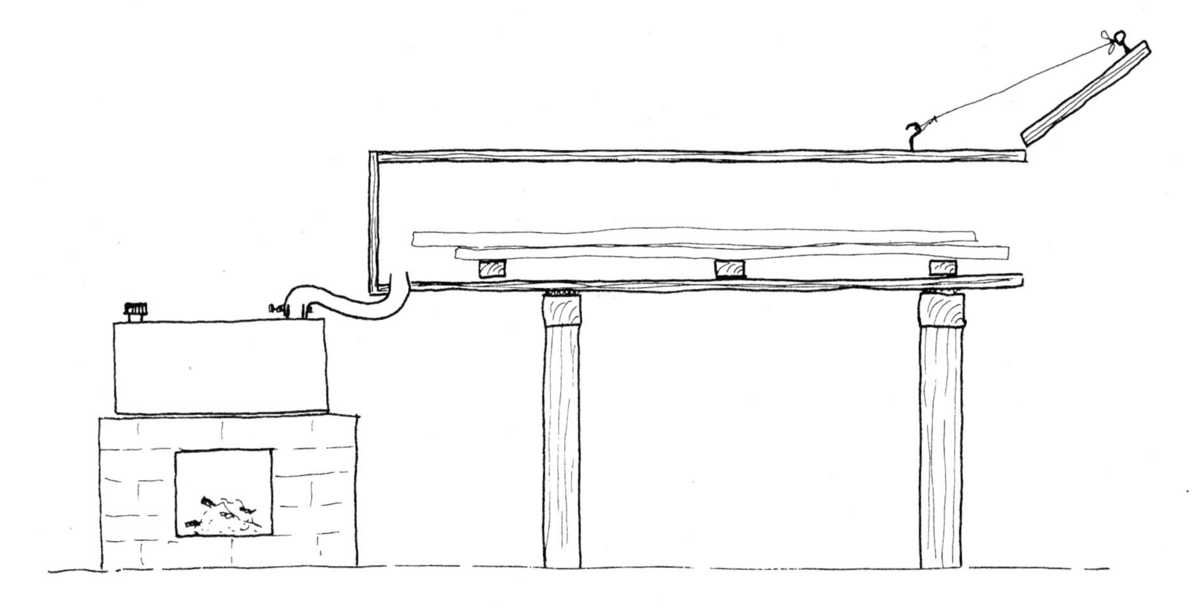

Fig. 10.12 A chest steamer – the door is closed during use.

Some stick makers use hot water when shaping the handle of a stick (I find it better, although there can be a tendency for the bark to peel). In this case a simple bucket of heated water will suffice.

Steam: Which type of steamer you build will largely depend on how much steam bending you intend to do. The simplest is probably a vertical metal cylinder mounted on top of a bucket or similar vessel fitted with an electric element (**fig 10.11**). Fix hooks inside the top of the cylinder from which to hang the product. This system also has the advantage that condensation runs back into the water reservoir.

For larger outputs a horizontal chest is most commonly used (**fig 10.12**). A Suffolk rake factory that I often visited had an iron chest 2.4m (8ft) long by 0.5m (18in) square, with a flap door at one end; it could hold 40 or 50 stails. You can make the chest out of marine plywood and fit it with shelves to accommodate a range of products (**fig 10.13**). Steam can be generated by means of a brick boiler built underneath the chest, or from a free standing generator feeding via a pipe. In the second case old oil drums or similar provide a good means of containing fire and water cheek by jowl.

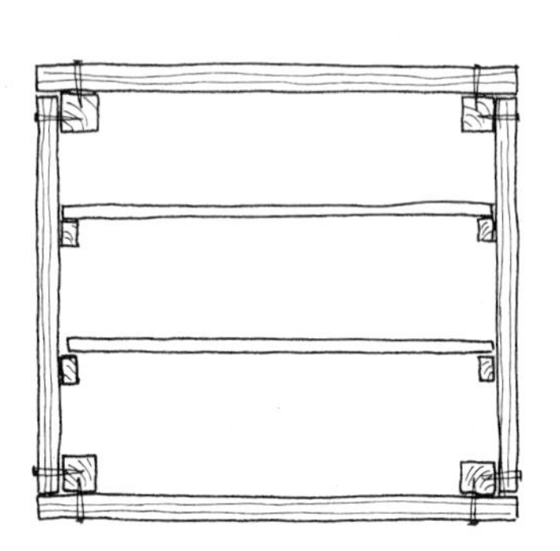

Fig. 10.13 Cross section of a chest steamer showing construction and shelves.

Always ensure the steaming chest has a small pressure relief hole; site this away from the inlet to get a flow of steam throughout the chamber. You can reduce your steaming times by insulating the chest in some way.

Charcoal kilns

Traditional clamps, together with charcoal making are described in Chapter 12; here we look at the equipment commonly used today.

Oil drum kiln: Old oil drums, usually obtainable from a friendly farmer, are an ideal tool for understanding the principles of charcoal burning, and for making small volumes of charcoal.

Take your oil drum, a cold chisel, clump hammer and some earmuffs. Firstly drive five evenly spread holes, c.50mm (2in) diameter, in the base of the drum. Then use the chisel to cut out the other end of the drum, making the cut about 25mm (1in) from the edge. After removing the end, knock up the rim you have left to make it wider, and flatten out the lid you have cut out. The lid should now just sit on the enlarged rim. Place the drum base down on three or four bricks so that the air can get to the holes in the base and you are ready to start (**fig 10.14**).

Moveable ring kiln: If you have a good volume of wood to char on one site, these kilns, which can

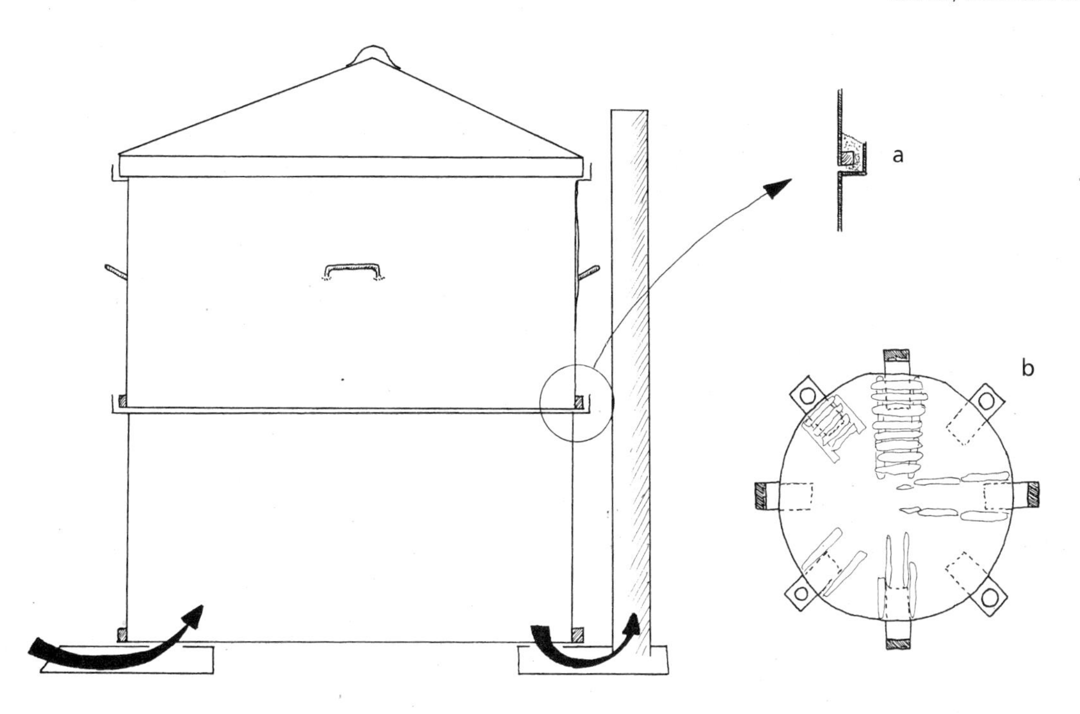

Fig. 10.15 A moveable two ring kiln: a. the two rings are sealed with sand; b. align the logs adjacent to air inlets and outlets so they are not blocked and the kiln can be lighted.

produce up to half a ton of charcoal in one burn, are ideal. Although there will be small differences in design from kiln to kiln, the principles are fairly consistent.

The body of the kiln is made of 3mm corrosion resistant steel, welded into a cylinder of c.2.3m (7ft 6in) diameter. Its base is strengthened by a solid ridge, and the top is formed into a 50mm x 50mm (2in x 2in) rim (**fig 10.15**). For a two ring kiln, the depth of the body is usually c.900mm (35in). If you are working alone, a one ring kiln is essential for you will not be able to lift a ring on your own, and this can be made deeper, at c.1.3m (4ft 3in). If a top ring is used, it should be made to the same pattern, so that its ridge sits in the rim of the bottom section. Since two people are needed to position the top ring, it must be fitted with four handles made of 10mm (3/8in) steel rod.

The whole body is capped with a conical lid of 2mm mild steel which is fitted with four equally spaced steam release valves that can be shut as required. The lid sits in the rim at the top of the body, and may have a handle.

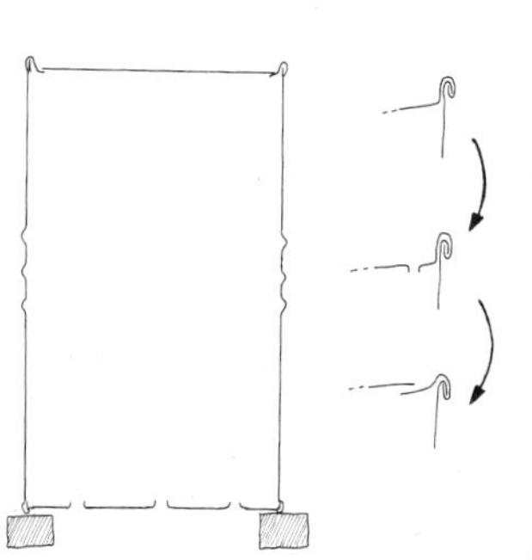

Fig. 10.14 Oil drum for charcoal making; note how top is cut away and then re-shaped to form a removable lid.

Eight air inlets/outlets are equally space at the base of the kiln, upon which the bottom ring rests. Alternate airways have holes to accept 120mm (4 3/4in) thin-walled steel pipes that act as chimneys. These are c.2.3m (7ft 6in) high, and fit loosely in their sockets so that they can be easily removed to close down the kiln at the end of the burn. These airways are c.500mm (20in) long, about half this length protruding under the base of the kiln. The gap between the bottom ring and the ground is sealed with soil.

You should be able to buy a second-hand kiln, but otherwise they can be made in local workshops equipped with basic welding, rolling, drilling and cutting equipment.

Further reading:

Abbott, M. ***Green Woodwork***,
Guild of Master Craftsmen Publications, 1989
Hill, J. ***The Complete Practical Book of Country Crafts***, David & Charles, 1979
Hollingdale A. ***Charcoal Production – a Handbook***
eco-logic books, 1999
Underhill, R. ***The Woodwright's Shop***,
University of North Carolina Press, 1981

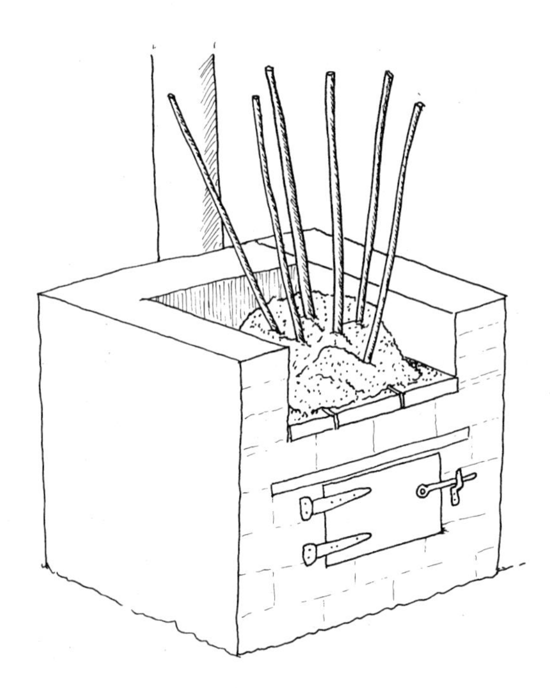

Chapter 11
The Key Skills

Learn your green woodworking skills step by step; always walk before you run. In this chapter we look at the most important of those skills. Once you have mastered them there will be little you cannot turn your hand to, and in learning them you will understand more about wood and tools.

Sharpening Edge Tools

This is a crucial skill, for blunt tools mean hard work, poor quality products, and more risk to yourself. You can judge the sharpness of a blade in several ways: firstly feel the edge for burrs; secondly look at the cut surface of the wood for score marks; and lastly examine the cutting edge in a good light for the telltale 'line of light' (**fig.11.1**) which shows it is blunt. These all flag up the need to hone or grind the blade.

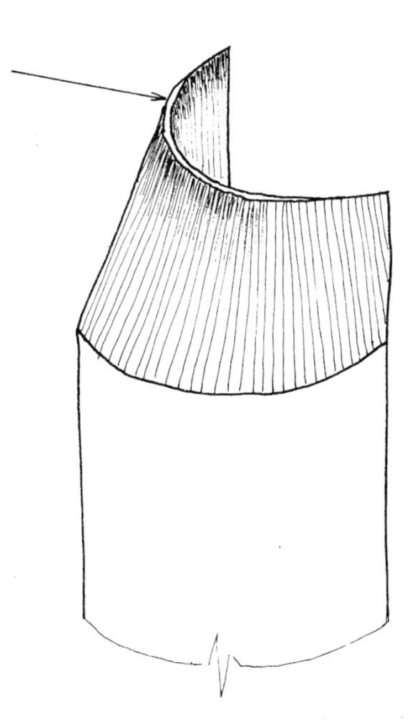

Fig. 11.1 The 'line of light' that indicates a blunt cutting edge.

Principles: (see **fig. 11.2**) When sharpening billhooks and axes keep their shoulders well back; they should cut through wood, not act as a wedge. Any tool with only one sharpening bevel must be ground dead flat on the reverse side, or it will not bite into the wood or cut straight. Keep the correct angle on the bevel of chisels and gouges so that they cut properly. Avoid overheating the cutting edge when grinding or the steel may lose its temper, and turn when used. There are few short cuts when sharpening – it is a slow, precise job.

Grinding: Grinding is required to achieve the correct profile at the cutting edge of a blade. Traditionally this was done on a large 460mm x 102mm (18 x 4in) medium coarse sandstone wheel rotating in a sump containing water (**fig. 11.3**). I still use one. The water both cools the blade and removes tiny metal particles that may clog the stone and it is still a good means of sharpening tools with long cutting edges. Modern power driven grinding stones are fast and efficient, but being narrow can run the risk of an uneven finish on longer blades and higher tool temperatures if not water cooled. You should also consider using modern diamond grinding stones. Hand held, they require little lubrication, never overheat and are fast.

Grind the tool carefully to the correct profile, correct angles and to produce a small burr which you remove by honing. Grind your edge tools as little as possible, for every ride on the grindstone removes metal and shortens the tool's life. Only grind a blade when it is damaged or has lost its profile.

Honing: This is achieved using an oilstone or whetstone (**fig. 11.3**). Whetstones tend to be coppice tools, lubricated with a little spittle. To hone billhooks, axes etc., use the whetstone in a circular

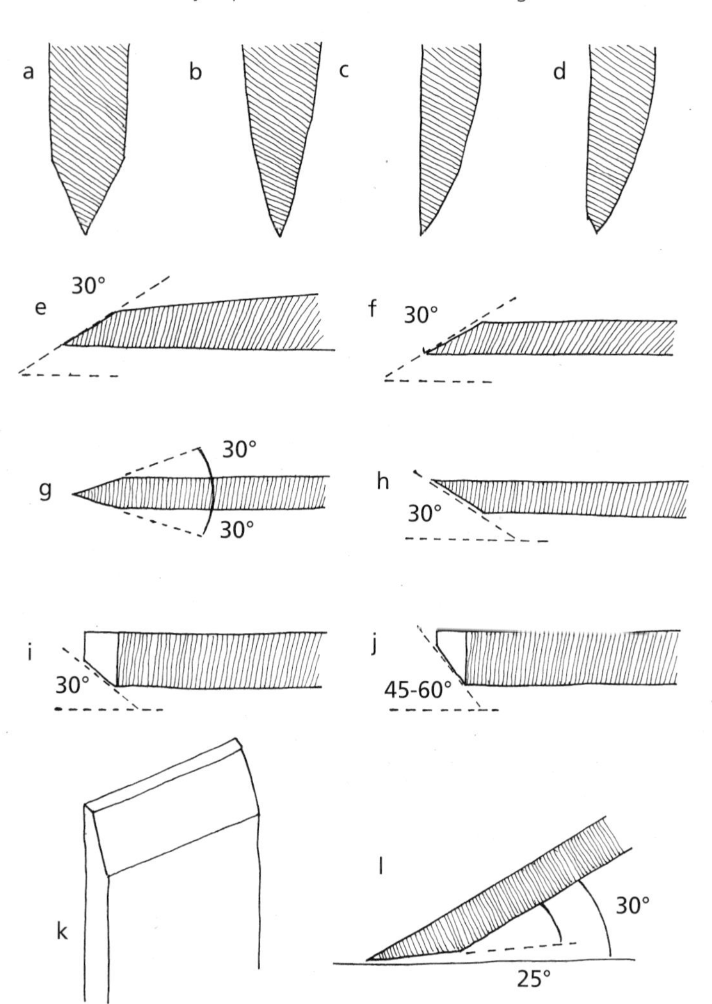

Fig. 11.2 Blade profiles: a. poor billhook – shoulders too thick; b. good billhook – shoulders well back; c. side axe – correct profile; d. side axe – wrong, starting a double bevel; e. morticing chisel; f. firmer chisel; g skew chisel; h. plane iron; i. Spindle gouge; j. bowl gouge; k. and l. double edge on carpentry chisel – grind to 25°, hone to 30° (note turning chisels have same grinding and honing angles).

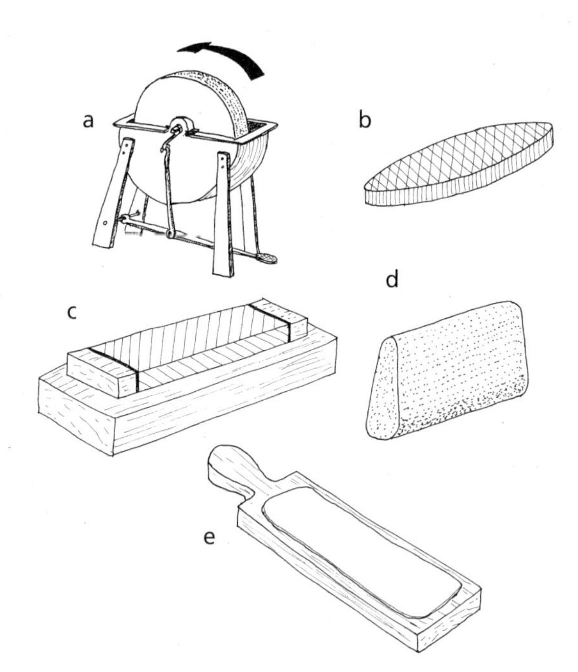

Fig. 11.3 Sharpening stones: a. treadle sandstone in water bath; b. whetstone; c. oilstone with wooden blocks; d. slipstone for gouges; e. the strop – a piece of leather glued to a block of wood.

motion along the cutting edge (**fig. 11.4**), first on one side then the other, carefully keeping the profile you want. You will feel and see the burr become a flexible 'wire edge'; remove it by stropping or by rubbing the cutting edge down the corner of a piece of wood. As soon as it is removed your blade is perfectly sharp. Confirm the keenness of the edge by the absence of any line of light.

Workshop tools are usually honed on oilstones. Use a medium grade c.200mm x 50mm (8in x 2in) stone in a lidded box to keep dust off. A small wooden block at each end allows the full length of the stone to be used. You can lubricate the stone with a light oil, although mixing it with paraffin will give more bite. I prefer a fine sharpening stone used with cutting fluid, although I am just trying fine diamond stones, which are faster, wear more slowly, and only need water as lubrication.

Skew chisels, plane blades, etc: Hone these on the stone using either a straight back and forth motion or a continuous figure of eight movement (the latter gives a more even wear on the stone). Place your left hand towards the end of the blade (**fig. 11.5**) in order to apply downward pressure on the bevel and place the right hand further up to control the angle the blade makes with the stone. Too low an angle means you are honing the shoulder and not sharpening, too great an angle will result in a second, steeper bevel at the cutting edge which will be less efficient. Avoid rocking the blade as it goes back and forth along the stone for this will round the bevel. Try to keep your hands and arms fixed and rock your body from the hips to make your strokes parallel.

Keep rubbing one side until you can feel a burr when you draw your finger off the edge of the blade; turn the blade over and rub the other side. When the burr, or wire edge, is flexible enough to

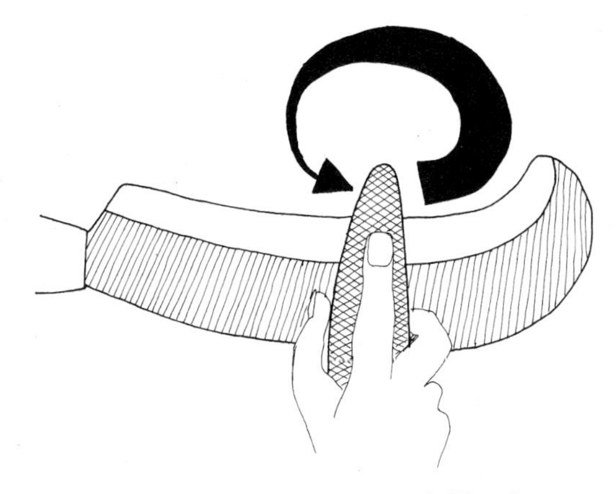

Fig. 11.4 **Using the whetstone on a billhook or axe.**

Gouges: To hone the outer bevel of the gouge, use a fine stone. Hold the chisel at right angles to the stone, lift the handle until the whole bevel is flat on the stone, and use the hands as already described to maintain the angle and apply pressure. Rub the gouge along the whole length of the stone, twisting it at the same time so that every part of the bevel is honed (**fig. 11.6**). Continue until you can feel a burr on the concave side. Remove this using a slipstone lubricated with a drop of oil. If the slipstone is smaller than the gouge, rock it to ensure the whole edge is rubbed. Keep it flat in the gouge and do not create a second bevel. Alternate honing on stone and slip will remove any burr.

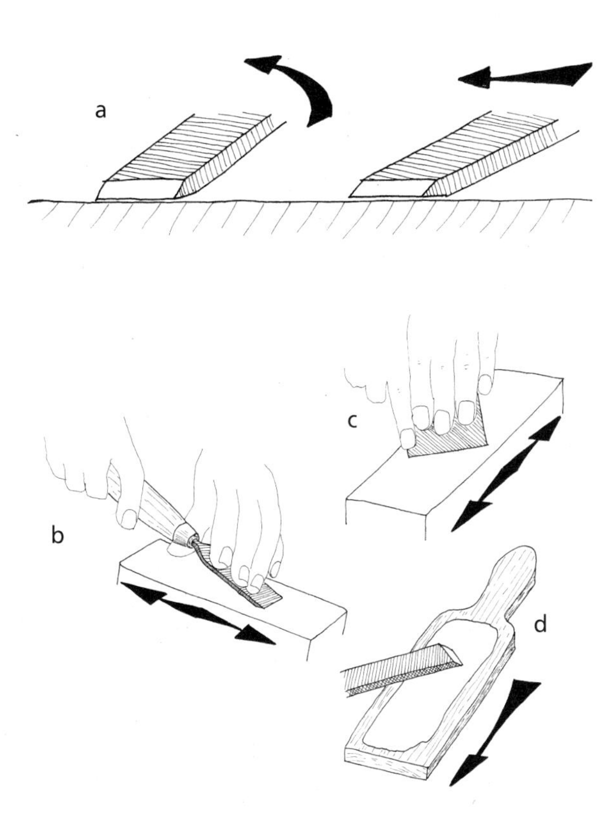

Fig. 11.5 Sharpening chisel/plane blades: a. lift the blade to the right position, then keep it parallel when honing; b. and c. note the hand positions for chisel and plane blade; d. when stropping move tool in one direction, turning over as required.

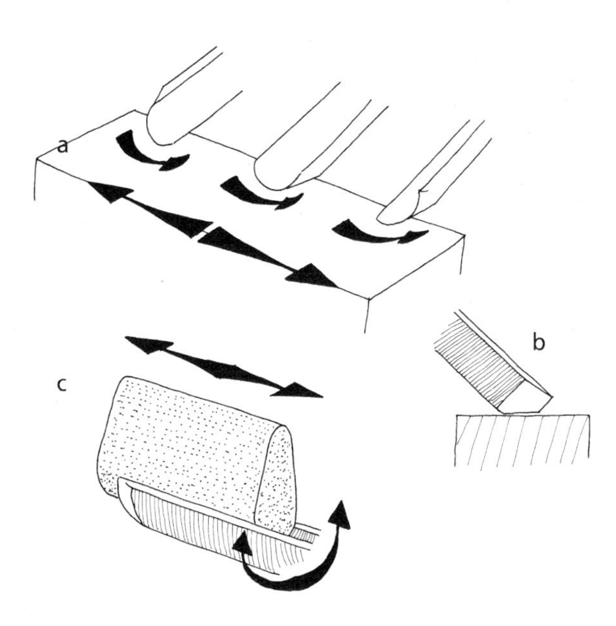

Fig. 11.6 Sharpening the gouge: a. roll the gouge from one side to the other as it moves from one end of the stone to the other and back; b. keep the bevel flat on the stone; c. use the oiled slipstone backwards and forwards and side to side to remove the burr.

rock from one side to the other as you draw your finger off the edge, remove it by shaving the edge across the corner of a piece of wood, or by using the strop. Use firm pressure, and move the blade only one way along the strop, first one side, then the other. Look for the absence of a line of light to confirm the perfect edge.

Riving

Riving wood is as old as woodmanship and with good reason, for it has so many advantages.

- You can split curved poles into equal clefts, impossible with a saw.
- There is no kerf, hence less waste.
- Riving is faster than sawing.
- Riving reveals weaknesses allowing you to reject the wood before it spoils a good product.

- Clefts are stronger than sawn wood because they follow the natural grain, whereas sawing often crosses the grain creating points of weakness.
- Clefts are more waterproof and durable than sawn wood because the open ends of the wood vessels are not exposed.

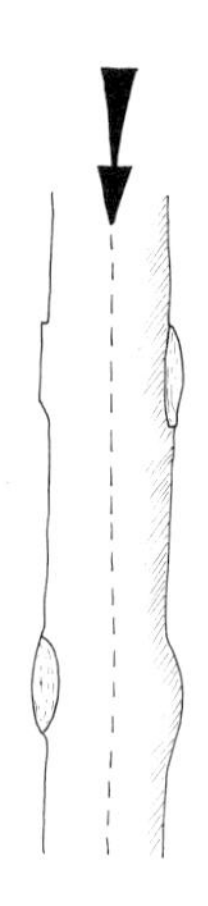

Fig. 11.7 Riving: where possible rive between knots

Basic Principles: Always start at the thinner end of the material, so should your split run out slightly at the end, you will still have two usable clefts. Where possible, rive the wood into two equal parts; it is much easier to control the direction of the split with equal pressures on either side. Where branches arise on either side of a stem, always try to rive between the knots they create, rather than through them to avoid weak, thin clefts (**fig. 11.7**). The ways a round log can be split are shown in **fig. 11.8**.

With even pressure on both clefts, a split will run true; uneven pressure will cause it to run towards the cleft under most tension (**fig. 11.9**). Understanding this will enable you to correct a split that has started to run out: apply tension to the thicker cleft by bending it, and the split will run back towards it. With thicker wood a riving brake makes it easy to apply the required tension in a controlled way.

Selecting wood for riving: Ash, hazel, willow and chestnut are probably the very best; old elm, hornbeam, box and apple probably the worst (see Chapter 2). But within any species there are variations caused by the environment, management, or the genetic makeup of a particular tree. Properly stocked, fast grown, well cut wood will always give the best results. In ***all*** species the butt end is usually the most intractable. Sere wood will not rive.

The condition or greenness of the wood is also very important. As wood dries it toughens. This can be an advantage, and hazel or ash coppice cut in February and March is best stored for six weeks if used for broches or hurdles. Willow and chestnut are best used immediately, as is any wood where shrinkage is key to the final artefact (some furniture). Store wood in shade so it seasons slowly and

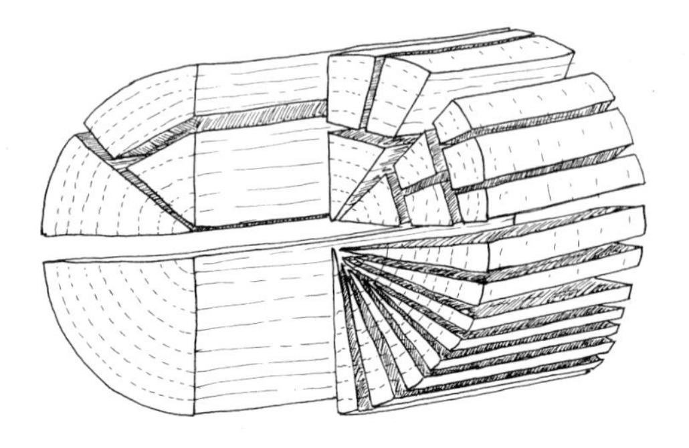

Fig. 11.8 Riving: the ways in which a round log can be riven to produce various types of cleft.

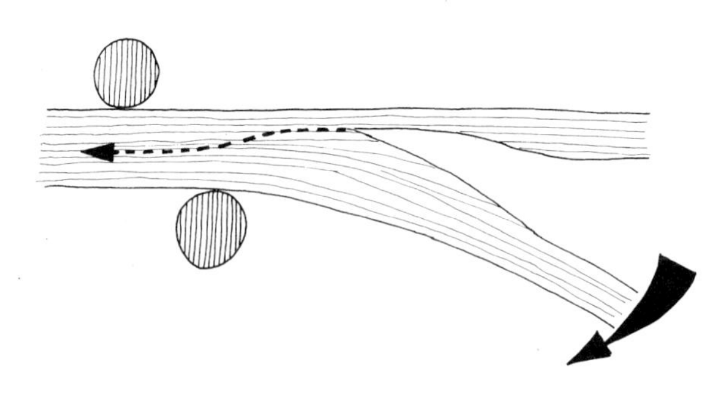

Fig. 11.9 How an off centre split can be re-centred by tensioning the thicker cleft.

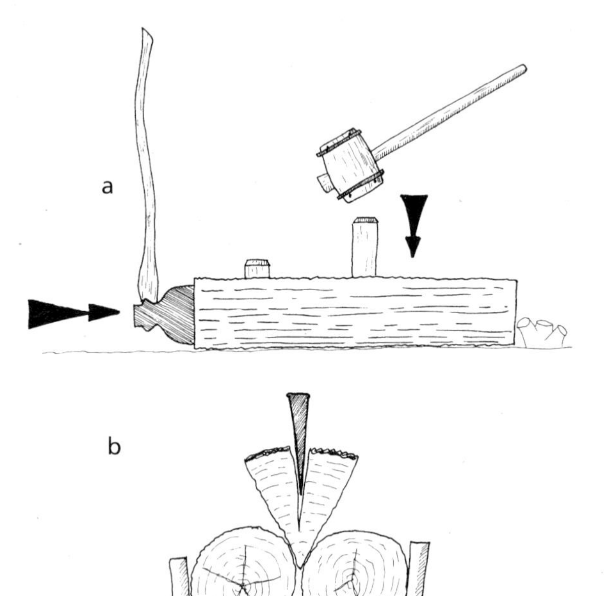

Fig. 11.10 Wedging large poles: a. using axe and beetle to start the split and wooden wedges to continue; b. supporting a cleft to wedge it further.

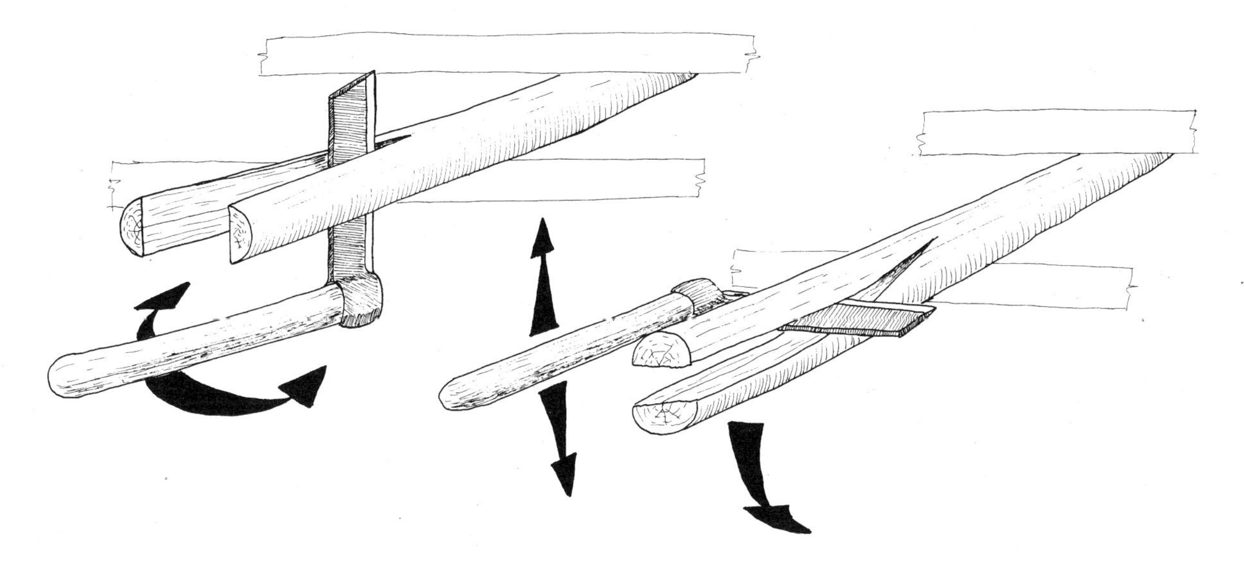

Fig. 11.11 Using the froe: when split is straight lever from side to side; when split is off centre put thicker section under tension.

with small rods do not trim the knots flush until you use the wood, for these points will dry first. o produce the finest clefts it may be necessary to hold wood under water to retain its pliability (see swills and bonds).

Wedging large poles: Large poles are best riven with wedges, the job being too heavy for the roe. Lay the pole on the ground, the thicker end against a firm stop (**fig. 11.10**). Start the split with one or two metal wedges, or an axe. Continue the split using wedges. Wooden wedges are kinder for high quality work or soft woods. If the split moves off line, drive a wedge in on the proper line, and then use an axe to sever the tongues of wood holding the clefts together. Repeat these radial splits as required. Wedges are unsuitable for tangential clefts since you have no means to control run-out.

The froe and riving brake: A riving brake (Chapter 8) together with a froe, makes riving poles both quick and easy. Drive the froe into the smaller end of the pole while it is more or less vertical in the brake. Then with the pole supported by the horizontal bars of the brake, lever the froe left and right to extend the split (**fig. 11.11**). Keep moving the froe forward to keep close to the point of splitting, which you must watch to ensure it remains central. The feel and sound of the clefts coming apart cleanly is something you will soon learn to recognise. If the split does move off centre, put the thicker cleft under pressure by levering it between the horizontals of the brake; it will come back into line. At all times use the froe to lever the clefts apart; the only time you may need it to cut is if you hit an intransigent knot, and then a sharp blow with the beetle will drive the froe through it.

With the froe you can make fine clefts for pales or shingles, and also rive tangentially. This takes more care since too much pressure will make the split run out. Always progress steadily and avoid trying to extend the split too far with each movement of the froe. When you can make 24 usable palings from a 150mm (6in) pole, you have mastered the craft!

Billhook or adze for small rods: For several products you will need to master riving long thin rods evenly using a hook. Cut at an angle into the rod as close to the small end as possible. Lever your hook to and fro to start the split running, and then continue this process down the rod with your left hand grasping the rod just ahead of the hook (**figs. 11.12** & **11.13**). This is perfectly safe since you are levering, not cutting. The crisp sound of the wood parting and its feel in your hand will tell you if you are doing a good job. For slightly thicker material I prefer to put the rod through my legs, and use the long nose of the hook to lever the clefts apart keeping its the blade close to the rod, and using my legs to apply tension if the split starts to run out (**fig. 11.14**).

You may find it helps to use a riving post when riding thin rods – see Chapter 6 and **fig. 6.22**.

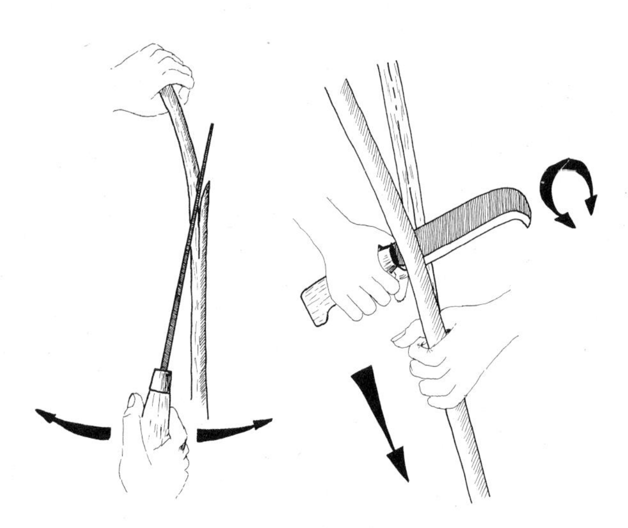

Fig. 11.12 To start the split in a hazel rod, bend it and then cut to the centre with the hook.

Fig. 11.13 Split the hazel rod by twisting the hook from side to side.

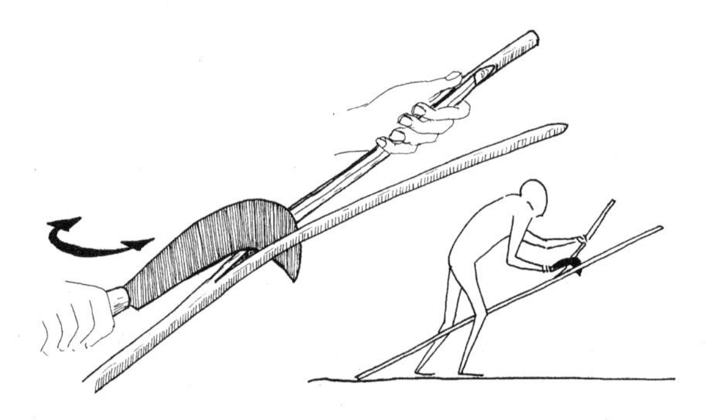

Fig. 11.14 Use the nose of the billhook to lever hazel rods apart; pass it through the legs to apply lateral pressure if required.

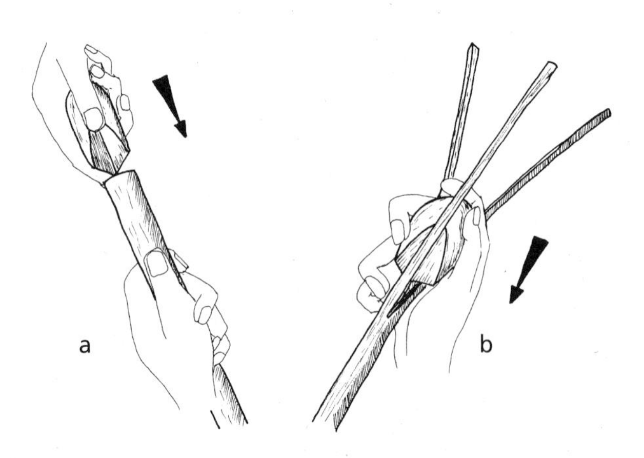

Fig. 11.15 Using the cleave: a. starting the split; b. pulling the cleave through a rod to make three clefts.

Using the cleave or bond splitter: To split small 12mm (1/2in) rods into fine clefts, the cleave is the tool to use. Cleaves will not cut through knots, so select and trim your material carefully, and cut the end square. Force the cleave centrally into the end of the rod then pull or push the cleave steadily through the rod, producing three even clefts as it passes (**fig. 11.15**). If one cleft starts to thicken, bend it a little more and it will thin again.

Turning

Whichever type of lathe you use the skills required are the same – and need lots of practice.

Preparation: A majority of your wood will be green although you can use some seasoned. Trim your clefts to make at least an octagonal shape (**fig. 11.16**) to reduce turning time, waste and to give a smoother start. Use a bradawl to mark the centre points of your work piece (you may find if it is fairly round that a 'centre finder' – **fig. 11.17** – helps) and lubricate these points with a drop of beeswax. Fix the piece between the centres and rotate it several times; then re-tighten the centres so the piece is firm as well as running smoothly. Set your tool rest so that it is central to your cutting area and as close to it as possible. It may well be necessary to move the rest as your work proceeds. You are now ready to begin.

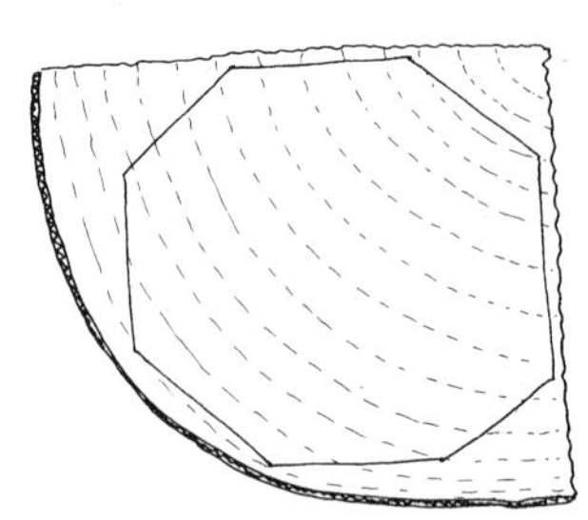

Fig. 11.16 How to shape a cleft for turning; further shaping to make the piece rounder is even better.

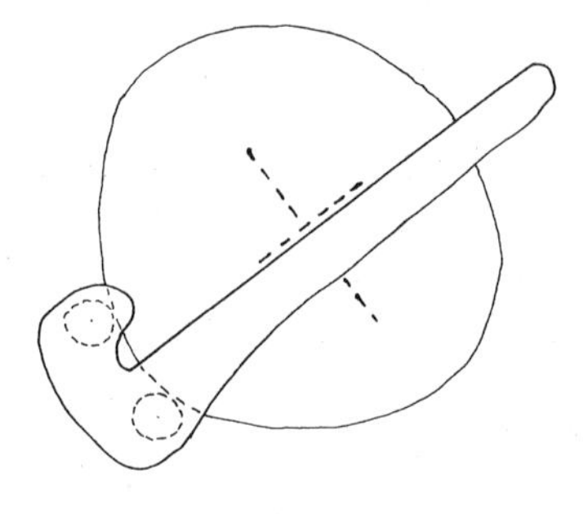

Fig. 11.17 Using a 'centre finder'.

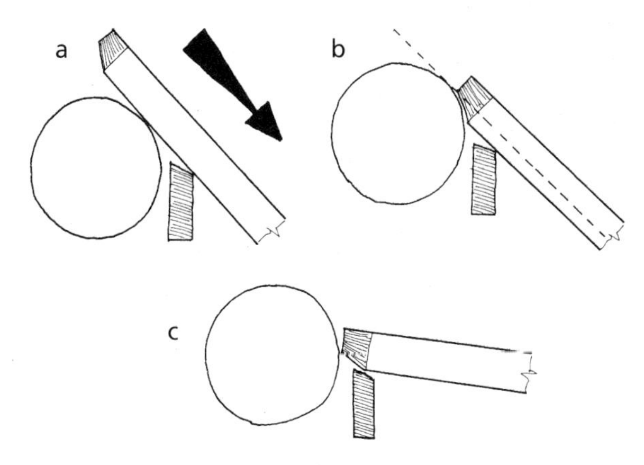

Fig. 11.18 Achieving the right cutting angle: a. start with chisel high on workpiece; b. move chisel down until it starts cutting – the optimum position; c. chisel too low – it is scraping, not cutting.

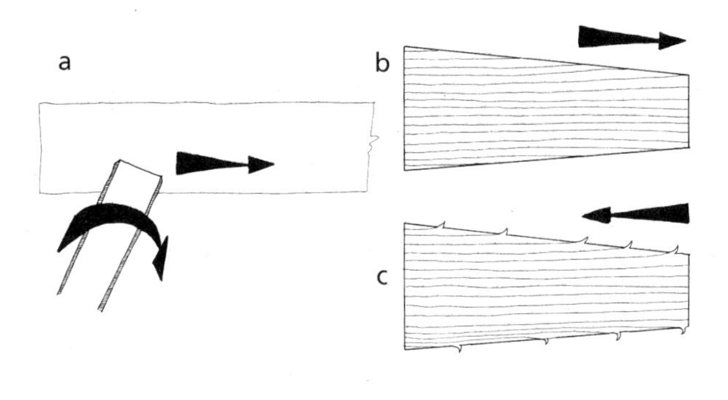

Fig. 11.19 Using the gouge: a. point chisel in direction of cut and rotate slowly; b. cut 'downhill'; c. how cutting 'uphill' lifts the grain.

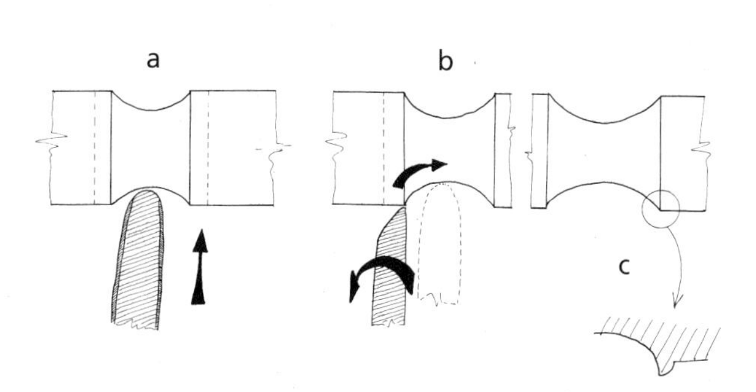

Fig. 11.20 Forming a hollow/cove: a. remove waste using chisel straight on; b. final shaping and smoothing; c. you can leave a fillet at the edge of the cove.

Using the gouge: Use this tool first to size and rough finish your piece. It must be used with its bevel at a tangent to the work piece, cutting as high as possible. To achieve the optimum cutting position place the shank of the chisel on both rest and work piece, and slide it gently down until the cutting edge starts to cut (**fig. 11.18**). With green wood the chisel will remove coarse long shavings that peel away as the piece quickly takes shape. Don't scrape with the gouge; it will tear the wood and produce dust instead of shavings. As with any cutting tool, when shaping always cut downhill, with the grain. Point the gouge slightly in the direction the tool is moving, and rotate it to use all of its cutting edge (**fig. 11.19**).

To form a hollow, use a gouge smaller than the hollow you want to achieve. Use the gouge straight on to remove waste from the centre of the hollow (easier with a finger shaped, not square ended tool. Then with the gouge on its right edge, start at the left of the hollow and cut down towards the centre, rotating the chisel anti clockwise at the same time. Repeat this, reversing all the actions, to produce a symmetrical hollow and repeat as needed to obtain the required depth (**fig. 11.20**).

Using the skew chisel: This (or a large firmer chisel) is used to produce a smooth surface on the work. It takes more skill to master than the gouge. On a skew chisel the corner of the blade greater than 90° is the heel; the other is the toe. It is the

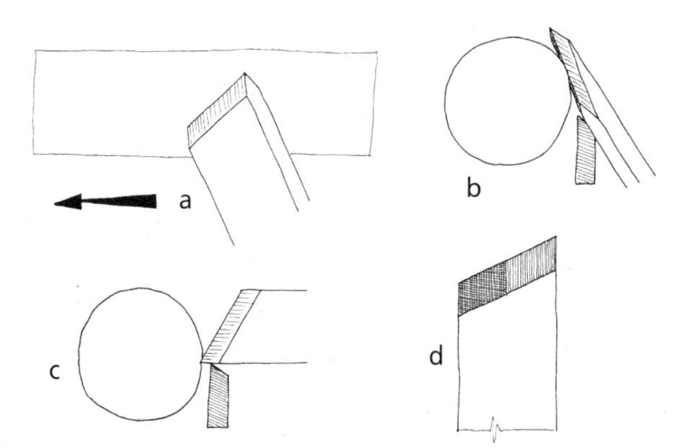

Fig. 11.21 Using the skew chisel: a. point chisel in direction of working; b. position of the skew on the workpiece – keep the toe clear; c. using the toe of the skew to make a cut into the workpiece; d. the hatched portion of the blade is the area you should normally use.

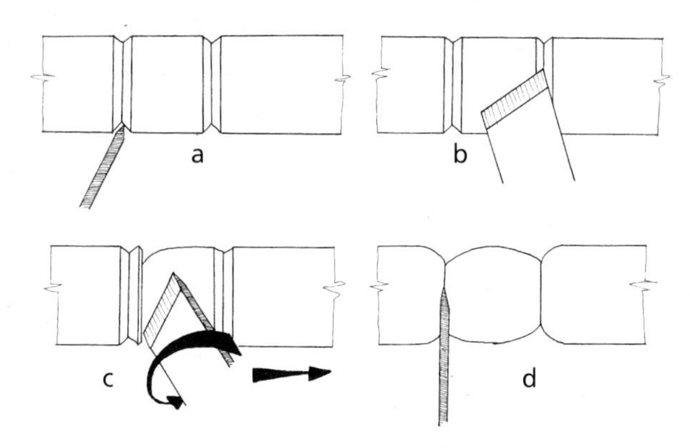

Fig. 11.22 Forming a bead: a. form a deep cut at either end of the bead using the toe of a skew chisel; b. start shaping from the centre; c. rotate the chisel from the centre to the deep cut; d. chisel position at end of cut.

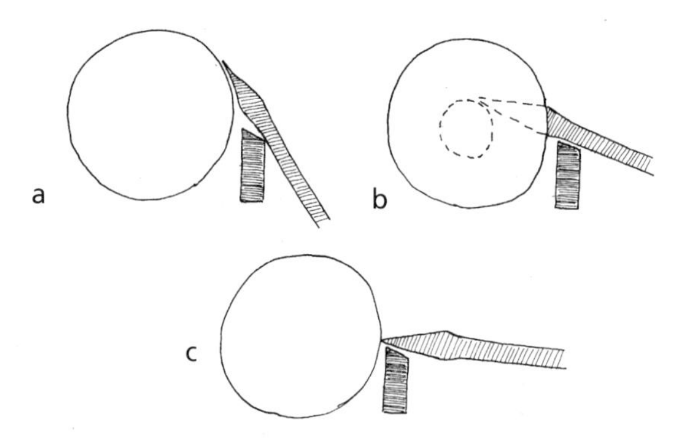

Fig. 11.23 The parting tool: a. and b. keep tool high on workpiece to keep it cutting; c. tool too straight – scraping not cutting.

heel that does the cutting when smoothing and the toe when cutting in at 90 degrees to the centre. Again follow the rules of cutting high, keeping the bevel on the work piece, cutting downhill, but most of all keeping the toe clear of your work when smoothing and making beads or it will dig in and gouge lumps out of your careful work. Point the chisel in the direction you are moving it and cut steadily along the piece, usually from the centre to each end (**fig. 11.21**).

Beads are cut with the skew chisel. To do this, first make deep cuts at each end of the bead using the toe of the chisel. Then form a 'v' by making angled cuts again using the toe of the chisel and cutting in towards your very first cuts (**fig. 11.22**). To round the bead place the heel of the chisel at its centre and make a curved cut by simultaneously moving the chisel handle to the right, rotating the chisel blade anti-clockwise, and slightly lifting the chisel handle so that the blade finishes in a vertical position at the left end of the bead. Repeat this action the other way round to form the right hand side of the bead. This basic cutting motion will, of course, form any convex curve.

The parting tool: Use this to make a broad incision in the wood; it is frequently used at the end of a piece. Keep the cutting edge as high as possible on the wood to keep it cutting and not scraping (**fig. 11.23**). Parting tools tend to tear the wood at either side of the incision; tidy this with the toe of the skew chisel.

Different shapes: Once you have mastered these basic tools there are many shapes you can make. These are detailed in Chapter 15.

Bowl turning: To turn large diameter pieces you cannot simply use a slice of tree trunk, for as we have seen it will split and warp. You have to take a tangential block (**fig. 11.24**) and hollow that side closest to the heart. Once you have cut a block out roughly round it as shown. If you are using a treadle lathe you will need to screw the piece to a faceplate (**fig. 11.25**). If you want a flat bottomed bowl it is best to plane the base smooth and then screw that face to the plate with 13mm (1/2in) screws. If you want a more curved bowl you have to fix the plate to the top first, turn the base, and then reverse it to hollow the bowl; this is a real problem because if you are slightly off centre with your second fixing, the walls of the bowl are uneven.

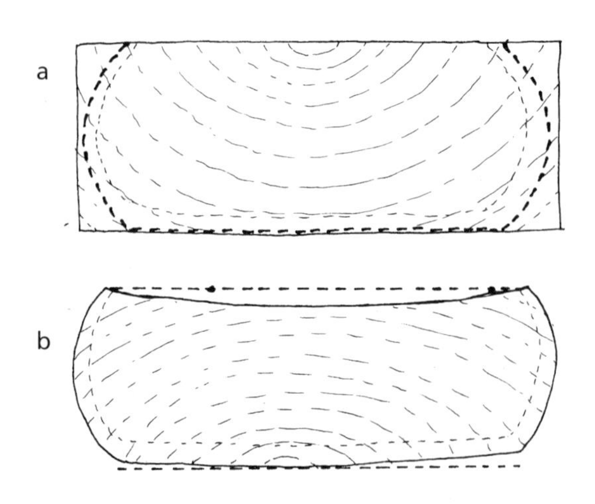

Fig. 11.24 Bowl shrinkage: a. the best way; b. how a bowl hollowed from the wrong side can distort on drying.

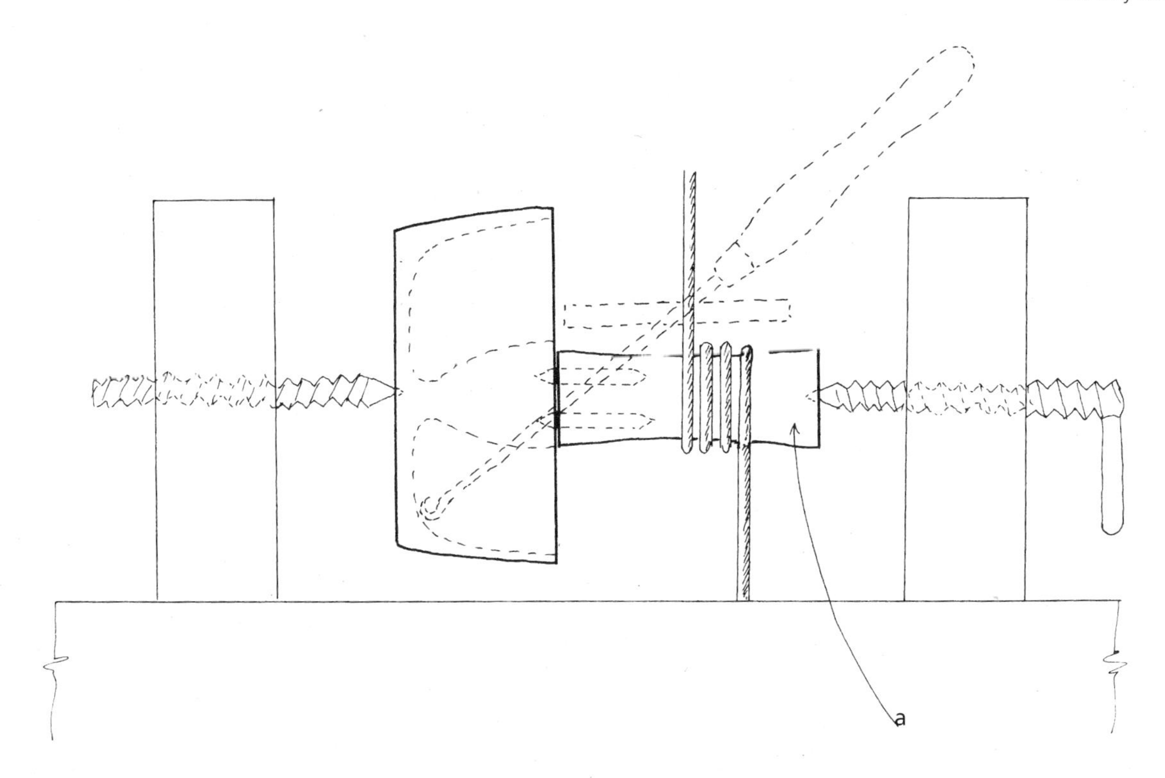

Fig. 11.26 Holding a bowl on a pole lathe, using a mandrel (a) to drive it and a bowl cutting hook chisel in its working position.

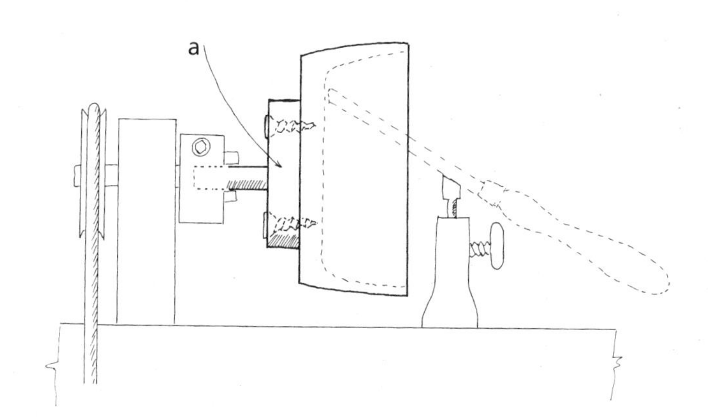

Fig. 11.25 A bowl held on a face plate (a) on a treadle lathe with a bowl gouge in its working position.

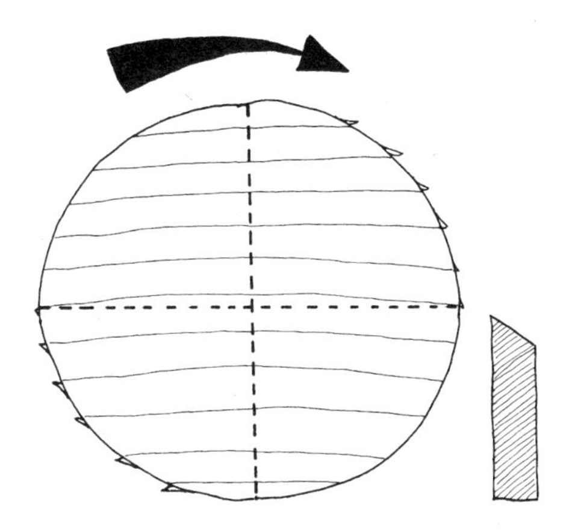

Fig. 11.27 How the alternating grain in a bowl can be raised during turning.

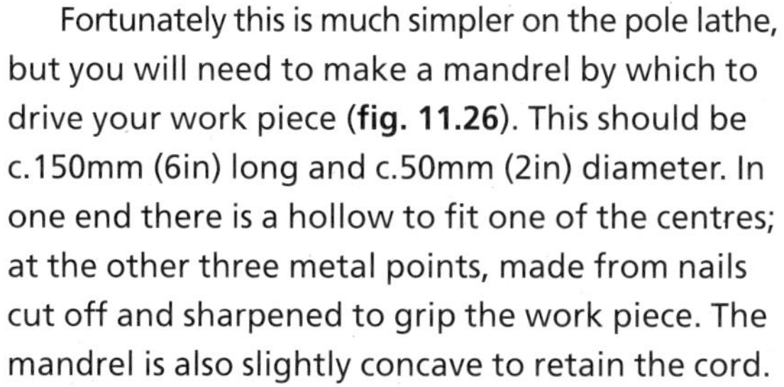

Fortunately this is much simpler on the pole lathe, but you will need to make a mandrel by which to drive your work piece (**fig. 11.26**). This should be c.150mm (6in) long and c.50mm (2in) diameter. In one end there is a hollow to fit one of the centres; at the other three metal points, made from nails cut off and sharpened to grip the work piece. The mandrel is also slightly concave to retain the cord.

Adjust the tool rest to accommodate the larger diameter work piece and to allow you to work on the end face. Shape the outside of the bowl with gouge and skew chisel, the inside with a bowl gouge (sharpened at c.55° angle), perhaps a scraper or a special bowl turning hook. Whichever tool you use you will quickly experience the problems of alternating grain (**fig. 11.27**) tending to give a rough-smooth-rough-smooth finish on every rotation. Your tools must be very sharp, and you will probably end up, like me, doing a lot of scraping! Once you have shaped the outside, turn

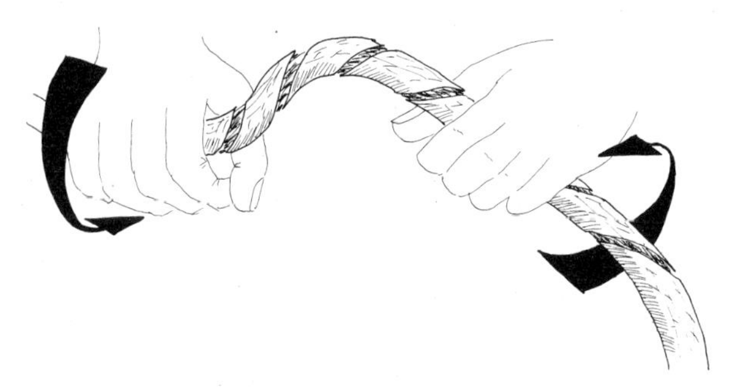

Fig. 11.28 Winding a rod to make a withe.

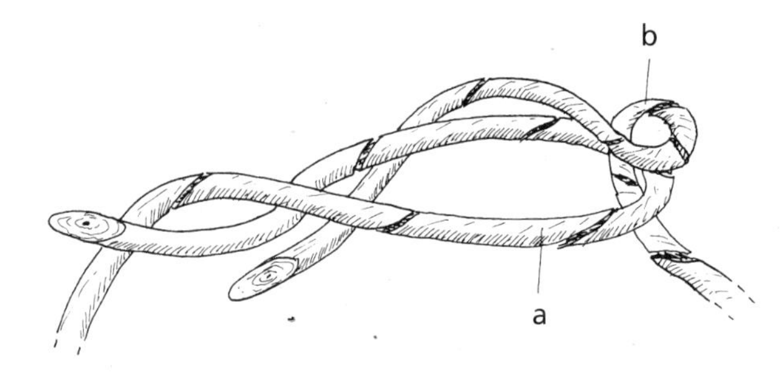

Fig. 11.29 A completed withe bond with its loop (a) and twisted knot (b).

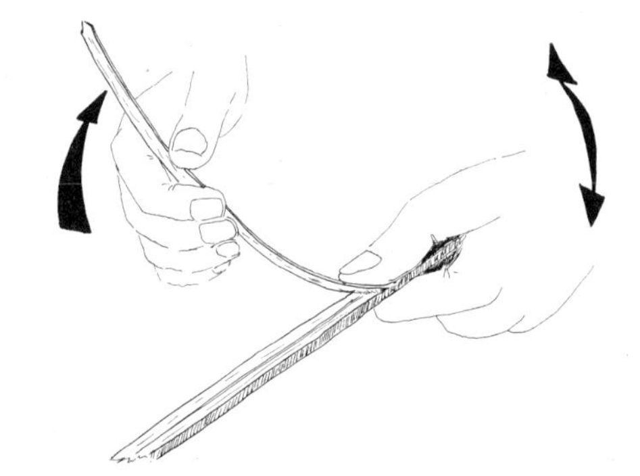

Fig. 11.30 Peeling thin bonds of ash or hazel – use the left hand to control the thickness by bending the workpiece.

bowl and mandrel round to do the inside. Use a gouge or a special hook chisel. Get the rest as close as possible to the point of cutting, use the hook down into the bowl (**fig. 11.26**) and the gouge as in **fig. 11.25**. This is a long slow job. Aim for a tapered wall thickness from 6mm (1/4in) to 18mm (3/4in) at the base. Reduce the waste core to c.25mm (1in) where it contacts the base, remove it from the lathe, then with your heart in your hands, give it a sharp knock to break the core off. Clean up the base of the bowl with a spoon chisel. Platters are made using similar principles; use the hooked chisel, treat them as a shallow bowl, but don't use the mandrel on the front face.

Writhing and peeling wood

There are a number of jobs for which wood is required to perform as if it was rope. Besom bonds, withe bonds, hurdles and crates, and basket making are a few examples using this more extraordinary property.

Writhing or winding rods: Small rods <18mm, (3/4in) of hazel, elm and birch can be twisted to make an immensely strong 'rope'. Consider a rod as similar to a rope, made up of many parallel fibres. If you separate these by twisting, the whole rod becomes very flexible and capable of turning very tight corners without breaking. Select rods that are clean and free from major knots. Rods wind much better when they are warm, and break if they are frozen, so leave them by the fire to become supple. To wind the rod, put the butt under your foot so that the rod curves up to your hands. Twist the end until you hear and feel the fibres separate; progress this separation down the rod by 'pedalling' the rod with two hands (**fig. 11.28**), moving down the rod as you go. The twisted rod will naturally form a loop, and if you pass the butt

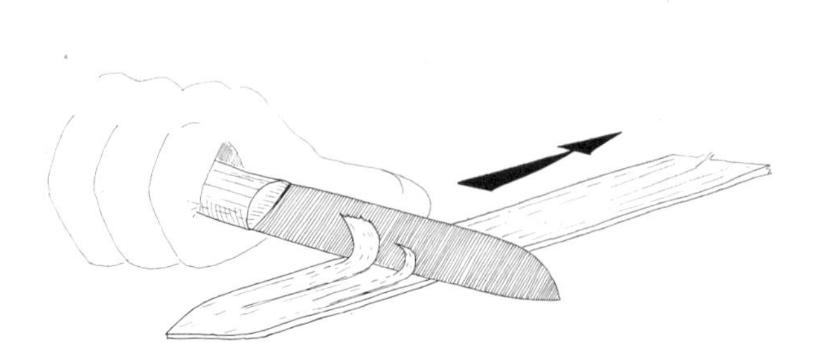

Fig. 11.31 Smoothing a bond by pulling it under a knife which is held rigid.

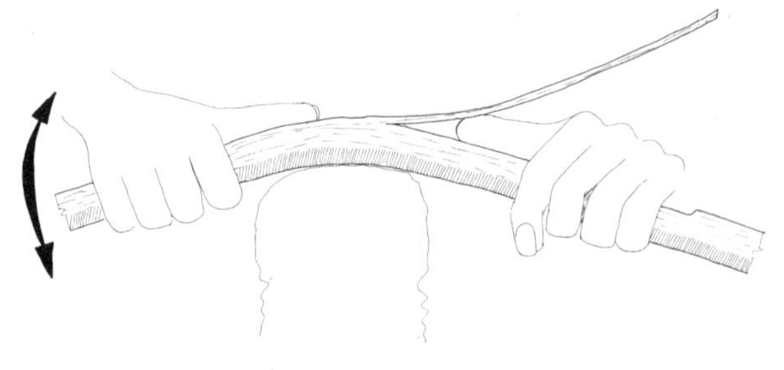

Fig. 11.32 Peeling thin clefts of hazel from a rod; use a knife to start the cleft, then progress using your thumb or the knife to peel it away.

through this it will stay round until you use it. Of course when making baskets or hurdles the butt end will already be fixed in the work piece.

To knot a bond, pull the butt through the running loop that formed when you were winding it, wind it some more and it will naturally form a knot that will tighten as it dries (**fig. 11.29**); just tuck the butt end away.

Bonds/laps: These are thin, narrow clefts, particularly of ash and oak, used for binding besoms and in some basketry. Start with clean 30mm (1 1/4in) ash rods, and rive them into three using a cleave. Remove the pith and some wood with your knife to leave a thick, flat cleft. Now insert your knife and lift a 1.5mm (1/16in) cleft. Once you have peeled back enough, grasp the cleft in the jaws of your horse and carefully peel back the thinner cleft (**fig. 11.30**). Adjust the thickness by bending the wood with your left hand – bending will make the thin cleft thicker as the split moves to the wood under tension. Once your cleft is complete you may need to carefully shave any thicker parts by drawing the cleft under your knife (**fig. 11.31**). With care, bonds or wider strips for basket making can be lifted from round rods of hazel and ash, using just a knife and your knee as a lever; again, the more you bend, the thicker the cleft (**fig. 11.32**).

Another method of making ash bonds is to soak a log with both inner and outer bark removed, and then hammering it vigorously to lift flakes the thickness of one annual ring. Pre-score the wood with your knife to the width of bond you want.

Bramble: This is one of the best bindings, being remarkably tough. Use the long, straight fast growth, remove the thorns, and carefully split the stem in half with a knife. Remove the pith from each half by drawing them under your knife, which you hold still to act as a scraper, and use the binding before it dries.

Oak/Ash: To make clefts for swills, quartered oak logs are soaked overnight and then boiled for an hour before splitting into fine 1.5mm (1/16in) strips. The splits can be radial or tangential, and once started with a knife or hook, clefts are pulled apart (**fig. 11.33**); use your legs to help apply tension when the split starts to run out. The clefts are then dressed with a draw knife.

Bark: The inner bark of young lime and elm can be used for woven chair seats. It is best taken from poles which are long and straight with a minimum of knots, and that have been felled in spring when the cambium cells are dividing quickly and hence separate easily. Remove the outer bark very thinly with a draw knife used bevel down and slowly. Then score two knife marks through the bast c.30mm (1 1/4in) apart, marking the strip to be removed (**fig. 11.34**). Prize up the bast at the end of the pole and steadily peel it away. It should come away cleanly in a strip c.3mm (1/8in) thick leaving the perfectly smooth inner wood; if fibres of the bast are being left on the inner wood and the strip is thinning, use your knife to lift these fibres and return the strip to its full thickness. Poles with big knots, epicormic growth, or that have been barked by deer make the bark strips of poor quality.

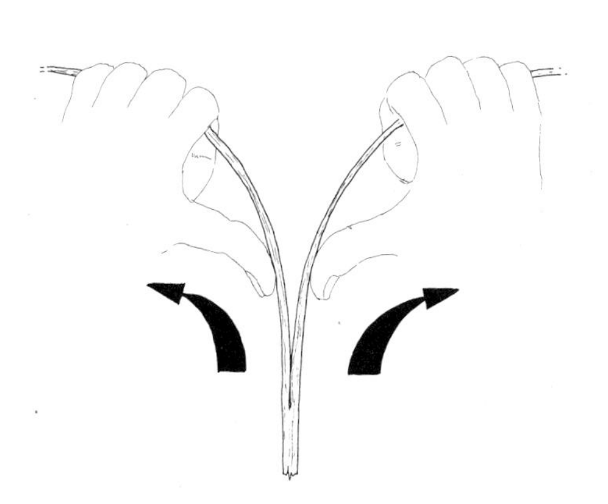

Fig. 11.33 Levering apart very thin clefts of steamed/boiled wood. Start the split with a knife; progress as shown.

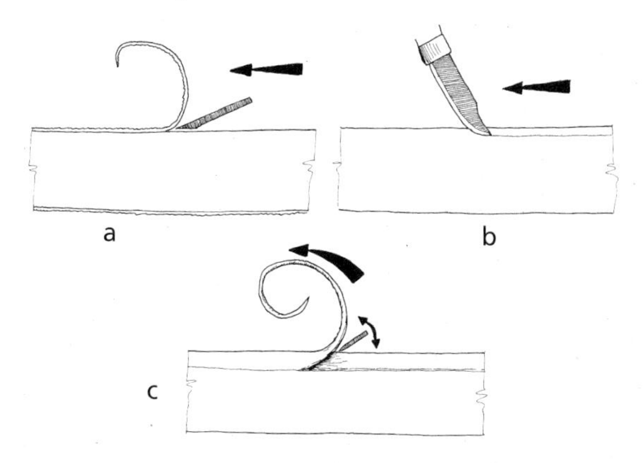

Fig. 11.34 Bark for chair seats: a. removing the outer bark; b. marking through the bast; c. peeling off the bast strip using a knife to free it if necessary.

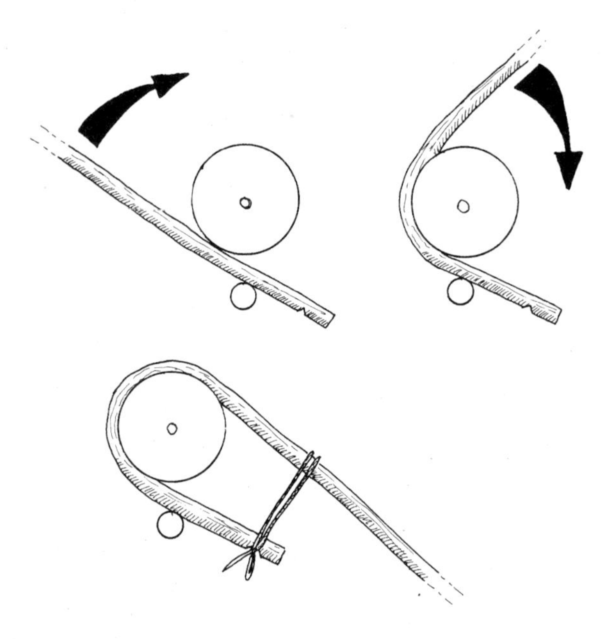

Fig. 11.35 Shaping a steamed walking stick handle around its circular jig. It is left tied for a week to set.

Shaping and steaming

Wood can be shaped whilst it is still green. Ash, beech, yew, elm, oak and chestnut are all good for bending, green or steamed. The amount of bending you can effect with green wood is limited to gentle curves, sufficient to produce stick furniture, but once released the wood often relaxes.

Steaming wood makes it more plastic for bending. It is better if your wood has time to toughen a little first, and lose some of its free water. Holding 50mm (2in) poles for six weeks, for example, reduces splitting and lifting of the bark. Use saturated steam at atmospheric pressure to soften the wood. Soaking in hot or boiling water can darken the wood, and if you are working wood with the bark on it can become too soft. Select the wood carefully so there are no knots in awkward places, that there are no cuts that will start a split, and that the wood is of an even thickness so that it will not 'fold' where it is too thin. Make sure you have a mould around which to shape the piece, otherwise you may be horrified at the result! As a rough guide, wood will require one hour per inch thickness to reach the right degree of malleability. Bend the piece whilst it is still hot, but do it steadily so as not to cause a fracture (**fig. 11.35**). Most steam bent work is best left in its jig for a week to set, and since after even this time it will ease back a little, make your curves a little tighter than you require in the finished product. Remember as well that you can use steaming to straighten curved wood as well as to shape it.

Further reading

Abbott, M., ***Green Woodwork***
Guild of Master Craftsmen Publications, 1989
Hill, J., ***Complete Book of Country Crafts***
David & Charles, 1979
Tabor, R., ***Traditional Woodland Crafts***
Batsford, 1994
Underwood, F. & Warr, G., ***Beginners Guide to Woodturning*** BTCV, 1981; Toolcare, 1998

Chapter 12

Gardens, fuel and buildings

Products for gardens

Traditionally many greenwood products were used in gardens. Although this market has declined, if you are cutting a woodland this is still the best way of utilising a lot of material you would otherwise burn.

Pea sticks

Pattern: c.1.5m (5ft) long with a 300mm (1ft) clear stem at base, flat, fan shaped with plenty of twigs, and the butt cut at an angle (**fig. 12.1**). Put 25 in a bundle.

Tools: Just a good billhook.

Materials: Elm and hazel less than 10 years are best; oak, maple and ash are useless.

Method: Cut pea sticks whilst working up felled wood. Trim to the right size and shape. Store off the ground weighted on top to flatten them (**fig.12.2**). Tie in bundles.

Fig. 12.1 Flat, fan shaped pea stick with angled cut at base.

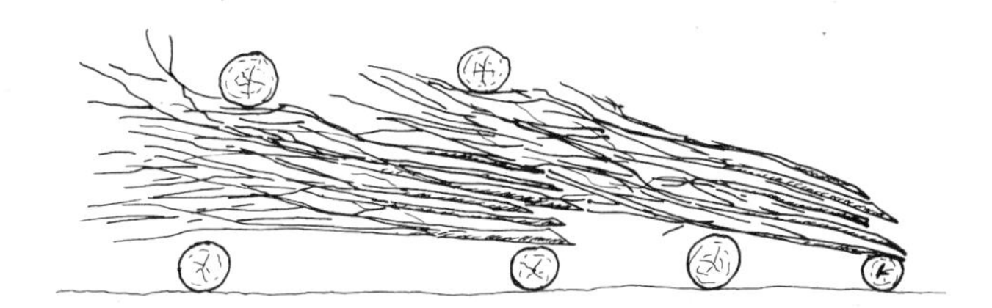

Fig. 12.2 A 'ringe' of pea sticks, weighted to flatten them.

Bean rods

Pattern: c.2.1m (7ft) long, reasonably straight and c.19mm (0.125in) diameter at top. Ideally pointed at the butt.

Tools: Billhook, chopping post, and progs for bundling.

Materials: Any suitable poles; ash, hazel and chestnut are best.

Method: Cut selected poles to size. Thread all knots and buds. Sharpen to 3mm (1/8in) square tip. Support in crotch posts and bundle in 10's or 20's.

Flower stakes

Pattern: c.1.2m (4ft) long, straight up to 25mm (1in) top diameter (**fig. 12.3**). Cut the top to a 'V' so it can be hammered without splitting and sharpen the butt.

Tools: Billhook, chopping post and progs for bundling.

Materials: Any straight rod of right size.

Method: Cut to size. Thread all knots and buds. Sharpen butt with four cuts, and top with two cuts. Bundle in 15's or 20's.

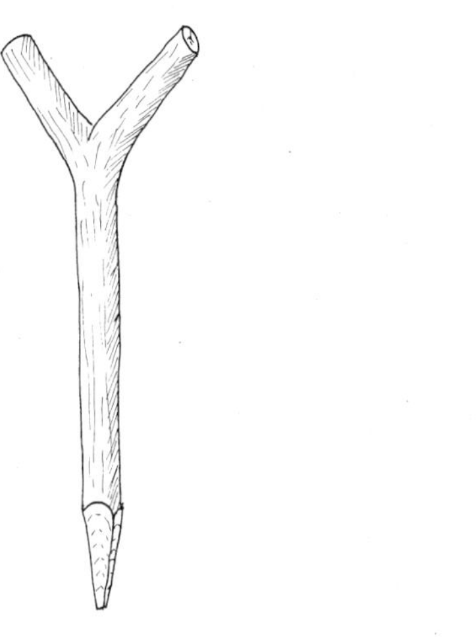

**Fig. 12.4
A lug or prop.**

Fig. 12.3 A flower stake, sharpened and with a 'V' top that will not split if hammered.

Fig. 12.6 A pergola: these are best treated with preservative.

Lugs, props and crotches

Pattern: Lugs are heavy 60mm (2 1/2in) butt size crotches for supporting the laden boughs of fruit trees (**fig 12.4**). Smaller ones are used to support shrubs. They must be straight, and sharpened at base, with a crotch 100mm (4in) deep. Clothes props should be 38mm (1 1/2in) butt, 2.1m (7ft) minimum length, and rinded at the top to avoid staining washing.

Tools and devices: Saw, side-axe, chopping block and shave.

Materials: Any wood will do.

Method: Cut crotch to size, remove buds and knots. Sharpen butt and half-sharpen straightest arm with side-axe so crotch can be driven into the ground. Remove bark from clothes prop with shave.

Tree stakes

Pattern: 60mm (2 1/2in) diameter, sharpened at butt and normally rinded.

Tools and devices: Saw, side-axe, block, shave, rinding brake.

Materials: Chestnut best; treat other woods with preservative.

Method: Cut to length, remove bark and sharpen butt leaving a 3mm(1/8in) square tip that will not turn when driven.

Trellis, arbours, pergolas, rustic poles

Pattern: This is really to customer choice, depending on whether the poles are to look 'rustic' or very straight. Any poles in the ground should be barked and treated with preservative. Bark can be left on other poles and the whole treated with varnish, preservative or other wood treatment. Sizes vary from 20mm (3/4in) to 75mm (3in) diameter. A range of trellis patterns is shown in **fig. 12.5**. Pergolas (**fig. 12.6**) are best from prefabricated panels that can be erected on site; the same basic size of panel can be made into four or six sided structures. They are best pegged to the ground so that they do not move in heavy wind. Some infill panels using round or cleft rods are shown in **fig. 12.7**.

Fig. 12.5 Varieties of trellis-work made with round poles.

Fig. 12.7 Patterns for infill panels for pergolas or special fencing, all in round wood.

Tools and devices: Saw, side-axe, block, draw knife, brake.

Materials: Chestnut is best near the ground, but hazel and birch are good for rustic work.

Method: Cut to size, utilising any suitable or interesting shapes. Carefully remove knots – not too flush – and do not nick the bark, lest it peel too soon. Shave and sharpen as required. When erecting a trellis, drill through the poles before nailing to avoid splitting the wood.

Finishing: Many customers like to purchase these items already treated a preservative finish. Wood preservatives are now available in a range of colours. Oil varnishes are particularly good for withstanding weather.

Fig. 12.9 A compost container made of four panels fixed to posts.

Garden waste containers and tree guards

Patterns: The commonest is a circular woven structure (**fig. 12.8**). Round rods between 12mm (1/2in) and 25mm (1in) are woven between c.37mm (1 1/4in) stakes that are driven into the ground. Size as required.

An alternative is panels made from cleft rods nailed to a frame, and supported by four stakes (**fig. 12.9**). Size as required.

Tools and devices: Billhook and sledge hammer.

Materials: Use hazel, birch or willow for weaving; stakes of hazel, elm or chestnut.

Method: Cut stakes to length, sharpen butt, and drive into ground at c.210mm (8in) intervals. Trim weaving rods of knots and buds and weave between stakes. Cut weavers to start and finish on inside. Twilley (**fig 13.24**) the top two rods and tuck the ends into the weave so they don't lift.

Fig. 12.8 A woven garden waste container.

Garden borders/dividers

Patterns: These are made either from woven hazel or willow; wired round logs, or clefts nailed to stakes (**fig. 12.10**). Sizes and patterns are to the customer's needs.

Tools and devices: Saw, billhook, mallet, froe and brake; and shave as appropriate.

Materials: Hazel or willow for weaving, chestnut for others if untreated.

Methods: Make woven borders as you would tree guards, winding the top rods around the end posts and tucking them into the weave. For round logs, after they are cut to size, staple to wire, and then fix this to stout posts in the ground. For cleft borders, split poles on froe and brake, remove the bark, nail to short stakes and drive into ground.

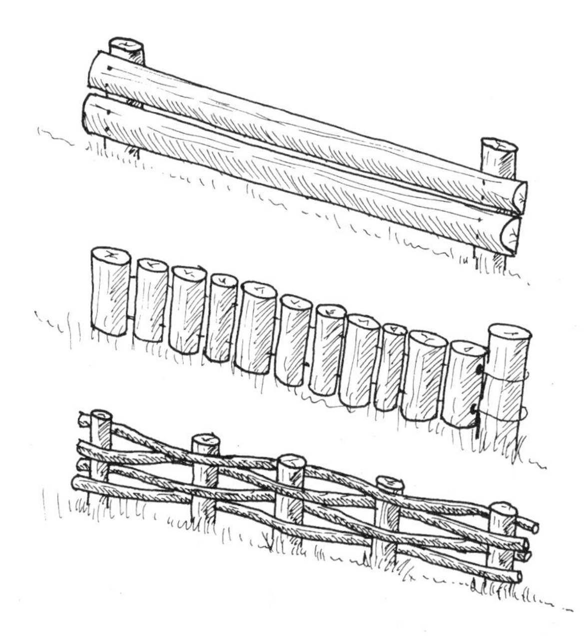

Fig. 12.10 A variety of garden flowerbed borders.

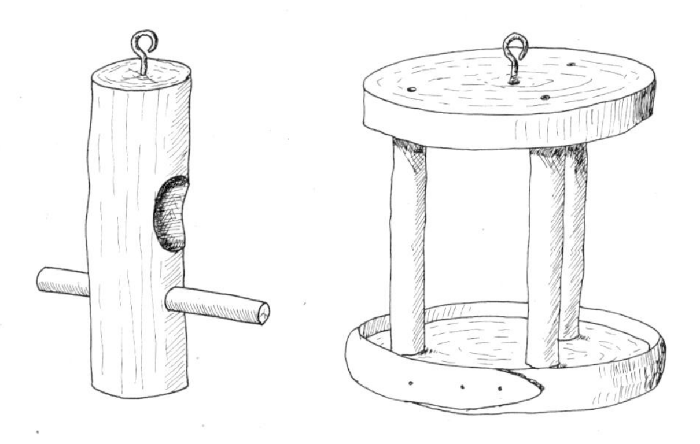

Fig. 12.11 Two patterns of bird feeders.

Bird feeders

Patterns: These are as endless as your imagination! A couple are illustrated (**fig. 12.11**). The first is simply a 50mm (2in) log with a 25mm (1in) hole bored through and a small rods as a perch. The second uses two 150mm (6in) diameter discs; the lower has a cleft hazel rim and the discs are joined by three 25mm (1in) diameter rods.

Tools and devices: Saw, brace and bit, hammer, gouge.

Materials: Any.

Methods: I think these are self-explanatory! But try to use seasoned wood for the large discs to avoid excessive splitting as they dry.

Garden Bowers

Pattern: These are best made in situ, and the particular form is open to discussion between customer and craftsman. A simple form is briefly described (**fig. 12.12**).

Tools, materials: Use hazel or willow and a billhook.

Method:

- Drive nine stout rods in a shallow semi-circle c.1.5m (5ft) wide.
- Weave around these rods to c.300mm (1ft) high, taking the weavers around the end rods.

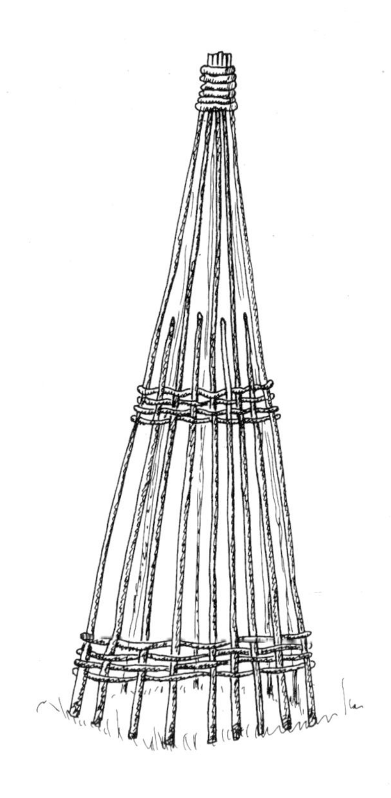

Fig. 12.13 A plant climbing frame.

- Bring the front two rods over and wind together to make an arch and then curve the centre rod over to meet this, winding it over the arch and then back on itself.
- Bring over the next two rods from the back to meet the front arch, and join them to it by winding them around this front arch down towards the ground.
- Bring over the last 4 rods from the side, winding them together and binding them to the three rods coming over from the back.
- Now complete the arbour by weaving between the framework of rods you have created, twisting them round at the ends to bind the structure. You can use small withe rods to bind around the lip once the weaving is complete.

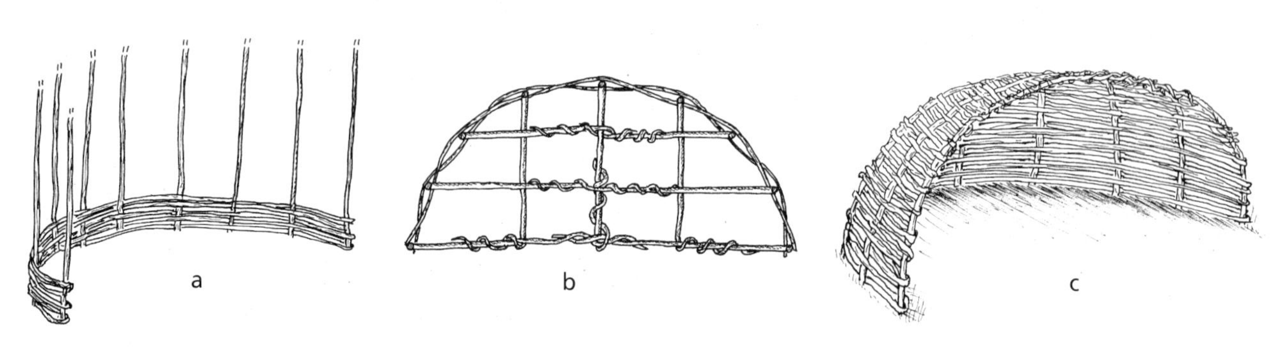

Fig. 12.12 Willow bowers: a. starting with semi-circle of rods; b. winding framework together; c. a finished bower.

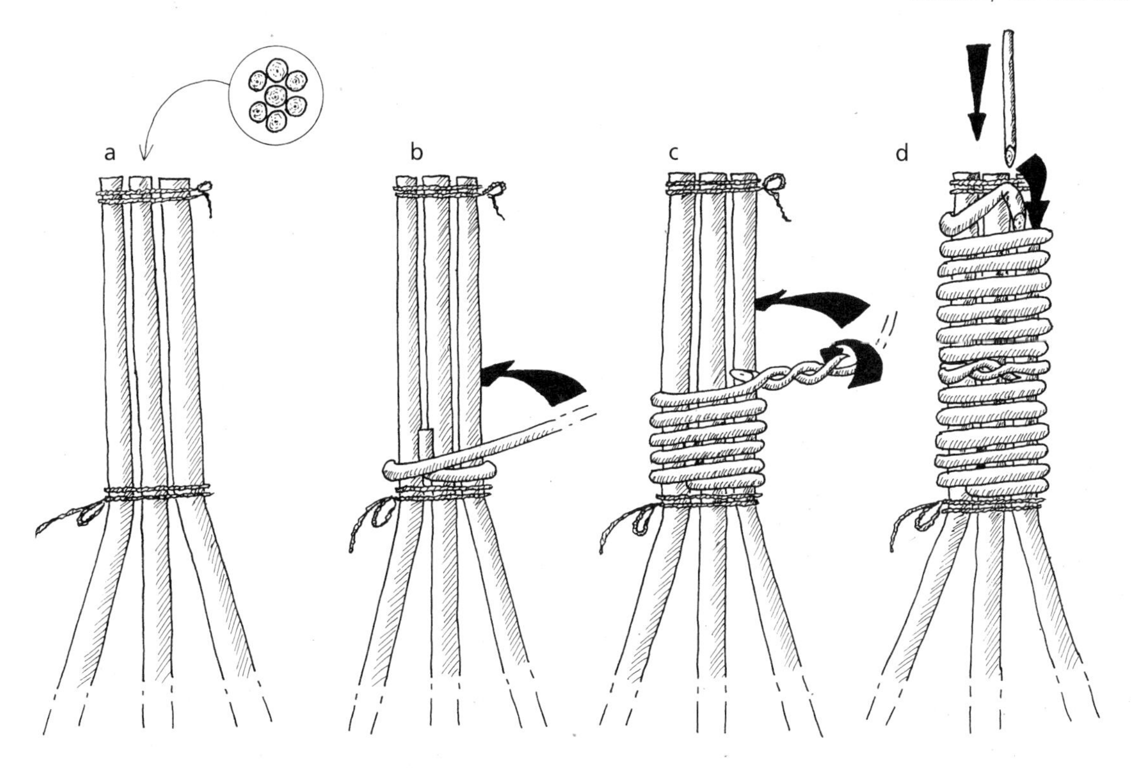

Fig. 12.15 Fixing the top of a climbing frame: a. temporary tying; b. winding the binding rod; c. joining binding rods; d. finishing – note the small stick used to make a cavity for the last end to be tucked away.

Plant climbing frames

Pattern: Usually conical structures bound together by fine rods (**fig. 12.13**) similar to putchers used to catch salmon. Sizes vary from 2.1m (7ft) high with a 350mm (14in) base diameter using 13 rods to 1.2m (4ft) high with a 250mm (10in) diameter and seven rods.

Tools: Small billhook or good knife; pattern or mould.

Materials: Hazel or willow for uprights; willow for weavers.

Method:

- A 2.1m (7ft) frame is described. Use a large sheet of plywood with holes drilled at appropriate place as a pattern (you can get all sizes on the same sheet). **Fig 12.14** shows a putchers mould which you can use.Drive the 13 sharpened uprights through the mould and into the ground. Choose straight rods c.19mm (3/4in) diameter.
- Start weaving c.300mm (12in) above the ground and twilley the rods (Chapter 13) for the first layer to bind them and to get spacing between the uprights. Use app. 6mm (1/4in) rods, as long as possible.
- Carry on weaving one rod at a time. When starting new rods join small end to small end and large to large to give a more even weave. Complete a strip c.100mm (4in) deep.
- Make another identical strip of weaving at c. breast height 1.5m (5ft). It is best to tie the uprights together before starting this in order to give the right shape. Use fine weavers for this.
- Cut off six alternate vertical rods c.50mm (2in) above the top weave (you will have two longer rods side by side).
- To bind the seven longer rods at the top, squeeze them together so that one is surrounded by six others. Tie temporarily at top and c.152mm (6in) lower with twine. Bind with one or two withe rods as shown. To tuck the end away, use a small stick to make a cavity, bend the last rod at exactly the point of this cavity, cut it back to leave 38mm (1 1/2in) to tuck in, remove the stick and force the end of the rod into place (**fig. 12.15**).

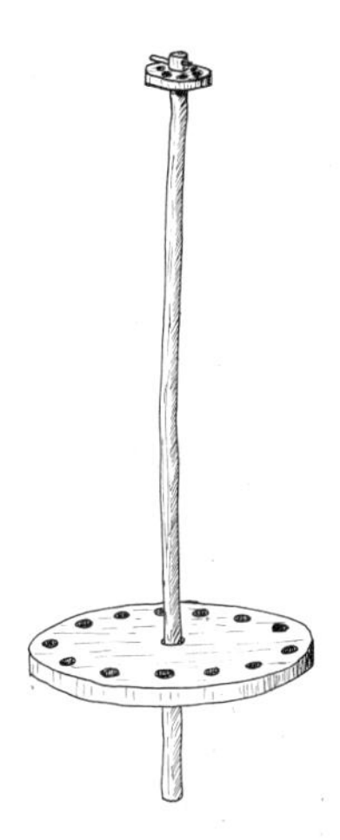

Fig. 12.14 A mould for making salmon traps.

Fuel

Woodworking always results in some waste wood. If you cut a section of coppice there will be quite a lot. Despite having a wood stove in your workshop (strongly recommended!), you may have to sell some wood as fuel.

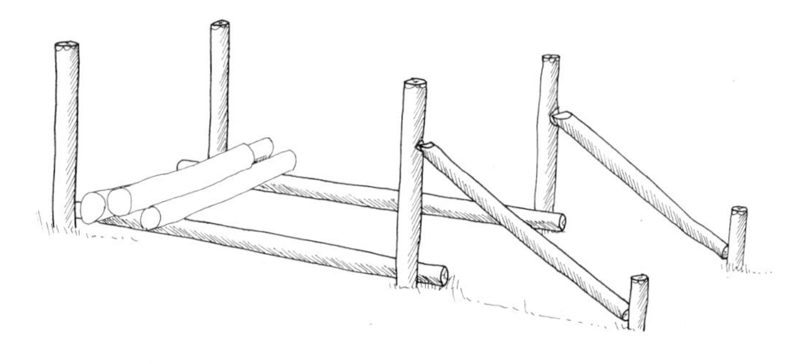

Fig. 12.16 A cord for storing wood.

Cordwood: Traditionally any 'lop and top' was 'corded'. A cord is a volume of round wood equivalent to 128cu.ft. (3.6cu.metres), and was measured by cutting the wood into 4ft (1.2m) lengths, and placing it in stacks 2.4m (8ft) long by 1.2m (4ft) high. A cord is reckoned to be 50 percent air, so the weight of seasoned wood in a cord is app. 1.25 tonnes. Use any wood and stack it down as you work.

Cordwood is best seasoned for two summers before sale, and thus should be stored off the ground using long poles as rails underneath the wood, with uprights at each end (in soft ground these may need bracing (**fig. 12.16**). Some customers like to buy wood in the cord so they can cut and split it to their particular needs.

Logs: Firewood logs can be sold delivered in bulk, or more expensively in plastic sacks. Small round wood is easiest, needing only to be cut to length; larger wood often requires splitting. Customers with small grates require logs to match, those with large open fires can utilise the large knotty pieces that are otherwise difficult to dispose of. Wood stoves provide a large outlet, but always need well-seasoned wood in order to avoid problems with tar. Ash, beech, oak, elm, maple and hornbeam are all first rate firewood.

A tractor driven saw bench is best for producing large numbers of logs. A chain saw can be used, but is it slower, much more tiring, and quickly wears the chain bar.

Faggots: When coppicing our ancestors did not waste the twiggy material that today we consign to the bonfire. It was bundled into faggots and used for firing bread ovens, drying hops, malting barley, preventing erosion on river banks and in ditches as a soakaway system. Alas, I know of no one still using them for heating, although river authorities continue to buy fascines.

Patterns: Faggots are bundles of rods and twigs 900mm (3ft) long by 610mm (2ft) in circumference. Fascines are made of c.20 hazel or willow rods of c.25mm (1in) diameter and 2.4-3m (6-8ft) long tied three times and with a finished diameter of 260mm (10in) (**fig. 12.17**).

Tools and devices: A good curved billhook and some short posts driven into the ground 450mm (18in) apart to hold the sticks.

Method: Lay a couple of well branched sticks out to the right length between the posts. Follow these with the sticks or brushwood, trimming any that are too straggly or too large. When you have sufficient, bind your faggot with one tie. Make fascines by laying 20 selected stems between the posts, and then tying.

Kindling: In Sussex kindling was sold as 'pimps', 150mm (6in) long by 75mm (3in) diameter bundles of twigs with a couple of pieces of cleft hazel. The trick is to tie the wood in long lengths, and then to cut between the ties.

Charcoal: Potentially charcoal is the largest untapped market available to English woodlands; would that it were profitable! It is made by heating wood in insufficient air for full combustion. The result is virtually pure carbon, black, with the gloss of a crow's feathers and the wood structure still visible. Charcoal is only c.15% of the original wood weight, and 75% of the volume. Wood should be seasoned for at least 6 months after felling before

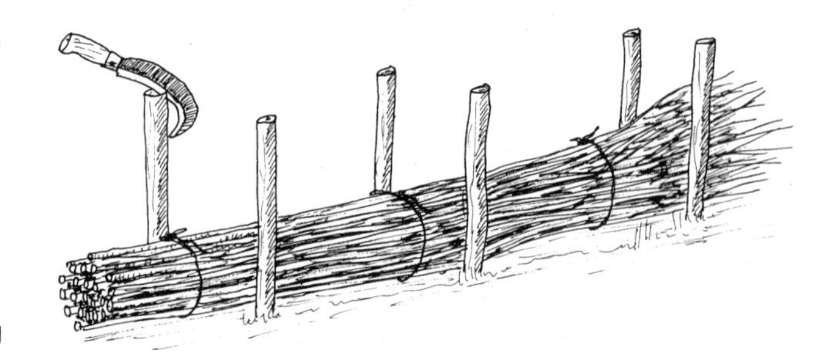

Fig. 12.17 Fascines: the posts hold the sticks together so they can be tied.

charring for best results. It should be less than 150mm (6in) diameter. Modern methods use steel drums or kilns, replacing the traditional earth clamp.

Oil drum method: Start here to understand the mechanisms of charcoal making (**fig. 12.18**).

- Place the prepared drum on three bricks so air can flow to the holes at the base.
- Light a fire in bottom of drum, and when burning strongly add the cut branchwood randomly in order to leave air spaces. Put larger pieces in first, then smaller on top.
- When the fire is hot and your spit really sizzles on the metal of the drum, seal around base of drum with soil leaving one 100mm (4in) gap, and put on lid leaving a small gap. If the heat is uneven across the drum, open a new hole on the colder side and close the first.
- When the dense white smoke (mainly moisture bound in the wood) turns to a thin blue, stop down all air access at the base and around the lid with sand, soil or sods. A burn should take about five hours.
- Cool for 24 hours, tip out, sieve charcoal through wire mesh or slats to required size, and bag up.

Portable kiln method: These are like very large steel drums, c.2.5m (8ft) diameter and at least 0.9m (3ft) high (**fig. 12.19**).

- Select a level site free from flooding.
- Erect circular body of kiln, on top of air vents if these are separate, and seal body to ground.
- Lay the first layer of poles radially across the base to provide air flow from the draught box and so that a lighted paraffin rag can be pushed to the centre where you should arrange a pile of kindling and charcoal (**fig. 10.15**).
- Load with wood, the first at right angles to the first layer, no longer than 0.9m (3ft), fairly tightly packed. Take care not to block your channel to the centre.
- Erect chimneys, put on lid, and insert lighted rag, using a long pole, to the centre to start the burn. Once going well, stop down air inlets.
- Burn for c.17-20 hours, and when smoke changes colour to thin blue, remove chimneys and block all holes. Fine tuning of air access will be needed during burn: keep heat fairly even around kiln, but don't let it flame, it must char.

Fig. 12.19 A modern portable kiln for charcoal making.

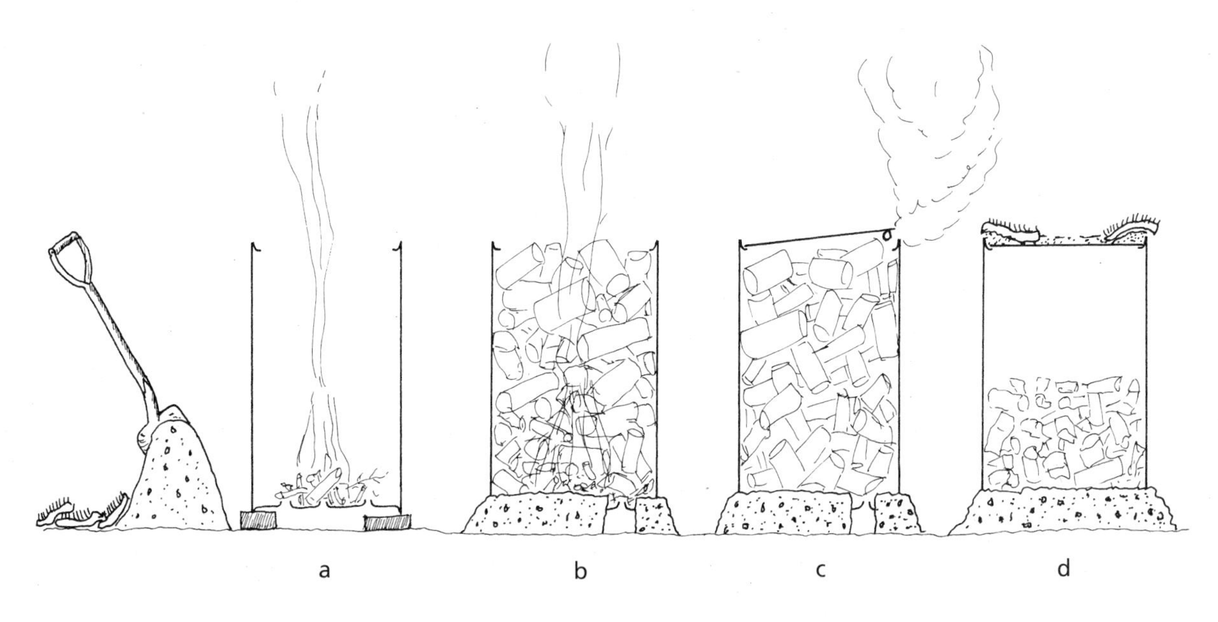

Fig. 12.18 Making charcoal in an oil drum: a. starting the fire; b. filling with wood; c. charring – limited air can enter at base and stick holds lid open enough to let the smoke out; d. drum sealed to stop the burn.

- Cool for at least 24 hours (don't be impatient – open it too early and it will blaze up, so have some water to hand), then empty, sieve and bag your charcoal – a filthy job for which you should wear a mask.

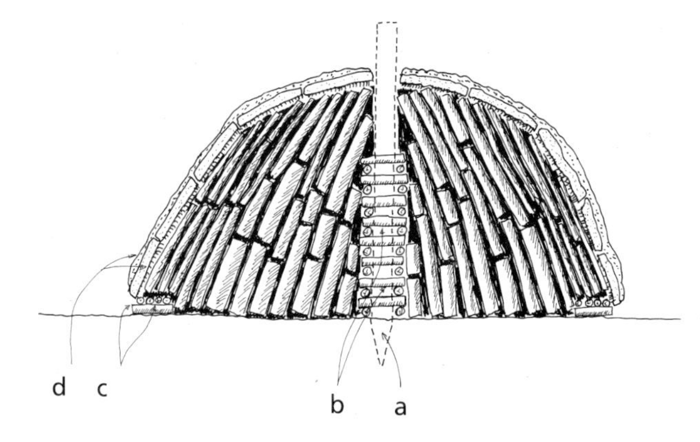

Fig. 12.20 A traditional charcoal clamp: a. motte peg; b. chimney; c. air inlets; d. sods and soil.

Traditional clamp method*:* For those who must do it traditionally, the method is (**fig. 12.20**):

- Drive a 1.8m (6ft) motte peg into centre of your flat hearth (c.3m/10ft) – not too hard for you must pull it out.
- Build a chimney of short logs around the post as shown.
- Build stacks of vertical wood around this, larger at centre, smallest at outside. Make an oval, not pointed stack.
- Cover the whole stack with vegetation (grass, bracken, etc) and then a layer of soil. Leave four holes at base N,S,E & W c.100mm (4in) diameter.
- Once you have a good fire going, seal holes and chimney. Watch clamp continuously and keep air out by repairing any cracks that appear in the covering as the wood settles, or open a hole at base if not going well.
- Smoke will seep out of clamp, white and wet at first, and slowly move down the sides of the clamp. When smoke is thin and blue stop all air access with soil and sods.
- Cool for 24 hours, break open, sieve and bag.

Charcoal sticks for drawing: Use fine willow sticks for these. Tie into bundles 150-200mm (6-8in) long, and char in a small steel container (oil drum or smaller). Pack the bundles tight in the container, and follow the normal process. Watch with more care that the temperature is even throughout the container. It should only take 2-3 hours. Unload carefully to avoid breaking the sticks.

Housing

Wood from coppices has always played a major role in our vernacular architecture, and there remains a market for some items in renovation, repair and in new timber buildings.

Thatching wood

Patterns: Many thatchers and all spar makers like to buy round wood to convert. It should be no shorter than 1.3m (4ft 6in), cleaned of major knots, not sere, damaged or barked, and be between 12mm (1/2in) and 50mm (2in) in diameter. Tie it in convenient bundles and store in the shade.

- Sways or binders – round or cleft 1.5m (5ft) to 2.4m (8ft) long and about 25mm (1in) across.
- Liggers or runners – clefts, shaved on the inner face and pointed at ends, 1m (3ft) to 1.5m (5ft) long from 38mm (1.5) rods.
- Broches, spars or spits – clefts preferably sharpened at ends, c.12mm (1/2in) across and usually 660mm (26in) long (**fig. 12.21**).

Material: Hazel or willow.

Tools and devices: Billhook, spar hook or adze, riving post and frame for bundling.

Method: For liggers and sways, trim rods and cut to length, then rive into four clefts. Trim off the pith to leave a flat surface, and give both ends a long pointed taper.

Broche wood is best left at least a month to toughen up. Cut to length and then rive these 'gads', to produce 12mm (1/2in) clefts. The diameter of the gad will determine how it should be split (**fig. 12.22**). Either hold the gad under your arm and rive it by twisting your hook (**fig. 12.23**), or use the adze and riving post (**fig. 6.22**). Sharpen each broche with three cuts (**fig. 12.24**).

Collect product in a frame, and bundle liggers and sways in 25's and broches in 200's.

Laths

Patterns: Plasterer's laths are 25-50mm (1-2in) wide by c.6mm (1/4in) thick and 1.2-1.5m (4-5ft) long clefts. These are used to key plaster or rendering to ceiling or wall (**fig. 12.25**). Slaters laths are stronger in cross section – usually 50mm (2in) by 25mm (1in).

Tools and devices: Saw, froe and beetle, and riving brake.

Materials: Oak and chestnut best; hazel and willow will do.

Methods: Having trimmed poles and cut them to length, rive into two. Rive the clefts again into

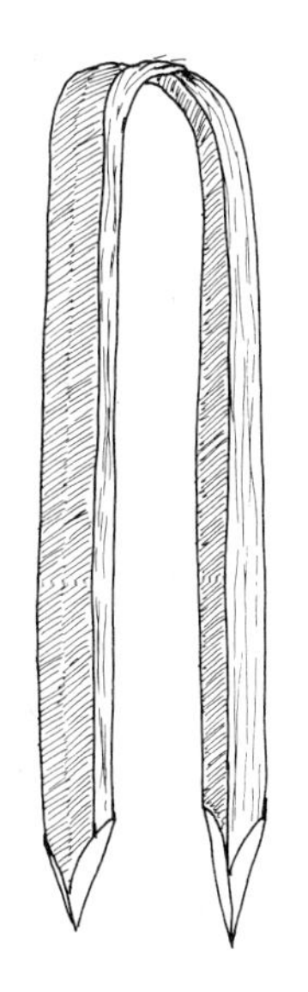

Fig. 12.21 A broche or spar twisted ready for use.

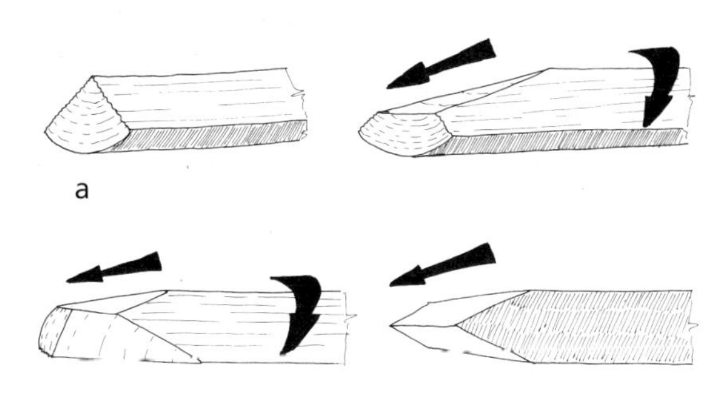

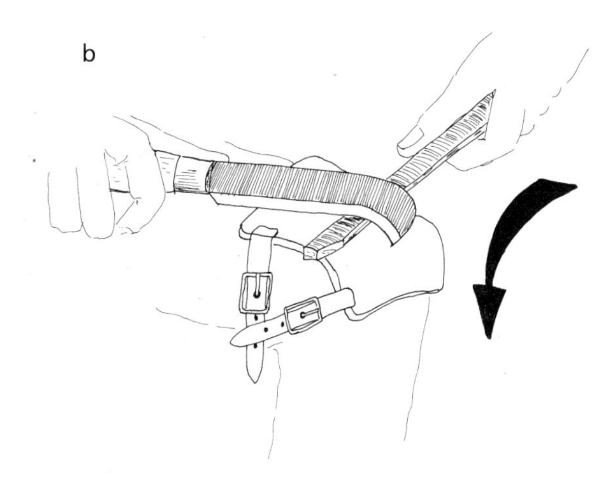

Fig. 12.24 a. three cuts used to sharpen a spar; b. holding the spar on a leather knee pad for sharpening.

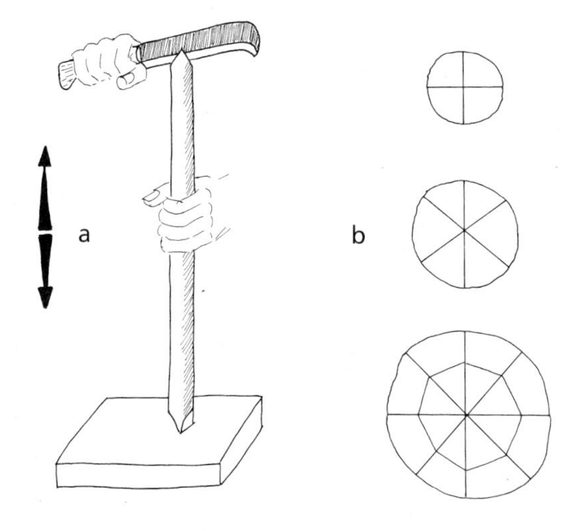

Fig. 12.22 Spars: a. starting to split a gad; b. riving patterns for different sizes of wood.

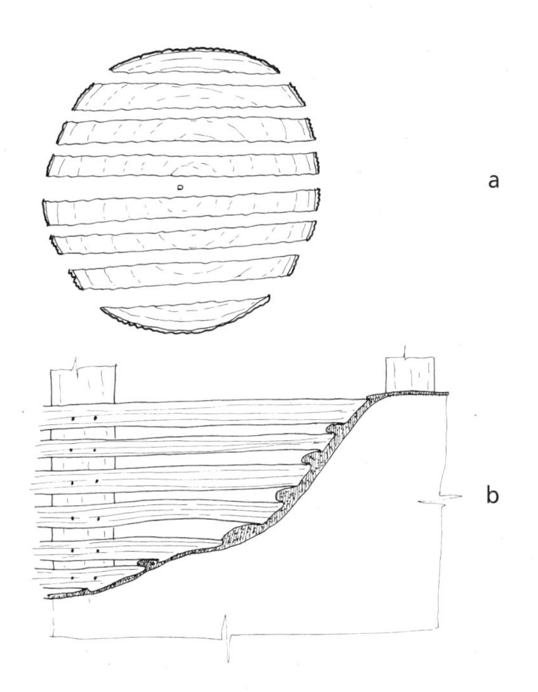

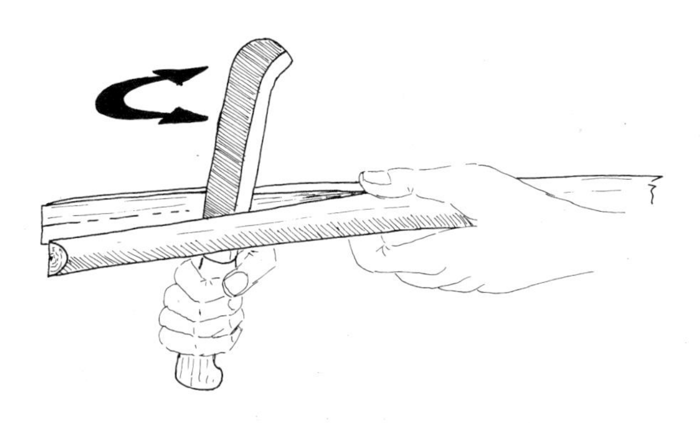

Fig. 12.23 Splitting out spars using a spar hook to lever the clefts apart.

Fig. 12.25 Laths: a. how laths are split from a round pole; b. laths fixed to a frame to hold plaster.

two tangentially, and repeat depending on size of wood until you reach target thickness. Leave the cleft surfaces rough and bundle for sale.

Wattle rods

Patterns: These are used to hold the daub infill in timber framed buildings. Usually supplied to builders in variable lengths c.12mm 1/2in) diameter and free from major knots. Stouter staves of 35mm(1 1/2in) diameter were used round which to weave the withe rods (**fig. 12.26**).

Material: Hazel and ash most commonly used.

Tools – methods: Merely select, size and trim appropriate rods and bundle in 25's.

Shingles

Patterns: Shingles are still used for roofing, although sawn cedar wood is more common than native oak. Although the 'standard' sizes are

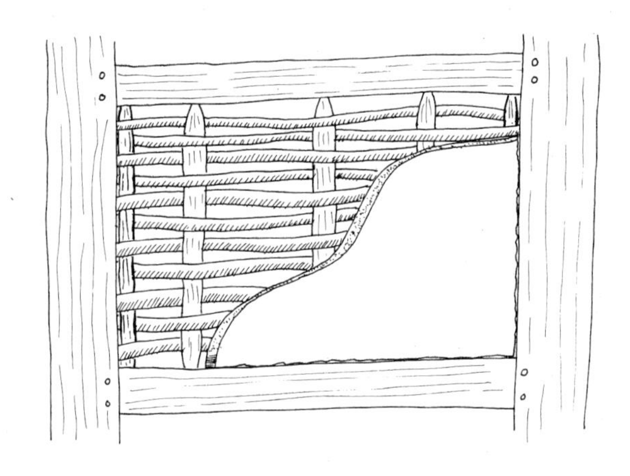

Fig. 12.26 Wattle rods woven between cleft uprights in a timber frame with daub covering.

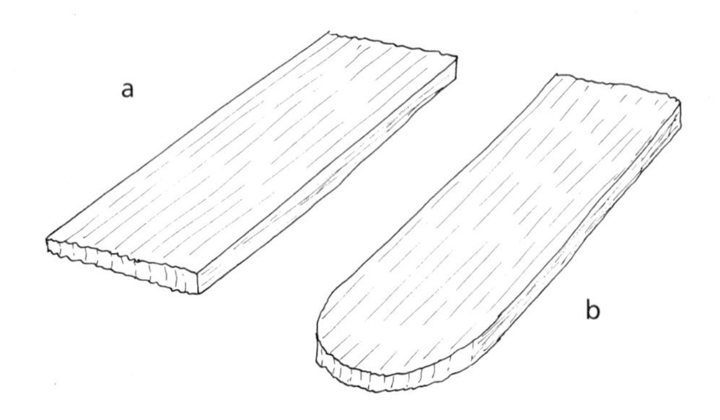

Fig. 12.27 Shingles: a. plain pattern; b. American pattern with rounded end.

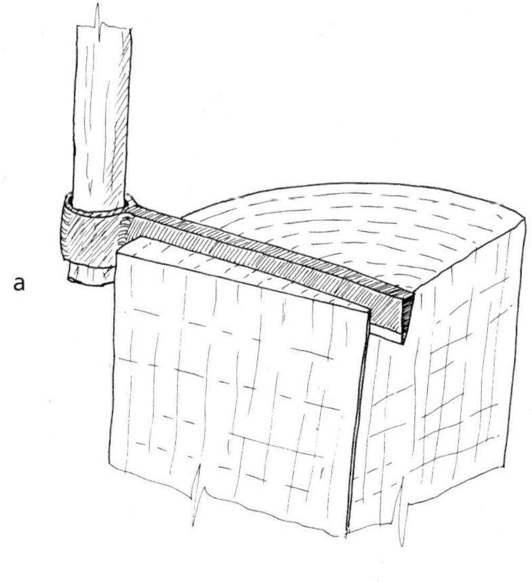

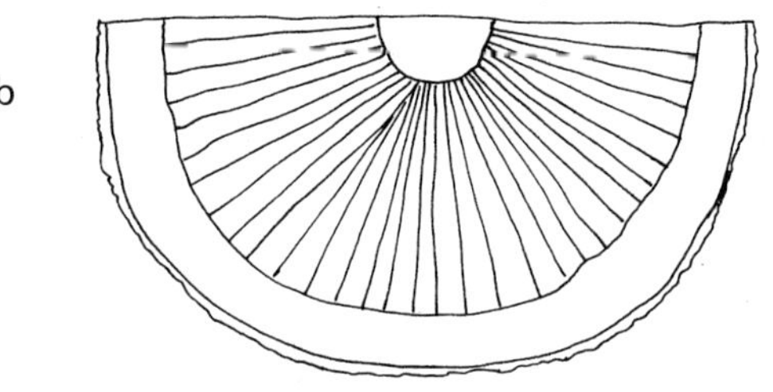

Fig. 12.28 Shingles: a. splitting shingles from a large cleft; b. the outermost sapwood and core are not used.

304mm x 150mm (12 x 6in) and 304 x 203mm (12 x 8in) variation in width is frequently allowed. Shingles 456mm (18in) long were called 'perfection'. Target thickness is 12 - 6mm (1/2-1/4in). In America round ends are common since they shed water better (**fig. 12.27**).

Tools and devices: Saw, wedges and beetle, froe, riving brake, draw knife and horse.

Materials: The very straightest butts of oak or chestnut c.75mm (3in) wider in radius than the shingle width you require.

Method: Cut butt to length required. Split into quarters with wedges. Remove sapwood and heartwood. Now use your froe to repeatedly split the clefts until the target thickness is reached. Tidy up with draw knife, evening the thickness if necessary, but always leave one face unshaved – this is the really waterproof one. Marking the log before splitting improves quality no end!

You can take 9mm (3/8in) clefts off the quarter butt (**fig. 12.28**), but they tend to thin at one end so that you must turn the butt over each time to keep a level face.

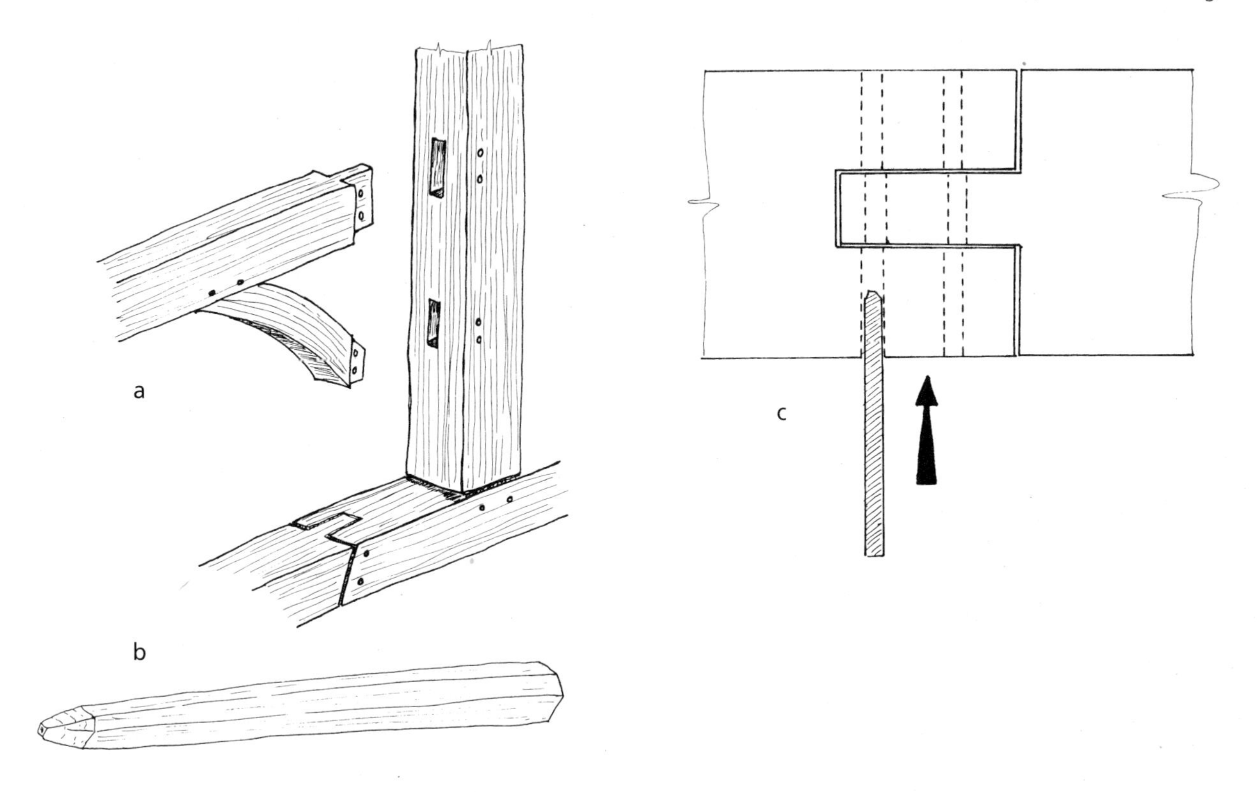

Fig. 12.29 Timber framing: a. typical joints; b. a trenail; c. holes in tenon slightly off centre so joint is tightened as you drive the trenail home.

Timber and trenails: Significant size timber is best left for professionals with specialist equipment. Smaller stems can be adzed square (Chapter 7) for minor use. Oak and chestnut are worth the sweat, and you can fashion small timbers good enough for a shed. Use appropriate shaped limbs for braces, and consider carefully the best joints to give the strength you require.

Trenails are the wooden pegs used to secure timber joints (**fig. 12.29**). If you do find a use or market for them, use oak or chestnut and split them as described for rake teeth, but don't round them, just chamfer the corners off with a knife – they hold better that way.

Further reading

Anon. ***Forestry Commission Bulletin 27 – Utilization of Hazel Coppice*** HMSO, 1956

Armstrong, L., ***Wood Colliers and Charcoal Burning*** Coach House Publishing, 1978

Howkins C. ***Trees, Herbs & Charcoal Burners*** 1995

Long J. ***Making Bentwood Trellises, Arbours & Gates*** Storey 1999

Hollingdale A.C. & others, ***Charcoal Production – A Handbook*** eco-logic books 1999

Paddon, A. & Harker., ***A Charcoal production using a portable metal kiln*** Rural Technology Guide 12, Commonwealth Secretariat Publications, 1980

Tabor, R., ***Traditional Woodland Crafts*** Batsford 1994

Underhill, R., ***The Woodwrights Shop*** University of N. Carolina Press, 1981

Underhill, R., ***The Woodwrights Companion*** University of N. Carolina Press, 1983

Chapter 13

Fencing

When fields were smaller and animals an essential part of the rotation on every farm, fencing was a major market for coppice wood. Today, it remains the most important outlet for chestnut and hazel coppice, although paling and panels for gardens are now more important than hurdles for sheep.

Hedging materials

Where hedges are still laid, stakes and ethers are used to hold and bind the laid stems (**fig. 13.1**).

Patterns: Stakes are usually 1.5m (5ft) long and a butt diameter of c.38mm (1½in). They may be sharpened. Stakes do not have to be perfectly straight, but must be good enough to be driven into the ground.

Ethering rods, which are woven between the stakes to keep the laid stems down, should be approx. 3m (10ft) long with a butt diameter of c.25mm (1in)

Tools, materials and method: A billhook and side axe will be all you need to prepare hedging wood.

Stakes can be of any wood since they do not have to last long. Ethers should be of hazel or willow to give the long, slim, flexible rods required.

Simply cut the material to the size required, remove any large knots, and put together in suitable bundles.

Stakes, spiles and posts

Patterns: Stakes are usually 1.7m (5.5ft) long with a top diameter of c.75mm (3in). They can be cleft as well as round, but if so, the cleft faces should still be c.75mm and cleaned of any spears.

The bark is normally removed, and stakes are sharpened to leave a small square at the tip that will not turn when driven. Real quality stakes have their tops 'half sharpened' to avoid wood flaking away when they are hit (**fig. 13.2**).

Posts are the same length as stakes, but are cut to 127mm (5in) diameter and not sharpened (you dig a hole and tamp the soil in around a post). Gateposts are best hewn from the round, that portion underground being left round, and the top adzed to shape (**fig. 13.3**).

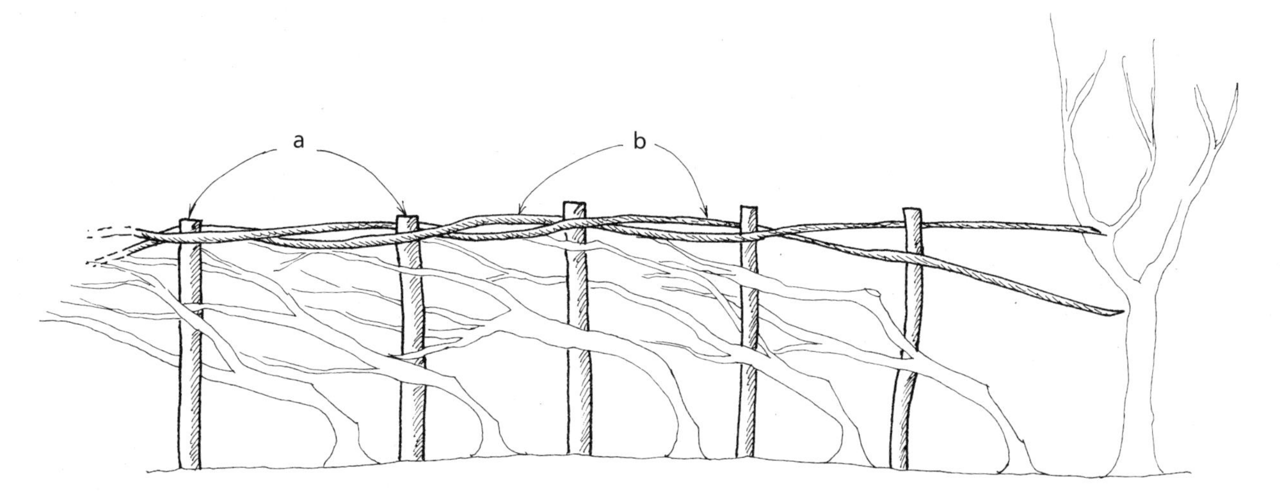

Fig. 13.1 A laid hedge with stakes (a) and ethering rods (b).

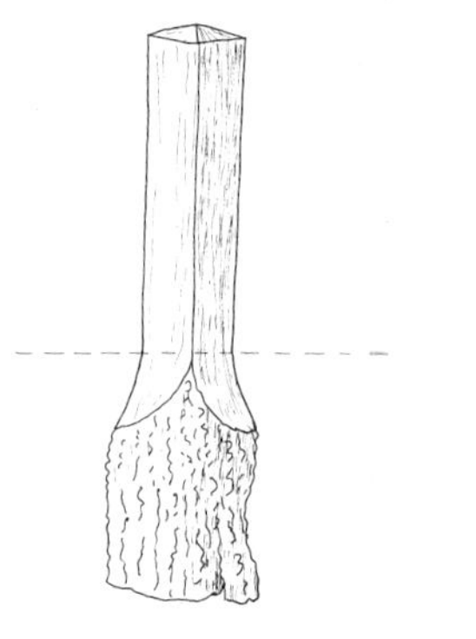

Fig. 13.3 A gatepost left round under the ground.

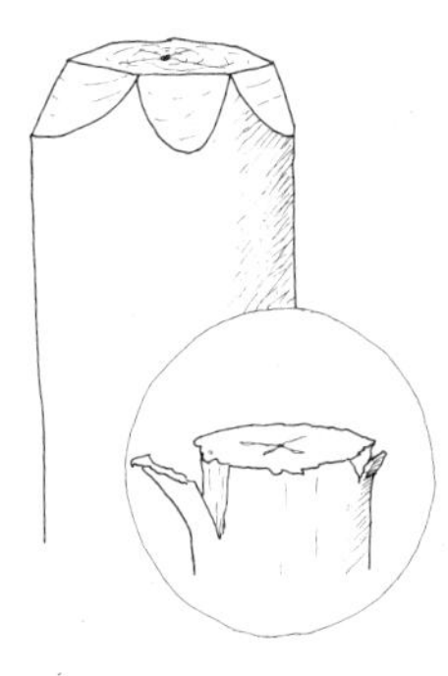

Fig. 13.2 Half sharpening the top of a post prevents it splitting when driven.

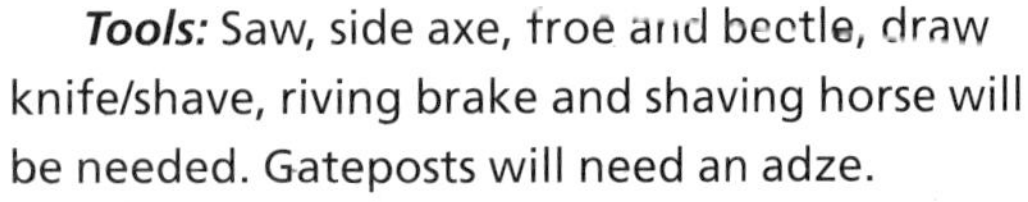

Tools: Saw, side axe, froe and beetle, draw knife/shave, riving brake and shaving horse will be needed. Gateposts will need an adze.

Materials and methods: Oak and chestnut are normally the only materials to use, but alder is used for river bank revettments where the stakes are continuously under water.

Cut stakes to length. Remove the bark using the shave or draw knife. Then, depending on the size of the pole, rive the larger ones (ie, 100mm (4in), rive once into two stakes; 152mm (6in), rive into four stakes). Remove any spikes and sharpen using your side axe, and stack in layers to season.

Square gateposts using your adze, and champfer the top to shed rain.

Fig. 13.4 Post and rail fencing.

Post and rail

Pattern: The normal pattern for post and rail (**fig. 13.4**) is a series of c.127mm (5in) diameter posts, spaced at 1.2 to 2.4m (4-8 ft) intervals, with mortices to hold two rails passing between the posts. Although rails can be nailed to the posts, this will be the first part of the fence to fail! Rails are quarter or half clefts shaped at each end to fit the mortice.

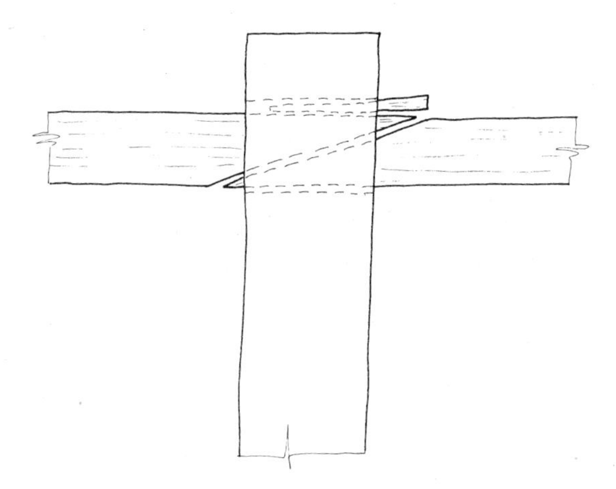

Fig. 13.5 Rails overlapped in the mortice and wedged.

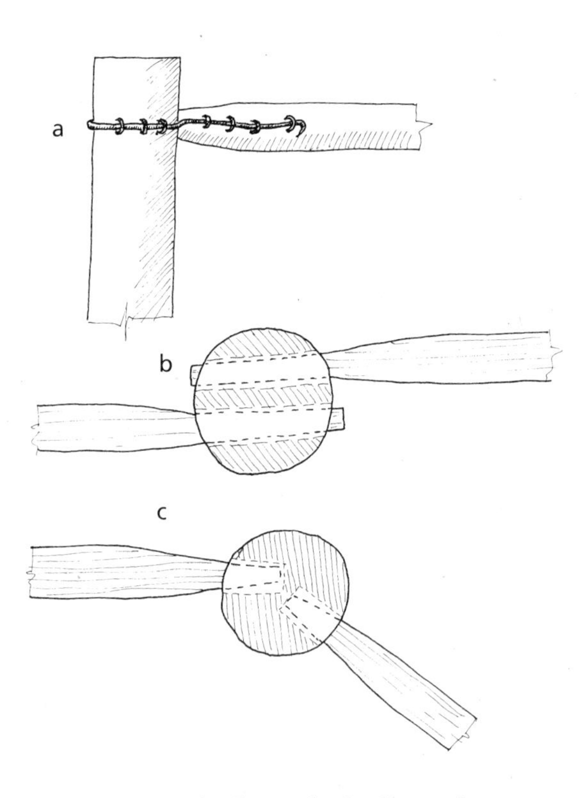

Fig. 13.6 Post and rail: a. rail wired to end post; b. double morticed post; c. post morticed to form a bend in the fence.

Mortices can be single or double (**fig. 13.6**). If single it is best if adjacent rails overlap within the mortice, and are wedged tight (**fig. 13.5**). End posts can be held to the rail using stapled wire (**fig. 13.6**). To go round corners, adjust the position of mortices – in this case they cannot pass through the post (**fig. 13.6**). For lighter work mortices can be large diameter round holes.

Tools and materials: Use the same tools as for stakes but with the addition of a brace and bit and/or morticing chisel.

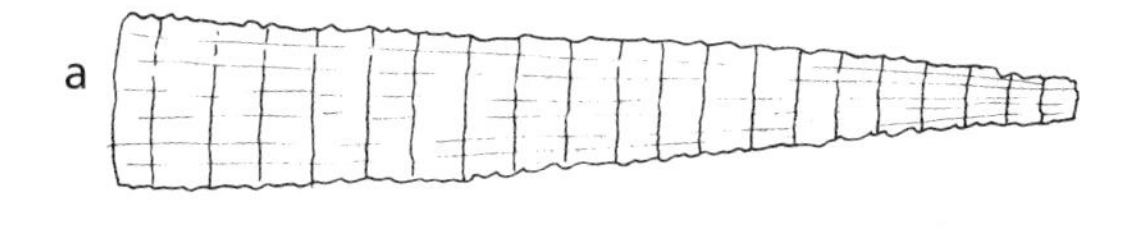

Fig. 13.7 Paling: a. paling; b. typical pale fence.

Oak and chestnut are best, being essential for posts. Rails may be ash or elm.

Methods: Prepare posts and rails as described for stakes. Use the side axe to shape the ends of the rails. Cut mortices in the posts to required pattern, sizes and angles.

If you are erecting the fencing remember: posts should go in pre-dug holes and the soil tamped back with a pointed tamper; fit rails into mortices before firming post in position; secure last post to rail firmly with wire and staples.

Pale fencing

The pale fence was once a regular feature around parks intended to contain deer and protect coppice. When properly made it is incredibly durable.

Pattern: The basic framework is post and rail as already described, to which are nailed feather edged pales (**fig. 13.7**). Pales are c.1m (3½ft) long, 76mm (3in) wide, with an outside thickness of c.19mm (¾in) and an inner thickness of c.6mm (¼in).

Tools and materials: These are as described for stakes and posts. The pales themselves must be of oak or chestnut; anything else will need regular treatment with a preservative.

Method: Making posts and rails has been described. Pales are made by taking a series of radial clefts from a rinded round pole (**fig. 13.8**); it should be possible to obtain between 24 and 36 pales from a 165mm (6½in) diameter knot-free pole. Trim back the feather edge of the pale to 6mm (¼in) thickness. Many misshapen pales can be used, but trim any that will not allow a regular spacing when nailed in place. Bundle your palings together if they are not to be used quickly, since they will warp as they dry.

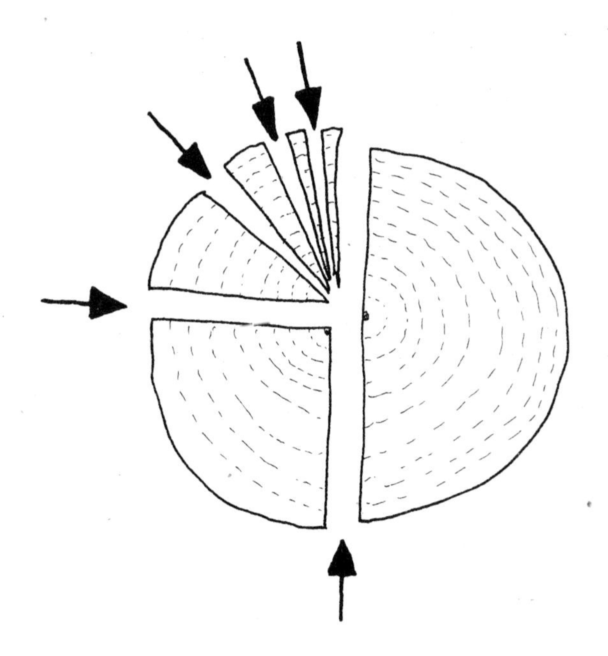

Fig. 13.8 How to rive pales from a round log.

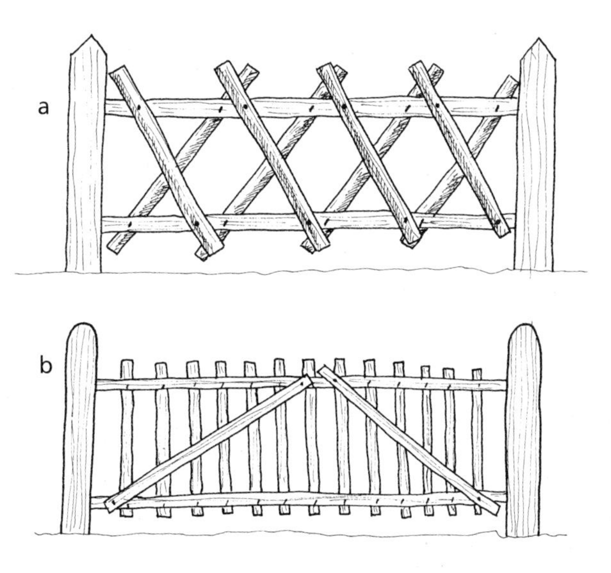

Fig. 13.9 Two examples of rustic fencing.

Rustic fencing

Patterns: This cottage fencing can be extremely varied – this is a good opportunity to make your own designs! The most common patterns use top and bottom horizontal rails to which barked round or cleft wood is nailed. These may be made as panels or erected in situ. A couple of very basic ideas are illustrated (**fig. 13.9**).

Tools, materials and methods: The tools you will need are those described for pale fencing. Once again the best material is chestnut, although hazel, ash or elm can be used for members not touching the ground.

Methods are self-explanatory, but just remember when nailing near the end of poles or clefts to drill pilot holes first in order to avoid the wood splitting.

Chestnut paling fencing

Pattern: Paling or spile and wire fencing consists of 25 to 44mm (1 to 1¾in) clefts of chestnut, anywhere between 0.6 and 1.8m (2-6ft) long held together by wire strands (**fig. 13.10**). The wire, usually 14 gauge soft wire in two double strands, is twisted between each paling to both grip it and provide a regular spacing. The gap between the palings can vary from 25 to 127mm (1 to 5 inches). Smaller lengths of paling require two lines of wire; longer lengths (>1.5m – 5ft) require three. The wire may be stapled to all or some of the palings to prevent them slipping out. The top of each paling is bluntly sharpened with three cuts in order to shed rainwater (not so that you can drive them into the ground!). All this detail is described in BS1722 pt.4.

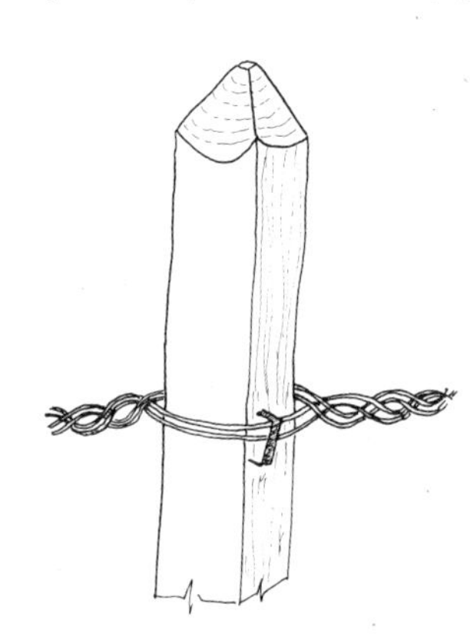

Fig. 13.10 Chestnut paling showing twisted wire and staple.

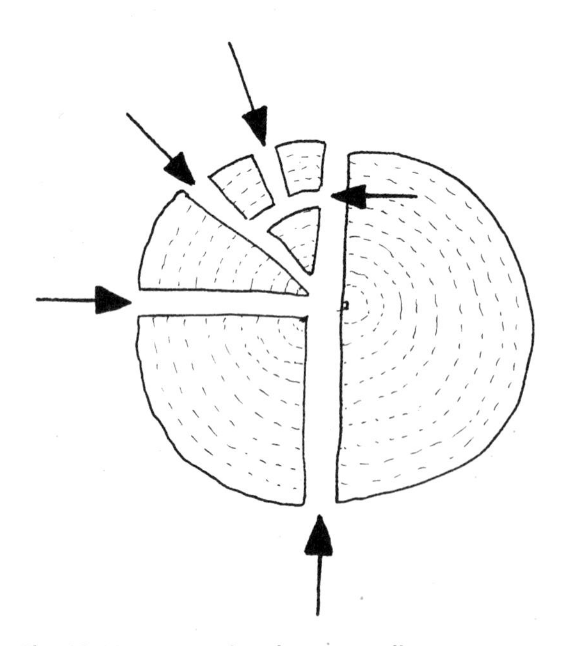

Fig. 13.11 How to rive chestnut paling.

Tools and materials: You will need saw, billhook, curved shave, shaving horse, froe, beetle and riving brake, side axe and chopping block in order to make palings.

You must use chestnut: it is the only tree with sufficient heartwood to produce durable small clefts.

Method: Cut poles to length and remove the bark using the shaving horse and shave. Then with the froe, rive the pole to produce clefts of the required size (see **fig. 13.11**). With good wood it should be possible to produce 24 pales from a 152mm (6in) diameter pole. Remove any spears on the cleft faces, and bluntly sharpen one end with your side axe. Bundle the palings before they warp.

Normally making the fencing is a factory task, using a long 'walk' along which a device moves which both feeds and twist the wires. On a small scale paling can be made by stretching the wire between two fixed posts app. 9m (30ft) apart (**fig. 13.12** – after Lambert). Insert the palings or spiles between the wires, then using the windlass, twist the wires. Twist a fixed number of turns for the spacing you require (six will give about a

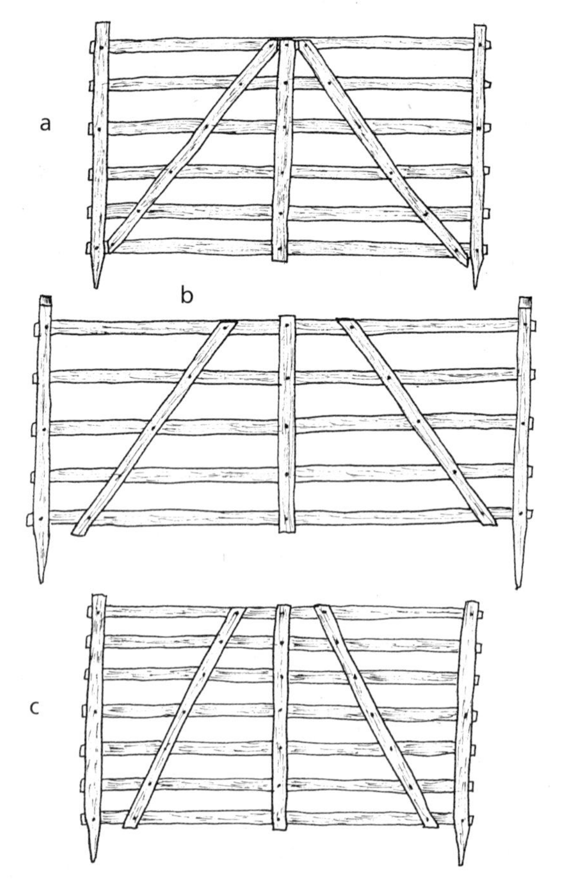

Fig. 13.13 Gate hurdles: a. Suffolk; b. Kent; c. Hampshire.

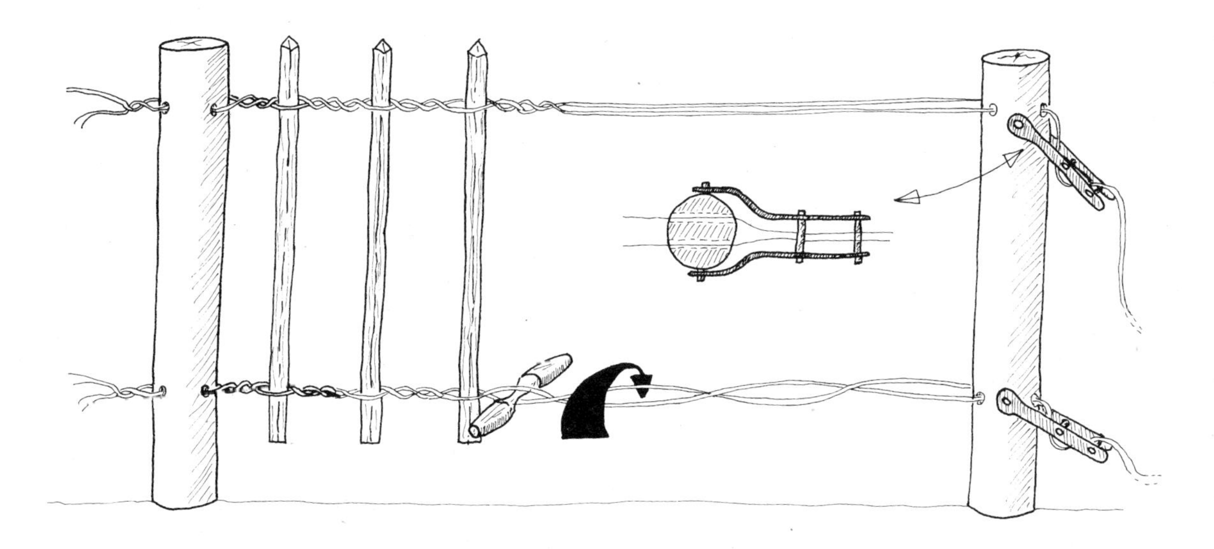

Fig. 13.12 A simple device for making paling fence (after Lambert).

76mm/3in) spacing) and remember to reverse the direction of the twist each time. Leave c.150mm (6in) of free wire at one end so that it can be joined to the next length of fencing when erected, and to tie in the loose end when the finished length is rolled for storage.

Gate hurdles

Patterns: As with many traditional products, the 'gates' used to pen sheep have strong regional styles, and examples are shown in **fig. 13.13**. Suffolk and Hampshire patterns have six and seven rails respectively; Kentish gates are longer, have five rails, and a longer foot that can be driven into the ground – hence the metal ferrule on the top of each head. All hurdles have their bottom rails more closely spaced to prevent older sheep putting their heads through.

Pig hurdles are the same pattern as the Hampshire sheep gate, but with stouter members. Bullock hurdles are both tall and long, with eight rails, all being made in very stout clefts.

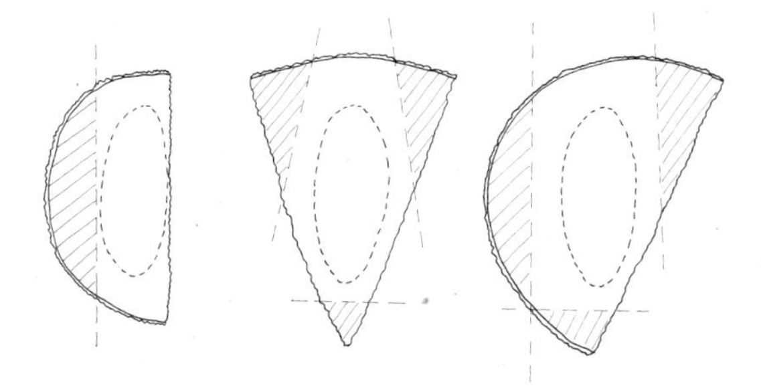

Fig. 13.14 How to shape ledges from clefts and negate any twist in the grain.

Tools and devices: You will need: saw, draw knife, shaving brake, froe and beetle, riving brake, side axe, pattern and rail gauges, pencil, brace and bit, twybil (or chisel and mallet), hammer.

Materials: Sweet chestnut is best, cleaving well and giving the longest life. Ash is very good, producing lovely straight clefts. Other woods used by craftsmen are oak, elm, hazel and willow.

Method:

- Cut poles to length, avoiding major knots, branches and curves; remove small knots with an axe. Rails should be cut 38mm (1 1/2in) longer than the hurdle width.
- Carefully rive the poles; the heads must be mirror half clefts, but rails can be quarter clefts if from large poles.
- Remove all bark and spikes from the clefts and shave the rails to c.25mm (1in) thick. Straighten any wind in the cleft by shaving one side more at either end (**fig. 13.14**).
- Complete the rails by shaping their ends using the gauge to check they taper to 19mm (3/4in) by 44mm (1 3/4in) in a flattened oval shape.
- Complete the heads by smoothing the cleft face, pointing the foot to a 9mm (3/8in) square point, and chamfer the top.
- To fit a ferrule, offer it up to the end of the rail before shaping; tap the ferrule with your hammer to mark its shape on the wood and then carefully shape the end of he rail to that shape. Ensure a tight fit, and nail into position (**fig. 13.15**). Ferrules are usually made to order by blacksmiths.

- Use an old hurdle as the pattern to mark the mortices. Place the heads cleft face upward exactly over heads of the pattern, and then lay out the rails so they overlay the heads. Put straightest and strongest rails at top and bottom; position any curved rails to minimise gaps. Mark the width of the rails on the two heads while they are in place (**fig. 13.16**). Leave the rails on the pattern.

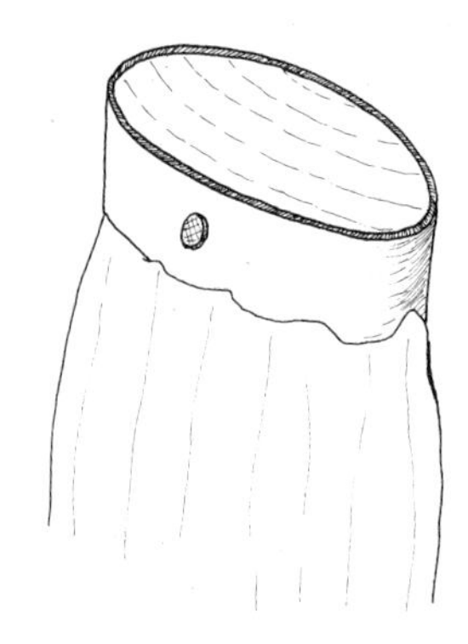

Fig. 13.15 Steel ferrule on a Kentish hurdle.

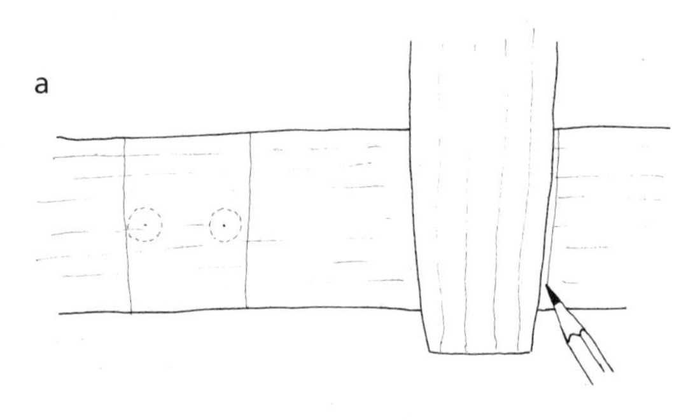

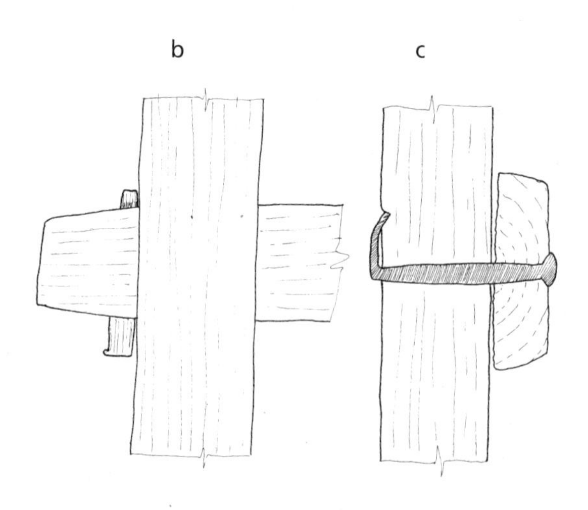

Fig. 13.16 Gate hurdles: a. marking mortices; b. all nails should be clenched; c. using a peg to hold the rails.

- To cut the mortices drill 14mm (9/16in) holes with your brace. Remove the waste wood between the holes using either twybil (**fig. 6.16 , 6.17**) or chisel and mallet. It is a good idea to run down the back of each head with the draw knife to remove any spikes raised by the drilling and morticing.
- Fit the heads and rails together. Fit one head first, and have two short posts against which to push when fitting the second head, and to force the rails through until they protrude c.19mm (3/4in). Nailing-up can be accomplished on the coppice floor, or better on a pattern table in the workshop. To avoid splitting the ends of rails, braces and strop, pre-drill the holes. Nail only top, middle and bottom rails to the heads; nail the braces and strop to every rail, but never to the heads. Use 65mm (1 1/2in) nails (cut rosehead nails are best since they grip tightly, but wire will do) and clench over the ends, burying the tips in the wood (**fig. 13.16**).
- Use you draw knife to champfer back the braces and strops flush to the top rail and remove any splinters. Store finished gate hurdles off the ground and flat; if you have a flat-sided level stack you are not going wrong!

Mini gates: These sell to gardeners wanting to keep border plants from overhanging lawns, or to keep pets off sensitive areas. They should be made as exact replicas of the full size hurdle with smaller rods, and oval mortices are replaced by a single 15mm (5/8in) hole. Use a pattern stick to mark the heads and a pattern table to make them up on; (Chapter 9) these will ensure all your hurdles are identical sizes.

Wattle hurdles and fencing

Making wattle hurdles or panels still rates as one of the supreme green wood crafts. To be able to make a tough, animal friendly and neat fencing panel using little more that your hands and a billhook – no nails, no wire – is to prove a real understanding of both product and materials.

Patterns: Like gate hurdles, there are regional differences in the way hurdles are woven. Some of these are shown in **fig. 13.17**. Sheep hurdles have a twilley hole so they can be carried and longer uprights at each end so they can be overlapped and fixed to a stake. The lamb creep hurdle allows lambs to hop through to fresh grass, but not the ewes. Sheep hurdles are usually 1.8m (6ft) long by 1m (3 1/2ft) high, woven around 10 uprights or

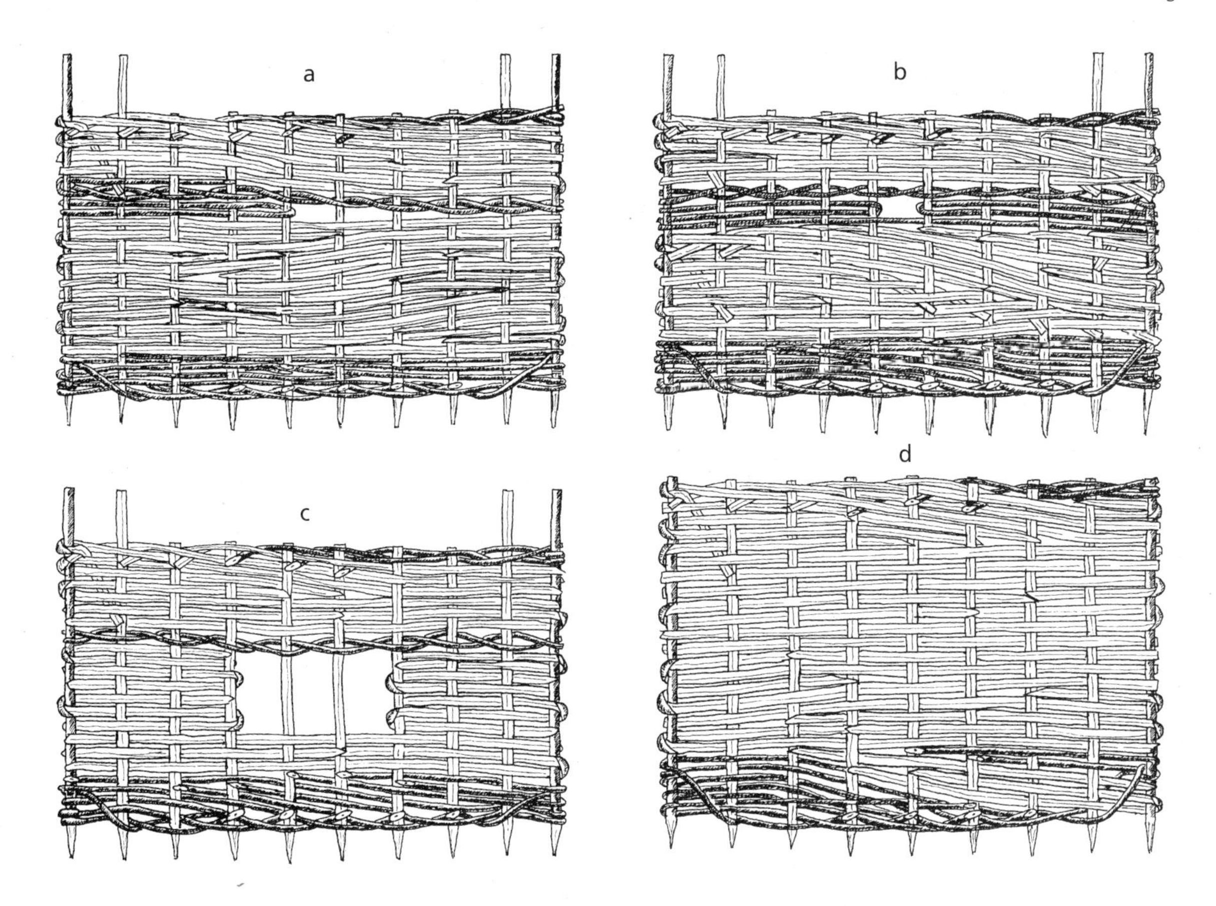

Fig. 13.17 Wattle hurdles: a. Dorset; b. Hampshire; c. Sheep creep; d. Garden panel.

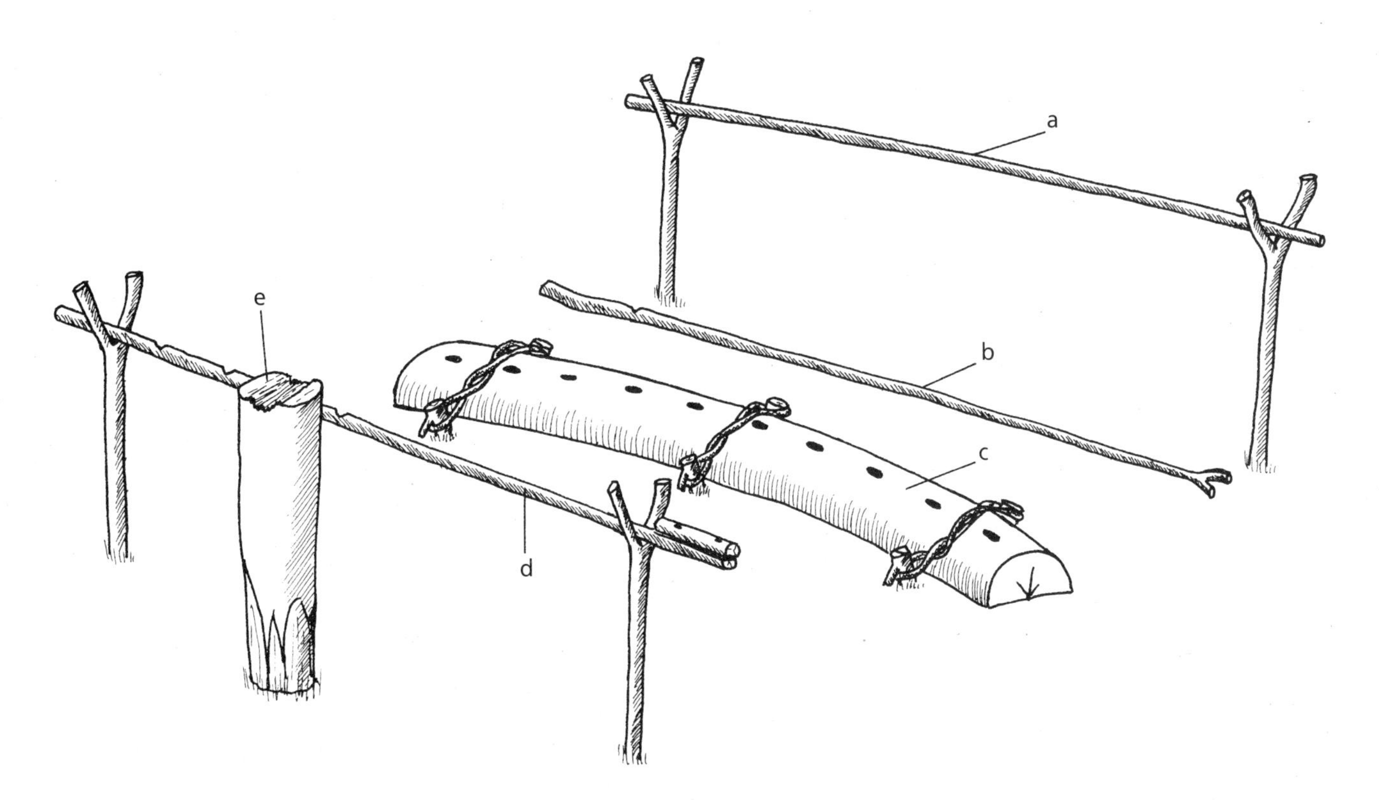

Fig. 13.18 Hurdle maker's set up: a. gallows; b. measuring rod; c. mould; d. measuring frame; e. chopping block.

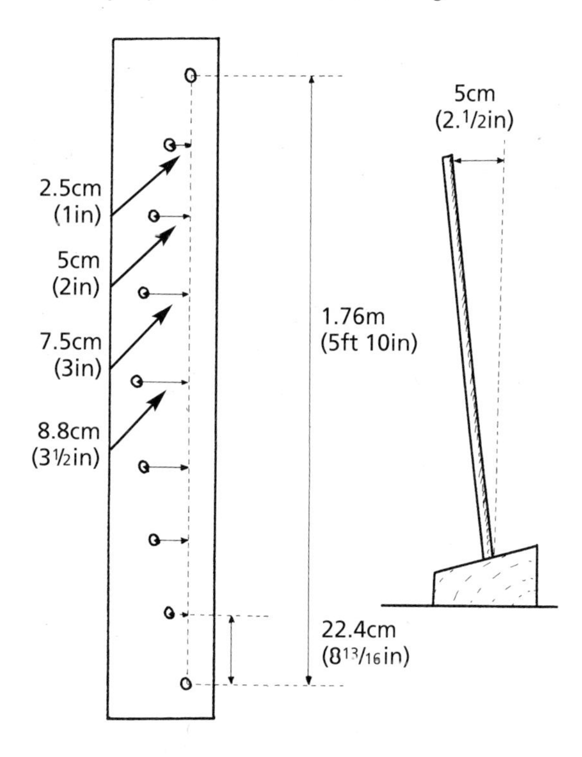

Fig. 13.19 Details of hurdle mould.

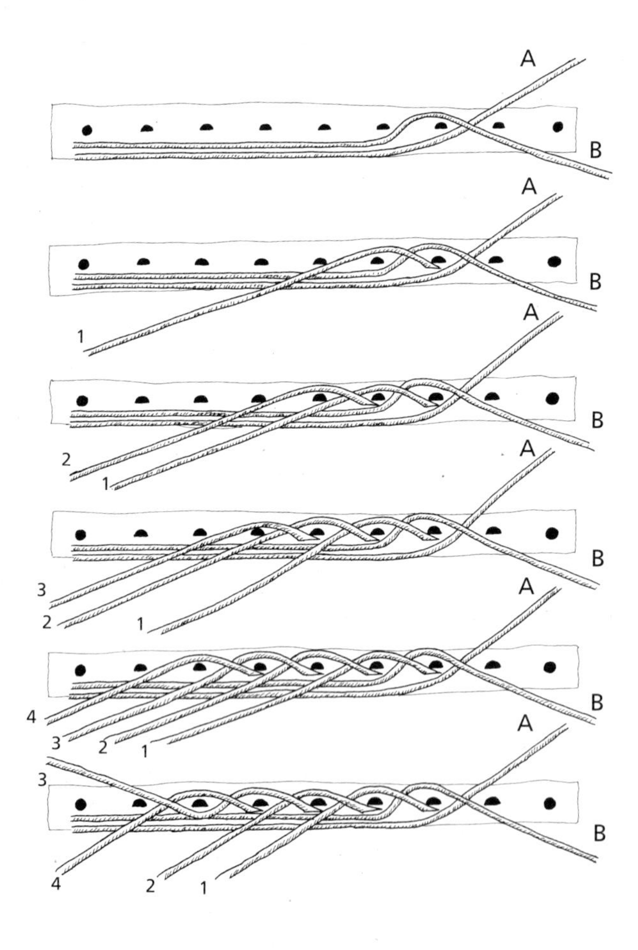

Fig. 13.20 Picking up the bottom of a hurdle: A & B are the spur rods, 1-4 are round rods.

zales. Because these hurdles are regularly moved, the bottom binders are twisted twice around the end zales to prevent the bottom falling out.

Garden screens or panels are the same length as a sheep hurdle, but can be from 0.9m (3ft) to 1.8m (6ft) high. But since they are moved about less, they have only nine zales and bottom binders that only pass once around the end zales.

Wattle fencing can be made in situ by weaving around posts driven into the ground. Only each end and the top of the fencing need to be securely bound in these circumstances.

Some wattle fencing is made by leaving the uprights in a stout wooden base which can be treated and thus offer a longer life. The weaving of the panel remains as already described. A final alternative is to produce a wooden frame and fill the centre with woven wattle rods, simulating a wattle and daub panel without the daub. This makes particularly good garden gates.

Tools and devices: To make free standing wattle panels from cut round rods, you will need: a billhook, gallows, chopping block, measuring stick, small beetle, hurdle mould and trimming hook or axe (**figs. 13.18** & **13.19**). If you prefer riving rods with an adze and riving post instead of a billhook, add these to the list.

Materials: Hazel is the stuff of hurdles, although willow is a good substitute. Zales can be made of ash or elm.

Method:

- Sort rods by length and quality, using best for zales and finishing rods.
- Select straight rods c.31mm (1.1/4in) diameter for zales, leaving end ones round and carefully riving others so they have no thin spots.
- Sharpen zales to a 130mm (5in) point and cut to length.
- Fit the zales into the mould; where the riven zales have curved, fit them so that they all curve the same way.
- To pick up the initial weave, use round rods c.19mm (3/4in) diameter. For a nine zale panel you need four (five for ten zales) 2.1m (7ft) long, and two spur rods 3.3m (11ft) long.
- Insert the two spur rods between zales two and three (**fig. 13.20**), leaving 900mm (3ft) beyond the end zale. Insert the remaining rods in front of zales four, five and six as shown.
- Using your foot to hold the rods down, lift rod three and take it behind zale eight, bending the rod and zale carefully to achieve this.

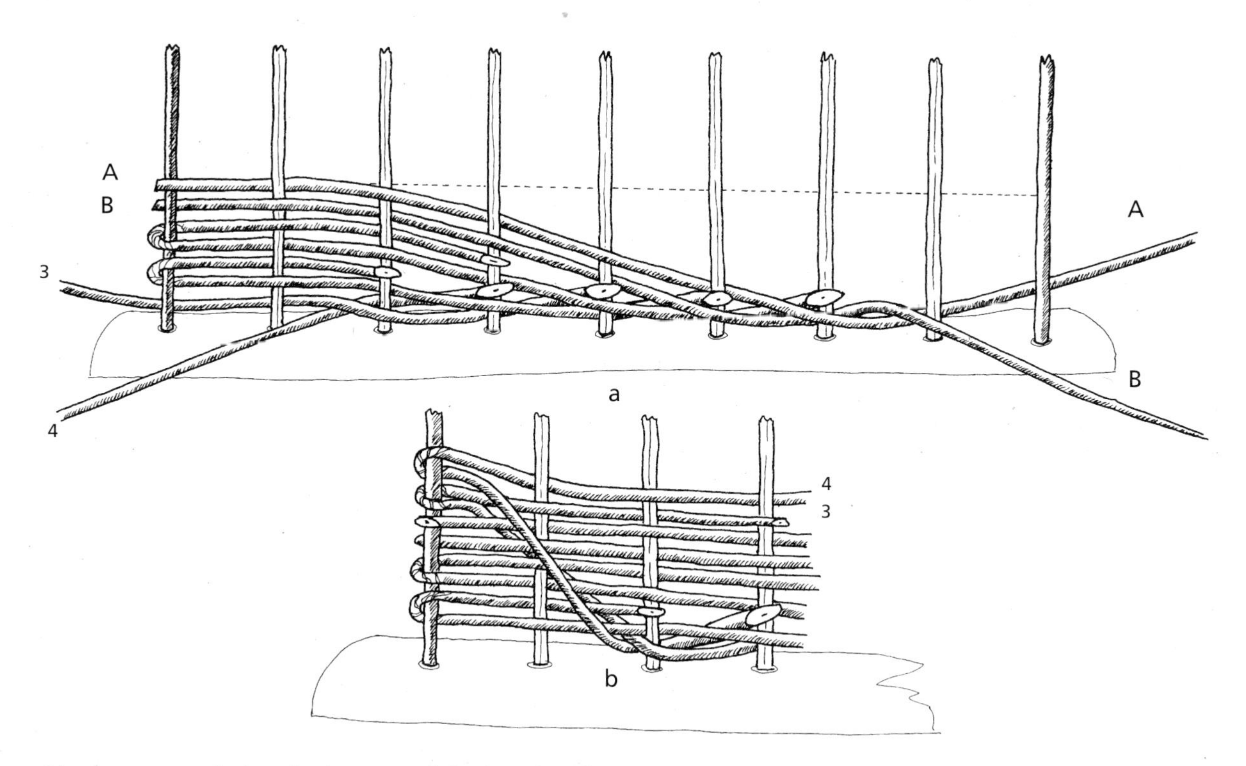

Fig. 13.21 Completing the bottom of the hurdle: fill in to the dotted line (a) with weaving rods before spur rods are brought up (b) to tie in the bottom.

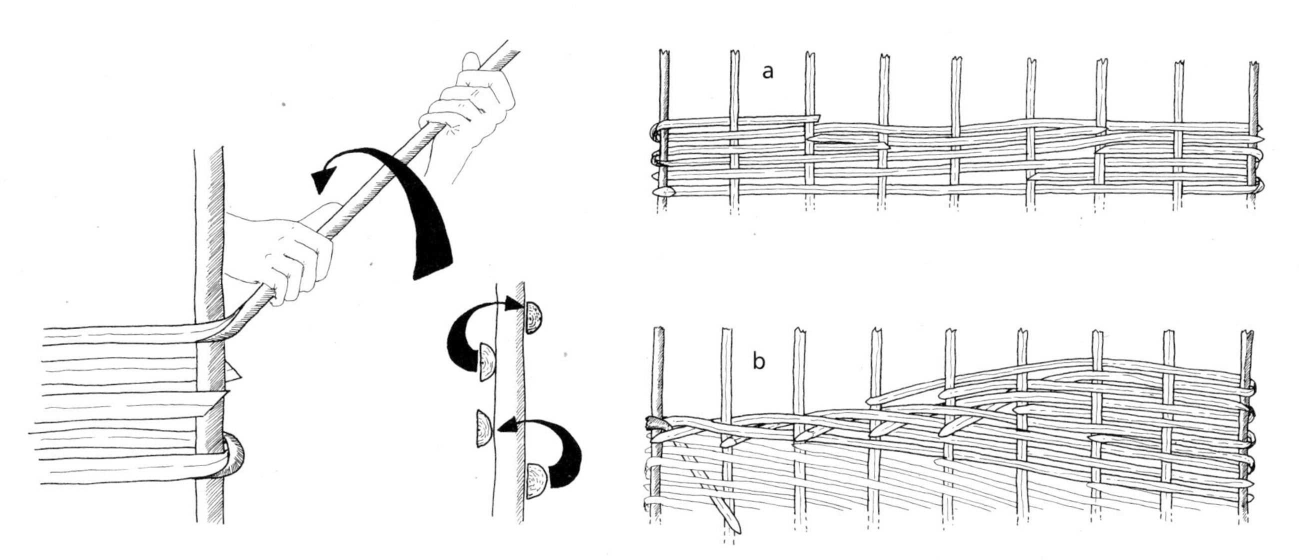

Fig. 13.22 Turning the weavers around the end zale.

Fig. 13.23
Weaving patterns: a. Dorset/Hampshire; b. Sussex.

- Now weave rods two and one to the end zale, pass round it, and weave back along the hurdle. To take the rod round the end zale, twist it to separate the fibres.
- Fill in the bottom of the hurdle so it is level by weaving cleft rods, and then tie in both ends using the spur rods plus three and four as shown (**fig. 13.21**).
- Raise the hurdle using cleft rods as weavers. Thin any thick spots and cut out thin ones to avoid distorting the hurdle's shape. Work the weavers and the zales so the former bend round the latter, producing a flat hurdle. Twist the clefts to go round the end zale as shown (**fig. 13.22**). Two patterns of weaving are shown (**fig. 13.23**).

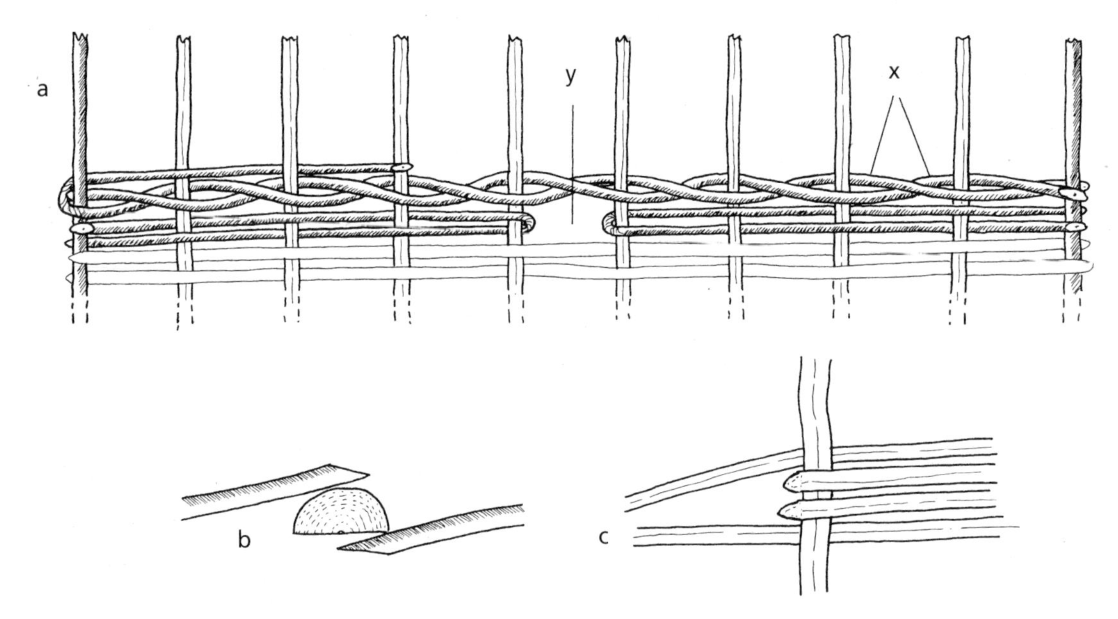

Fig. 13.24 Weaving: a. twilley rods (x) can be used to straighten the hurdle and create an opening (y); b. do not start and finish weavers on opposite side of a zale; c. do not finish two weavers at the same zale.

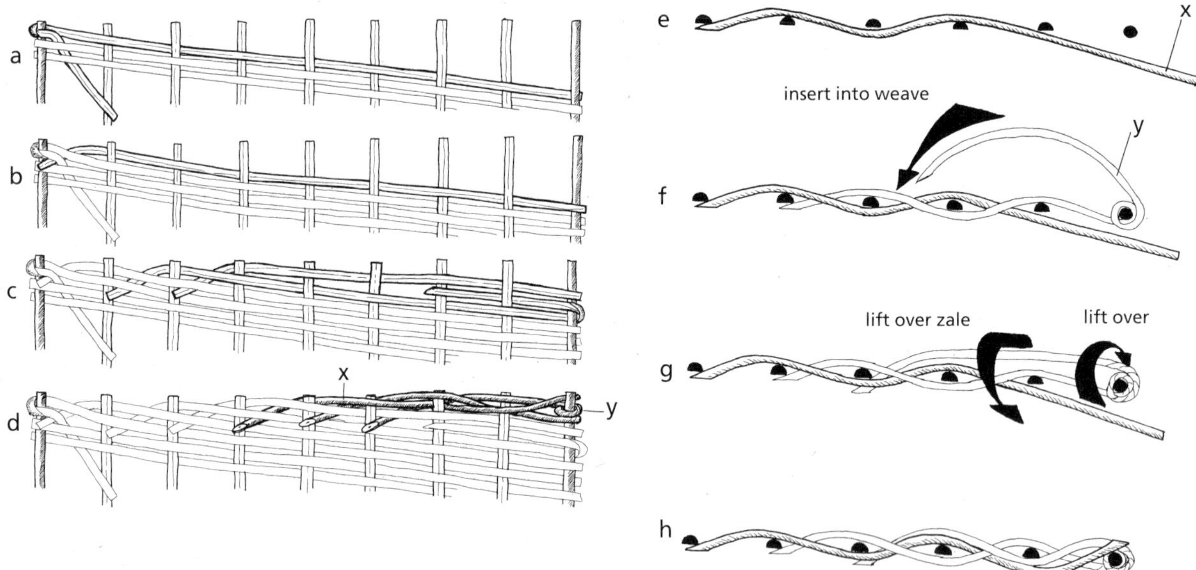

Fig. 13.25 Securing the top binding: a. spur inserted; b. first top weaver in place; c. top weavers two and three in place; d. stump rod (x) and finishing rod (y) in place.

Fig. 13.26 Detail (e-h) of how to weave the stump (x) and finishing rods (y).

- Keep the weave tight by using your club to hit it down. If the hurdle does distort, weave two twilley rods – being stiffer they will straighten the zales. Lay in butt ends first; avoid knots where you need to twist; don't finish two weavers at the same zale (**fig. 13.24**); nick very stiff weavers to bend them; finally keep the middle of the hurdle full – using short pieces if necessary.
- Finish weaving c.75mm (3in) below zale nine and c.200mm (8in) below zale one. To secure the top you need four cleft weavers 1.8 to 2.4m(6-8ft) long (five for a 10 zale hurdle) and two round finishing rods called the stump rod 1.2m (4ft) and the finishing rod 2.4m (8ft).
- Force the first weaver, or spur, down into the weave, take it around zale 9 as shown, and weave it normally. Insert and weave the other three top weavers as shown (**fig. 13.25**). Thrust the stump rod in front of zale six and weave it to zale one. Insert the finishing rod weave it to

zale one where you must twist it, wind it twice around the zale, then force it back into the weave in front of zale four, and finally lift it over zale two. Lastly lift the end of the stump rod over the finishing rod (**fig. 13.26**).

- Using your nug axe or hurdling bill to trim back the ends of the weavers; lift the ends away from the zales to do this (**fig. 13.27**).

A sharp kick should loosen the hurdle in the frame, and the job is complete!

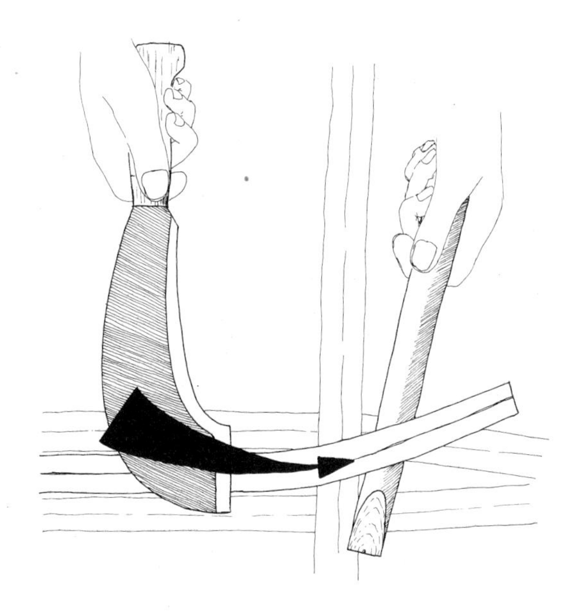

Fig. 13.27 Trimming up the weavers.

Cleft gates

Patterns: Gates, like hurdles were originally made in a wide variety of local patterns, alas no longer seen. A selection is illustrated in **fig. 13.28**. The key elements to any gate are: a vertical member at each end – the harr at the hinge end, the smaller head at the other – both stout enough to take mortices; between five and seven bars or rails that are morticed into both harr and head; a top rail, stouter than the others for the gate hangs from it, and which tapers to the head end to minimise the weight on the hinges; finally a diagonal brace is essential from the base of the harr to the top rail. Effective braces must be under compression in the finished gate. Vertical slats may also be used.

A typical field gate is 2.7m (9ft) wide by 1.4m ($4^1/_2$ft) high. The harr is 127 x 76mm(5 x 3in), the head 88 x 76mm (3.25 x 3in), the top rail 88 x 57mm (3.25 x 2.$^1/_4$in) and the other members 76 x 32mm (3 x $1^1/_8$in). Design others to similar proportions.

Tools and devices: You will need a saw, an adze if you are going to hew larger members, froe and/or wedge, beetle, riving and shaving brakes, draw knife, morticing chisel and bench, brace and bits, side axe. If you are going to make a lot of gates, a low table or frame upon which to make them is ideal.

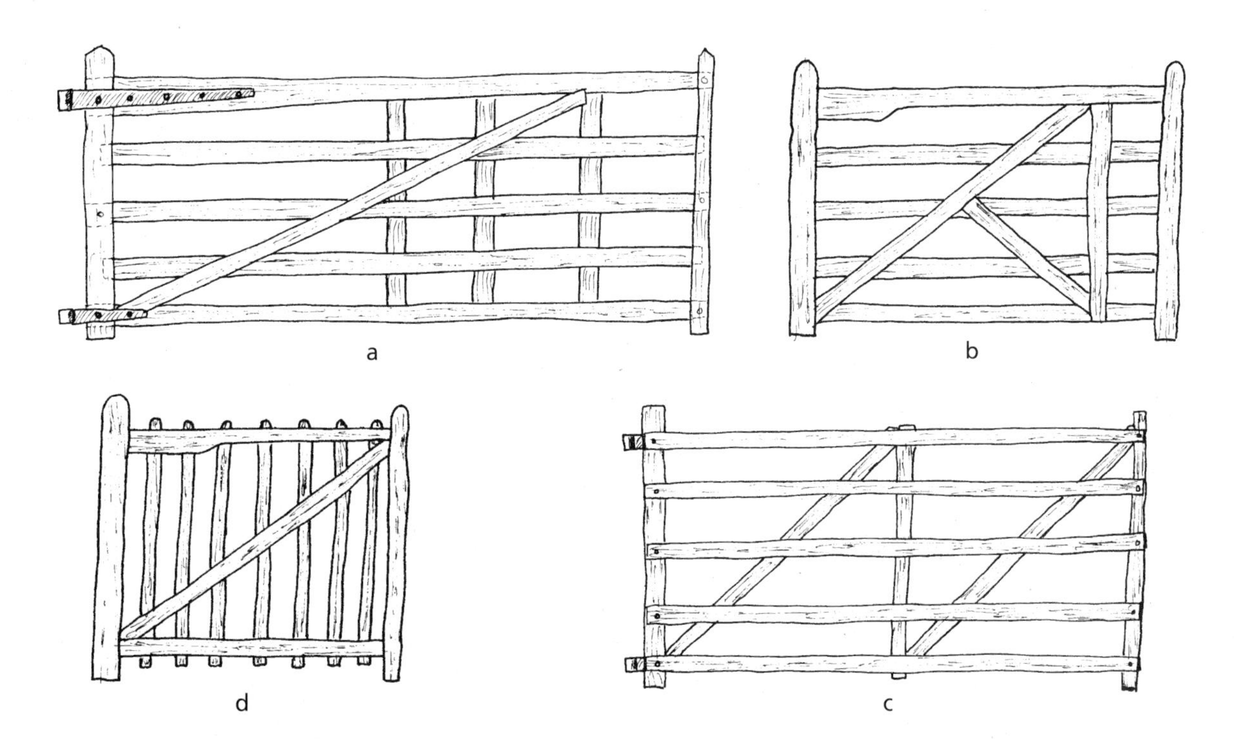

Fig. 13.28 Gates: a. field gate; b. horse gate; c. cleft ash gate; d. cottage gate.

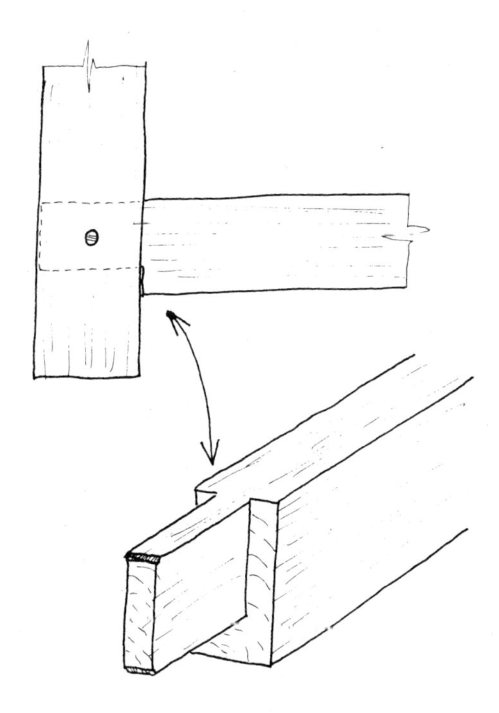

Fig. 13.29 Tenons cut with a shoulder to give more support.

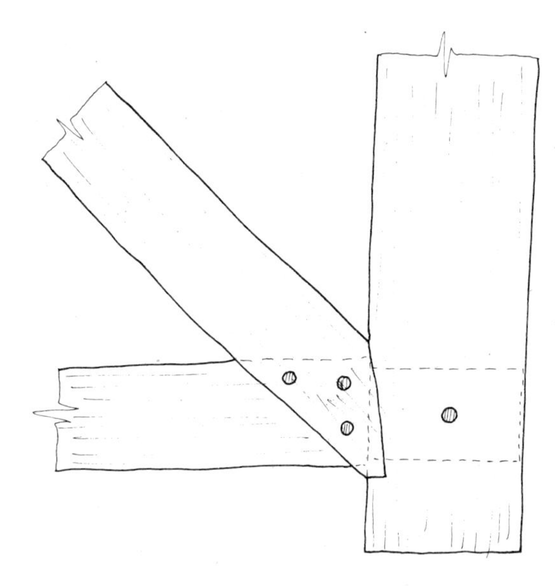

Fig. 13.30 Braces fit into a notch in the harr to give more support.

Materials: Again, oak and chestnut are the best woods for strength and durability. Lighter gates can be made of ash, but really need treating with preservative, particularly in the mortices.

Method:

- After carefully selecting the poles or trunk for each part, cut them to length.
- Rive poles to required sizes, remove bark, knots and rough spears.
- Shave smaller members to the final size/shape required. Remember to taper the top rail.
- Use side axe, adze or draw knife to shape the harr and head. The straighter and truer you can make these, the squarer and stronger your gate will be.
- Mark out and cut the mortices in harr and head.
- Carefully shape the tenons; (you can cut them with a shoulder (**fig. 13.29**) to help stop them dropping). Bore holes in mortices and tenons for the wooden pegs which will hold them. Position these to tighten the joints. (Note: on light gates you can overlap harr, head and rails, drill right through both members, and bold them together, thus avoiding morticing.)
- Cut braces and slats to final size/shape. Braces should locate in a notch in the harr and top rail of a heavy gate (**fig. 13.30**). Peg, bolt or nail all the components together, making sure any curves in the rails both compensate one another thus not twisting the gate and give an even gap between the rails. Clench over any nails. Remember to incorporate hinges when making up if they are integrally bolted with the other members.
- Finally use your drawknife to tidy up the gate; champfered edges not only look good but make a gate nice to handle.

Further reading

BTCV, ***Fencing*** 1997
Edlin, H., ***Woodland Crafts in Britain*** David & Charles, 1973
Lambat, F., ***Tools and Devices for Coppice Crafts***, C.A.T, 1977
Hasluck, P., ***The Handyman's Book*** Senate, 1998
Rose, W., ***The Village Carpenter*** Cambridge, 1937
Seymour, J., ***The Lore of the Land*** Corgi, 1984
Tabor, R., ***Traditional Woodland Crafts*** Batsford, 1994

Chapter 14

Tools and Tent Pegs

Increasing mechanisation of agriculture and horticulture has reduced the demand for wooden tools and tool handles. Demand is no longer sufficient to allow a craftsman to concentrate on making only one type of product, a situation that allowed him to refine his methods to a fine art. Once you have used a wooden hay rake or a besom in anger, you will appreciate how functional and beautifully balanced these tools are.

Besoms

These are the witches broomsticks of fairy stories. They are unbeatable for sweeping leaves off the lawn.

Patterns: A normal besom broom (**fig. 14.1**) is composed of a head (the twiggy bit) and a tail (the handle). They are normally about 1.5m (5ft) long overall, with a 1m (3ft) head and a 1.1m (3ft 6in) handle. The heads can be made to 254 or 305mm (10 or 12in) diameter, bound by two or three bonds or laps.

Besoms without a tail are known as swales. Still used in some steel works for brushing slag from the red-hot metal, they thus produce an extremely pure product.

Tools: Making besoms requires a saw, draw knife, curved shave, side axe, billhook, horse, knife, bond poker and chopping block. A bond poker (**fig. 14.2**) is like a large hollow needle which allows the bond to be poked under itself. You can use a small wooden wedge in its place. A besomer's vice (**fig. 8.16**) may help, and if you use wire, pliers/cutters are essential.

Materials: Heads should be birch twigs less than seven years old; they have the straightness and resilience needed. An alternative is heather gathered before it is too woody and brittle. Tails can be from any reasonably straight poles c.32mm (1¼in) diameter.

Fig. 14.1 A besom broom with ash bonds.

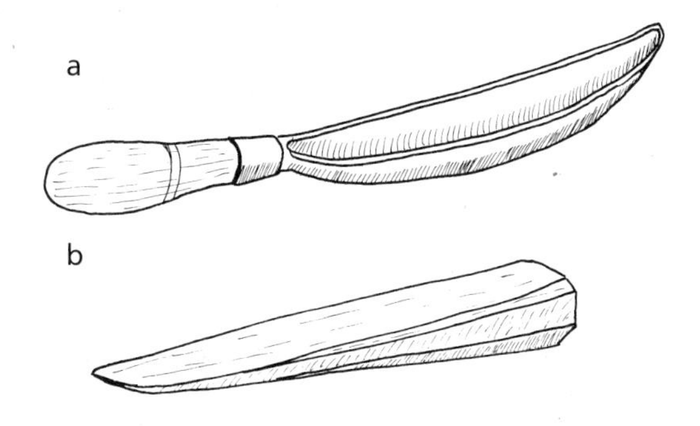

Fig. 14.2 A bond poker (a); alternatively use the small wedge (b) to force a gap between bonds and twigs through which the tail of the bond can be passed.

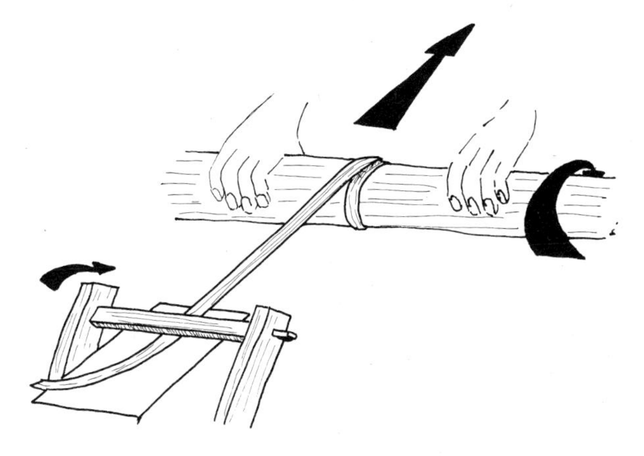

Fig. 14.3 Tightening the bond around the besom head.

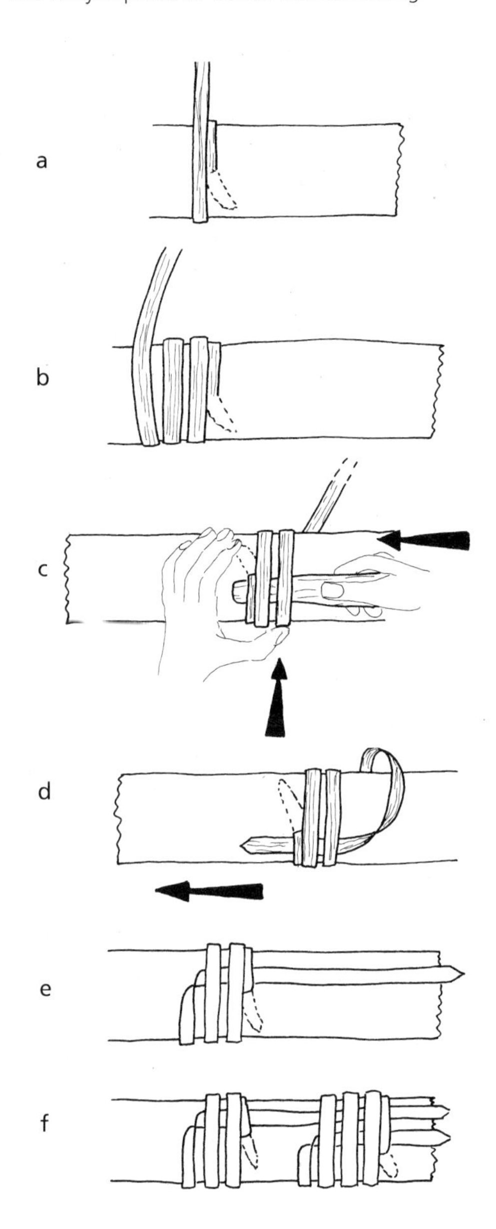

Fig. 14.4 Tying two bonds around the besom head; a. to e. shows the method on the first bond; the same steps are used for the second, to finish as in f.

Bonds are best made from ash or bramble, but hazel, oak and chestnut can be used, or wire for those not wholly into green woodworking!

Method:

- Produce your bonds as described in Chapter 11. These should be made as required and used immediately, before they go brittle. You can also use withe rods (also in Chapter 11).
- Pick the sticks to make the head, putting the longest in the centre. A bundle around which your finger and thumb tips just meet makes a 305mm (12in) head; if the first joint of your thumbs overlap it is a 254mm (10in) head.

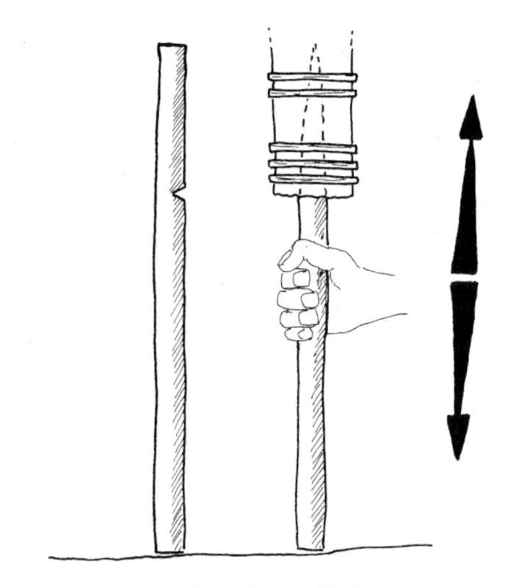

Fig. 14.5 Fitting head to tail: the momentum of the head forces it over the tail. The gauge is on the left.

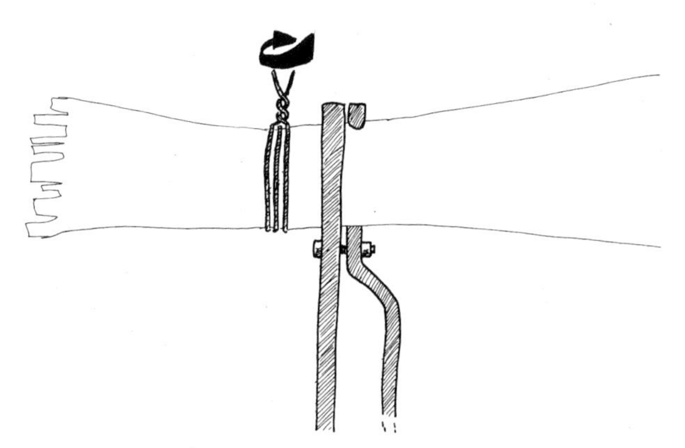

Fig. 14.6 The besomer's vice. The wire tail is bent over when twisted sufficiently.

- Bind the head with two laps. Do this at your horse so that you can use the vice to hold one end of the lap and pull hard on the head to tighten the binding (**fig. 14.3**). For natural bonds use the method shown in **fig. 14.4**, which will give secure bonds that tighten as they season.
- Chop the end of the head square with the axe.
- Cut the tail to length. Using horse, draw knife and curved shave, produce a smooth, shaved handle, gently pointed at one end.
- Force the sharpened end of the tail into the head, and drive it in by banging the tail on a block; the weight of the head will drive it down onto the tail (**fig. 14.5**). Use a gauge so that the tail enters by the correct amount (c.0.5m, 18in).
- Cut a small ash peg, drill a hole between the two laps and into the tail, and then drive in the peg to prevent the tail coming out.

Table 14.1 Patterns of hay rakes

Type	Head Width	Handle length	Number of teeth	Type of teeth	Type of Handle
Hay	710mm (28in)	1.98m (6ft 6in)	15	Wooden	Split
Seed	710mm (28in)	1.98m (6ft 6in)	19	Wooden	Split
Twitch	710mm (28 in)	1.83m (6ft)	12	140mm rose head nails	Split Split
Garden	450mm (18in)	1.52m (5ft)	13	90mm rose head nails	Split
Wire tooth and stay	710mm (28 in)	1.98m (6ft 6in)	12	Steel nail	Unsplit with wire stay
Drag	1.2 to 2.1 m (4ft to 7ft)	1.98m (6ft 6in)	23 per 1.2m	Wooden	Split with wire braces
Bow stay	710mm (28in)	19.8 m (6ft 6in)	12	Wooden	Unsplit with bow stay

Note: A besomer's vice can be used to hold the head tight whilst tying. If you use wire, make three loops around the head before twisting the free ends together (**fig. 14.6**).

Wooden rakes

There are endless variations of rake designed for hay making, preparing seed beds, for general garden work, for weeding or for breaking down rough ground.

Patterns: Some different patterns are shown in the above table (**see also fig. 14.7**).

Tools: To make a basic hay rake you will need a tine cutter to make the teeth, saw, froe and beetle, draw knife and shaving brake, stail engine, brace and bit, head clamp or vice, hammer and mallet. You may also need a pair of tin snips to cut the small tin bands required.

Materials: Heads can be of ash or birch, the teeth must be of ash and the handles or stails are best of ash or sallow.

Method:

- Select straight knot free poles c.38mm (1½in) diameter; steam and straighten if required.
- Cut poles to length, shave them, and then smooth using stail engine or a curved shave.
- Carefully cut along the centre of the last 533mm (21in) of the pole (the device in **fig. 14.8** is superb if you plan to make a lot). Note: For a bow stay rake do not split the handle but use a steamed 13mm (½in) rod passing through the handle into the head as shown.

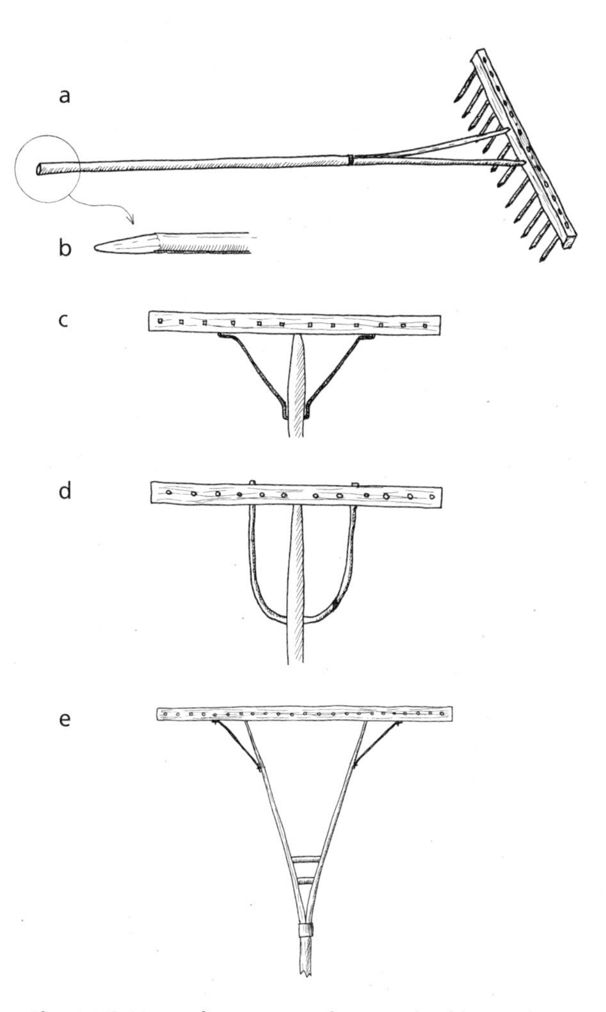

Fig. 14.7 Hay rakes: a. wooden toothed hay rake; b. sharpened end on Dunmow pattern so it can be stood upright in a field; c. nail tooth and stay; d. bow stay; e. drag rake.

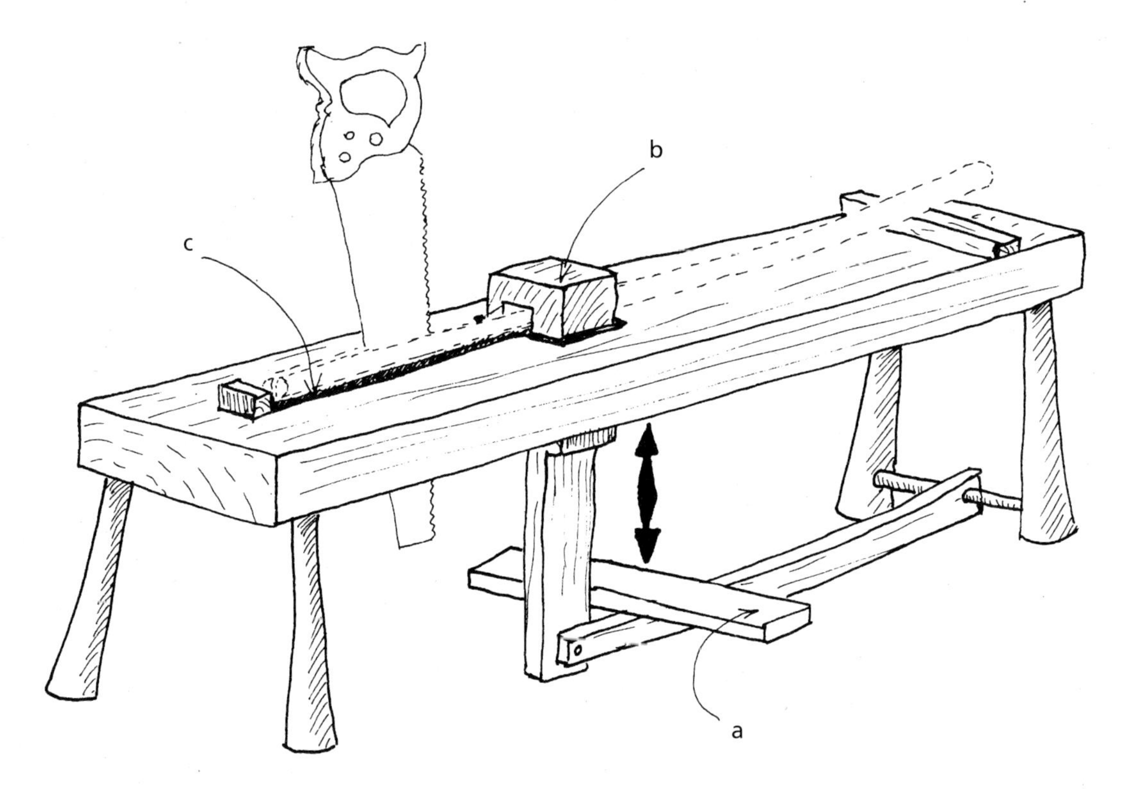

Fig. 14.8 Device for sawing rake handles: pushing on the foot plate (a) closes the vice (b), holding the stail above the sawing aperture (c).

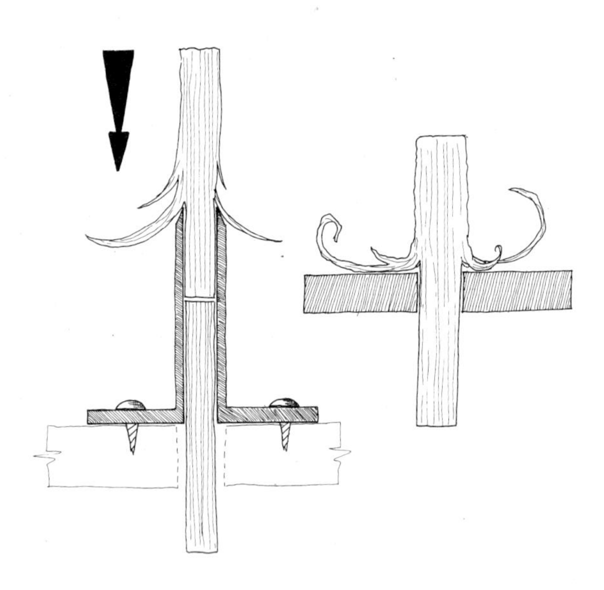

Fig. 14.9 Tine cutters, one using a sharpened tube, the other a flat steel plate. Hit the tine with a mallet to force it through.

- Nail a 19mm (3/4in) wide by 114mm (4 1/2in) long piece of tinplate around the stail at the end of your cut to prevent splitting. Shave the split ends to size c.13mm (1/2in) diameter.
- Split out a quarter cleft from a log, cut to length, and shave to shape for a head.
- Mark teeth positions with a gauge, and drill teeth holes at 90° to face.
- Mark and drill holes for stail in head at 75°.
- Make tines by cutting a log to165mm (6 1/2in), tying it with twine, and then splitting with a froe to make square clefts about 20mm (3/4in) diameter. Bang these clefts through a tine cutter (two forms illustrated in **fig. 14.9**) to make 15mm (9/16in) round teeth. Season tines well before use to avoid them shrinking in their holes.
- Clamp the head in a vice to avoid it splitting and drive teeth into their holes (a little water will help).
- Sharpen teeth with two cuts, using the draw knife, on side away from the handle (**fig. 14.10**).
- Fix the head to the stail with two nails using pre-drilled holes.

Beetles and Mallets

These are ideal when you are hitting wooden objects such as posts, flower stakes, wedges and tent pegs.

Patterns: A typical mallet (**fig. 14.11**) has a head c.101mm (4in) in diameter and 152mm (6in) long which may be round or octagonal. It is usually fitted to a handle c.457mm (18in) long which is tapered so that its wider end tightens in the head without need of a wedge.

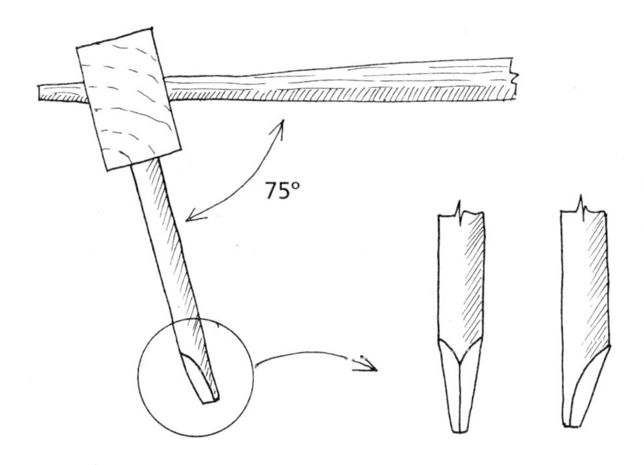

Fig. 14.10 Tines are most easily finished with two cuts of the draw knife. Note also the angle of the head.

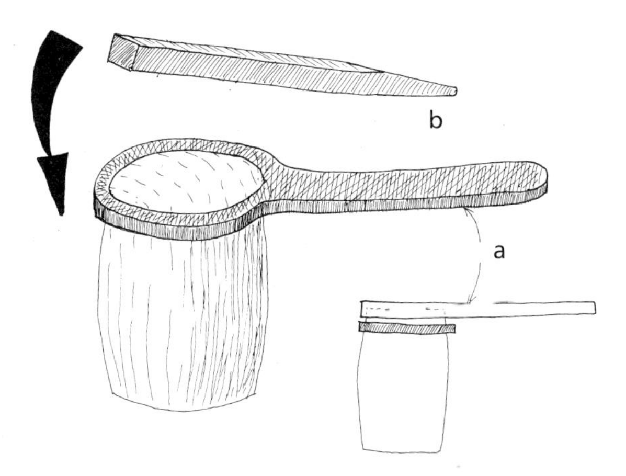

Fig. 14.12 Beetle: rings to prevent the head splitting are heated then forced on with handled ring (a) and heavy bar (b).

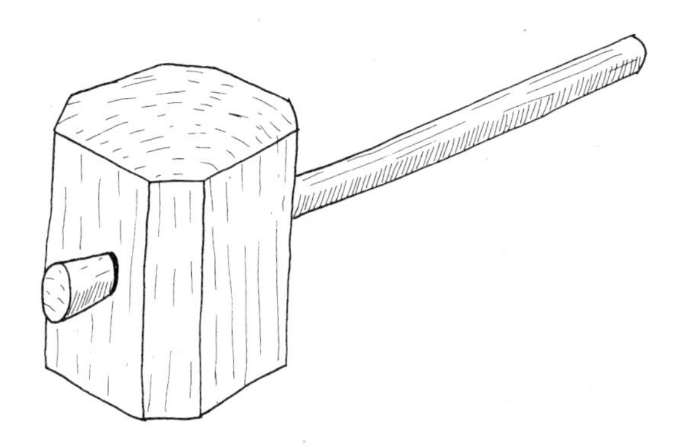

Fig. 14.11 A simple garden mallet.

Beetles are larger; their heads are often 152mm (6in) in diameter, fitted to a 1m (3ft 6in) handle. The heads are round, slightly tapered to each end, and may be fitted with steel rings designed to avoid any splitting.

Tools: Saw, wedges and sledge hammer, side axe, brace and bit, pole lathe or stail engine to make handles and possibly turn the head. A handled ring and heavy bar will be needed to fit rings.

Materials: Beetle and mallet heads are most commonly of elm, but if you can get large enough pieces, apple or pear wood is even better. Handles are best in ash.

Method:

- Split a large log into quarters, then using axe and/or lathe, shape the cleft into a head.
- Drill hole through head for handle c.38mm (1½in) for beetle; c.31mm (1¼in) for mallet.
- Turn or shave selected ash pole to just fit the hole in the head, but leave last 50mm (2in) tapered to be c.6mm (¼in) larger.
- Rings for beetles, if fitted, should be of 25 x 6mm (1in x ¼in) steel, welded into a ring c.3mm (⅛in) larger than the end of the head (remember this tapers so the ring jams very quickly). Heat the ring to as high a temperature as possible in a fire, place it over the head and knock it down using the handled ring and a bar to ensure it goes on straight (**fig. 14.12**).
- Once the ring is c.6mm (¼in) below the end of the head, dowse it in cold water, and drive in two cut nails above the ring.

Staves

There is a steady market for staves, mainly to Morris dancers, in whose hands they enjoy a short life.

Patterns, material and methods: Particular sizes depend on individual customers, but the most popular are 1m(3ft 6in) long at 32mm (1¼in) diameter.

Ash is best, but hazel is quite satisfactory. Maple is unsafe because it fractures too easily.

Select straight lengths, free from major knots, then smooth with a billhook. The bark can be removed with a curved shave if required. Store staves carefully so they do not season too quickly, causing splits along their length.

Tool handles

There is a special pleasure in making the handle for a favourite tool. Well done, it will give pleasure every time you feel its patina in your hand. And there is still a market for good handles.

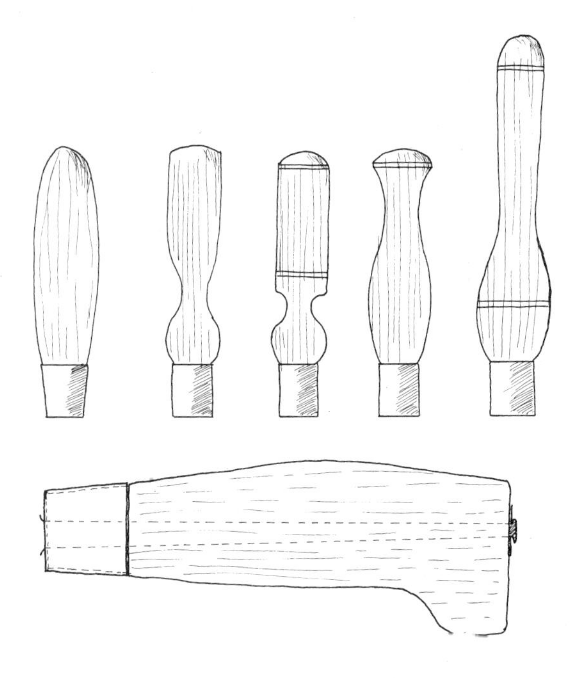

Fig. 14.13 **A range of ferruled handles for chisels, files, etc. The longer handle is for a turning chisel. The billhook handle needs a hole right through it to take the tang.**

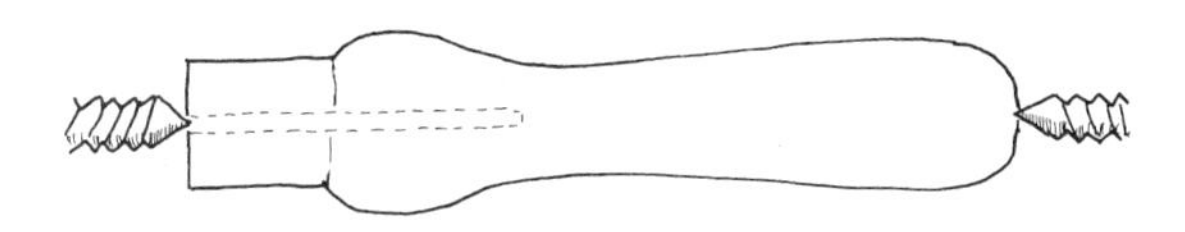

Fig. 14.14 **Drill a guide hole into the workpiece before turning, use it as a centre, then enlarge when the handle is ready for use.**

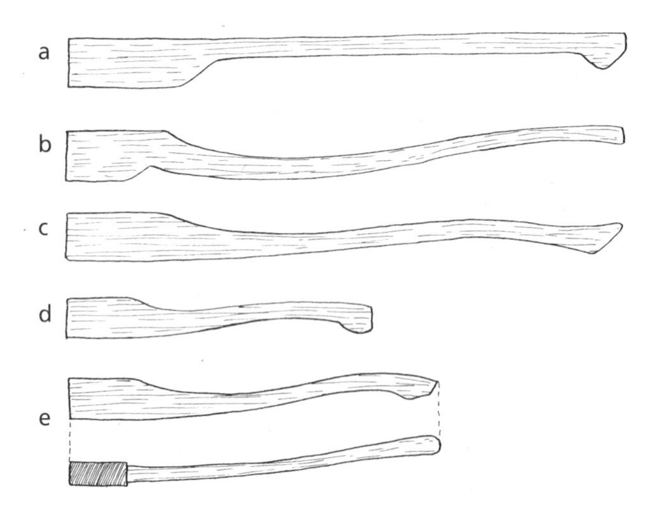

Fig. 14.15 **Axe handles (helves): a. English straight handle; b. Pembrokeshire; c. Fawn foot; d. Side-axe; e. Swayed handle for a hewing axe.**

Turned handles: There are no end of these, used for handling chisels, files, sickles, and even billhooks.

Patterns: Patterns and sizes are almost endless (**fig. 14.13**), but chisel handles can be very plain, whereas sickle and billhook handles must be shaped to offer grip when the tool is swung. Without exception they should have a ferrule.

Tools, materials and methods: Froe, draw knife, lathe, chisels and drill are sufficient.

Ash and beech make good handles; box is best for chisels since its hardness resists the mallet. Ferrules you can buy, but if you are not fussy, use copper pipe.

Shave a cleft already cut to length so it is easy to turn. Drill a small hole into one end for c.50mm (2in): this will act as one centre, and the pilot for the final hole for the tang. Now turn your handle, leaving the ferrule portion oversize. Let the handle season well. Then turn the ferrule section to size and knock on a hot ferrule that will shrink tight into place. Finally, using the hole you first drilled as a guide, drill the final hole for the tool tang (**fig. 14.14**).

Cleft handles: The subtle patterns of axe or billhook handles cannot be make on a lathe; their strength and functional beauty rely on hand shaping cleft wood.

Patterns: Axe handles vary by county, country and the tool they are to fit; a few examples are described in Table **14.2** and **fig. 14.15**.

Tools: Saw, froe and beetle, side axe, draw knife, centre grip and spoke shave are needed.

Materials: Use only ash for axes; ash, beech or willow for billhooks.

Method:

- Cut a suitable log to length and split out a sufficiently large knot free cleft (**fig. 14.16**).
- Mark your pattern onto the cleft, and trim it roughly with axe or draw knife (**fig. 14.17**).
- Fix the cleft in the centre grip and produce the final shape with a draw knife, rotating the cleft as required. Finally use a spoke shave to obtain a fine finish. Always cut with the grain.

Scythe snaiths

I really thought green woodworkers had lost the battle when, last year, I found aluminium snaiths in my local hardware shop! If you want the real thing (**fig. 14.18**), here's how to do it.

Tools, materials and method: You will need saw, steamer, setting frame and curved shave. Use ash or sallow wood.

Table 14.2 Patterns for axe and billhook handles

Style of handle	Length	Features
English felling	900mm(3ft)	Straight with caulked end
US fawn foot - felling	900mm(3ft)	Fawn foot pattern
US fawn foot - snedding	760mm(30in)	Fawn foot pattern
Side axe	350mm(14in)	Slight curve, caulked end
Hewing axe	760mm(30in)	Curved, caulked and swayed
Pembrokeshire	830mm(33in)	Curved – no caulking
Billhook	140mm(5.5in)	Caulked with ferrule

After selecting your pole and cutting it to length, steam it for 1.5-2 hours. Then whilst hot, wedge it into the frame (Chapter 8 and Appendix 1); leave it for a week to set. After removal from the jig use the curved shave to remove all bark and obtain a smooth finish.

Turn the nibs (small handles) on the pole lathe. The metal work required is shown in **fig. 14.19**; you will need a friendly blacksmith to fashion this.

Stable and hay forks

An ever-increasing horse population should generate a steady market for stable forks. Wooden hay forks are traditional in the US, being elegant as well as effective.

Patterns: Stable forks are 1.2 to 1.5m (4-5ft) long with two curved tines held apart by a small triangle of wood (**fig. 14.20**). Hay forks have anything between two and five curved tines, held apart part way down their length by a dowel.

Tools: Saw, froe, draw knife, drill, steamer, setting jig, hammer and curved shave.

Materials: Use ash for its resilience and good bending performance.

Method:

- For a stable fork, cut pole to length then rind and smooth it.
- Cut along centre from end for c.510mm (20in), and nail a tin strip around shaft (as for hay rake).
- Steam or soak head in hot water. Whilst hot, separate tines, nail a 'V' of wood in place to keep them splayed, then fit into jig to give a curve if required. Leave one week to set.
- For hay fork split out a cleft large enough for the number of tines required, and using draw knife and shave shape the handle and head.
- Cut into the head end to create the tines. Drill a hole and pass a rivet through to prevent splitting and two holes for the dowels (**see fig. 14.20**).

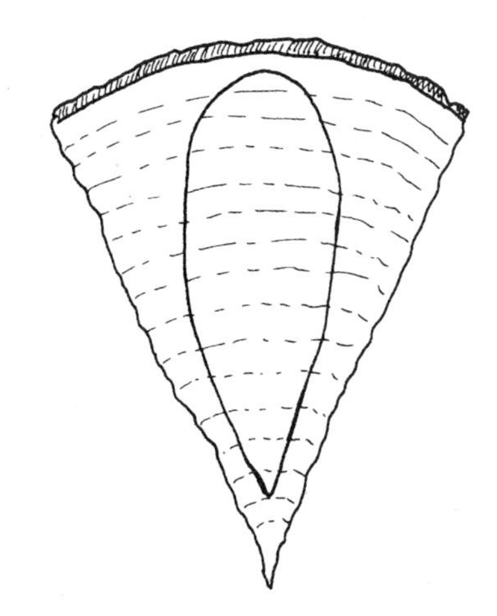

Fig. 14.16 Use a cleft large enough to make a handle.

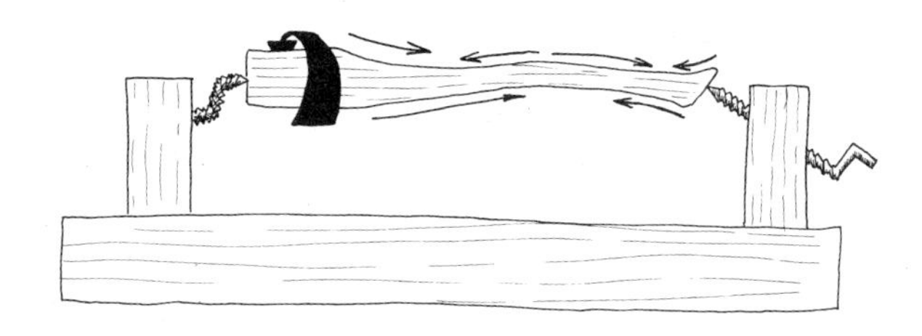

Fig. 14.17 Shaping an axe handle on a centre grip; always cut with the grain.

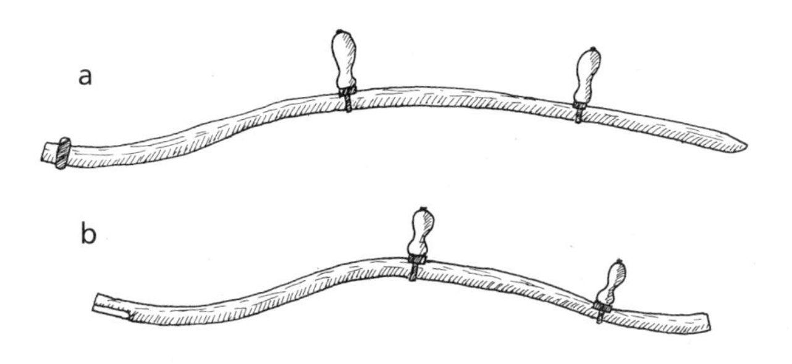

Fig. 14.18 Scythe snaiths: a. English pattern; b. American pattern.

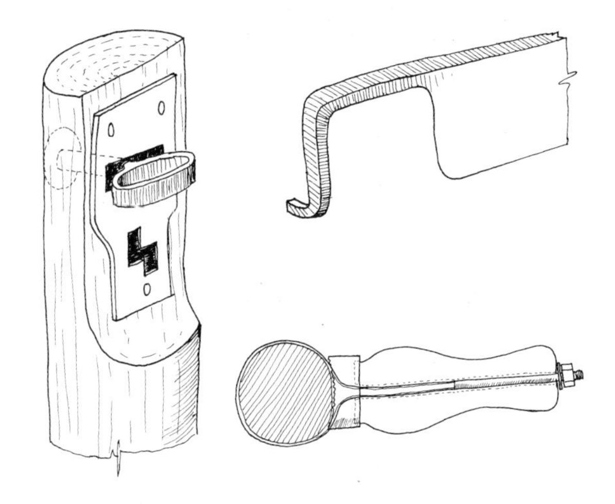

Fig. 14.19 The metal fixings required to hold a modern blade and the nibs (small handles) to the snaith.

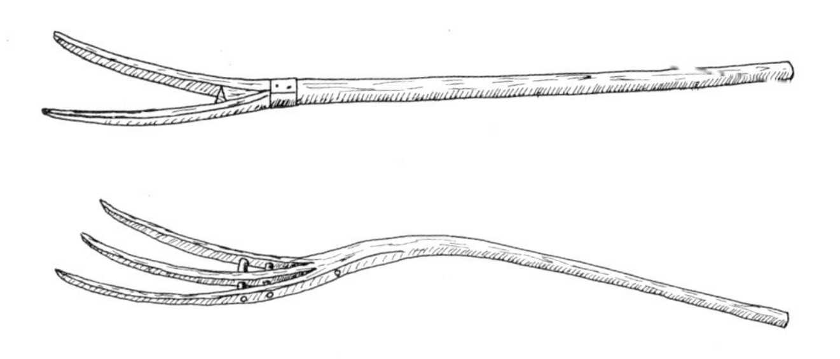

Fig. 14.20 A stable fork and a three tine hay fork.

- Soak or steam head, and whilst warm force tines apart with small wedges and drive the two dowels into place and pin them to the tines with small nails. Finish shaping tines.
- Soak or steam head again and put into jig (**fig. 8.22**). Leave for 1-2 weeks to set, then smooth off any rough points.

Tent pegs

Fortunately no metal peg grips quite as well as a good wooden one, so scouts and marquee owners still use them.

Pattern: The key elements to a proper peg are good champfers to avoid splitting or fraying the rope; a square point that will not turn and smooth curves so it will drive easily. Lengths vary from 229 to 457mm (9-18in).

Tools: Saw, froe and beetle, draw knife and shaving horse (or stock knife).

Materials: Ash and beech are best, but you can use chestnut.

Method:

- Cut suitable knot free logs to required length and rive into clefts c.19mm (3/4in) thick.

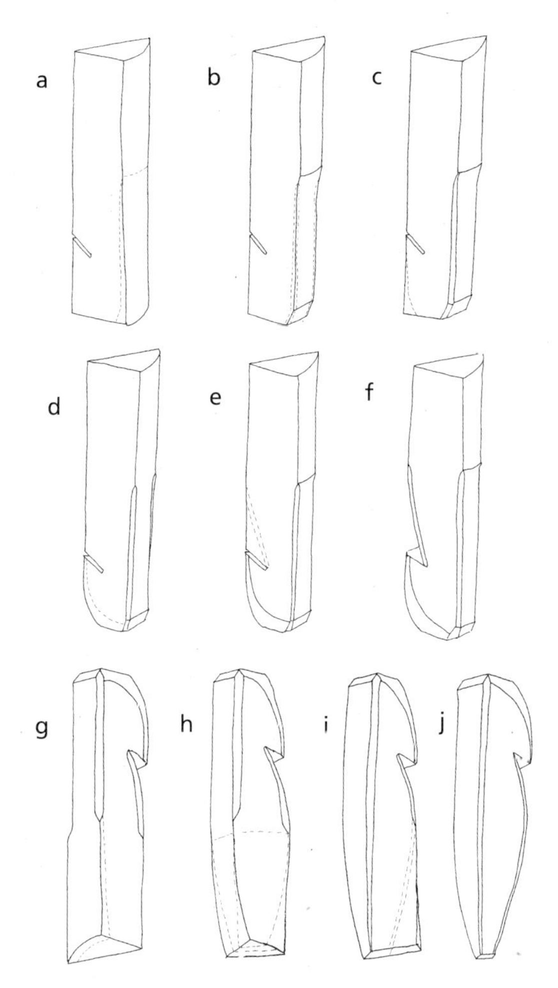

Fig. 14.21 Tent pegs: a. shape half the back; b. chamfer edges; c. shape top; d. chamfer top edges; e. and f. cut and chamfer notch; g. shape second half of back; h. bring in sides to a square point and chamfer; i. shape front edge to curve to a small square point and chamfer; j. finished peg.

- Make an angled saw cut in the cleft app.20% of length in from one end.
- I am told a good man with a stock knife can finish the peg with 18 cuts. I find it easier to using a draw knife on the shaving horse. The key steps are shown in **fig. 14.21**. Always cut with the grain.
- Cross stack pegs to season.

Further reading:

Edlin, H. ***Woodland Crafts in Britain*** David & Charles, 1973
Langsner, D. ***Country Woodcraft*** Rodale Press, 1978
Smedley, N. ***East Anglian Crafts*** Batsford, 1977
Tabor, R. ***Traditional Woodland Crafts*** Batsford, 1994
Underhill, R. ***The Woodwright's Shop*** University of North Carolina Press, 1981

Chapter 15

Turnery and Treen

Small products in wood

In this chapter we shall look at a range of products, some of which you can make on a lathe, some by simple shaping. It is an area where you really can invent your own products and stamp them with your individual style.

For centuries most implements, toys and kitchen utensils were made of wood. Indeed treen, which literally means 'make of wood', is a word from our Saxon past. It is sad that so many items today are plastic, but there is a market for novel and high quality products – and what is more satisfying than using the products yourself.

I shall not describe in detail how to make each product, but rather cover the general principles, how to form particular shapes, and then describe a range of products that will provide some ideas.

Some general principles

Before you start making turnery products, just consider the following – it may avoid some disappointment.

Tools and skills: To make most of these products you need a pole or treadle lathe and suitable chisels. Finer work will require smaller chisels and vice versa. You can make everything described here with:

- A 32mm (1¼in) roughing-out gouge.
- A 6 or 12mm (¼in or ½in) gouge.
- A 25mm (1in) and 13mm (½in) skew chisel.
- A 50mm (2in) firmer chisel (optional – the wider skew chisel will do).
- A parting tool (only essential for the treadle lathe).
- Appropriate drills.
- A draw knife and spoke shave for shaping wood.

Practice the key skills described in Chapter 11, and also the guide to turning different shapes later in this Chapter.

Choice of wood: Choose the right wood for the job. For products that will come into contact with food choose close grained non-tainting woods: sycamore, maple, cherry and beech are best. Yew is ideal for paper knives or items where constant flexing is needed. Attractive grain or colour such as elm, black hearted ash, or spalted beech are ideal for decorative work. Chapter 2 has more on each species.

Design: Work out the size and design of your piece before you start cutting. Once you have produced a basic cylinder, mark the position of the key shapes on it in pencil to give you points to work to. If I produce a particularly elegant piece (not very often!), I keep a pattern of it so I can repeat it.

On the lathe: It is generally better to keep the heavier end of the workpiece at the head stock end of the treadle lathe, and remember to allow extra wood at this end to part off the workpiece. This does not apply to the pole lathe.

Long thin items such as spindles may need support along their length to prevent flexing during turning (see Chapter 10 for how to do this).

Finishing: All turnery is best burnished with a handful of shavings whilst still on the lathe. This imparts a lovely patina which you can enhance with other materials later.

Final finishing with wax, oil or varnish will depend on the item and its intended use. Kitchen items are best treated with oil, such as walnut. Where possible dunk the item in hot oil to expel

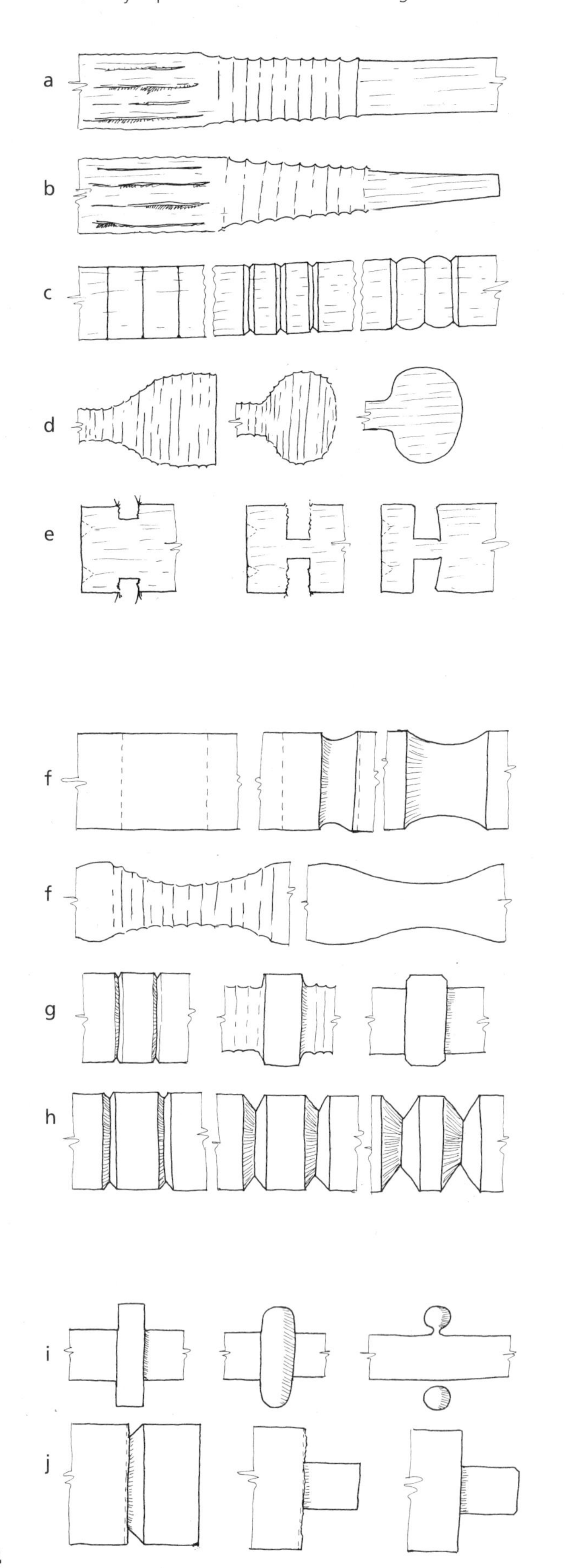

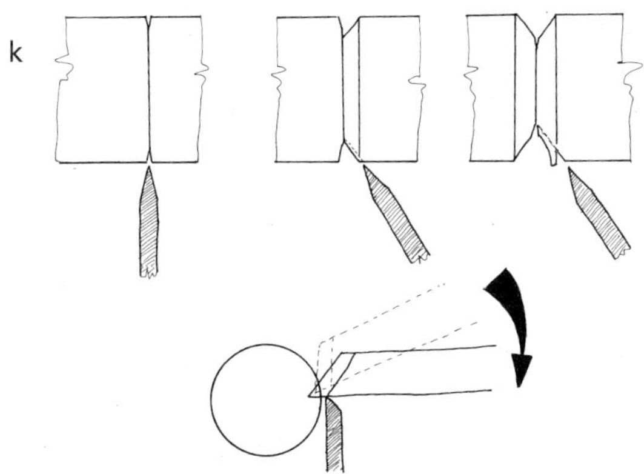

Fig. 15.1 Basic turnery shapes: a. cylinder; b. taper or cone; c. beads; d. knob; e. parting and square ends; f. hollow or cove; g. raised bead; h. 'V' cut or deep groove; i. free ring; j. rebate with square shoulders; k. making a deep 'V' cut.

some of the air in the wood. Warn your customers in case of allergy. For many items a coating of beeswax gives sufficient protection – it is best applied and polished whilst your piece is still on the lathe. Varnish will give a very high gloss and provide water resistance. These finishes are best applied after the piece has been seasoned. Seasoning should be a slow process to avoid drying cracks.

Making shapes

Figure 15.1 (a-k) illustrates a range of shapes you may use. For repetitive pieces like legs, accurate spacing will be very important visually. The tools required and guideline methods are as follows:

Perfect cylinder: Use the large roughing-out gouge to get to size, then achieve final finish with large skew chisel or firmer chisel. Try to move the chisel steadily and continuously a long the workpiece. Test your result with a straight edge.

Taper: Size and produce shape using large roughing-out gouge, then smooth using large skew or firmer chisel. Always cut 'downhill', with the grain.

Beads: First mark out the beads on the already smoothed workpiece. Cut the beads with skew chisel as described in Chapter 11. Use the larger skew chisel if your workpiece is greater than 380mm (1½in) diameter.

Knob: To make a ball shaped knob at the end of a piece, use a small gouge to achieve the shape required. Roll it down each side of the knob from the top. Follow this with the small skew chisel to produce a smooth finish. Use the heel of the blade, but be very careful as the chisel becomes more vertical for it will tend to dig in.

Parting and square ends: On the treadle lathe it is necessary to use the parting tool at the chuck end to mark/make the end of the product. This is described in Chapter 11. The parting tool leaves a poor surface, which should be smoothed by using the toe of a skew chisel. If the item you are making is to stand on this base, create a very slight hollow by twisting the parting tool.

Hollows or coves: Mark the extent of each hollow on an already smoothed piece. Use a 12.7 or 19mm (1/2in or 3/4in) gouge to make the hollow using the method described in Chapter 11. A hollow with one vertical side is made by using the gouge repeatedly from one side to make the curve and then using the toe of the skew chisel to smooth the vertical side.

Shape long, shallow hollows by cutting with the gouge from each side, with the grain. Finish the slopes with the skew chisel, but use the gouge for the bottom of the hollow.

Raised beads: These can be square, although are more normally rounded. Mark their position and use the toe of the skew chisel to make deep cuts at the edges of the bead. Use the same tool or the gouge to remove the waste wood from either side, leaving it smooth. Again, use the skew chisel to smooth the side of the bead and shape it as required.

Free ring: To make a free ring, as used in a rattle, make a raised bead with a rounded top as described above. Then use the toe of the skew chisel to slowly undercut from each side, rather as you would when flattening and slightly concaving a base. When the two cuts meet the ring will come free. Any ridge left by the ring can be smoothed using the skew chisel. Friction between the inside of the ring and the remainder of the piece will smooth the former.

Vee cut: Small vee cuts for decorative purposes can be easily make with the skew chisel. Use its toe to make a cut at the centre point for the vee, then twist the chisel a small amount either way to make a small vee. For a larger vee make a deep central cut with the toe of the skew. Then cut in towards this at an angle from each side. Lever down on the handle to force the toe of the blade through the wood and keep the bevel on the cut face. Repeat until the vee is the size you require.

Rebate with square shoulders: This may be required where a rebate is needed to fit into a hole to join two pieces together such as a candlestick into a base. Mark the point of the shoulder, and score with the toe of the skew chisel. Use the skew or gouge to remove waste from the rebate up to the scored cut. Repeat until the required size is reached. Remember on the vertical surfaces to use the toe of the chisel to avoid digging in. Another way may be to use the parting tool to produce the shoulder, but the surfaces will need to be cleaned up with the skew chisel.

A range of products

There are literally hundreds of different small products you could make. In this section I shall briefly describe some to show the scope that is available. Each one is illustrated.

Small turnery

***Garden dibbers* (fig. 15.2)**: These are ideal to start with, requiring only a turned handle and a conical section to make the hole for the seed. They come in various sizes, and are best with 25mm (1in) markings on the conical section.

***Gardener's line* (fig 15.3)**: Make these very similar to a dibber, but in place of the handle turn an even section around which a cord or line can be wound.

***Bag carriers* (fig. 15.4)**: Extremely simple to make, these carriers or handles for plastic carrier bags consist simply of a fist long smooth cylinder with a notch at each end into which locate the cut-out handles of the carrier bag – a real finger saver.

***Door wedges* (fig. 15.5)**: More effective than door stops, these comprise a wedge with a turned handle at one end. Turn the handle first, then shave and champfer the wedge from the remaining part of the billet. These can be made to any size.

***Paper knives* (fig. 15.6)**: Turn as attractive a handle as you can for these, doing the turning before shaping the blade. The blade should have a point suitable to get into the end of an envelope, thin enough – 2-3mm (1/16-1/8in) – at the back and tapering to a cutting edge.

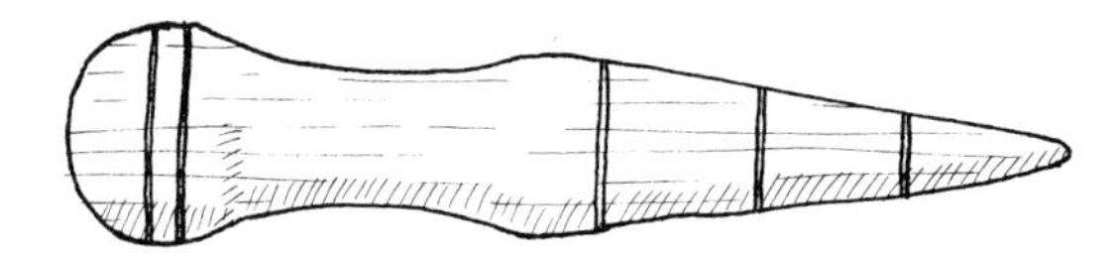

Fig. 15.2 Garden dibber, marked in inches.

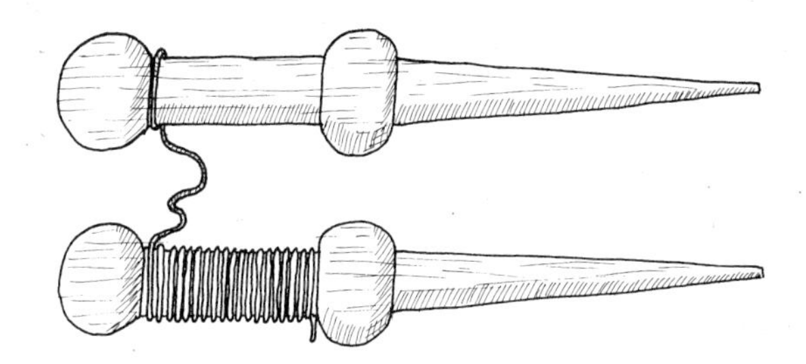

Fig. 15.3 A gardener's line.

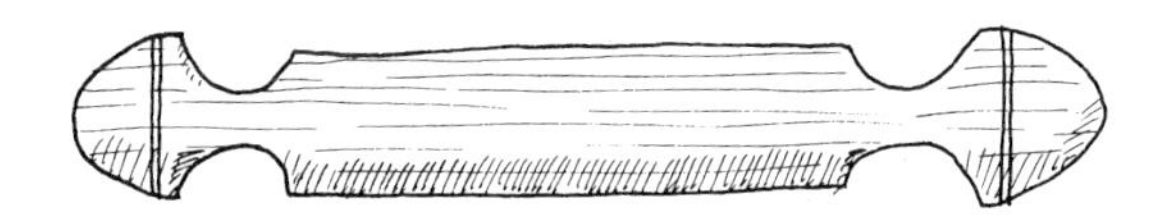

Fig. 15.4 Bag carriers.

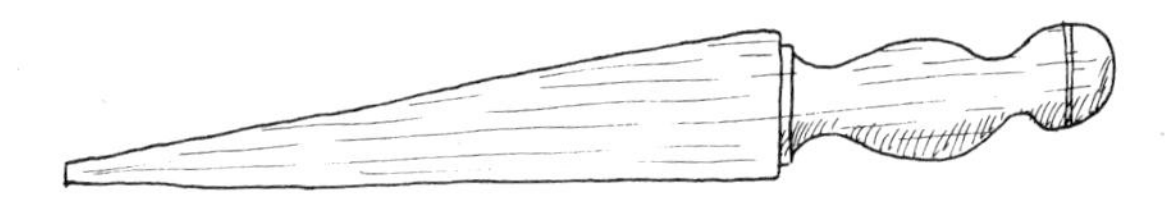

Fig. 15.5 Door wedge.

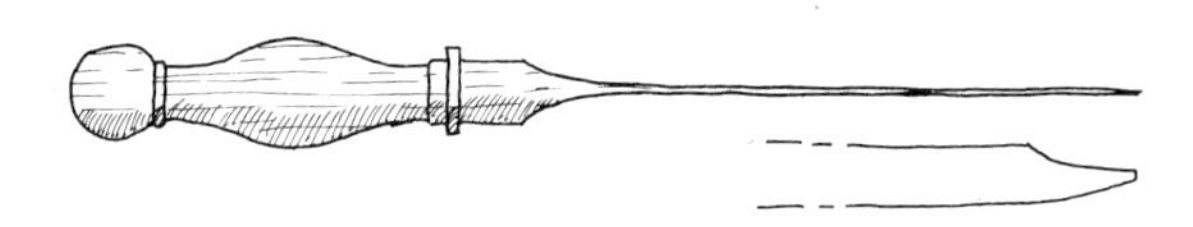

Fig. 15.6 Paper knife; note how to shape the end.

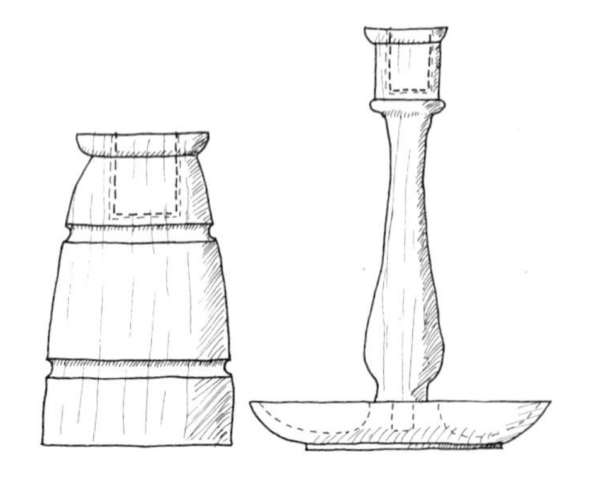

Fig. 15.7 Candle sticks: the heavy dotted line is the metal liner. The second stick is made in two parts.

***Candlesticks* (fig. 15.7)**: One-piece candlesticks need to have sufficient weight and width at the base to make them stable and a sufficient rim to catch most of the wax. Two piece candlesticks need a rebate at the bottom of the stem to fit into the base. Before turning the blank remember to drill a pilot hole in it which you should use as the tail stock centre and later enlarge to hold the candle. Line this candle hole with copper pipe and a suitable diameter coin in the base.

***Night light holders* (fig. 15.8)**: These are very simple, but are special if you can use attractive wood. You can either turn them, or make a suitable hole in an attractive shaped piece of wood. The hole does not need lining.

***Light pulls* (fig. 15.9)**: You can make several of these from one billet and then separate them. Make a pilot hole before turning the wood, and finally drill a short, but larger diameter hole in the bottom to hide the knot at the end of the string.

***Foot rests/massagers* (fig. 15.10)**: These consist of a roller shaped into a continuous, slightly concave, series of beads c.31mm (1¼in) diameter that can be rolled under the foot. A more complete version incorporates three of these rollers fixed into a wooden frame so they can rotate freely. Make a smooth concave roller first, cut a series of vees, then round off the edges.

***Mushrooms* (fig. 15.11)**: These are a good use for small branch wood with the bark left on, and they should be turned to retain some of this bark. The long 'lawyers wig' pattern is shown. Use seasoned wood, cutting off 76mm (3in) from the end to avoid splits already formed in the wood. After turning do not dry too quickly, and varnish soon.

***Clothes pegs* (fig. 15.12)**: Turn these first on the lathe, making a smooth cylinder with a knob at the end. Then make the cut to produce two jaws. These must be shaved with a knife to open a mouth and be rounded so as not to split.

Needle holders/lidded pots: These can only be made on a treadle lathe, only if you have a chuck to hold a drill bit and lastly only if you have seasoned, close grained wood. See basic steps in (**fig. 15.13**).

Toys

Rattle: Traditional rattles require the turning of two or three tree rings trapped by the handle at one end and a knob at the other. Turn the handle first, the rings as shown in **fig. 15.14**, and finish off with the knob. Rattles are frustrating, but a good test of your burgeoning skill and confidence.

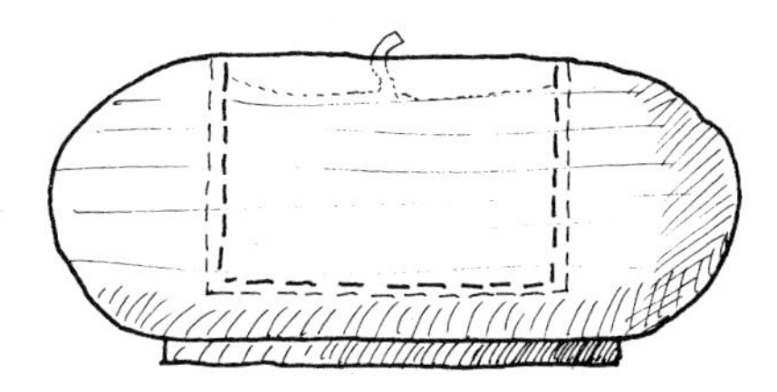

Fig. 15.8 A night light holder.

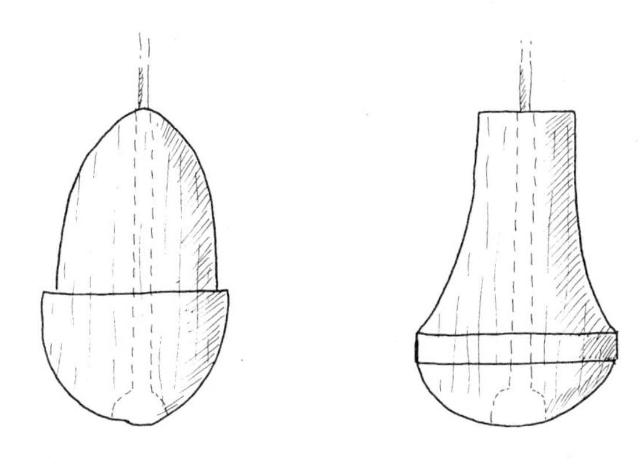

Fig. 15.9 Light pulls. Allow a larger hole at the bottom to hide the knot.

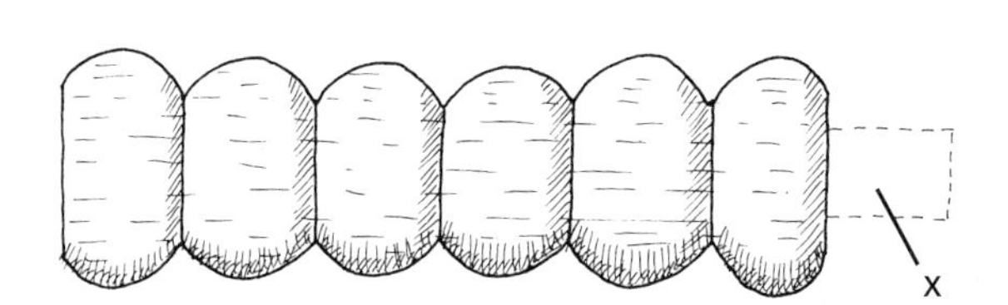

Fig. 15.10 Foot rest/massager. A spigot (x) can be made at either end to fit into a wooden frame.

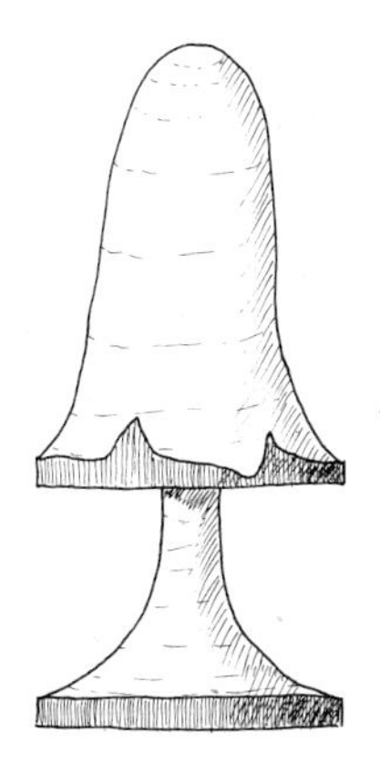

Fig. 15.11 Mushroom shapes: usually made from round wood. This example is a 'Lawyer's Wig' pattern.

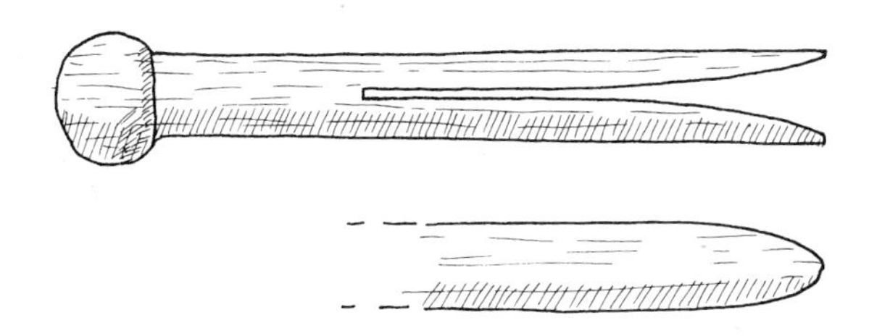

Fig. 15.12 One piece wooden clothes peg.

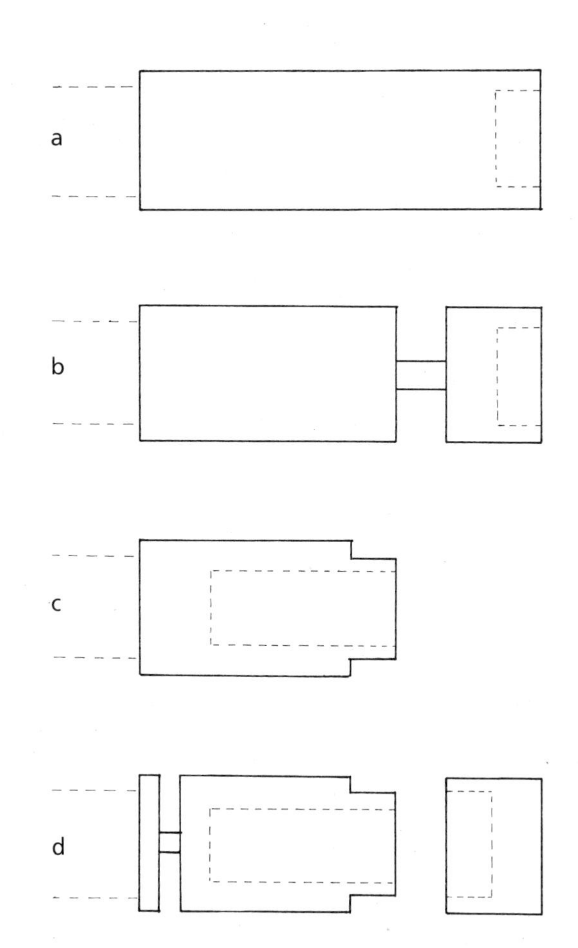

Fig. 15.13 Making a lidded pot: a. turn the recess in the lid; b. part the lid from the body; c. hollow the body and turn a rebate that the lid will fit; d. part off the base of the body.

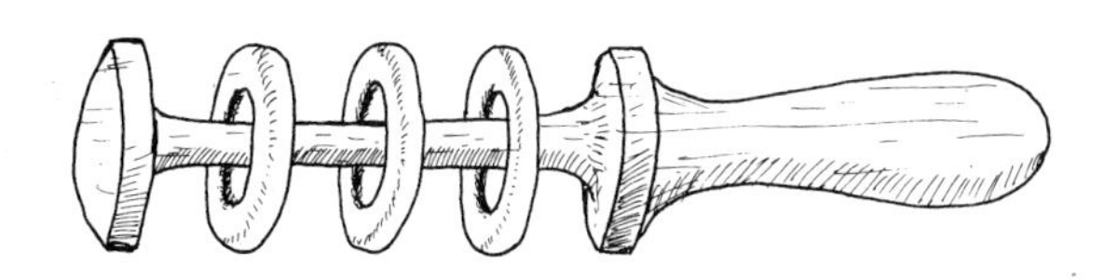

Fig. 15.14 A traditional rattle.

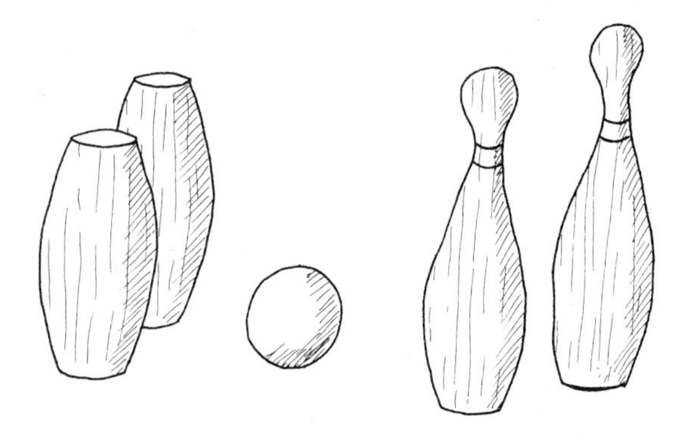

Fig. 15.15 Two patterns of skittles and a wooden ball.

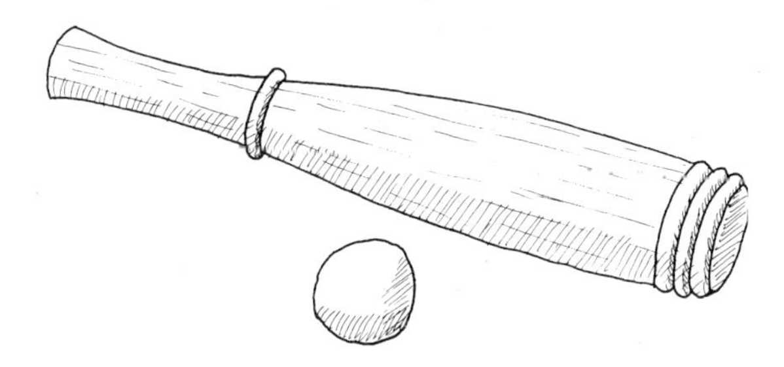

Fig. 15.16 Bat and ball.

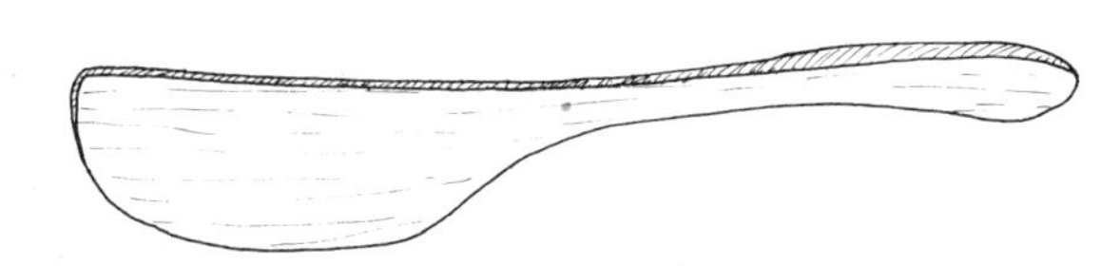

Fig. 15.17 Pot scraper.

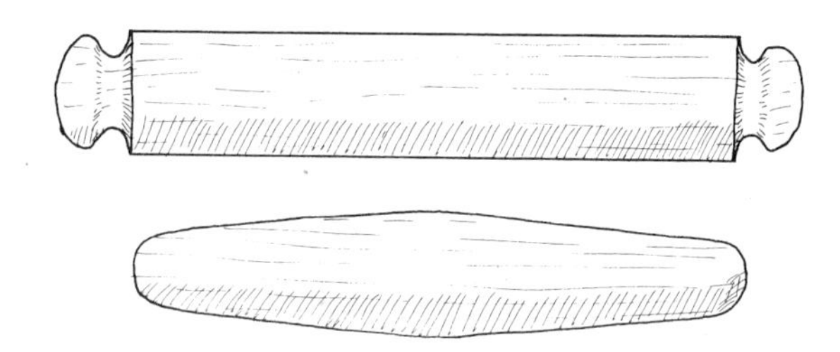

Fig. 15.18 Two patterns of rolling pin.

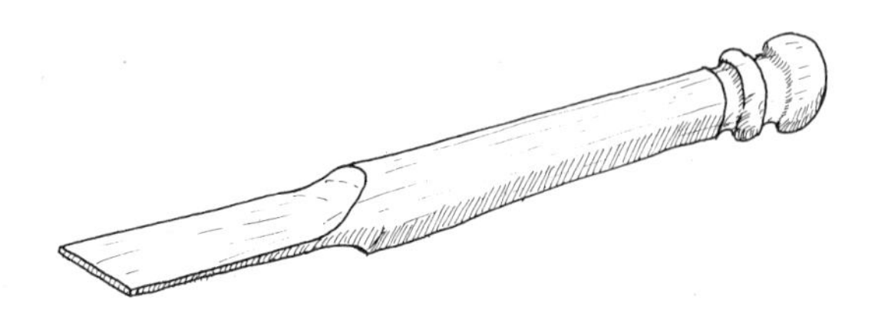

Fig. 15.19 A mustard 'spoon'.

Skittles **(fig. 15.15)**: These can be bottle shaped or the more traditional oval shape, and in a variety of sizes. Oak, apple and elm are the best woods to use since they will split less. The pieces should be well seasoned after turning and before final use.

Bat and ball **(fig. 15.16)**: Turn a simple rounders bat that tapers towards the handle, and provide a knob or swelling at the end of the handle so that it does not fly out of the users hand. Turn a round ball to go with it.

Stick and bat game: For this produce a bat similar to that described above. The stick should be c.152mm (6in) long and tapered from the centre towards each end. The idea is bang on the end of the stick whilst it is on the floor to flip it into the air; as it comes down the player must hit it with the bat as far as he can. Greatest distance wins.

Kitchen products

Pot scraper **(fig. 15.17)**: This should be make from a tangential cleft from quite a large log. Carefully shave and cut the wood to the desired shape and thickness c.3mm (1/8in). Finish off with 180 grade garnet paper and treat with oil.

Rolling pin **(fig. 15.18)**: This may seem simple, but it does require concentration and care to make an even pin. Round straight pins are most popular. When smoothing the surface try to run steadily and continuously with the skew chisel to avoid the ridges created by stopping and starting.

Mustard spoon **(fig. 15.19)**: As you can see, this is more spatula than spoon, having a flat working surface rather than a bowl. Produce this as you would a paper knife – turn the handle first, then smooth the end to shape.

Spurtle **(fig. 15.20)**: This is the Scottish tool for stirring porridge – and it works. About 308mm (12in) is a good length. Make the short handle attractive but simple, and make a blunt point at the business end.

Kitchen roll holder **(fig. 15.21)**: Make a turned stem with a nice knob or shape at the top that will protrude beyond the roll. Rebate this into a base which can be round or square, but must be at least the same diameter as the full roll. This is a great project for young pole lathers wanting to make something for mum.

Egg cups **(fig. 15.22)**: These are really very small bowls. Leave enough wood for the pole lathe cord to run on, and then shape the outside. Hollow out the inside using a small gouge or hook, leaving a central pillar of wood to run on the centre; finally

Fig. 15.20 A spurtle.

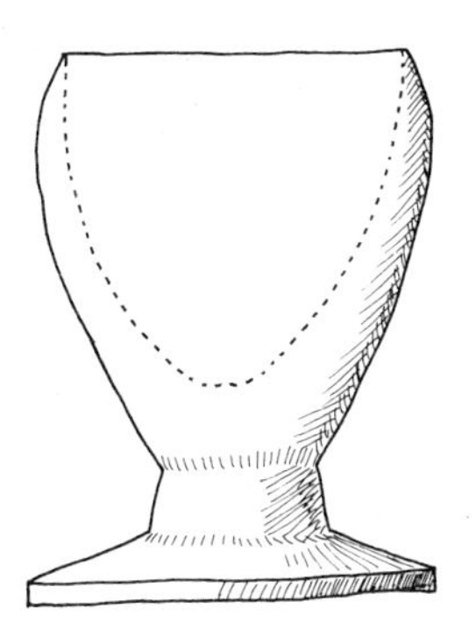

Fig. 15.22 Egg cup.

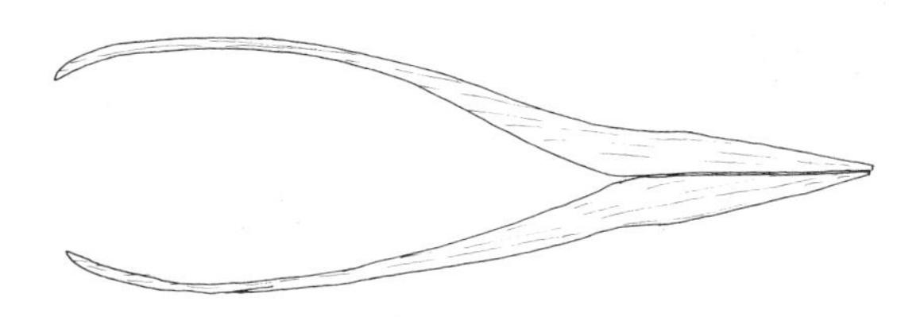

Fig. 15.23 Salad tongs; the jaws need only be 25mm(1in) wide.

cut this out and clean up the inside of the bowl. On the treadle lathe just fix the workpiece to a face plate.

Salad tongs **(fig. 15.23)**: These make a change from the usual spoon and fork. Cut and shape two identical halves as shown, preferably in yew which has the ability to bend, bend and bend again. Carefully glue the two halves together and finish with garnet paper and oil.

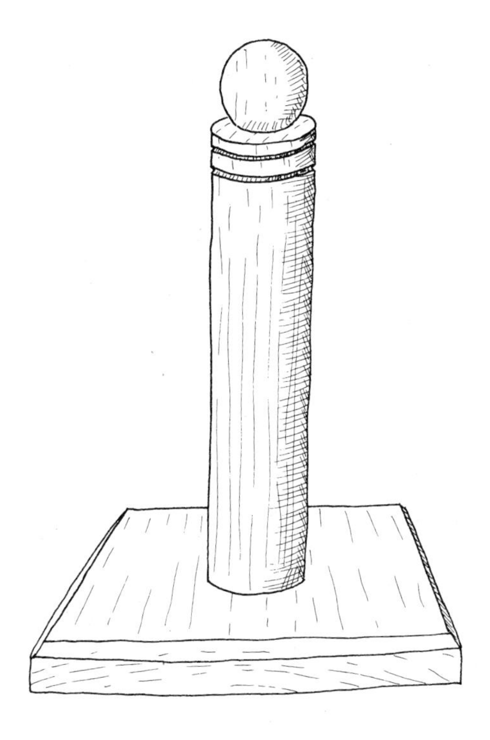

Fig. 15.21 Kitchen roll holder.

Bowls and platters: These can be made to various sizes and some variation in form. You will need a hooked knife to do a good job of turning these. This knife leaves a faintly ribbed surface that I think adds to the charm of the piece. The basic methods are described in Chapter 11, but work at it, for to master these products will provide untold satisfaction.

Further reading:

Abbott, M., ***Green Woodwork***,
Guild of Master Craftsmen Publications 1989
Underwood, F. and Warr, G., ***Beginners Guide to Wood Turning***, Newnes 1981

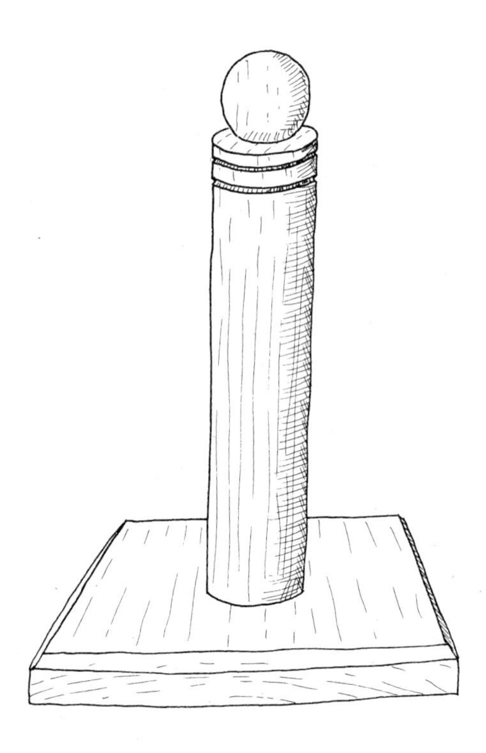

Chapter 16

Benches, Chairs and Stools

To many green wood workers making furniture is their ultimate aim. To sit on a chair fashioned with your own hands from a tree is a unique experience. If you have mastered the skills of green woodworking making basic furniture is within your grasp.

You can make chairs, tables, stools, screens, planters, magazine racks, plate stands, etc. The design you use is limited only by your imagination and ingenuity. I shall briefly describe the basics, but the books listed at the end of this chapter contain more detail.

Rustic twig and stick furniture

This furniture style has a long history. It was made by native Americans, and is described in 18th Century furniture catalogues. Although it declined after the 19th Century twig furniture is currently enjoying a revival.

Patterns: Twig and stick furniture is made of round wood. This can be used as straight poles or sticks to produce a formal design, or as branched, curved or woven rods to produce a very individual appearance.

Twig furniture has simple butt, lap and overlap joints (**fig. 16.1**) that are secured by flat headed

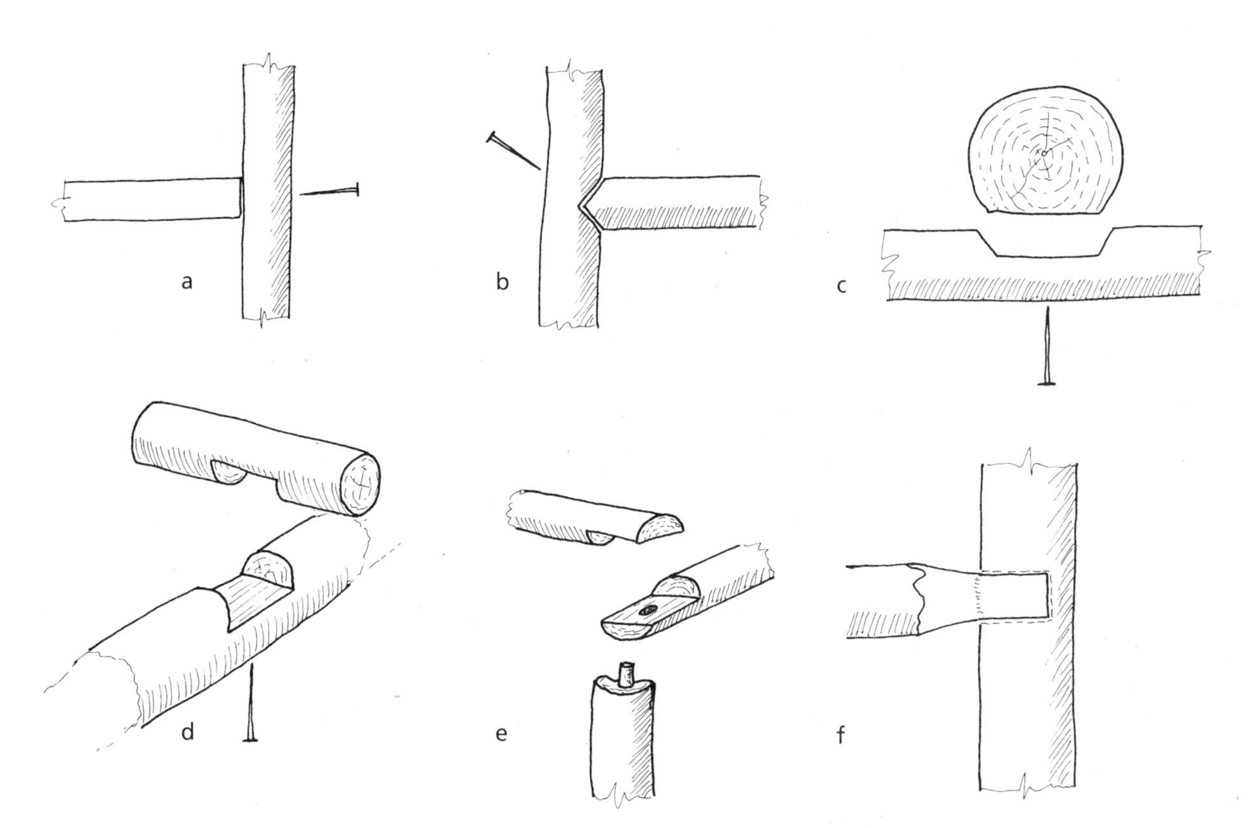

Fig. 16.1 Joints for stick furniture: a. butt; b. 'V' butt; c. part lap; d. half lap; e. corner half lap; f. round mortice and tenon.

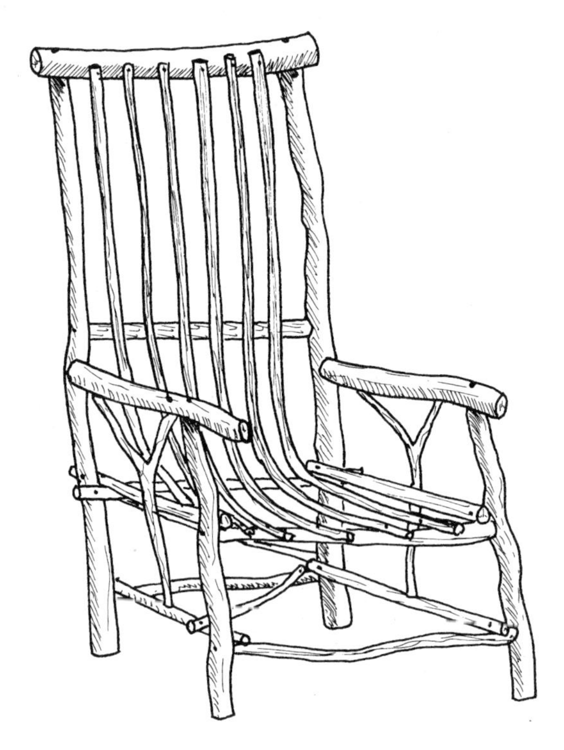

Fig. 16.2 A stick armchair.

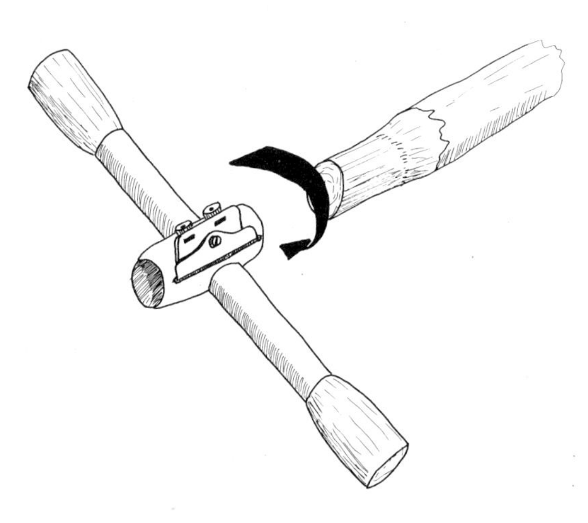

Fig. 16.3 A modern rounder.

galvanised nails driven through pre-drilled pilot holes. In the case of a chair, this enables a sturdy frame to be produced to which a back in much smaller woven rods can be added. Lastly a seat base of round or cleft wood can be applied to the frame. A typical design is shown in **fig. 16.2**.

Stick furniture more commonly has its main members joined by round mortice and tenon joints. Mortices are made by drilling round holes in one member, and tenons by shaping the other by shaving or by means of a rounding plane (**fig. 16.3**). Two designs are shown in **fig. 16.4**.

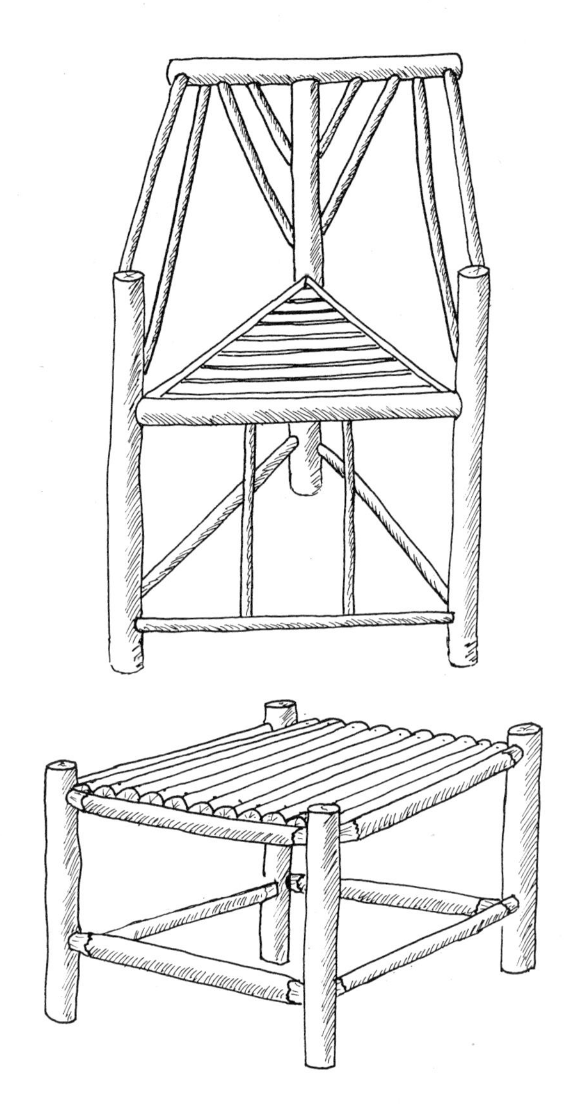

Fig. 16.4 Two extremes; a simple stool and a complex corner chair, both in morticed round wood.

Tools: To make a full range of furniture you will need saw, hammer, chisel, brace and bits, rounding plane/stail engine or draw knife.

Materials: For indoor use you can use almost any wood. For use outside avoid the softer woods that rot more quickly (Chapter 2). Look carefully at any branch wood you have, whether twisted or forked, to see how it might be used to create interest or to offer strength.

Methods:

Twig chair **(fig. 16.5)**

- Draw out your design and make a cutting list.
- Cut the parts of the frame from 50mm (2in) branches for the main members and 25-38mm (1-1½in) branches for smaller members.
- Nail four legs (A) to the arms (B) and four braces (C) to make two sides. Pre-drill all nail holes and use simple butt joints.

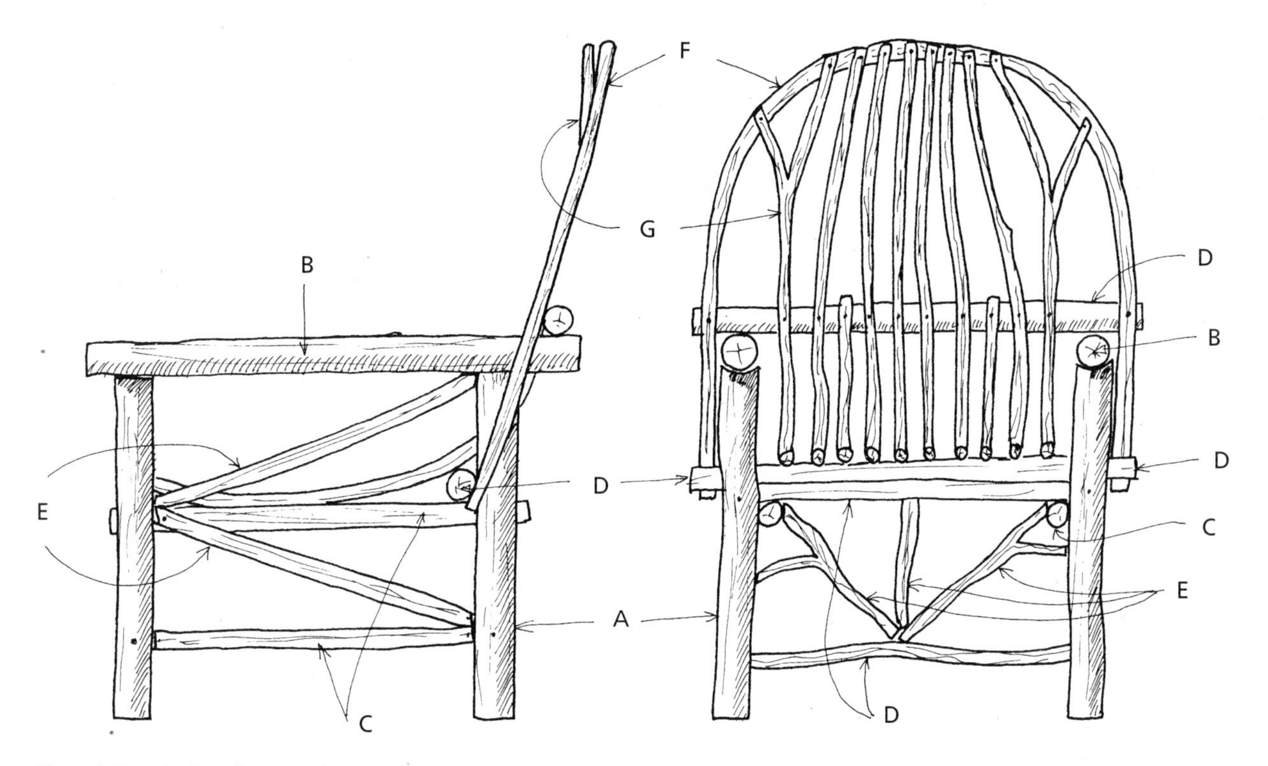

Fig. 16.5 A design for a twig armchair.

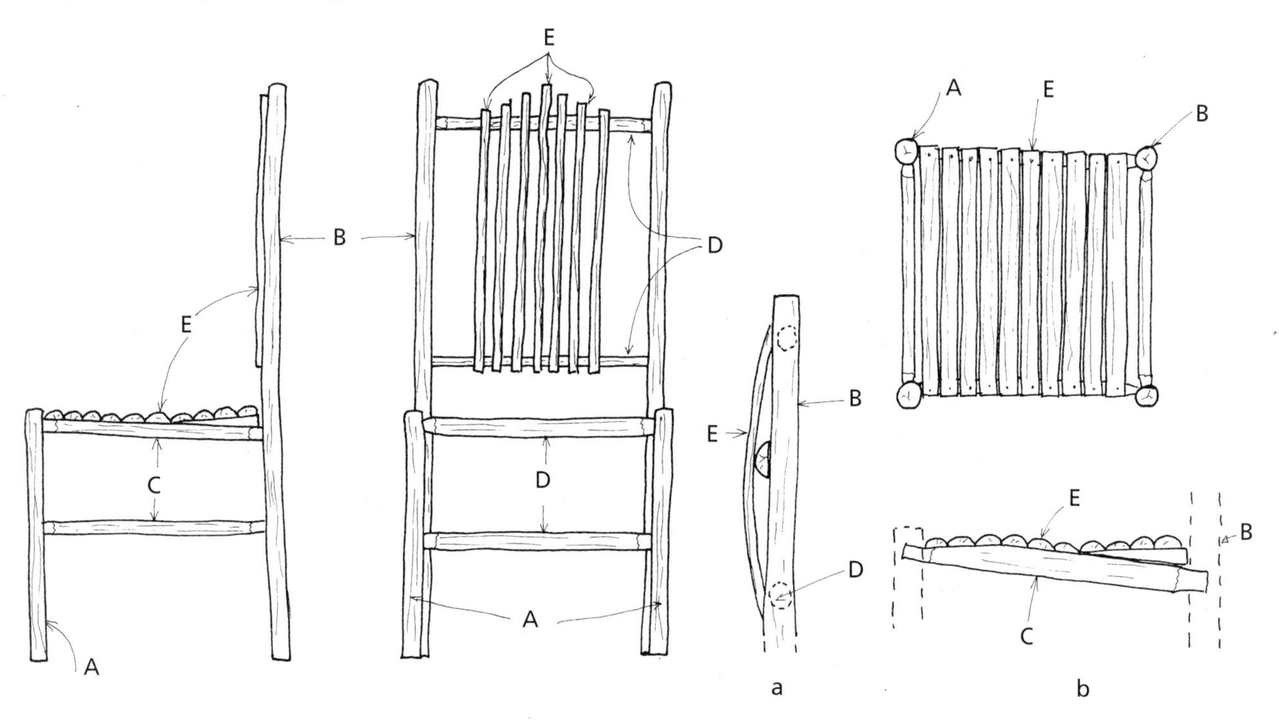

Fig. 16.6 A stick chair: a. and b. show how the seat and back can be profiled.

- Nail five horizontal members (or stretchers) (D) to the two sides to make the basic frame. Add braces (E) as required to strengthen the frame.
- Position and nail the bow back (F) to the horizontals.
- Take ten19mm (1/4in) rods (G), preferably pre-warmed to make them pliable, bend to shape for seat, and nail in place. Avoid knots at the curve, and use commander to get a consistent shape. Trim up and smooth any rough ends on corners (I like to put a small chamfer or all cut ends to avoid the bark pulling back).
- Finish your chair with linseed oil/turpentine mixture, or polyurethane varnish for outside use.

***Stick chair* (fig. 16.6)**

- Draw up your design and cutting list considering how you can build shape into your plan to make the chair appealing and comfortable.
- Cut the parts to length, using c.38mm (1½in) rods for larger members and c.25mm (1in) for the rungs. Chamfer the ends slightly.
- Mark and drill 19mm (¾in) dia. holes in the legs (a1-2 and b1-2) to accommodate the rungs. If using a twist bit go no deeper than 25mm (1in). Round and taper the ends of the rungs using a rounding plane, shave or tenon cutter. Tenons should be dried for a week to shrink before assembly. Check your joints fit, and shave as needed.
- Glue each joint and assemble the side (C1-4) to the legs (A& B). Ensure joints are fully home and the two sides are flat.
- Glue front and back rungs (D1-6) to legs to complete the frame.
- Nail the small rods (E) (pre-drill the holes) for seat and back into place.
- Tidy up and finish as for the twig chair.

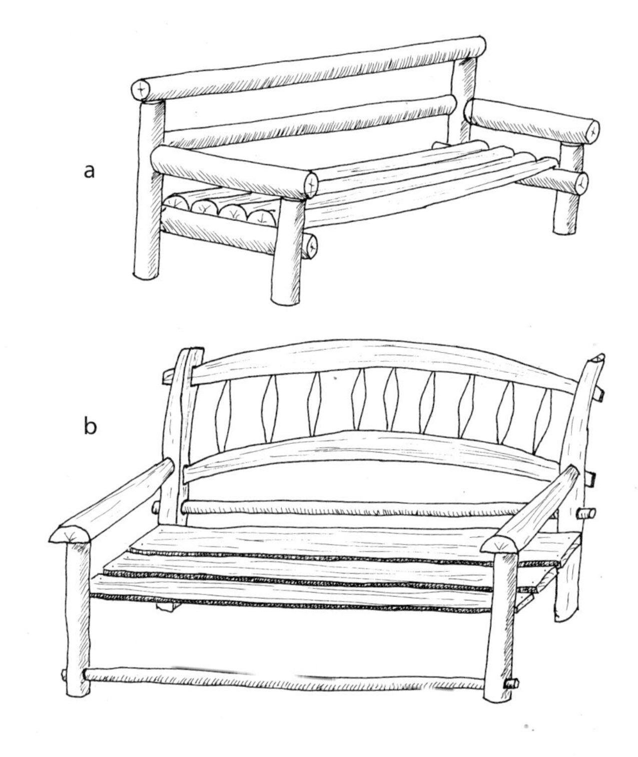

Fig. 16.7 Benches: a. made from round poles; b. made from cleft wood.

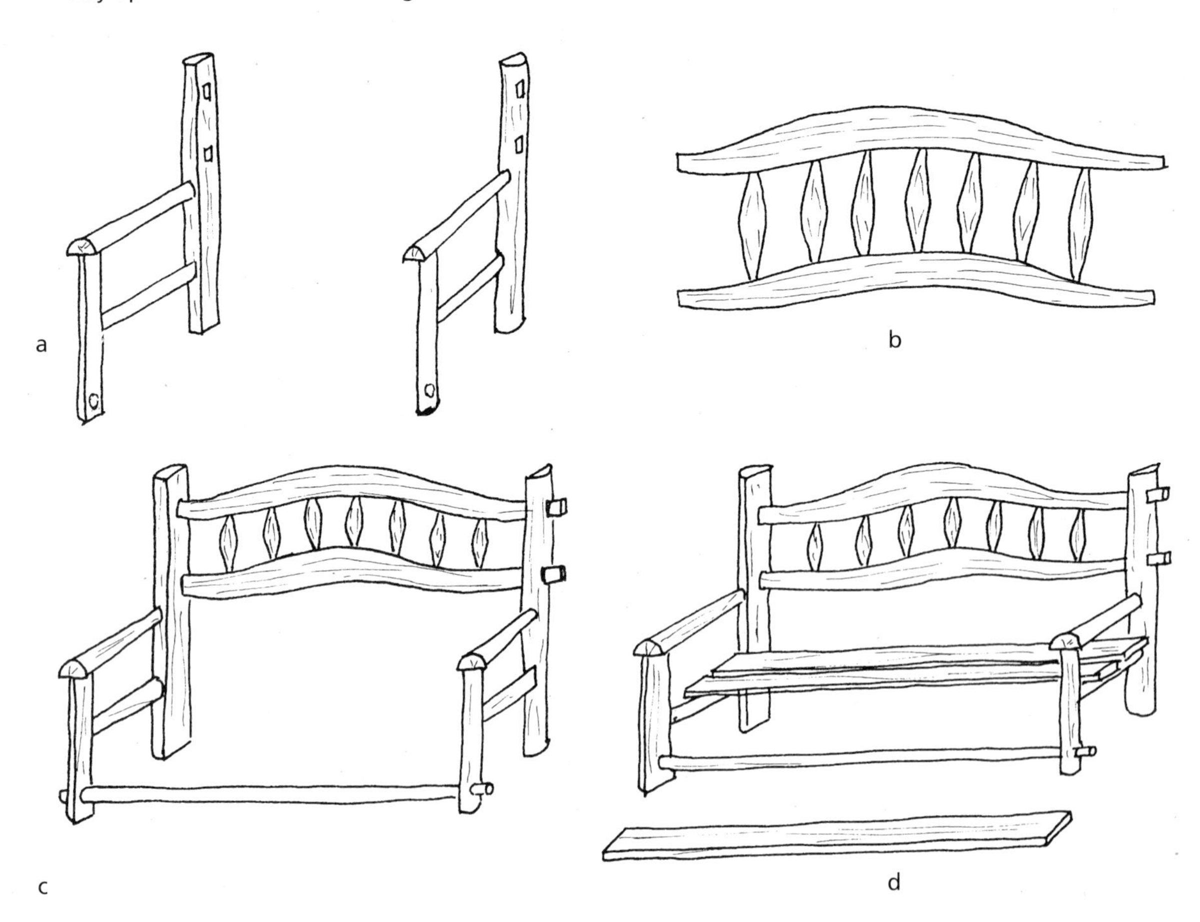

Fig. 16.8 Making a cleft wood bench: a. assemble the sides; b. construct the back; c. join back and sides; d. fit the seat.

Round and cleft pole benches

These are a marvellous example of what can be done with round wood using basic tools. This furniture could be made in the coppice as easily as in a workshop.

Patterns: Sizes can vary from large chairs to three- or four-seater benches. Shapes can vary from chunky and square, to elegant shapes utilising the natural curves in the wood (**fig. 16.7**).

Tools: You will need saw, side axe (preferably), froe and brake, draw knife, brace and bits, chisel and a hammer.

Materials: Chestnut is undoubtedly the best wood, followed by oak, for this furniture is going to be outside in all weathers.

Method (**fig. 16.8**):

- Design the bench and make a cutting plan. Use app. 76mm (3in) poles for the main members including the cleft back, and 51mm (2in) poles for the stretchers and 'sticks' at the back.
- Cut the poles to length, remove the bark and chamfer ends of those remaining round.
- Rive those poles required split, keeping mirror clefts together for legs, arms and back rails. Shave the cleft surfaces smooth, and for the back rails and seat slats, shave to an even flat surface on both sides.
- Mark positions of mortices, and make them with brace and chisel, or leave as round holes as required. Shape ends of other members to fit these.

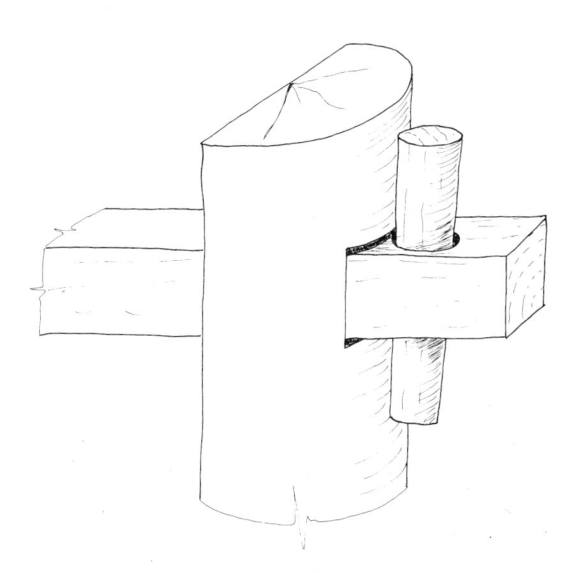

Fig. 16.9 A pegged mortice and tenon joint (round mortices are much quicker than traditional square ones).

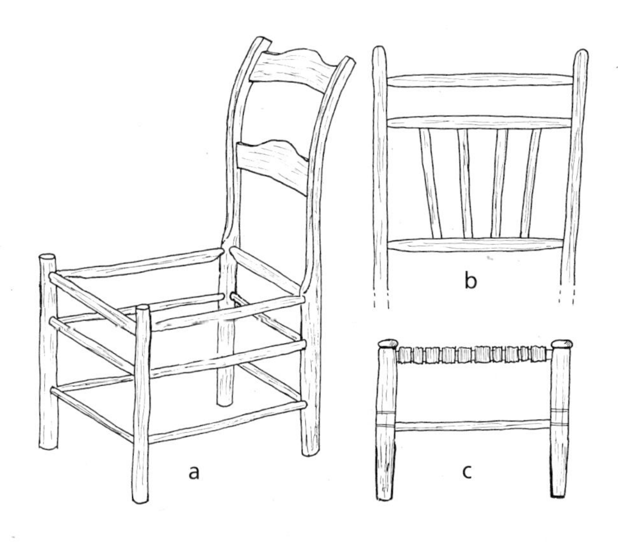

Fig. 16.10 Post and rung furniture: a. slat back; b. spindle back; c. stool.

- Put the parts for each end together, using galvanised nails driven right through the mortices to secure the parts, or take the tenon right through and drill and peg it (**fig. 16.9**).
- Shape the back sticks, forming ends c.19mm (3/4in) round. Fit into holes in the back rails.
- Fix the back panel and the main members to the side panels, fix by nailing, and thus complete the basic frame.
- Nail the clefts for the seat into place.
- Tidy up the bench removing any spurs and smoothing the edges with a draw knife.
- Finish with linseed oil and turpentine to give protection.

Post and rung stools and chairs

In my view a well made post and rung chair with a woven bark seat epitomizes all that is best in green woodworking. A post and rung stool is a brilliant project to start with.

Patterns: As the title suggest this furniture is based on four vertical posts with simple rungs joining the posts (**fig. 16.10**). The chairs have either flat slats or spindles at the back and the seats are woven using bark, ash clefts, rush or cotton tape. The posts and rungs can be turned, decorated, or shaped using edge tools. Size your chair to suit you; using dimensions from one you are comfortable with.

Tools: You need saw, draw knife, shaving horse, side axe, lathe and chisels, froe and brake, brace and bits, spokeshave, knife or firmer chisel and holding device for drilling the posts.

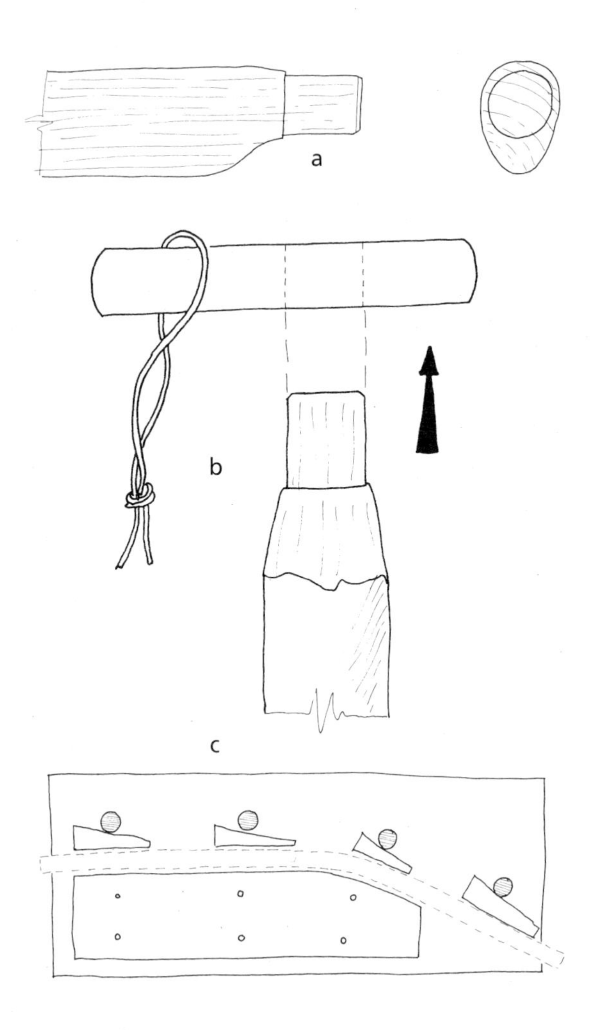

Fig. 16.11 a. round tenon (note: this is an oval rail for taking the woven seat); b. using a gauge to check the tenons; c. mould for shaping a leg.

Materials: Although a wide range of woods can be used, trees with a good straight grain will give the best results. Ash, chestnut, fast grown oak, cherry and coppice elm make lovely chairs. Elm bast is best for woven seating, but young oak and lime can be used. Use waterproof PVA glue to hold joints.

Method:

- Cut logs to size and split out clefts for posts and rungs.
- Shape and shave clefts to approximate size. Top rungs must be shaved to an oval shape (**fig. 16.11**). Remaining post and rails can either be turned or shaped with a curved shave. Whilst turning add any decoration; a small V marking the centres for the rungs is a good idea, as is a taper at the bottom of the posts.
- The parts should now be seasoned for a few weeks; they will become slightly oval. Rungs must be very well seasoned (airing cupboard or by the stove); then they will expand slightly when put together.
- Season the rear posts for a chair in a mould to shape them (**fig. 16.11**); warm them before bending.
- Split out flat clefts for slats if required; shave them smooth, mark the shape required with a template, cut out, and put in a mould to season to the required curve.
- Drill c.19mm (3/4in) mortices as deep as possible (use a mirror to judge the depth) (**fig. 16.13**) in posts for front and back rails. Mortice back posts for slats if required.
- Make round tenons at the ends of the rungs after you have made the mortices and you know the exact length required. Use a gauge and keep them tight (**fig.16.11**). If you do make them loose, use blind wedges to tighten them (**fig. 16.12**).
- Glue front and back panels together putting a thin covering of glue on tenons and mortices. Carefully drive the tenons fully home in the mortices, and wipe off any excess glue. The slats are best pegged as well as glued.
- After these panels have set, drill mortices in the posts for the side rungs. These should overlap the existing mortices by app. 2.5mm (3/32in) so they lock the former in place (**fig. 16.13**). Where the hole must be at an angle, use a jig or bevel (**fig. 16.20**) to get it right.
- Glue side rungs into the front and back panels to complete the frame. Burnish with shavings, and apply any finish you require before weaving the seat.

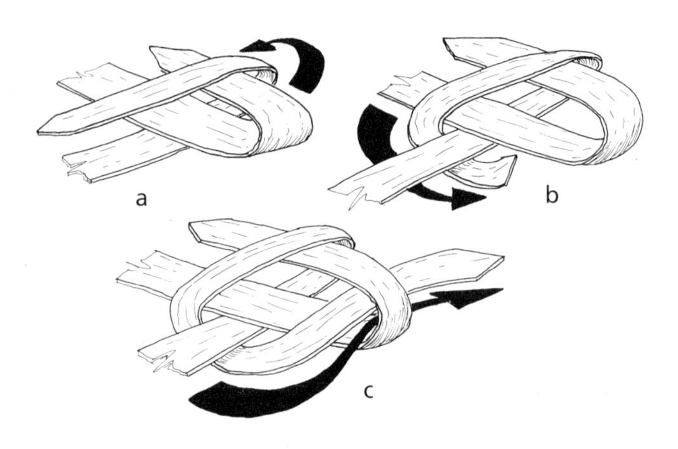

Fig. 16.14 Bark seating: a.- c. tying a knot to join two lengths.

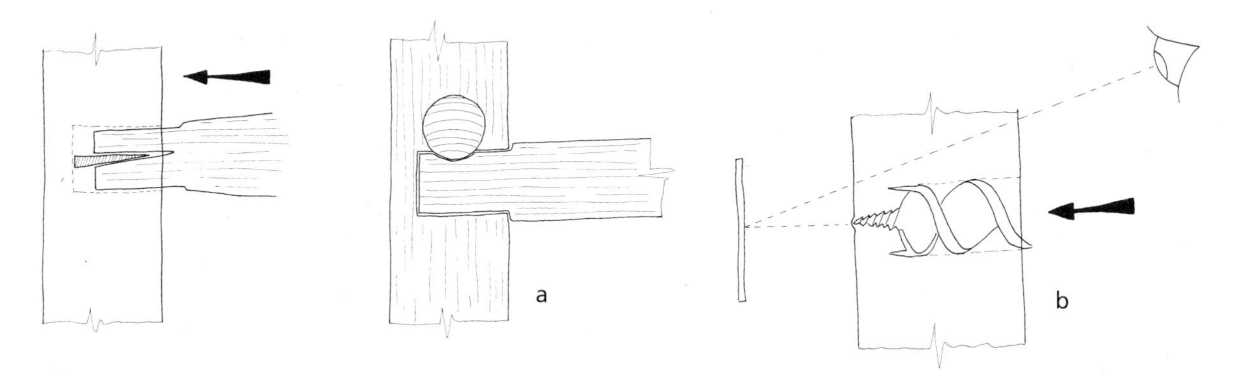

Fig. 16.12 Blind wedging.

Fig. 16.13 a. overlapping the mortices to lock the lower one in place; b. using a mirror to judge the maximum mortice depth.

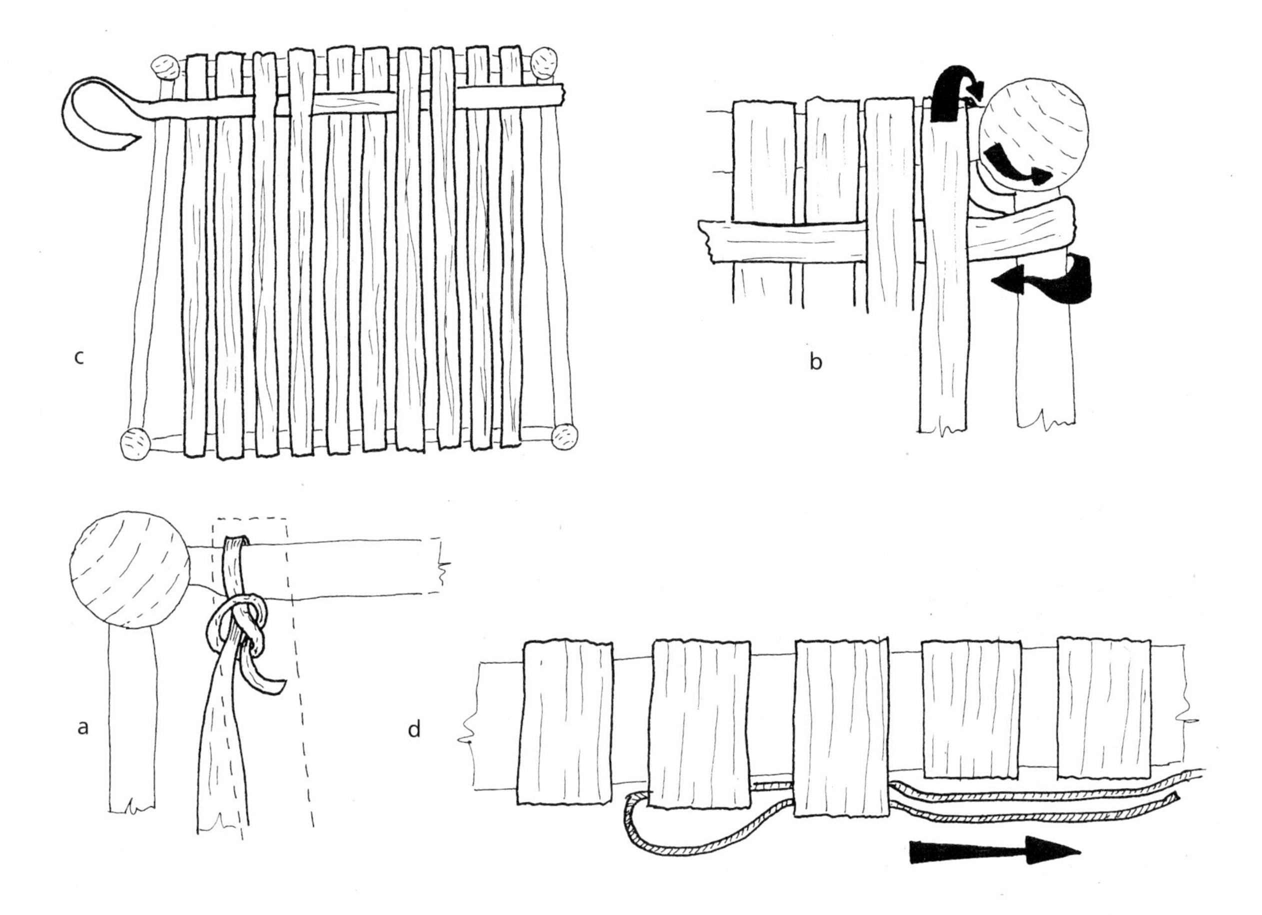

Fig. 16.15 Bark seating: a. tying the first end to the frame (note how the knot will be covered by the next pass); b. taking the last warp around the leg to start the wefts; c. taking the weft across the warps; d. tucking away the last weft.

- For a bark seat first soak your bark in warm water and trim it up; it does not matter if it is not all of the same width. Keep it wet whilst weaving.
- To join two lengths of bark, narrow the ends of each piece and tie together using a weaver's knot (**fig. 16.14**).
- Start by tying one end to the back rung and then form the warp by looping the bark around the front and back rungs, joining additional sections as required (**fig. 16.15**). Keep knots on the underside of the weave and the bark uppermost. Don't over tighten. Cover your first knot with the first warp loop.
- When the warps are finished take the strip to the nearest side rung and start the wefts (**fig. 16.15**). Keep the warps wet and pliable

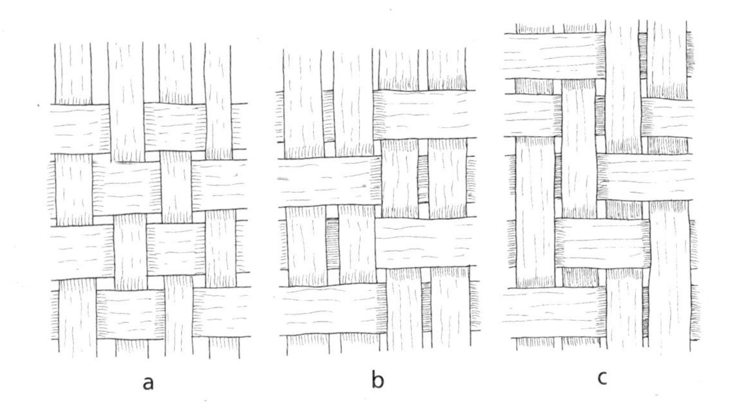

Fig. 16.16 Weaving patterns for bark seats: a. one over - one under; b. two over – two under; c. herringbone.

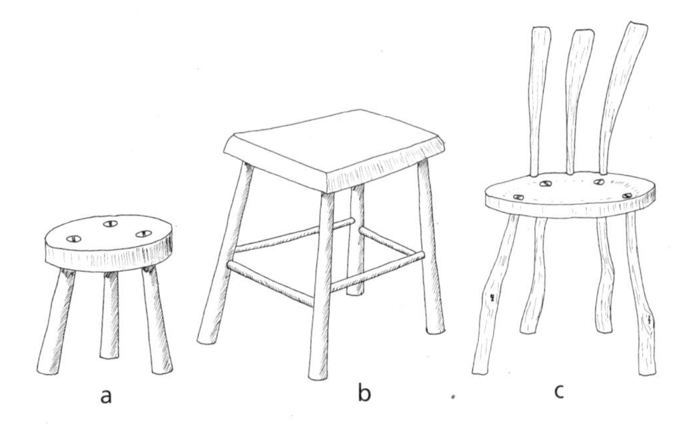

Fig. 16.17 Slab and stick furniture: a. round milking stool; b. square top stool; c. modern chair design in coppice wood.

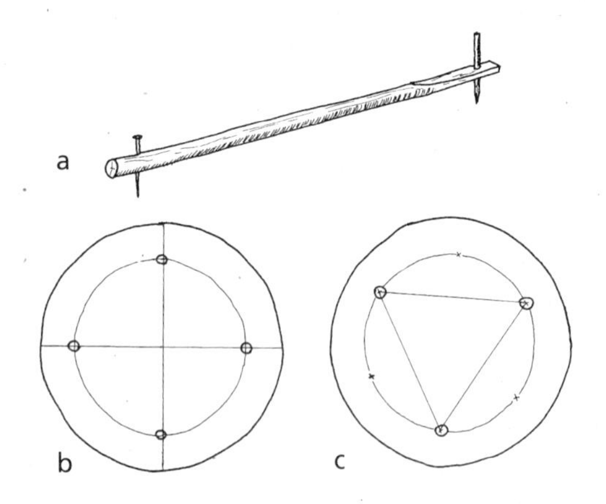

Fig. 16.18 Marking out stool slabs: a. nail and pencil compass; b. marking four legs on right angle lines; c. marking three legs (use the compass set at the radius of the circle, to mark six points around it; use every alternate point as a centre for a leg).

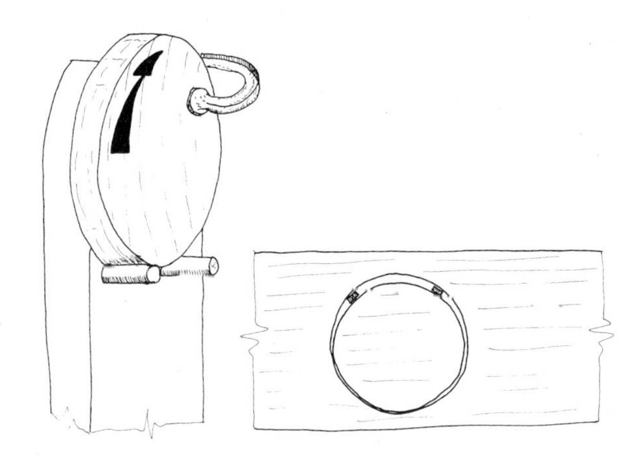

Fig. 16.19 Holding a round slab either by wedging the slab in the hole in the plank from which it was cut or by clamping it to a vertical post fitted with two supporting dowels.(after Abbott)

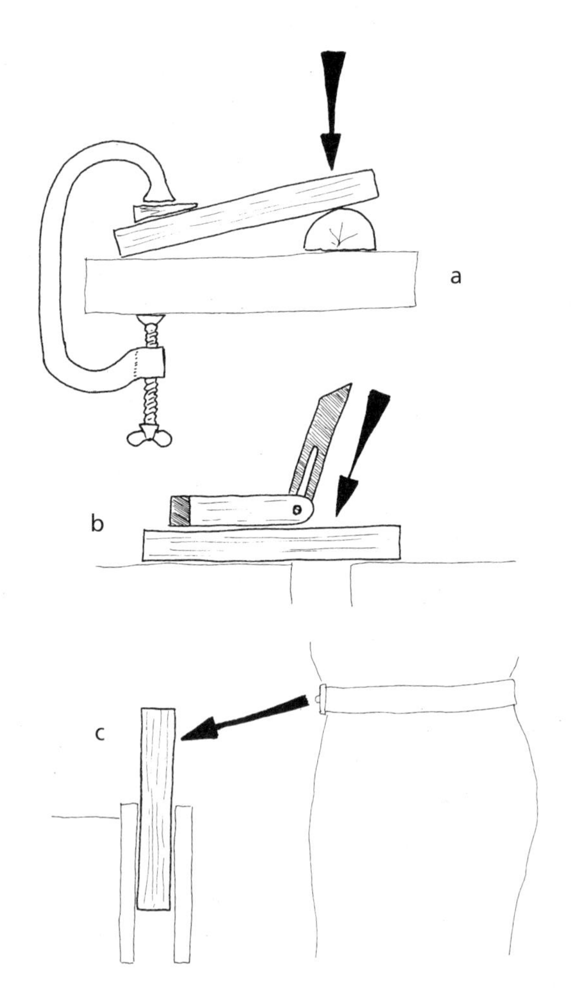

Fig. 16.20 Getting the right mortice angle: a. use a half round log to tip the seat and drill vertically; b. use a sliding bevel and align the drill with it; c. put the seat at the same height in a vice and use a fixed point (your belt buckle) to give the angle for the drill.

whilst weaving. You can weave simple one over and under, two over two under, or herringbone pattern (**fig. 16.16**).

- Use a knife or small wedge to lift the warp enough to push the weft through. Pull tight as you go. The last end should be tucked away into the weave underneath (**fig. 16.15**).
- A chair has wider rails at the front; this will leave two triangles unfilled by warps. After the weave has dried and shrunk cut some strips to fit and just weave them in place without tying their ends.
- No finishing agent is usually applied to bark – just allow the patina of use to develop.
- Alternatively canvas or cotton strips can be used; two contrasting colours look good and it is usual to tack the ends to the rails.

Slab and stick seats

These have a chunky, solid appearance which can reveal the beauty of your wood. My introduction to slab and stick was a child's stool made by a Kentish woodman; with the exception of the mortices, it was made entirely using a side axe. Windsor chairs appear in the next section.

Patterns: A round or square solid seat cut from a plank of wood and into which the legs are morticed, is the essence of slab and stick furniture (**fig 16.17**). The legs can be square or round, shaved or turned, with or without stretchers to brace them. In the more basic items, such as three-legged milking stools, the mortices go right through the seat and the legs are wedged; in better quality stools they are blind. Back posts can also be morticed to the slab to make a chair (**fig 16.17**).

Tools: You will need a saw, froe and break, draw knife and shaving horse, lathe (or spokeshave), a large shaping saw, brace and bits and a chisel for shaping wedges.

Materials: Elm is always favoured for seats since it rarely splits, but I have seen plenty in ash. Ash, beech, cherry or sycamore are fine for the legs, with oak for wedges.

Method:

- First make the legs. Cut a pole to length, split out suitable clefts, and shave them roughly to shape. Either finish off on the lathe or with a spoke shave. Do not shave the head of the legs exactly to size until they have been properly seasoned. If you use the lathe, you can decorate the legs. Long legs need stretchers as shown.

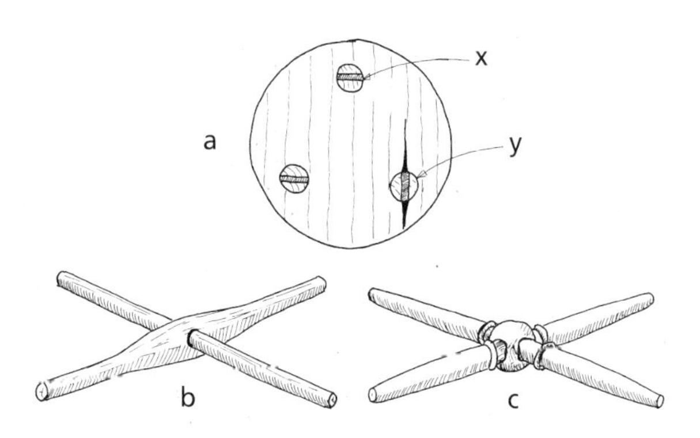

Fig. 16.21 Slab stools: a. put wedges in correctly (x) to avoid splitting (y); b. simple stretchers, one passing through the other; c. fancy stretchers morticed into a central ball.

- Make the seat from 32mm-38mm (1¼-1½in) plank. Mark out the seat using a string or nail compass if it is round (**fig. 16.18**).
- Clamping the plank to your bench, cut out the seat with your saw.
- Use a spoke shave to smooth the edge and top surface of the seat, always cutting with the grain. See **fig. 16.19** for means of holding a round seat during shaving.
- Mark the position of the mortice holes using the compass – see **fig. 16.18**.
- Drill mortice holes 25mm (1in) for legs and 3mm (½in) for stretchers). Drill from the top if they are going through the seat or from the bottom if they are blind. Make mortices the depth of the wood, and use one of the methods in **fig. 16.20** to get the correct angle.
- When the legs are fully dried, bring them back to the lathe or horse and shape the ends to the size of your mortice holes.
- If the legs are to be wedged, cut into the top of the leg c.25mm (1in). Prepare wedges the same length, the full diameter of the top, and c.3mm (⅛in) thick.
- Put legs in mortices, check length of stretchers and cut these to size. Drill a clearance hole in one stretcher to pass the other through (**fig. 16.21**). An alternative using a decorated stretcher is shown.
- Apply glue to the tenons and wedges. Mate stretchers to legs, then drive the legs home into the seat, their split ends orientated as shown (**fig. 16.21**) so as not to split the slab. Drive the wedges home. Blind tenons need only gluing and driving home.

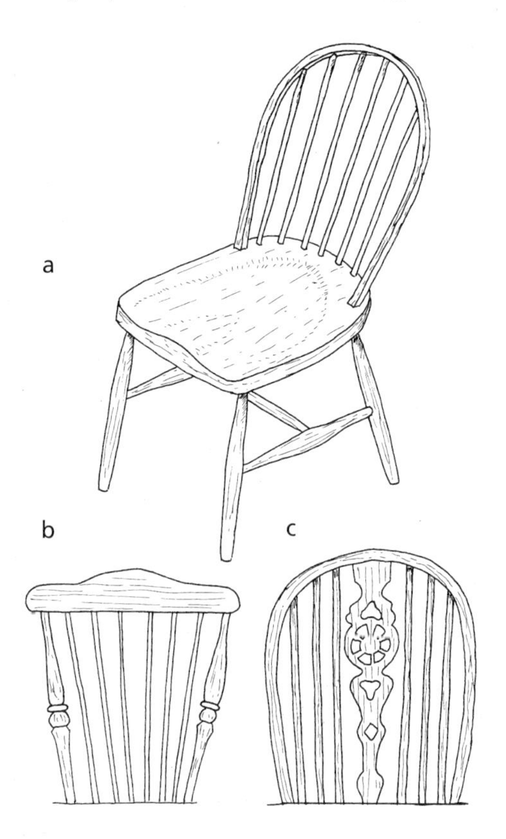

Fig. 16.22 **Windsor chairs: a. bow back; b. comb back; c. wheel back.**

- Clean up tops of the tenons where they come through the seat then polish and finish the stool as required. If the stool wobbles, even the legs as shown in **fig. 16.29**.

Windsor chairs

Perhaps the ultimate in chair design of the slab and stick type, it was making the legs and stretchers for Windsor chairs that gave bodgers their livelihood. I often think how much more satisfaction they would have had from making the whole chair – as no doubt you will.

Patterns: These are stick-backed chairs with solid wooden seats (**fig. 16.22**). The seats are usually shaped; the legs are usually turned with decoration (**fig. 16.23**); the leg stretchers are in some form of H configuration; and the backs may be 'comb', 'bow' or 'wheel' type, all composed of sticks or splats, and occasionally with two additional braces. Arm chairs and high-backed patterns are also made.

Tools: You will need bow and shaping saws, froe and brake, draw knife and shaving horse, lathe, spokeshave(s), curved adze or large gouge, brace and bits, sliding bevel, firmer chisel 25mm (1in), mallet, bench, steamer, various moulds/formers/gauges.

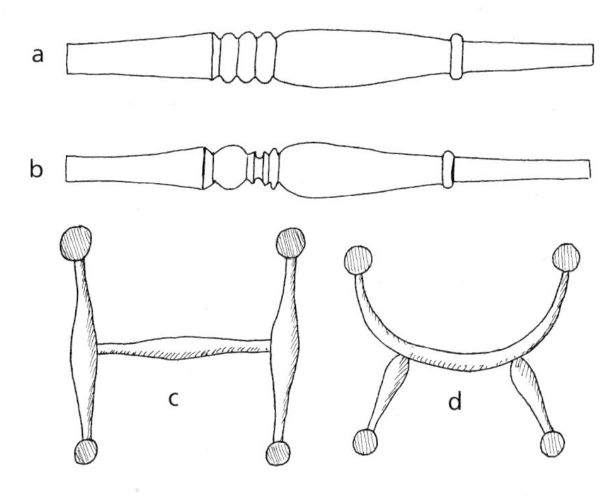

Fig. 16.23 Windsor chairs: a. and b. turned legs; c. and d. patterns for stretchers.

Materials: Elm makes the best seat, with ash, cherry, sycamore or coppice elm for the other components.

Method: Making Windsor chairs is complex. This account is necessarily very brief, but contains the key elements; practice and the recommended reading should provide the rest.

Seat: A good chair has a good hollow, so give your seat a good shape. Cut it from 40mm (1½in) plank.

- Cut the seat to the outline required (**fig. 16.24**).
- Drill 22mm (⅞in) holes for the stiles; angles shown in **figs. 16.24 + 16.26**.
- Mark the shape on the surface of the seat and remove waste wood using an adze or a large gouge. Work across the grain to avoid digging in.
- Smooth the surface and sides, and chamfer all the edges with one or more spokeshaves (a chair maker's travisher which is curved both ways is ideal of course), and then finish with a scraper.

Legs: Use 480mm (19in) long clefts shaved to a round to make legs, patterned or plain. Trim the ends slightly 3mm (⅛in) oversize to allow for shrinkage; aim for 25mm (1in) at tenon end. Give legs time to season.

Stretchers: Prepare these from clefts as you would legs, using billets 254mm (10in) long. Produce a gentle taper from the centre to each end, with a centre diameter app. 19mm (¾in) and ends 13mm (½in), which will allow shrinkage. Dry stretchers very well before final use.

Stiles (for comb back): Turn the two stiles. A typical pattern (**fig. 16.22**) has a maximum diameter of c.35mm (1⅜in), c.25mm (1in) bottom diameter and 16mm (⅝in) top diameter.

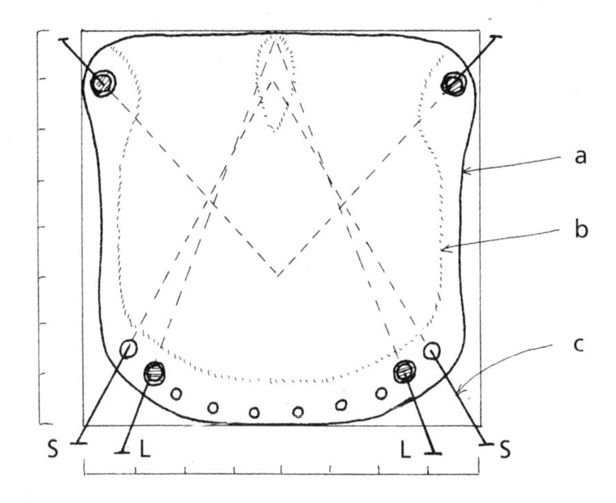

Fig. 16.24 Pattern for a seat (each scale division is 51mm (2in)): a. thick line gives outer shape of the seat; b. hatched lines show the profile for shaping the surface of the seat; c. dotted straight lines show the angle of the legs L and stiles S.

Spindles or sticks: Spindles are slightly tapered, sticks are straight – take your choice. Turn from 400mm (16in) clefts and app. 16mm (5/8in) diameter. After seasoning reduce the ends to 13mm (1/2in). Use a support on the lathe to stop the sticks whipping as you turn them (see Chapter 10). Sticks for bow-back chairs should be 500mm (20in) long.

Comb: This must be curved and thick enough to receive the stiles and sticks. Split out a cleft so that after shaving it is 500mm (20in) long, 83mm (3 1/4in) deep and 25mm (1in) thick. Steam (if required) and hold in a jig 4-5 days to set (**fig. 16.25**).

Bow: For this you need long straight-grained knot-free wood. Ash or yew is best. Split a cleft from a suitable log 1.3m (4ft 6in) long and shave/plane to a finished size of 25mm (1in) square. Avoid nicks across the grain that may cause splits on bending. Steam for one hour and bend in a jig, leaving five days to set and then three weeks to season.

Assembling legs to seat:

- Turn tenon ends of seasoned legs to 25mm (1in).
- Mark the leg positions on the seat as shown (**fig. 16.24**), and a line to show the direction to angle the drill.
- Drill 25mm (1in) holes for front legs @ 8 degrees (using sliding bevel to gauge this), and back legs @ 18 degrees (**fig. 16.26**). Go as deep as possible (use a marker on the bit) without coming through.

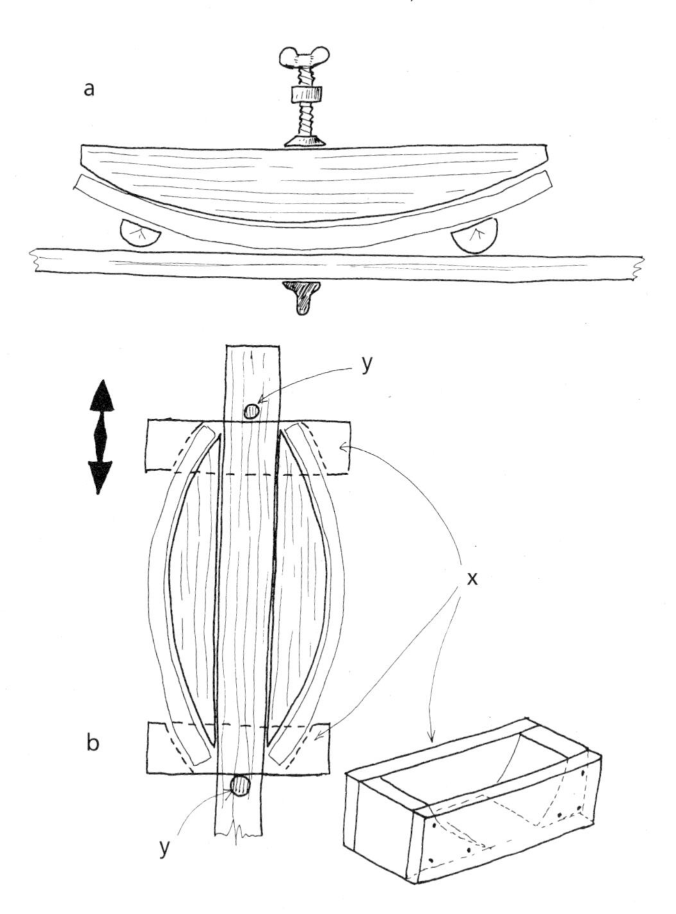

Fig. 16.25 Bending comb backs: a. using clamp, shaped former and two clefts; b. using shaped formed and holding the backs in two wooden 'cups' (x) held by removable dowels (y).

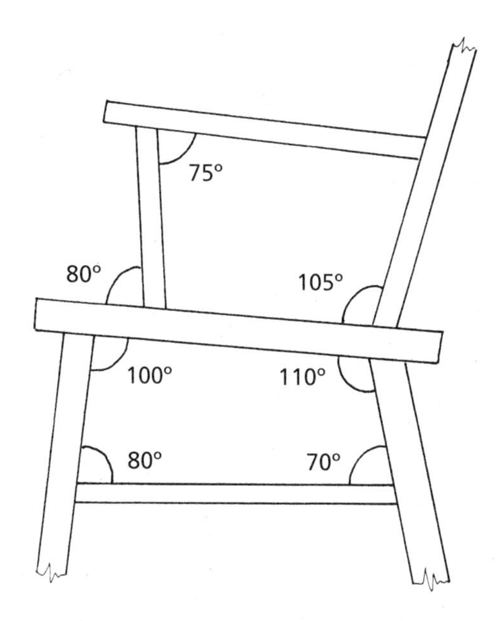

Fig. 16.26 Suggested angles for the joints of an armchair.

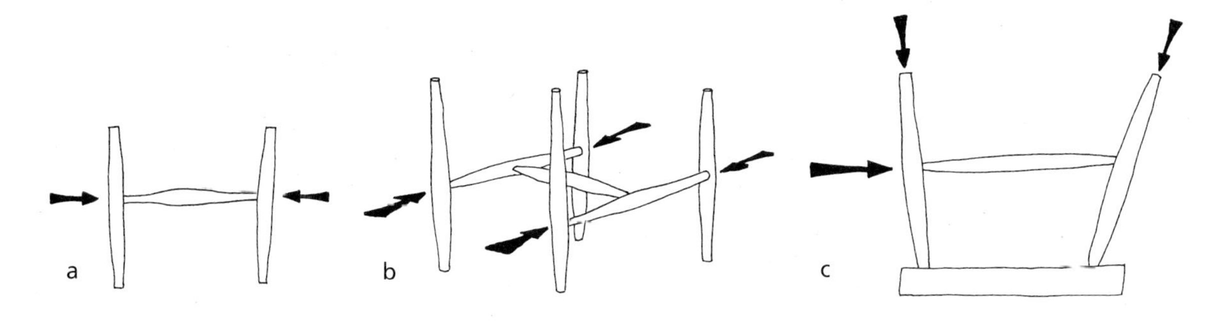

Fig. 16.28 Assemble legs and stretchers: a. put stretchers together into 'H' shape; b. fit legs to stretchers; c. drive legs into seat and tighten legs onto stretchers.

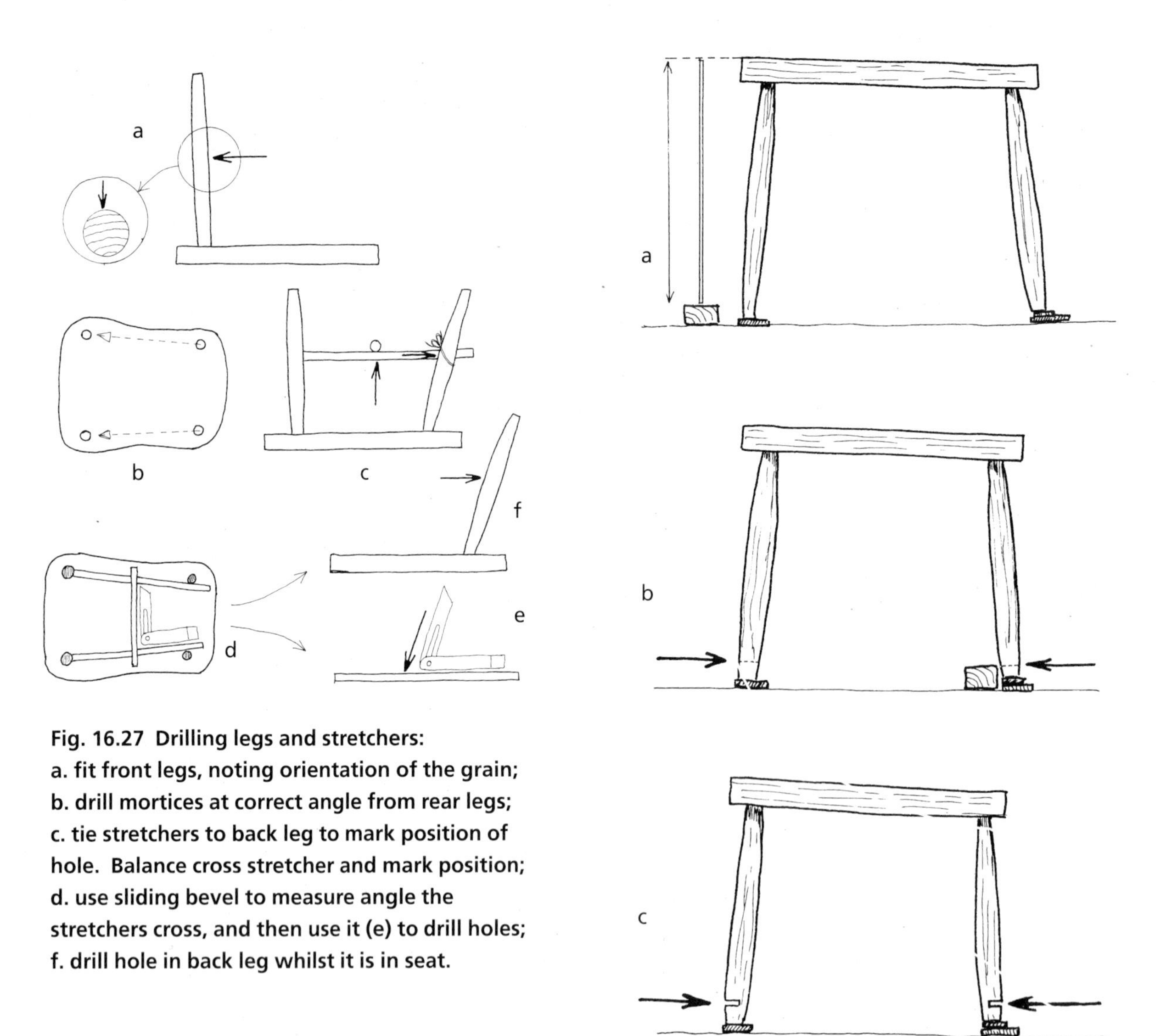

Fig. 16.27 Drilling legs and stretchers:
a. fit front legs, noting orientation of the grain;
b. drill mortices at correct angle from rear legs;
c. tie stretchers to back leg to mark position of hole. Balance cross stretcher and mark position;
d. use sliding bevel to measure angle the stretchers cross, and then use it (e) to drill holes;
f. drill hole in back leg whilst it is in seat.

Fig. 16.29 Levelling the legs: a. measure height, using a block 45mm (18in) rule and cut to size; b. use block to mark every leg with length required; c. cut legs to the height marked.

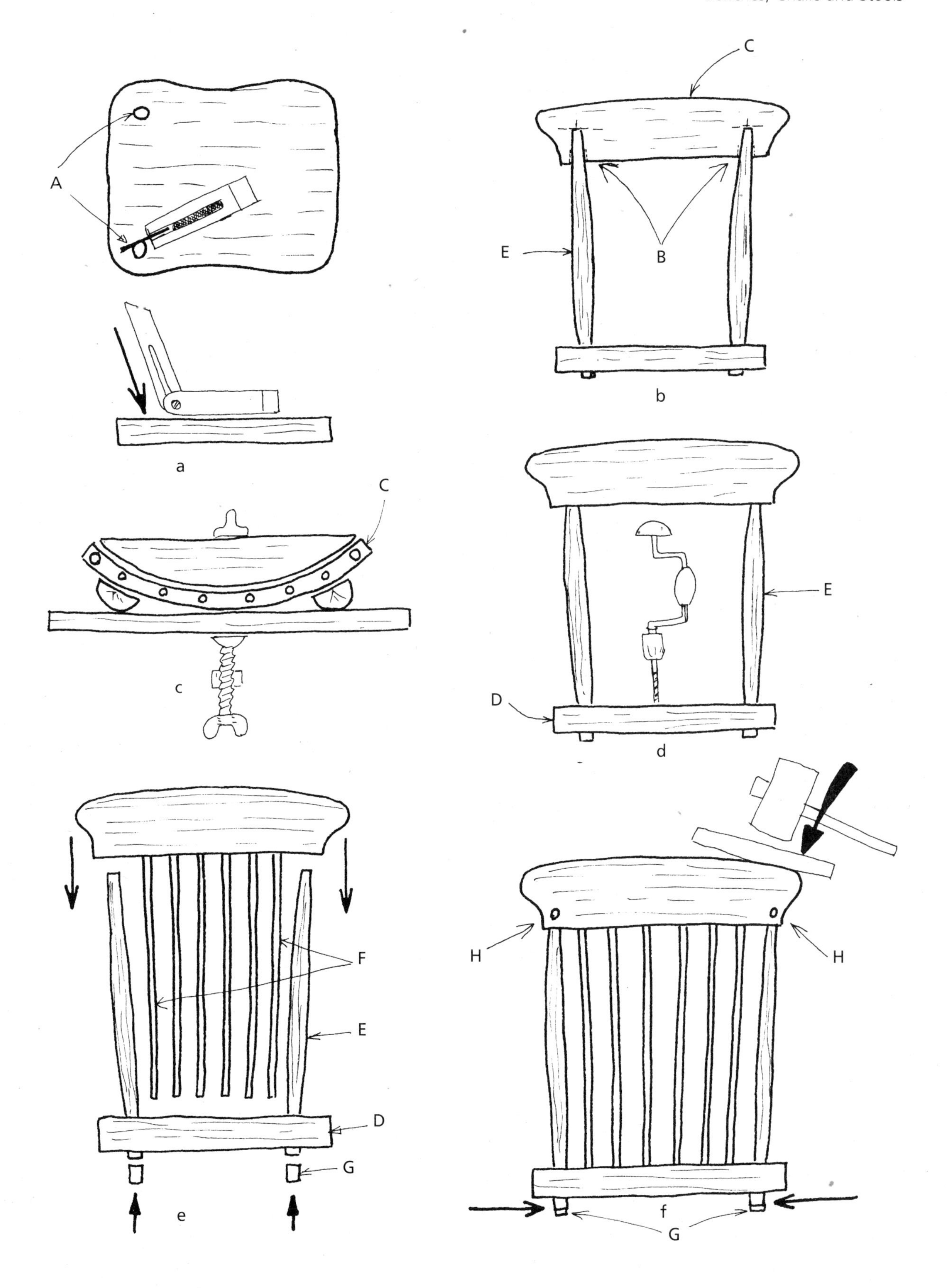

Fig. 16.30 Assembling a comb back: a. drill stile holes A using sliding bevel to give angle; b. mark stile (E) sockets B on comb C; c. drill holes in comb; d. drill spindle holes in seat D using stiles (E) to give correct angle; e. fit stiles E to seat D first, then comb and spindles F; f. knock together and wedge G and peg H.

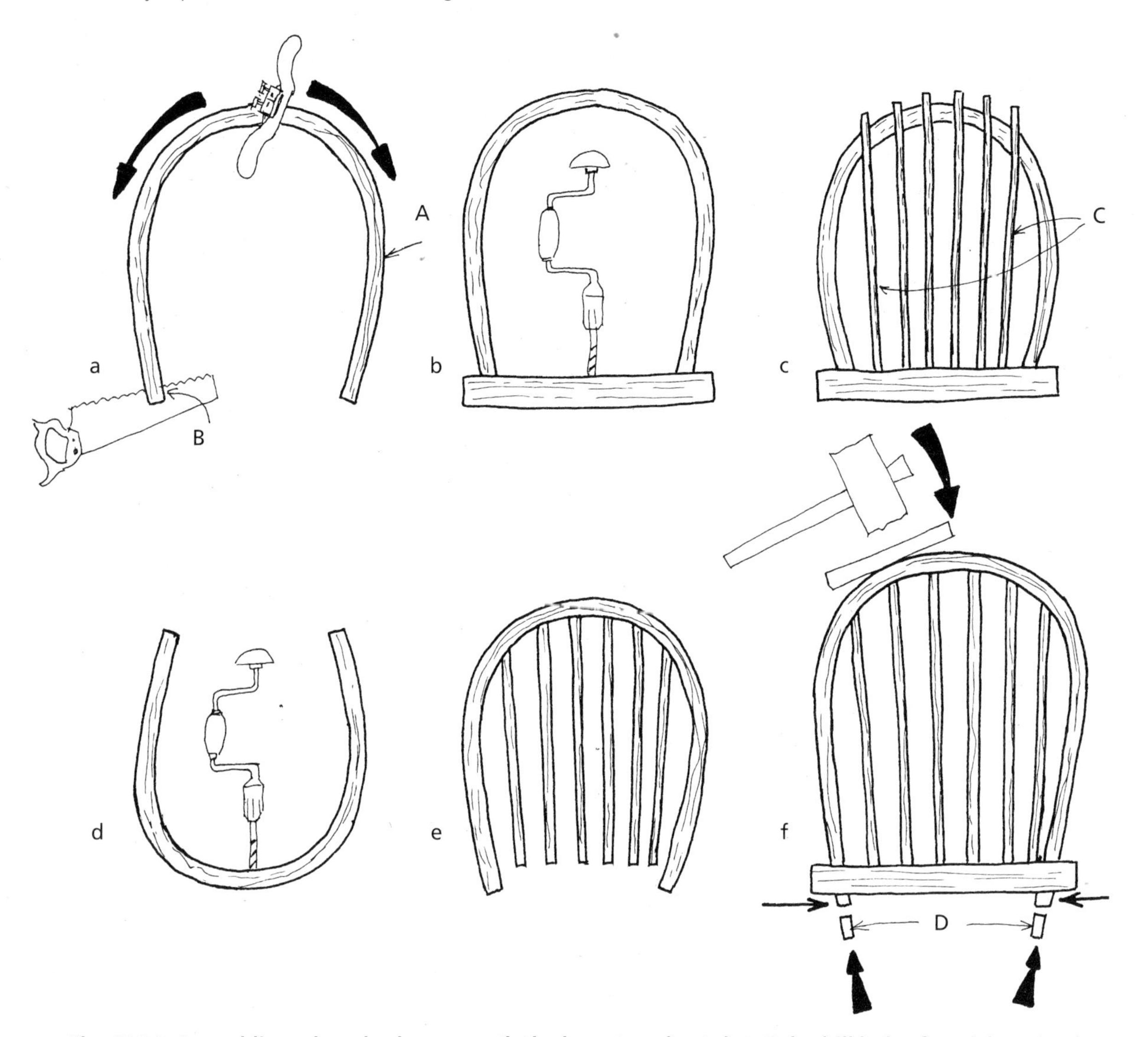

Fig. 16.31 Assembling a bow back: a. smooth the bow A and cut slots B; b. drill holes for sticks using bow for angle; c. measure sticks C; d. drill bow for sticks; e. fit sticks to bow; f. knock together and wedge tight D.

- Mark stretcher positions on legs 250mm (10in) from top (**fig. 16.27**). Mark leg so that the hole will cross the grain, not split it. With front legs in the seat, drill stretcher holes c.19mm (3/4in) deep. Put rear legs into mortices.
- Put side stretchers in place in front legs and mark where to cut off to fit back legs (allow for mortice depth). Put centre stretcher across other two and mark off length required. Set bevel to the angle between the stretchers, remove stretchers from legs and drill holes in side stretchers at required angle (**fig. 16.27**).
- Finish off sizing stretchers and drill stretcher holes in back legs (remove front legs to do this).
- Now glue together. Glue all of the holes, assemble in the order shown in **fig. 16.28**, then clean off any surplus glue.
- To level the legs (**fig. 16.29**), stand on a flat surface and use waste shavings to get the front a comfortable height above the back c.25mm (1in) – but what feels best for you. Measure down 450mm (18in) from top of seat at front, and cut a piece of waste to fill the gap. Then use this block to mark cutting position on each leg. Cut parallel to floor half way through each leg – then remove the chair and finish cutting.

Assembling comb back (**fig. 16.30**):

- Turn seasoned stiles to fit mortices, saw slot in base c.32mm (1 1/4in) deep and prepare suitable wedges.
- Mark stile sockets on comb; drill mortices and spindle sockets.
- Mark on the spindles the length required (allow for two 20mm 3/4in mortices), turn and cut them to size.

- Drill mortice holes in seat for spindles using stile to give the angle required and spacing evenly between the stiles.
- Glue all holes, put stiles into seat, put spindles in comb and then comb on stiles, spindles into seat mortices and then knock together.
- Finally secure the comb to the stiles using 3mm (3/8in) wooden pegs glued into holes drilled right through. Clean up both the bottoms of the stiles where they come through the seat and the comb pegs. Apply your finish.

Assembling bow back **(fig. 16.31)**:

- Shape/shave the curved bow to your finished profile, making the ends 22mm (7/8in) cylinders.
- Cut 20mm (3/4in) slots into bottom of bow and prepare suitable wedges. Fit bow to seat (don't glue!).
- Drill the 25mm (1in) mortices for sticks in seat using bow to give angle. Shape one end of sticks to fit these.
- Put sticks into seat and mark their centres on the bow and their length allowing for mortices.
- Remove sticks, cut to length and whittle to size for mortices. Remove the bow and drill 13mm (1/2in) mortice holes to app. half the bow depth.
- Check it all fits and then glue all the mortice holes. Fit tops of sticks into the bow, then lower whole back into mortices in the base. Knock into place till bow comes through the seat. Wedge the bow.
- Clean off ends of bow, and finish chair as required.

Quality materials, tight joints and good tensioning will make a strong, durable chair.

Further reading:

Abbott, M., ***Green Woodwork***,
Guild of Master Craftsmen Publications 1989
Alexander, J., ***Make a Chair from a Tree***,
Astragal Press 1994
Dunbar, M., ***Make a Windsor Chai***r, Taunton
Langsner, D., ***The Chairmaker's Workshop***, Lark
Ruoff, A., ***Making Twig Furniture***,
Hartley and Marks 1995
Underhill, R., ***The Woodwright's Shop***,
University of North Carolina Press 1981

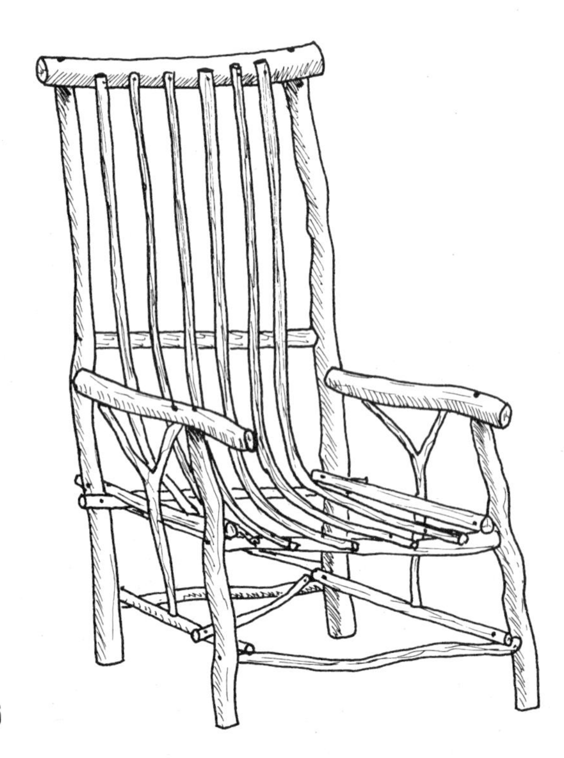

Chapter 17

Baskets

Making baskets is an ancient skill, probably as old as working flint. It is an immensely satisfying craft that produces items not only of use but also beauty. The styles, methods and nuances of basket making are wide ranging, so in this small section the descriptions are limited to key types that illustrate the different techniques.

Rigid cleft wood baskets

These baskets have frames which support thin but rigid cleft strips.

Trugs: These are the best known basket of this type and are still produced in large numbers by Sussex craftsmen. Trug is said to derive from 'trog', the Norse for a shallow boat, which the baskets clearly resemble.

Pattern: Trugs (**fig. 17.1**) are oblong baskets made of seven panels nailed to a wooden frame. They frequently have a handle that encircles the whole basket, and two legs. Market garden trugs have a braced handle but no legs, whilst farmers' 645mm (30in) bushel trugs, the largest of all, have nine braced panels with a gap at each end so it can be lifted by the rim (**fig. 17.1**).

Tools: Trugs are complex and you will need: saw, froe and brake, shaving horse and draw knife, steamer, setting frame, heavy 'mushroom' faced hammer and an anvil to nail on.

Materials: The frame can be of chestnut or ash; straight knot-free poles about 76 to 102mm (3 to 4in) diameter are ideal. Some craftsmen insist they should be split soon after felling to retain the bark. Slats are commonly willow, but can be oak or ash if you have large really straight grained poles.

Method: To make a 559mm (22in) trug you should:

- Cut poles to length; 1.22m (4ft) for the handle and either 1.83m (6ft) or two pieces 990mm (3ft 3in), for the rim.

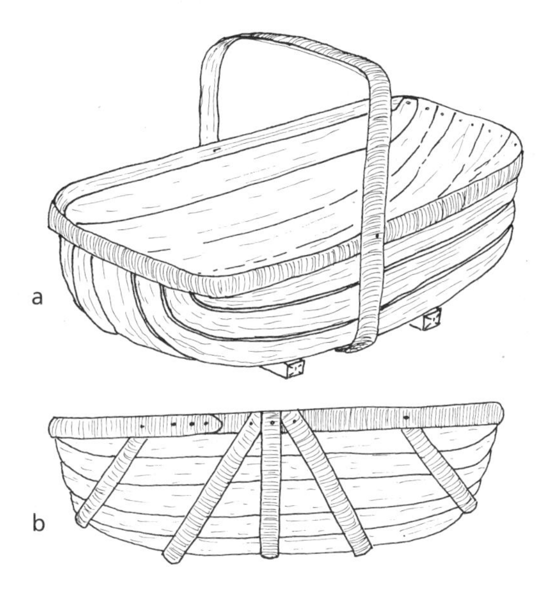

Fig. 17.1 Trugs: a. typical garden trug; b. farmer's bushel basket.

- Rive poles to make clefts c.24mm (1in) wide and shave the inside until it is c.13mm (1/2in) thick (**fig. 17.2**).
- Steam the clefts for about half an hour, and put into the setting frame (**fig. 8.23**); it is a good idea to have handle and rim on either side of this. Crucial to an evenly shaped frame are: an even cleft (no thicks and thins); enough steaming to make it pliable; and closely wedging frame to pattern.
- After about 4 days setting, scarf and nail the clefts into hoops. Nail the two together, clenching the nails over by hammering on the anvil.
- Cut a large diameter log – 152mm (6in) at least – to a length of 711mm (28in) and carefully split down to make clefts approx. 3mm (1/8in) thick. Carry out the final cleaving on steamed or boiled wood.

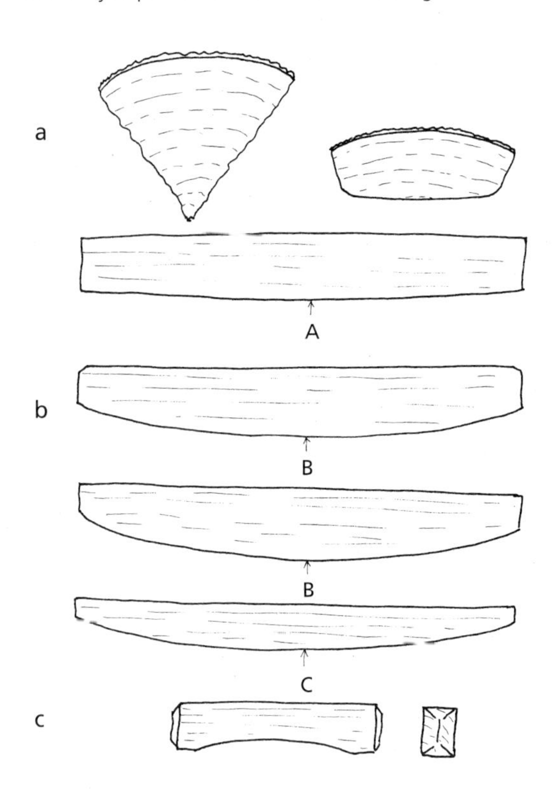

Fig. 17.2 Trugs: a. section of handle and rim shaped from a cleft; b. set of slats – one centre (A); four seconds (B) and two side (C); c. shaped foot.

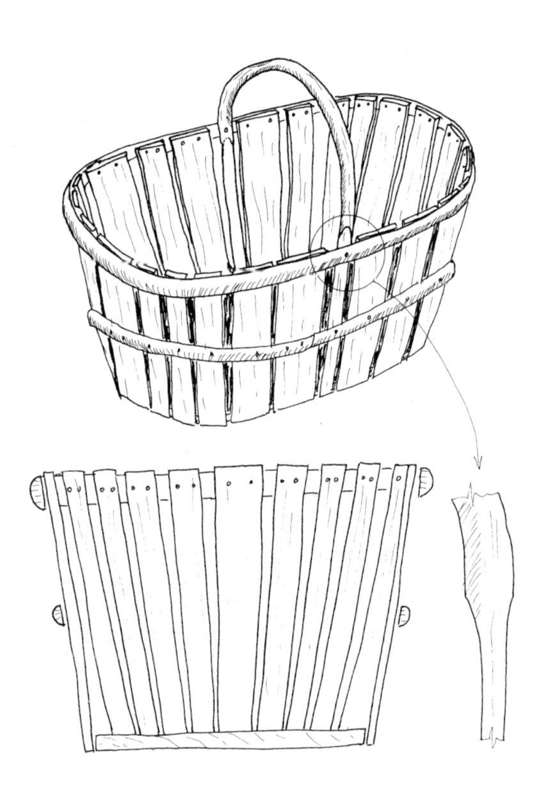

Fig. 17.4 A Devon splint basket with a section showing the size/shape of the splints and part of the handle showing how it is shaved thinner at sides of basket.

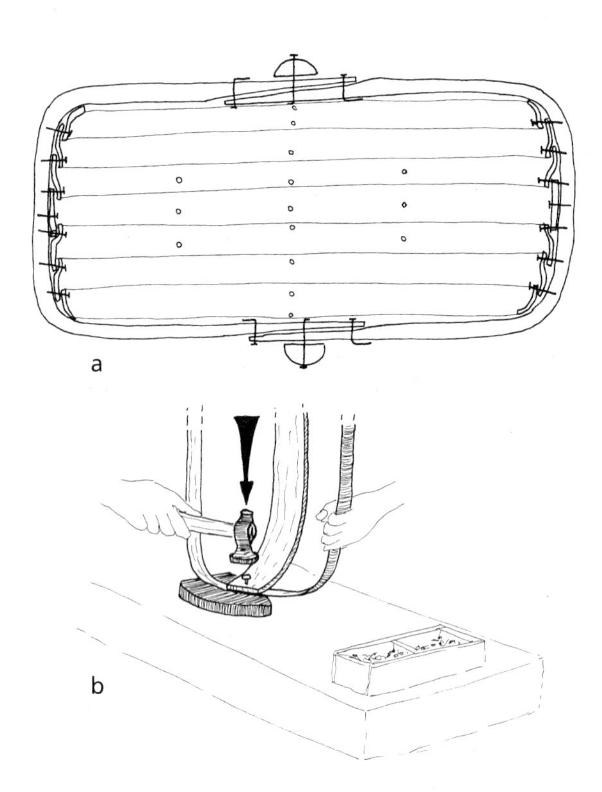

Fig. 17.3 Nailing trugs: a. nailing pattern – note overlapping of slats and rim; b. using the anvil whilst nailing.

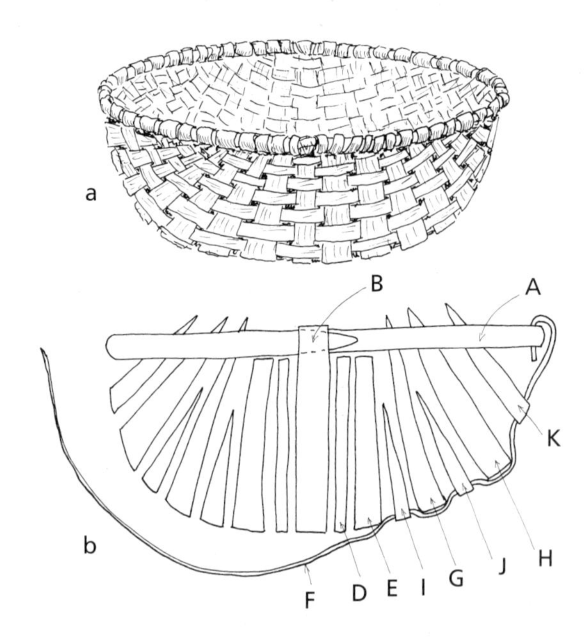

Fig. 17.5 Swill baskets: a. finished basket; b. the components – A bool; B lapping spelk; D first bottom spelk; E second bottom spelk; I top spelk; G first turn down; J kessen; H second turn down; K bool spelk; F taw. The knot for C is not shown – see fig. 17.8

- Shave clefts on your horse to get a smooth, even finish and shape and cut them to the pattern shown in **fig. 17.2** for centre, second and side slats. This shaving is easier with moist, warm wood.
- Store the slats in hot water to keep them pliable when nailing them to the frame, and lever them between setting pins to give a curved shape before commencing nailing.
- Nail the slats to the frame. Use flat headed copper nails. Fix the centre slat first, nailing it to the handle, then bowing it and nailing either end to the rim. Nail on the anvil and clench all nails. Next nail two 'seconds' and one 'side slat' to either side. Overlap the slats by approx. 6mm (1/4in) and nail through this point (**fig. 17.3**).
- Prepare two feet as shown in **fig. 17.2**. Fix these to the basket by nailing through the centre and second slats into the feet.
- Trim the ends of the slats level with the rim and remove any sharp edges to finish off the basket.

Splint baskets: Splints are thin clefts of wood used in making some traditional baskets. The baskets produced are tough and rigid, infrequently seen today. The Devon splint basket described is typical.

Pattern: This basket has a solid base, sides made of splints that are fixed to the base, a middle band and a top rim (**fig. 17.4**). Rims and bands are cleft, but the handle is left round. The splints are approx. 5mm (3/16in) thick, and 22 are used in a large basket (762mm-2 1/2ft long) and 18 in a small one (457mm-18in).

Tools: You will need saws (one for cutting curves), froe, riving brake, setting frame, draw knife and horse, mushroom hammer and anvil.

Materials: Handles, rims and bands are best made from hazel or ash, splints and base from ash or willow.

Method: For a 457mm (18in) basket the procedure is:

- Cut poles to length for top rim – 1m (40in), middle band – 914mm (36in) and handle 762mm (30in). Rive rims and bands in half, shave to a smooth finish. Shape rods for the handle as shown in **fig. 17.4**.
- Steam rims, bands and handles for 30 minutes, then place in setting frames for four days.
- Cut an approx. 228mm (9in) ash pole to length for splints and rive to approximate thickness. Shave to an even thickness. Shape to varying widths (**fig. 17.4**).
- Cut out a solid base from a 10mm (3/8in) plank (purchased or cut/riven yourself) to the shape required.
- Once set, scarf and nail the rim into a hoop. Nail the handle to this and then two end splints using two flat headed nails driven from the inside and clenched.
- Nail these two splints and handle to the base and then nail remaining splints similar to **fig. 17.4**.
- Scarf and nail the centre band to form a hoop, pull it up over the basket into position, and nail it to the splints from the outside, clenching all the nails.
- Tidy up any projecting splinters, and smooth the tops of the splints to complete the basket.

Woven cleft wood baskets

These baskets may or may not have a rigid frame, but all utilise clefts of wood thin enough to be woven whilst they are moist.

Swill baskets: Although swills or spelks came famously from Furness in Cumbria, similar products known as skips, slops and whiskets were made in Wales and the West Country.

Patterns: Swills are handle-less framed baskets with a woven boat-shaped body (**fig. 17.5**). Made in various sizes, the most common were 609mm (24in) long, 508mm (20in) wide and approx. 203mm (8in) deep. Regional patterns differ: the ribs in a whisket for example, pass from end to end of the basket, but in a potato basket pass from side to side.

Tools: To make swill baskets you will need: saw, draw knife and shaving horse, froe and riving brake, tank for boiling wood, setting frame, billhook, knives, bodkin, hammer and anvil.

Materials: Rims can be 10 years old rods of ash, hazel or chestnut. Oak is best for weavers, although ash or chestnut can be used. Hazel strips can be used for baskets where wide strips are not required. Wood for cleaving into fine, wide strips must be straight and knot-free and about 24 years old.

Method: Make a swill basket as follows:

- Season wood for about 6 months before use; it will toughen and run out less when riven if you do.
- Cut wood to 1.8, 1.2 and 0.6metres (6, 4 and 2ft) long for the taws and spelks (**fig. 17.5**), remove the bark and then quarter it.
- Boil clefts for c.1 hour, soak for 24 hours, and then reheat before riving and weaving.
- Split down the longer clefts radially or better tangentially, to make the approx. 1.5mm

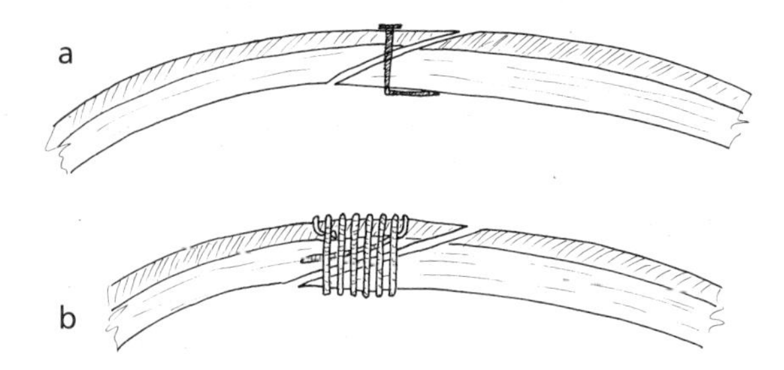

Fig. 17.6 Scarfing the bool rim: a. clenched nail; b. twine or bark tie.

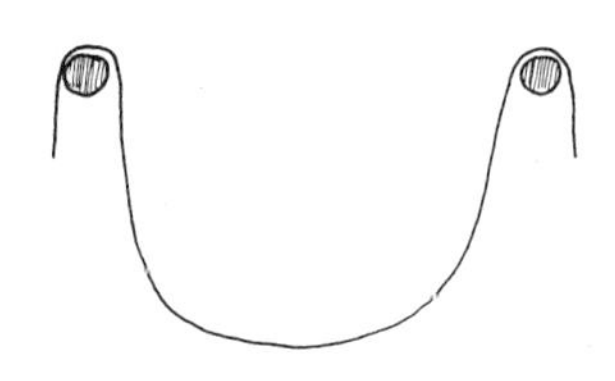

Fig. 17.7 The lapping spelk in place over the bool.

(1/16in) thick taws; these will vary from 13mm to 51mm (1/2in to 2in) wide. Split the 0.6m (2ft) lengths to c.3mm (1/8in) for the spelks. Carefully shave all the clefts to a smooth even finish (see Chapter 11), and keep moist until used.

- For the rim A (bool) take a 1.8m (6ft) x c.25mm (1in) rod, and shave about one third of its thickness away on one side. Steam for c.10 minutes, and then bend to shape on a setting frame with bark outermost. After setting scarf the ends and tie or nail together (**fig. 17.6**) to make the bool.
- Cut the spelks and taws to length but leave the shaping of their ends until you use them (**fig. 17.5**).
- Fold the lapping spelk B into position (**fig. 17.7**). It may need shaving thinner where it folds over the bool and fix it with a 13mm (1/2in) knot taw C as shown (**fig. 17.8**).
- Shape the first bottom spelks D and insert them into the knot taw (**fig. 17.9**). Insert the second bottom spelks E into a slit in the bool made with the bodkin. Get these spelks level – they form the base of the basket.
- Now weave the first taw F1 (approx. 13mm - 1/2in wide), as in **fig. 17.10**, going round the bool twice at each end.
- Shape the first turn down spelks G to c.25mm (1in) to a sharply pointed end, shaped on one side only. Force the ends into a slit in the bool. Secure by weaving second taws F2 as shown (**fig. 17.11**). Repeat for second turn down spelk H, (**fig. 17.12**) using two more taws.

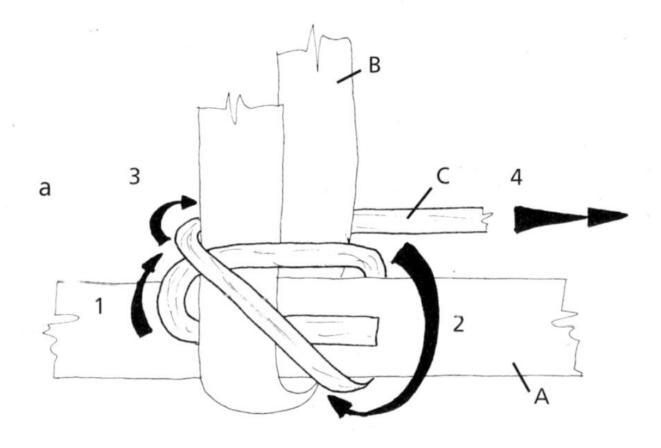

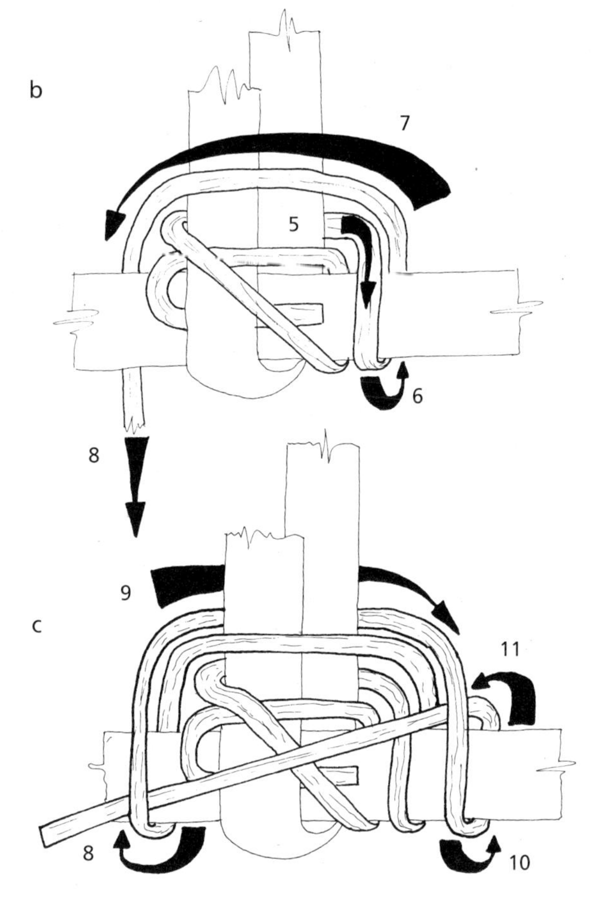

Fig. 17.8 Tying the lapping spelk B to the bool A using the knot taw C.

- Insert the final six spelks I, J & K into the weave, as shown, and then weave one long taw on each side. These start under the first bottom spelk, are woven '1 over 1 under' and taken twice round the bool, and finish on the other first bottom spelk (**fig. 17.12**).
- Finish off by weaving shorter wide taws at the base. Note the start/finish positions of these (**fig. 17.13**). Remember to leave a gap for a handle at the end (**fig. 17.13**). Shape the very last taw to fit the gap remaining, and leave the

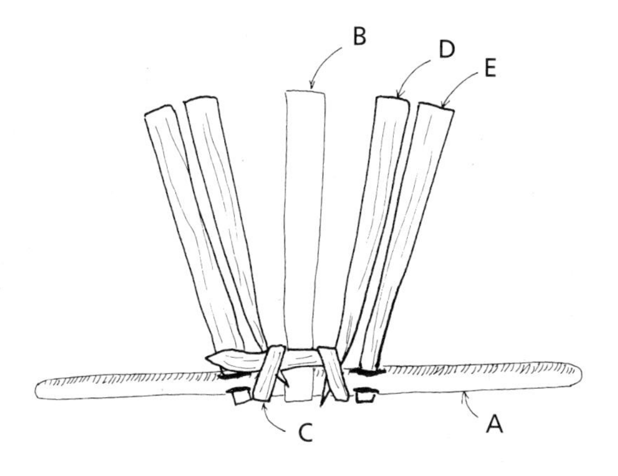

Fig. 17.9 The first bottom spelks D inserted into the knot taw C and the second spelks E inserted into slits in the bool A.

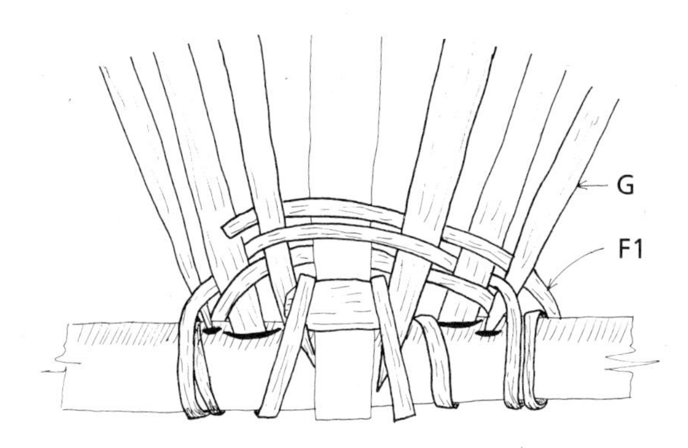

Fig. 17.10 The first taw F1 woven in place and the first turn down spelks G inserted into slits in the bool.

ends of the previous two taws out until this taw is in place; they can then be woven over the last taw to make it secure (**fig. 17.13**).

- Trim off any spikes, to finish the basket.

Woven cleft baskets without a frame: These elegant, practical baskets derive from the US, where 'white oak' basketry was an important craft (see Langsner).

Patterns: These baskets can be round or square bottomed, with or without a handle (**fig. 17.14**). They can be made in a range of sizes. It is usual to have a strengthening rim whilst the weaving is simple 'one over – one under' pattern. Every component is cleft wood.

Tools: You will need the same tools as listed for swill baskets. A drill will be needed to fix any handle.

Materials: Straight grained oak is best, being tough enough to split into thin clefts. Ash, chestnut and willow can also be used. Slow grown wood, with its clear annual rings, produces thinner clefts. You must have long straight lengths of knot-free wood. You will need elm or lime bast to bind the rims.

Fig. 17.11 Second taw F2 in place – note the start and finish positions and the double turn over the bool.

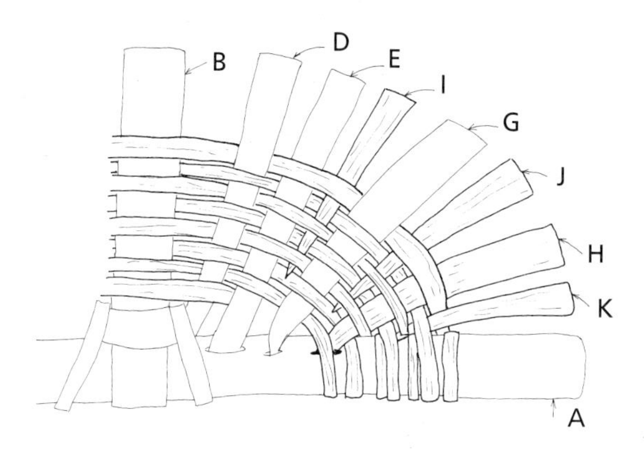

Fig. 17.12 Remaining spelks added and long taws woven to hold them in place.

Method: The way to make a square bottomed basket is:

- Make a clear design of your basket so that you know the size and amount of wood you will need.
- Cut poles to length; the most critical are the ribs which must be the width of the base plus twice the height of the basket. Allow an extra 304mm (12in) for lapping over the rim.
- Remove the bark, quarter the poles and remove most of the centre (**fig. 17.15**) to leave a shape that will give fairly even width clefts. Prepare tangential clefts as described in Chapter 11: ribs should be approx. 3mm (1/8in); weavers approx. 1.5mm (1/16in) and rims and handles approx. 6mm (1/4in) thick. Keep your clefts even, but thin the ribs where they will bend at both bottom corner and rim. Soak or steam your wood for this operation and keep it warm and moist whilst weaving.
- Start the basket by clamping one set of ribs (**fig. 17.16**) then weaving the others between them. Keep the base square by marking its size on the ribs. Use an odd number of ribs for a handled basket.

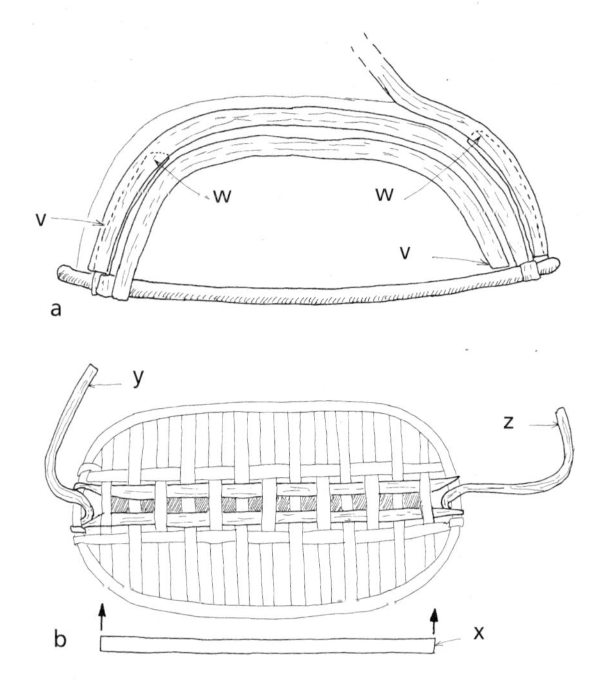

Fig. 17.13 Finishing the weave: a. note the start (v) and finish (w) positions of the bottom taws; b. the gap (shaded) for the last taw which is cut to size (x), fitted and the last taws (y + z) woven over it to finish the weave.

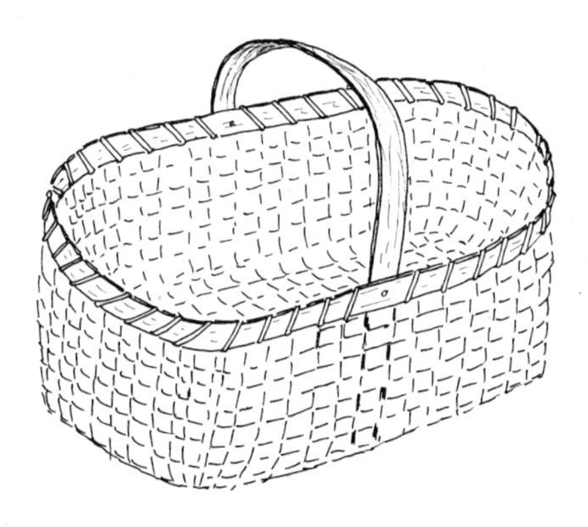

Fig. 17.14 Woven cleft basket.

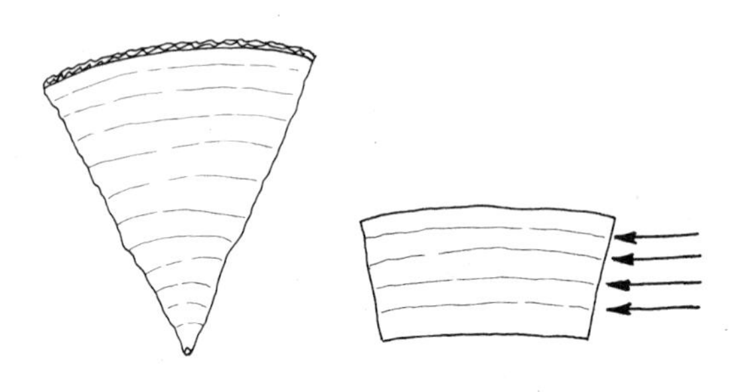

Fig. 17.15 How a segment is split down to make very fine one or two annual ring thick clefts.

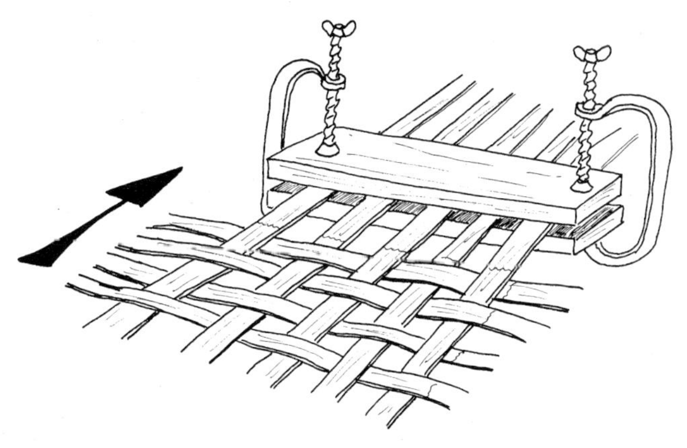

Fig. 17.16 Starting the weave: one set of ribs held in a clamp – note the marks on the ribs that define the size required.

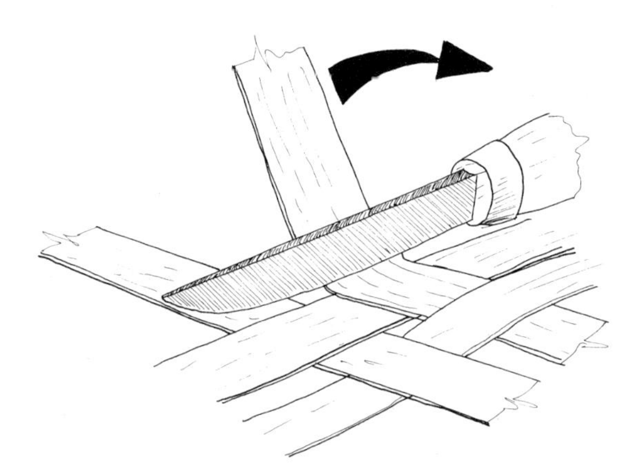

Fig. 17.17 Using a knife to bend the ribs at the point required.

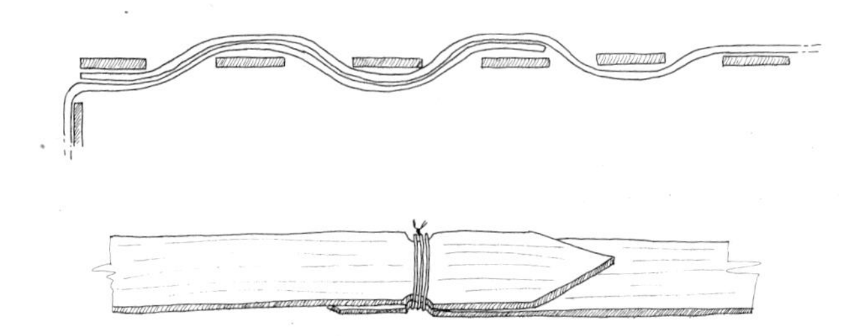

Fig. 17.18 Overlap the ends of the weavers as shown; some makers tie their weavers together.

- Bend the ribs up at the edge of the base (use a knife on your mark to bend them round (**fig. 17.17**) and hold with a hoop if necessary.
- Start weaving the sides with pieces long enough to overlap. Follow the method in **fig. 17.18** repeating until you have only 152mm (6in) of each rib protruding. Use clothes pegs useful to hold the weave in place as you go.

Fig. 17.19 Folding the ribs over at the top of the basket.

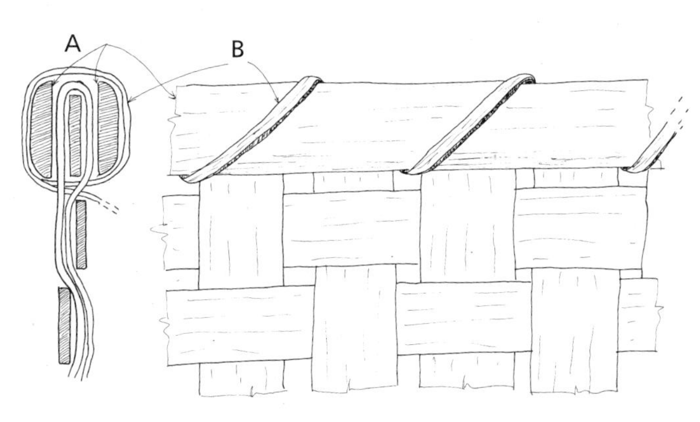

Fig. 17.20 Forming a rim: thicker clefts A are tied with lengths of elm bast B.

- Fold over the tops of the ribs and tuck into the weave as shown (**fig. 17.19**). Make sure ribs are moist for this operation.
- Shape a handle, and shave the ends so it can be forced down through the weave the full depth of the basket.
- Shape two thicker clefts to form the rim, scarf the ends, hold in place with a clamp and then use 6mm (1/4in) wide strip of elm bast to bind them in place (**fig. 17.20**).
- Finally secure the handle using a peg through the rim as shown (**fig. 17.21**).

Round framed baskets with handle: These baskets also use all cleft wood, but are based on a rim frame and handle, like the trug.

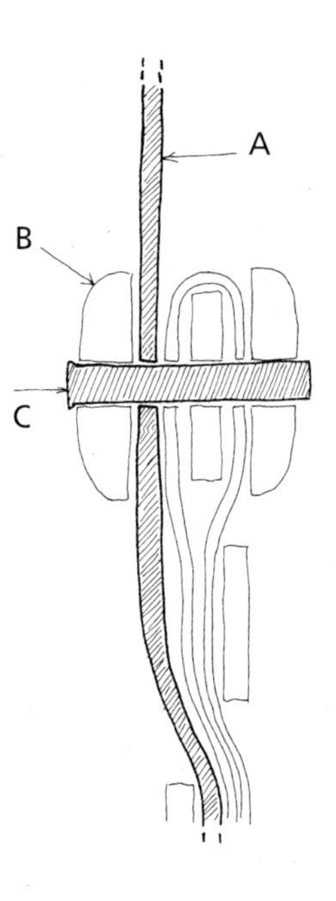

Fig. 17.21 Fixing the handle: cleft for the handle (A) is forced down into the weave and secured to the rim (B) by a peg (C).

Pattern: All of these baskets have a similar basic form and weaving pattern (**fig. 17.22**), but can be half-spheres, oval or melon shaped.

Tools and materials: These are exactly as described in the previous section.

Method:

- Prepare your split material as already described; handle and rim require 3mm (1/8in) thick by 25mm (1in) wide, the ribs are 3mm to 6mm(1/8 to 1/4) diameter, and the weavers 1.5mm (1/16in) thick and approx. 13mm (1/4) wide.
- Join both rim and handle into hoops using hook-and-eye joints (**fig. 17.23**), with the free ends on the inside of the hoop (fig. 17.25).
- Put one hoop inside the other and tack with small clenched pins. Now use a long narrow cleft to bind them together, creating an 'eye'. Two patterns are shown in **fig. 17.24**. Leave the ends long after going round each frame three times.
- Insert four ribs into the eye as shown (**fig. 17.25**) and weave remainder of binding through them to secure. Repeat at other end of basket (**fig. 17.26**).
- Work another weaver at each end, and then insert the four final ribs.
- Carry on weaving. Start new weavers by overlapping the end of the last one. Do one weaver from each end alternately until they meet in the middle. Tuck away the free ends to complete the basket.

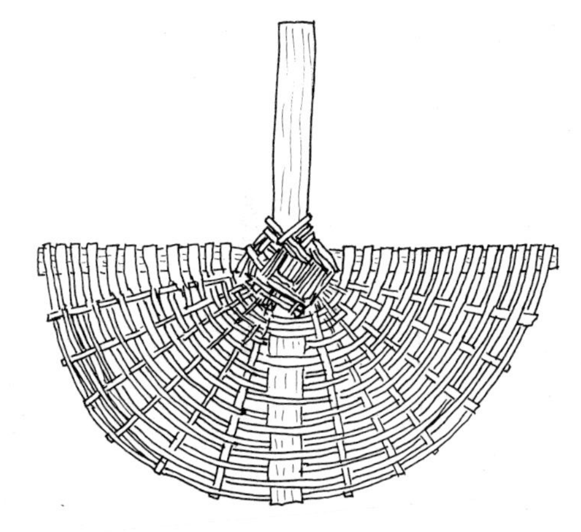

Fig. 17.22 A round, framed basket with handle (note – in practice the weaving would be closer).

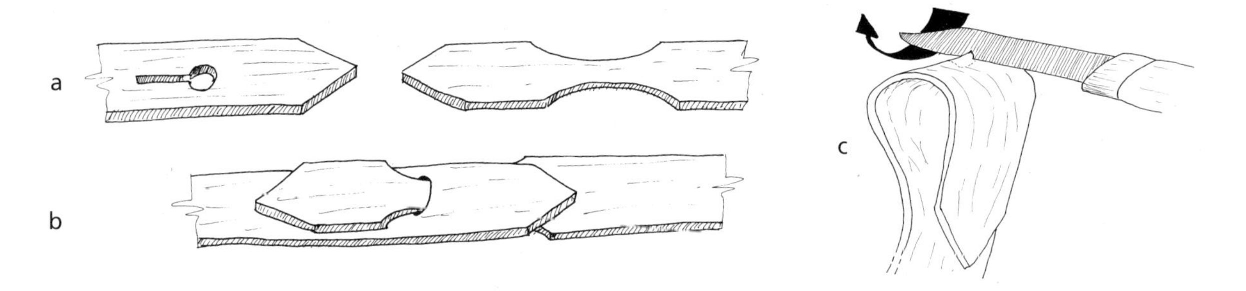

Fig. 17.23 Making rim and handle hoops using hook-and-eye joints: a. shape of hook and eye; b. joint put together; c. cutting the eye (do not fold the cleft the other way – it will split).

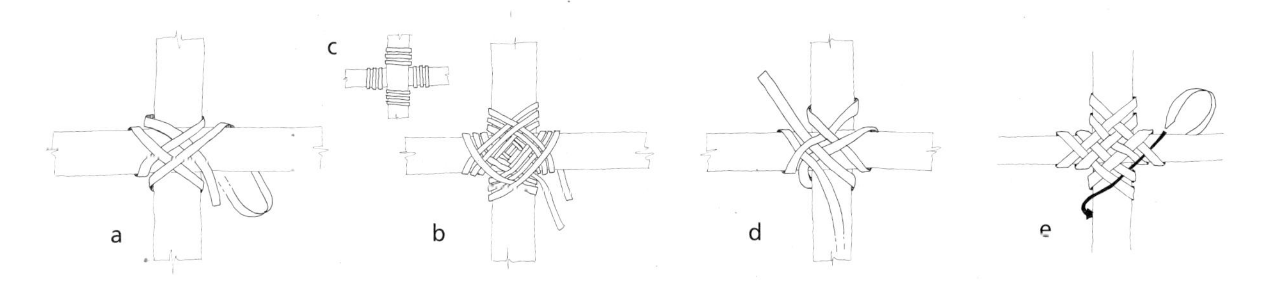

Fig. 17.24 Binding handle and rim together: a. one round of binding; b. thrice round completed; c. view of binding from other side; d. - e. alternative pattern of binding.

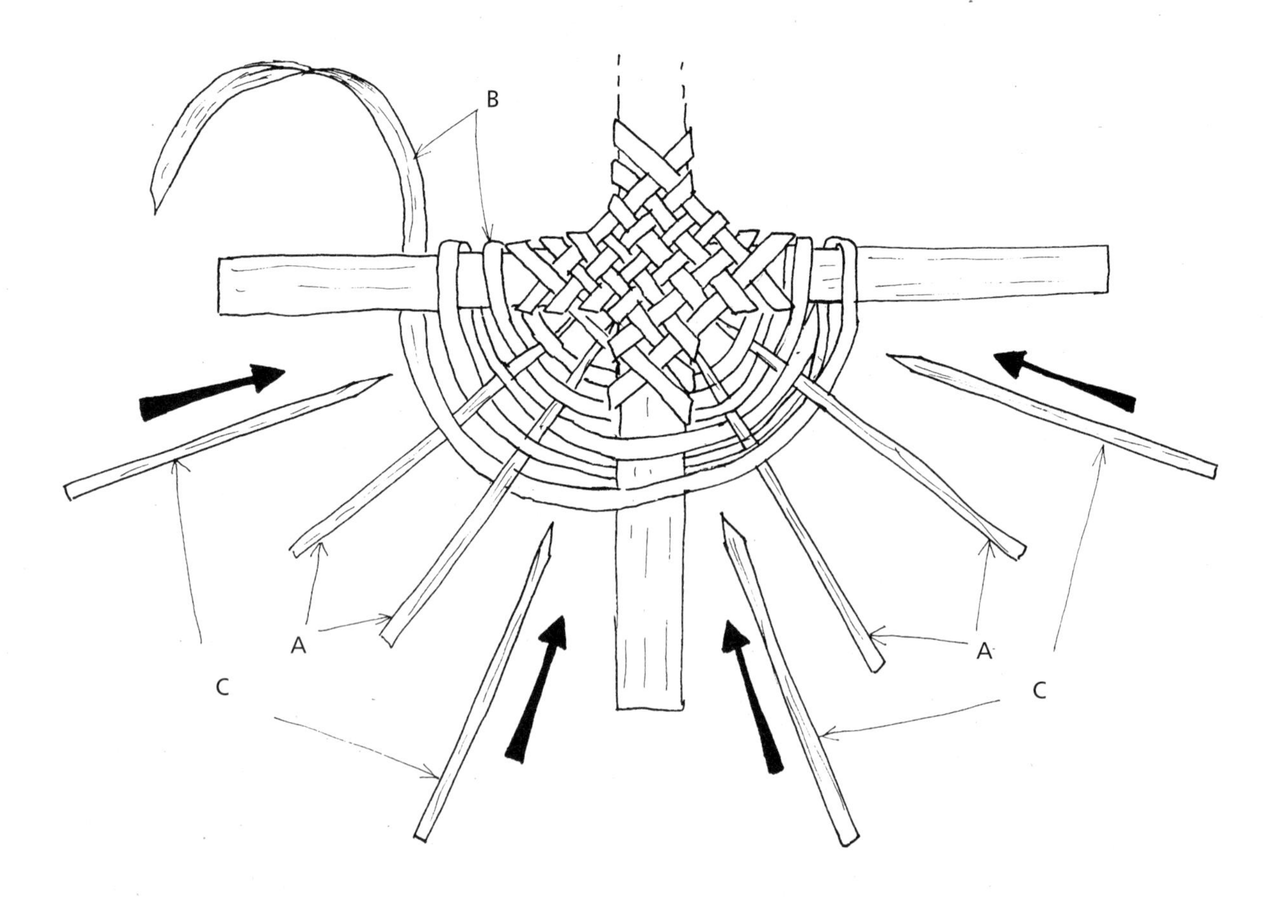

Fig. 17.25 Insert four ribs A into the binding. Weave remainder of binding B (or new length) as shown; insert last four ribs C.

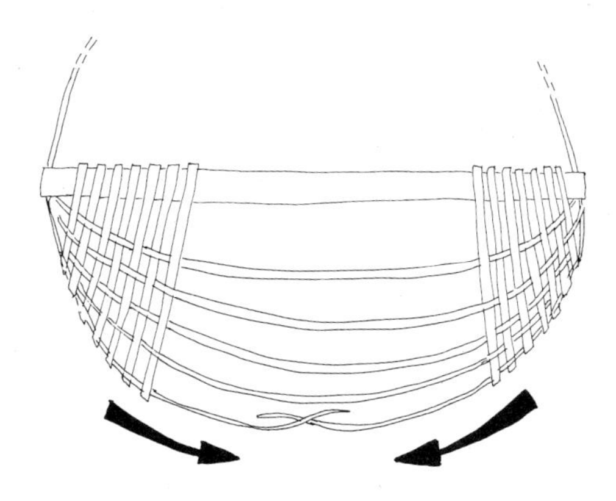

Fig. 17.26 Weave basket from both ends towards the middle until complete (note the hook-and-eye is on the inside of the basket).

Woven round stick baskets

These include the classic willow baskets we are all familiar with, but here I shall only consider two simple baskets made from coppice or hedgerow wood.

Oval and free form frame baskets: These beautiful baskets really capture the essence of products made by hand from native hedgerow and coppice shrubs.

Pattern: Baskets based on an oval (**fig 17.27**) or asymmetrical shape using a rim and cleft ribs, but no handle. Simple over and under weaving is used. The weavers are small round twigs or bramble stems.

Tools: Knife, secateurs, bodkin and thick gloves to shrie the bramble thorns.

Materials: Rims are best in hazel, ash, birch, sallow, chestnut or bramble. Bramble makes good long weavers, but small 3mm (1/8in) diameter twigs work well and are less difficult to prepare! If you can wrap them round your wrist without breaking, they will weave.

Method:

- Prepare a rim from a round rod by steaming and shaping it in a setting frame. Once shaped, scarf the ends and hold them together with tape or thin bark ties (**fig. 17.27**).
- Prepare three pairs of ribs from cleft or round rods approx. 6mm (1/4in) diameter tying them together and holding in a curve with string (**fig. 17.28**).
- Using a fine weaver of bramble or willow bind the first pair of ribs A to the rim as shown (**fig. 17.29**). Continue weaving, taking the weaver round the frame twice each time, until there is enough to insert two more ribs B. Sharpen these to the right length and insert them (**fig. 17.29**). Carry on weaving until the last two ribs C (**fig. 17.29**) can be inserted.
- Repeat this at the other end of the basket.
- Join the weavers butt to tip when starting a new one. I find it best with bramble to vary where the joins come.
- Carry on weaving from each end to meet in the centre. The weaving here should be straight across with no need for a double loop around the rim. Tuck the last weaver away securely to complete the basket.

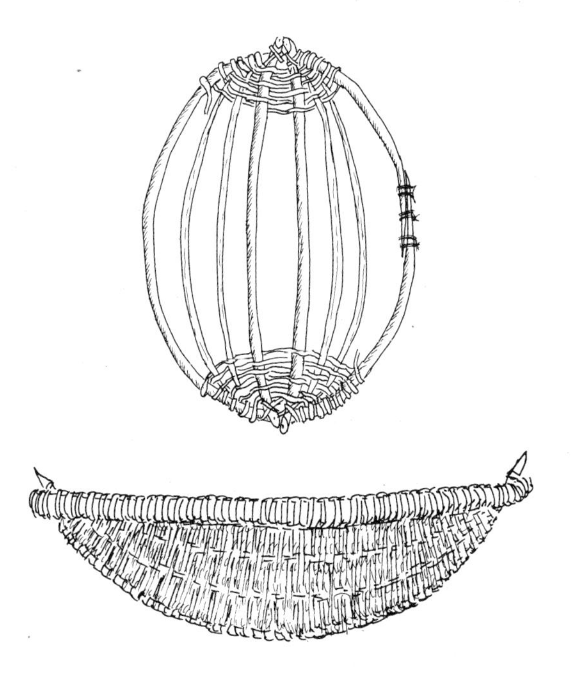

Fig. 17.27 Oval free form basket, based on a rim and six ribs. These can be made in interesting irregular shapes.

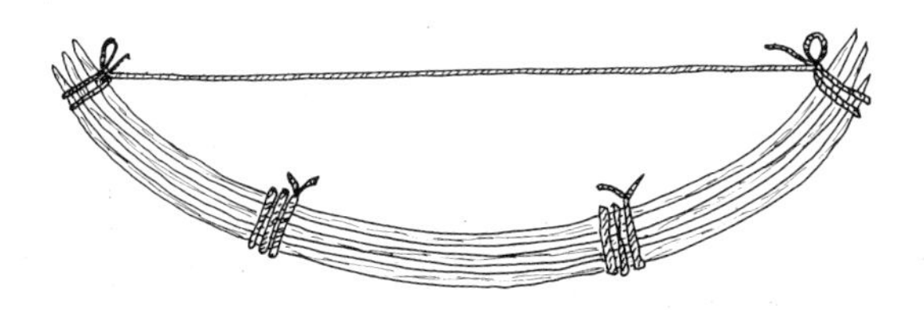

Fig. 17.28 Ribs tied to dry into the required finished shape.

Traditional unframed round basket:
Pattern: There are patterns for weaving bases, sides and borders too numerous to describe here. As an example I shall use a paired base weave, simple randing and a plain border.

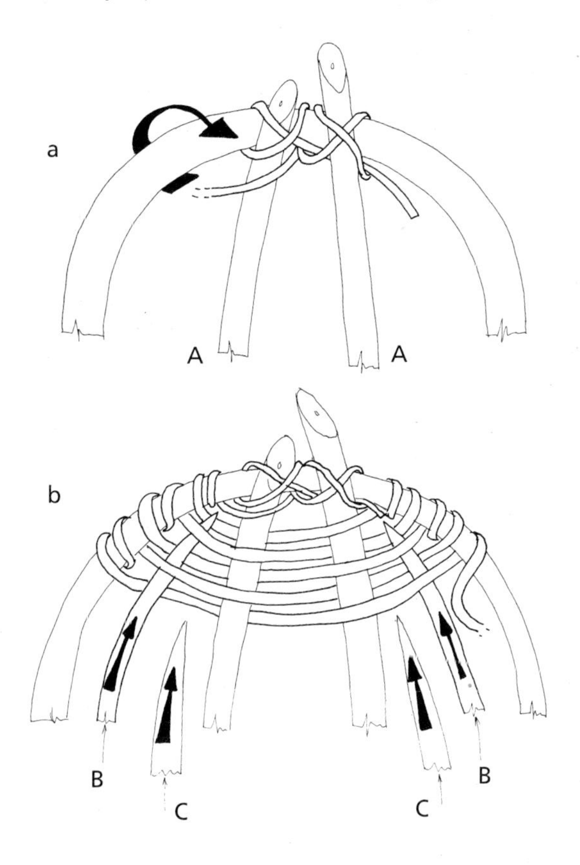

Fig. 17.29 **Fixing the ribs: a. tying the first two (A) in place; b. inserting more ribs (B+C) in the weave as it progresses.**

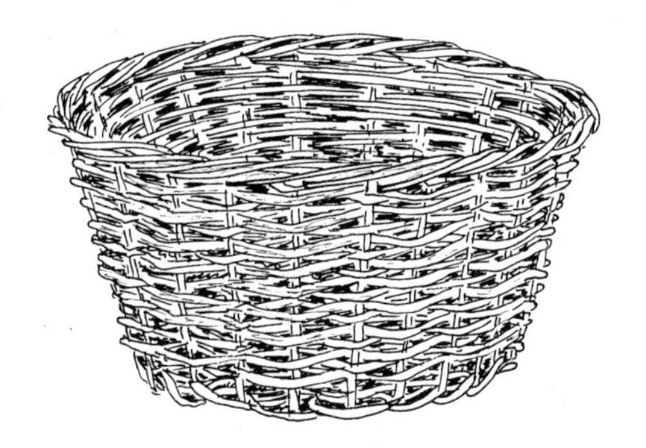

Fig. 17.30 A simple round basket.

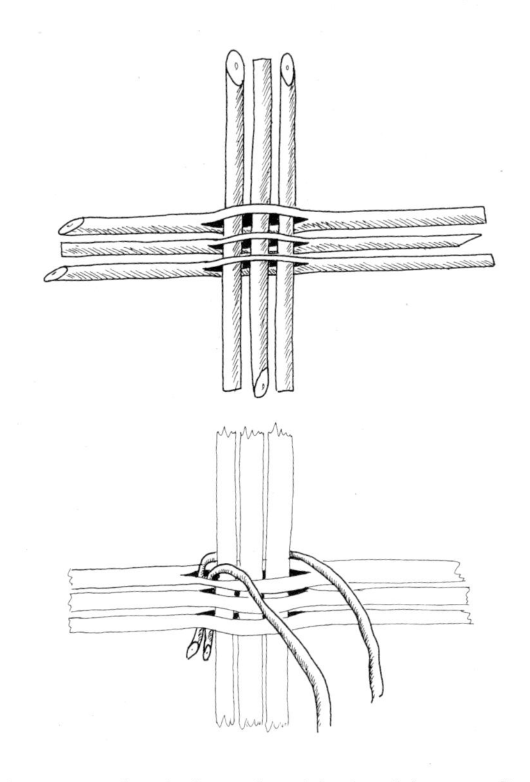

Fig. 17.31 The slath made with six sticks; two fine weavers are then inserted into it.

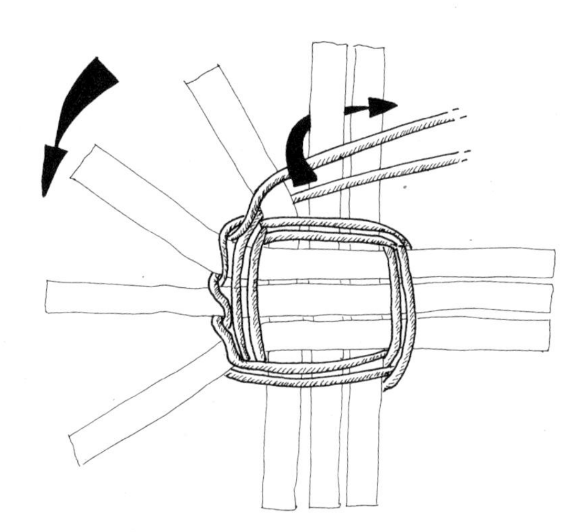

Fig. 17.33 Weave around each stick to form a wheel shape, still rotating the slath anti-clockwise.

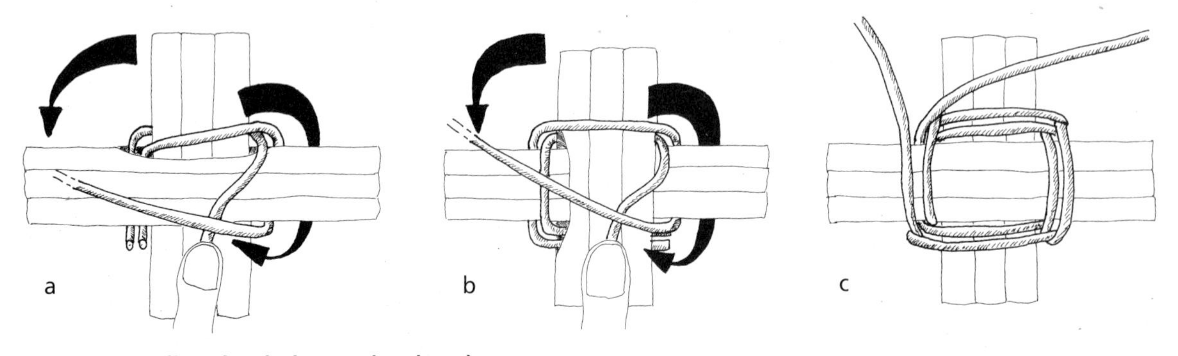

Fig. 17.32 Binding the slath together (a – c).

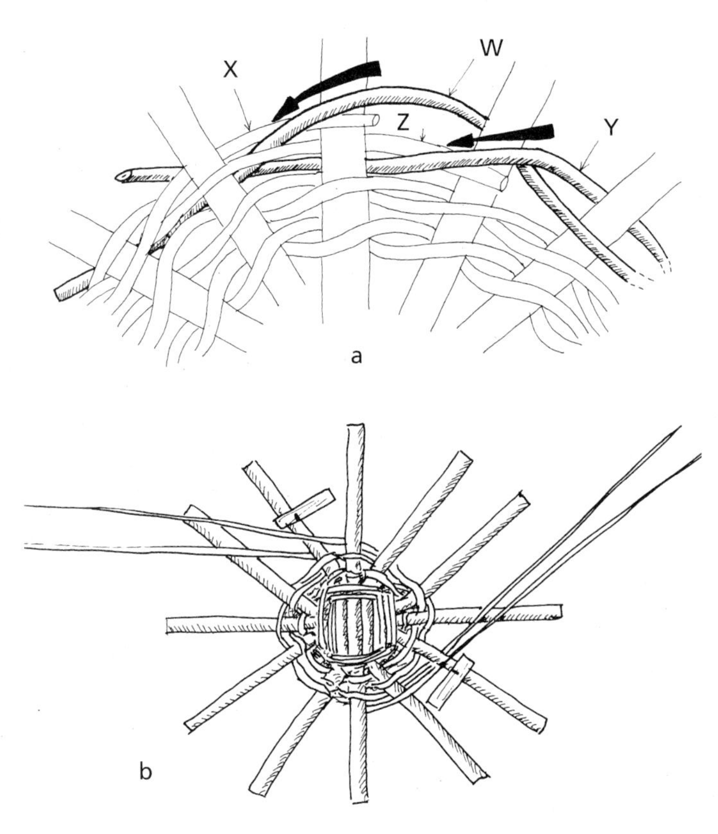

Fig. 17.34 Weaving the base: a. new weavers (W + Y) are inserted to carry on from X and Z which have been cut back to finish at consecutive sticks; b. using two pairs of weavers at opposite sides of the base produces a more even weave.

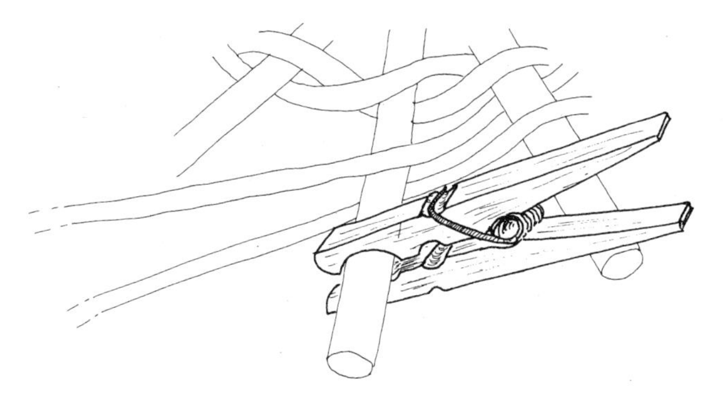

Fig. 17.35 Use pegs to stop the weavers sliding off the sticks.

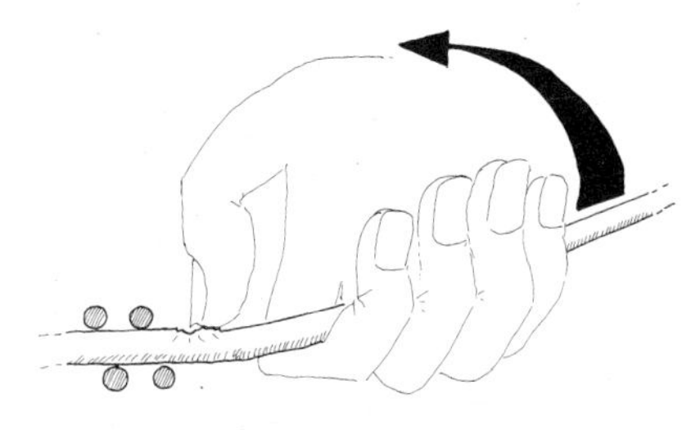

Fig. 17.36 Pricking up the side stakes using your thumb as the fulcrum.

Tools: The least you will need are knife, secateurs, a beater(heavy bar to knock the weave down), bodkin, a heavy weight, a measuring stick, some clothes pegs and a water trough.

Materials: The beauty of wild material is the range of colour and texture you can achieve. Use straight sticks of only one years growth, preferably without side branches and minimum of approx. 405mm (16in) long. Sticks with a large pith will be no good. Season the harvested sticks for at least one month, except bramble and elm which are best used within a week. Keep rods moist and warm at time of use. Use sallow, dogwood, lime or elm for side stakes or weavers, and bramble, field maple, hazel, spindle or honeysuckle for weavers.

Method:

- Start the base by forming a slath using six stout sticks (**fig. 17.31**). Use the bodkin to make a slit in the centre of three of the sticks, sharpen (slype) the ends of the other three and pass them through the slits as shown. Alternate the tips and butts.
- Insert two very fine weavers into the slit (**fig. 17.31**). Holding the slath and right weaver in your left hand, wind the other weaver over-and-under-and-over the slath as shown (**fig. 17.32**). Rotate the slath 90° anti-clockwise and repeat. Continue this binding for two rounds.
- Carefully lever the sticks apart, taking a weaver around each one in turn (**fig. 17.33**). Continue this pairing to separate the sticks like wheel spokes; keep the weave tight.
- When the first weavers run out, start a new pair where they finish and another pair at the opposite side. Start new weavers by inserting the end into the last woven row (**fig. 17.34**). Use pegs to hold the weave in place (**fig. 17.35**). When the base is large enough tuck the free ends under the last weave and trim back all the weavers and sticks.
- Take 24 even side stakes approx. 750mm (30in) long, slype the ends and push one into the weave on either side of each base stick – use your bodkin to make a channel. Prick up these stakes using thumb or knife to make the kink (**figs. 17.36 & 17.37**) and tie them together. Use the weight to stabilise the basket.
- Now start the upsett, which determines the shape and strength of the basket. Sharpen six fine waling rods. Insert three to the left of one base stick (**fig. 17.37**), the others to the left of the opposite stick. Weave these as shown

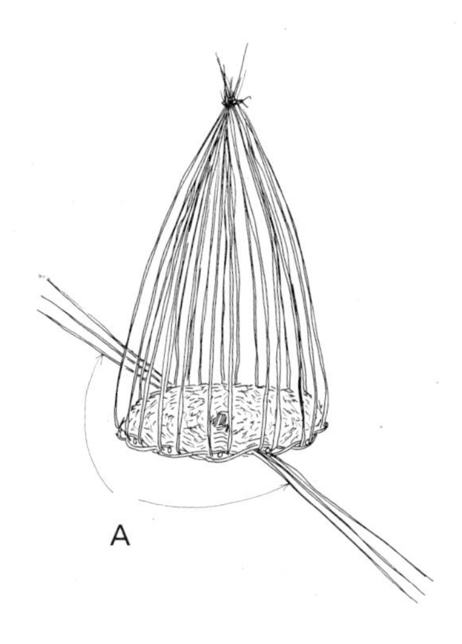

Fig. 17.37 Side stakes pricked up and tied together at the top; the six waling rods A for the upsett have also been inserted.

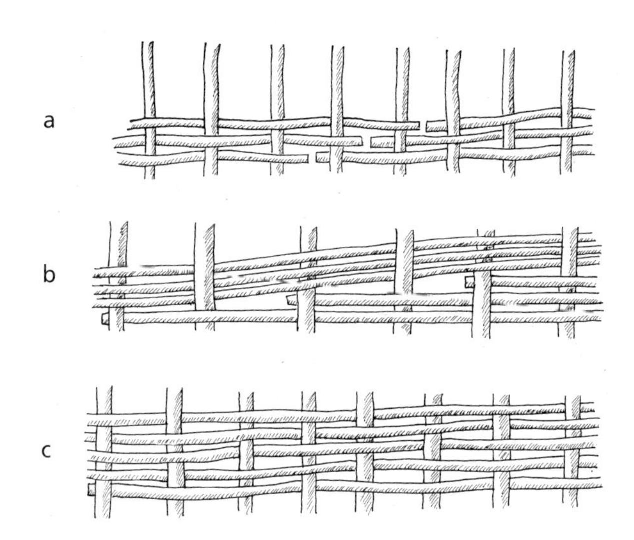

Fig. 17.40 Alternative weaving patterns for the sides of the basket. a. simple randing; b. three rod slewing (note the start); c. rib randing.

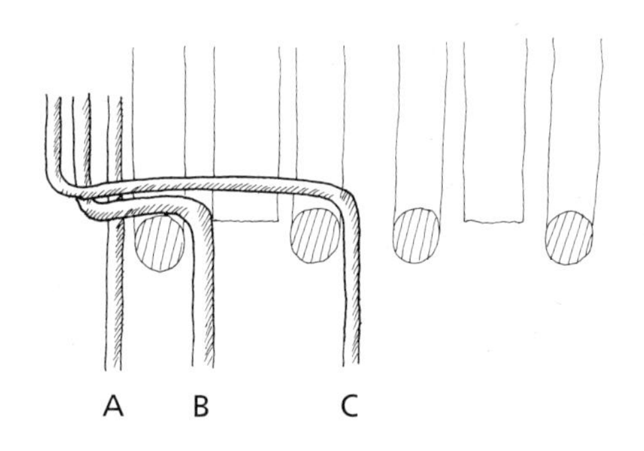

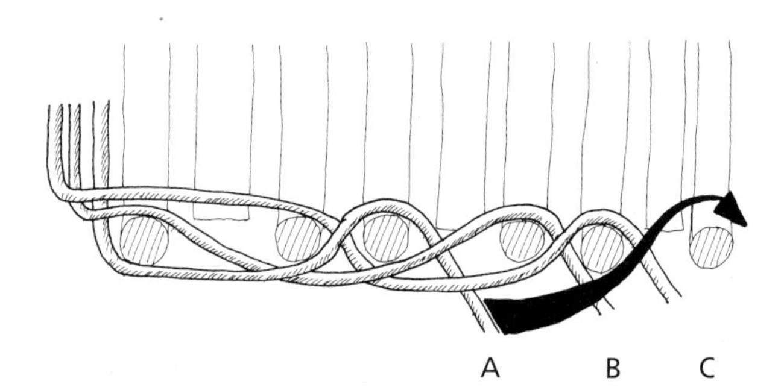

Fig. 17.38 Starting to weave the waling rods: always weave the rod to the left A, first and take it in front of two uprights, behind one, then out to the front. Repeat with B, then C.

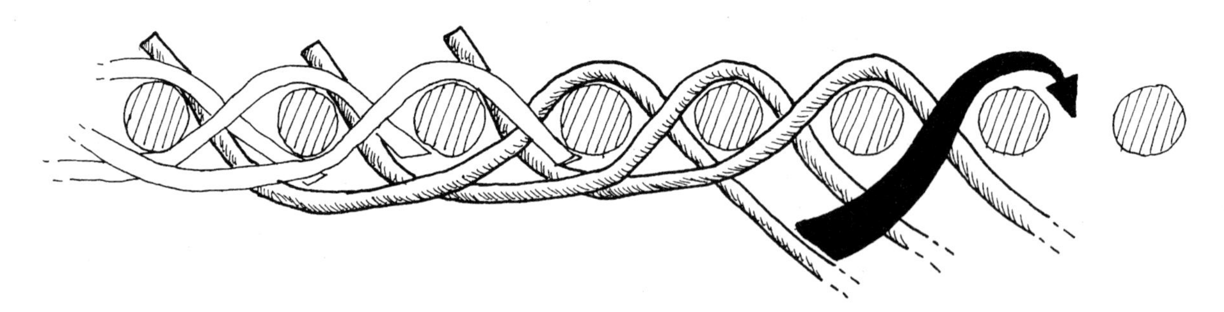

Fig. 17.39 Waling rods are trimmed to finish at consecutive side stakes and new ones inserted as shown.

(**fig.17.38**), adding further rods as required (**fig 17.39**). Keep the weave tight and close to the base; keep the side stakes evenly spaced.

- Now weave the sides. Use two weavers, weaving each alternately 'in front of a rod behind the next and back to the front'. Weavers must be thinner than the stakes. Bang the weaving down every few rounds and join new weavers butt to butt or tip to tip. Alternative weaving patterns are shown in **fig. 17.40**. Finish the side with three rounds of 'three rod waling', as you started.
- To make the border first kink the tops of each side stake over a piece of wood approx. 13mm (1/2in) diameter (**fig. 17.41**).

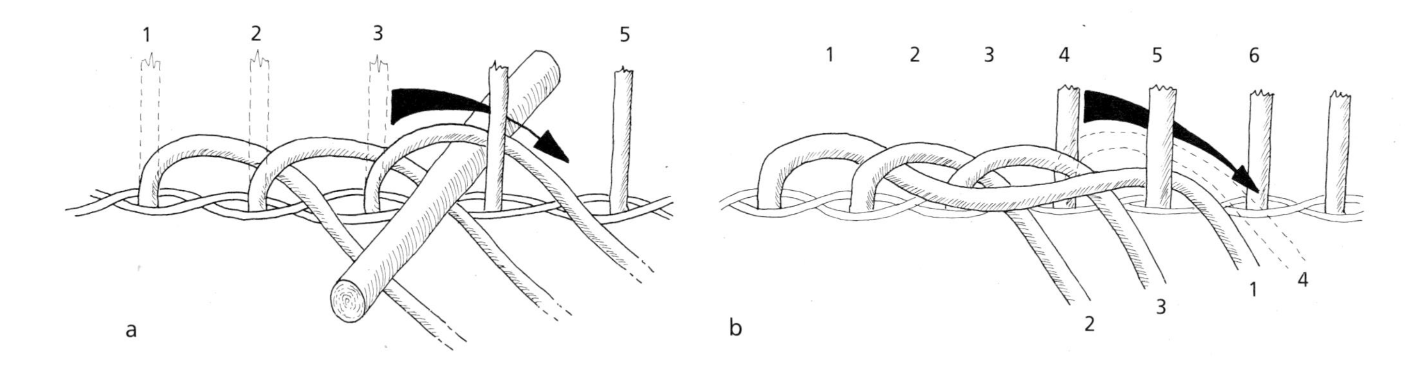

Fig. 17.41 Making the border: a. to start make a kink in every stake by bending it over a rod (this can be done as they are taken over for weaving). Take the first three stakes down as shown; b. continue continue weaving and pulling down stakes as shown.

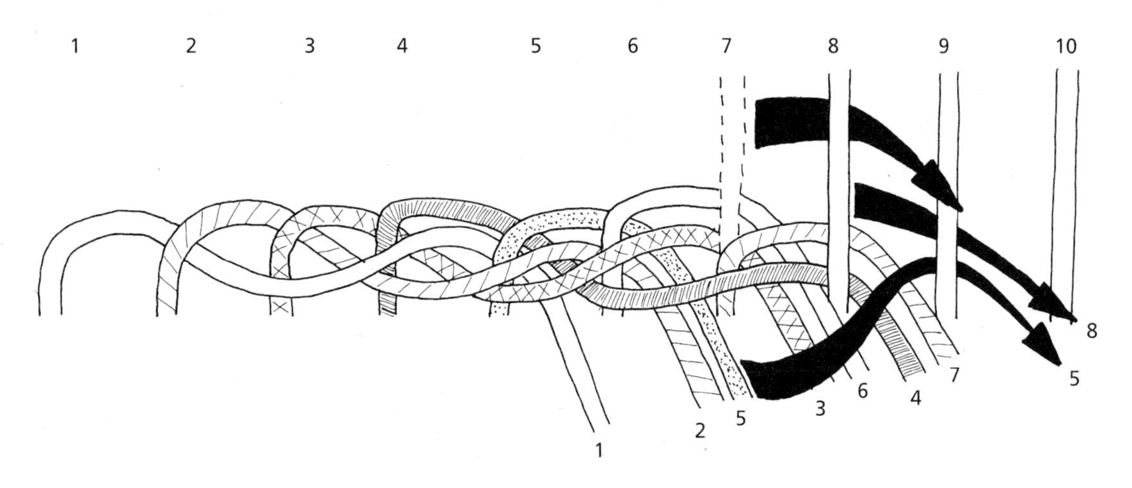

Fig. 17.42 Making the border: once there are three pairs of stakes (2 to 7) emerging at the front, continue weaving around the border as shown. Each time take the right hand stake of the left hand pair; one stake (1, 2, 3 etc.) is left protruding to be trimmed off.

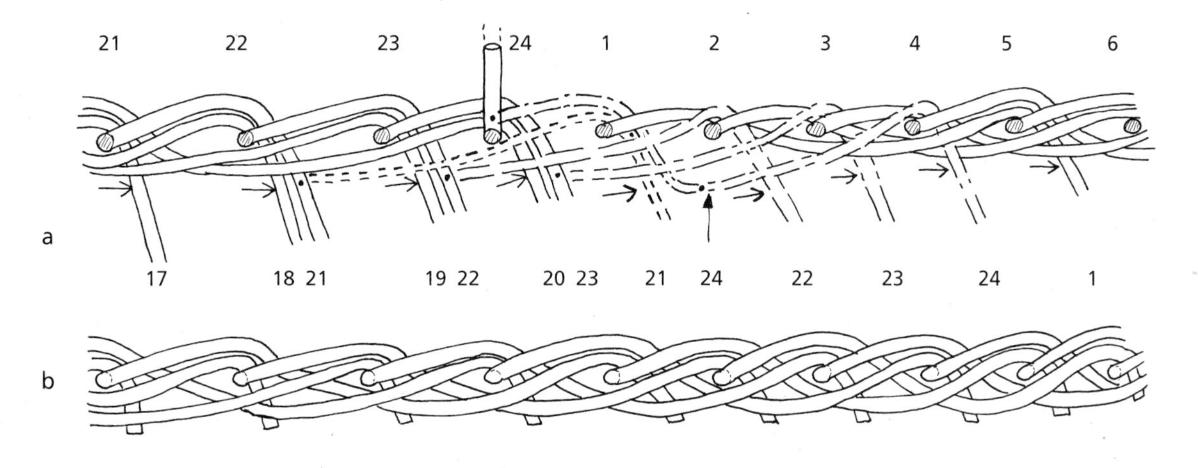

Fig 17.43 Finishing off the borders: a. putting away the final stakes. The slight gap created by kinking the first four stakes is essential here. The arrows indicate where stakes are trimmed off; b. the finished weave.

- For simplicity in the following description I have numbered the stakes from 1 to 24. Carefully bend the first stake 1 over behind 2 and back out in front of 3 (**fig. 17.41a**). Repeat with stakes 2 and 3.
- Now take stake 1 in front of 4, behind 5 and out in front of 6 (**fig. 17.14b**). Bend down stake 4 beside it. Repeat with stakes 2 and 3 to leave three pairs of stakes emerging at the front (1+4, 2+5 and 3+6).
- Take stake 4 and repeat this process, folding down stake 7 beside it (**fig. 17.42**). Carry on round the basket in this way, taking the next stake (i.e. 5 then 6, then 7) which will always be the right hand member of the left hand pair of laid stakes. Stop when only one stake (24) remains upright.
- To finish off take stake 21 in front of the last stake (24) and through the loop created by stake 1 (**fig. 17.43**). Soften these last rods to avoid them breaking. Fold stake 24 down beside it. Then tuck away stakes 22, 23 and 24 as shown.
- Finally trim all the ends with diagonal cuts, making sure they rest on an upright.

Your finished basket may not be perfect, but I will be surprised if you are not already planning your next one.

Further Reading

Barratt, M., ***Oak Swill Basket Making in the Lake District***, Barratt 1983

Collier, D. ***Basket Making***, Cassell 1918

Crawford M., ***Plants for Basketry***, AgroForestry Research Trust 1997

Gabriel, ***The Complete Book of Basketry Techniques***. 1995

Hill, J., ***The Complete Practical Book of Country Crafts***, David & Charles 1979

Langsner, D. ***Country Woodcraft***, Rodale Press 1978

Underhill, R. ***The Woodwright's Shop,*** University of North Carolina Press 1981

Vaughan, S. ***Handmade Baskets from Nature's Colourful Materials***, Search Press 1994

Chapter 18

A Medley of Sticks, Spoons and Whistles

In this chapter we look at a range of unrelated products. Although some, like hoops or crates, are rarely made today, the methods used in their construction may well find new applications.

Hoops

Wooden hoops were made to retain the staves of slack barrels, but today the principle is more used in flower tubs and trug baskets.

Patterns: Hoops are flattened clefts approx. 13mm ($1/2$in) thick with the bark left on one side, and between 32 and 44mm ($1^1/4$-$1^3/4$in) wide. The clefts are between 1.2 and 2.1m (4-7ft) long, as required, and both ends are scarfed so they can be overlapped and nailed together to form the hoop.

Tools: Hoop making requires a froe and riving brake (or adze), draw knife and shaving horse, and a coiling device or easel.

Materials: Mostly hazel , but the stout truss hoops used for nailing others are always made of ash.

Method:

- Cut straight rods 38-63mm ($1^1/2$-$2^1/2$in) diameter of appropriate length and split then into four equal clefts.
- Shave each cleft to an even flat strip with gently rounded edges (**fig 18.1**).
- Carefully slope each end to make a scarf joint of even thickness. Clefts are best shaped immediately, but can be stored and then soaked before bending.
- To shape the clefts either wind them within a circle of pegs on an easel (**fig. 18.2**) or use a coiling device (**fig. 18.3**) which forces the cleft into a curve. Tie or nail the hoops to maintain their shape whilst drying.
- An easy way to nail hoops together is to place them in a truss hoop with their scarfs overlapping, and pin them together (**fig. 18.4**).

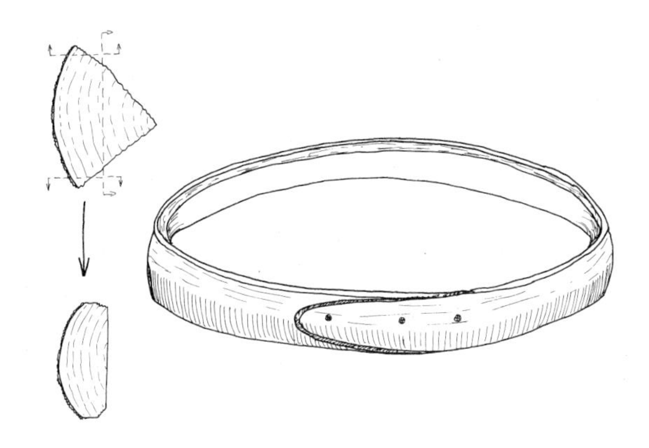

Fig. 18.1 Barrel hoops showing how a cleft is shaved to make the hoop and the finished hoop, scarfed and nailed.

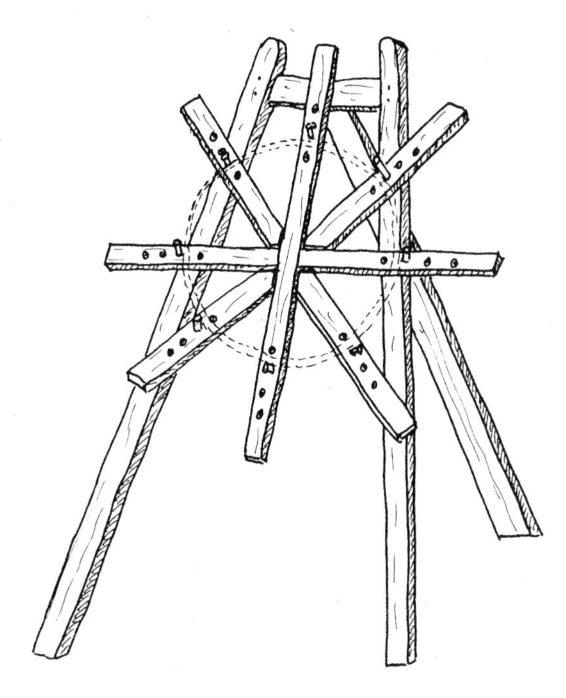

Fig. 18.2 Hoop making easel: the freshly shaved hoops are coiled round inside the pegs, the positions of which can be changed to give different diameters.

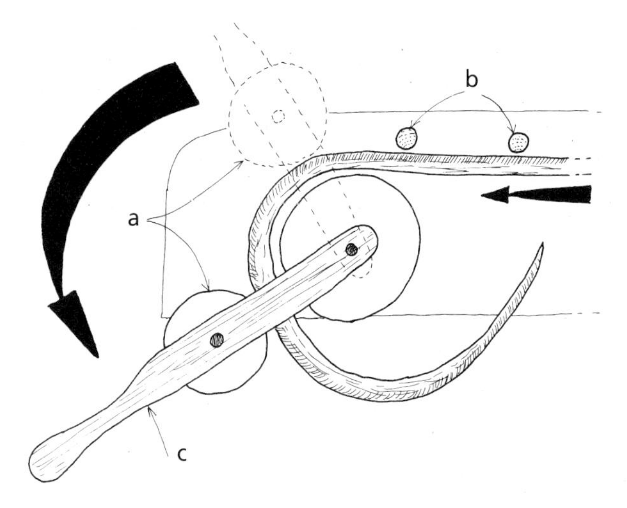

Fig. 18.3 Hoop bending: an alternative to the easel is this device with two rollers, the outer (a) of which can describe an arc As the cleft is fed forward under the retaining pins (b), lever (c) is adjusted to and fro to give the required bend.

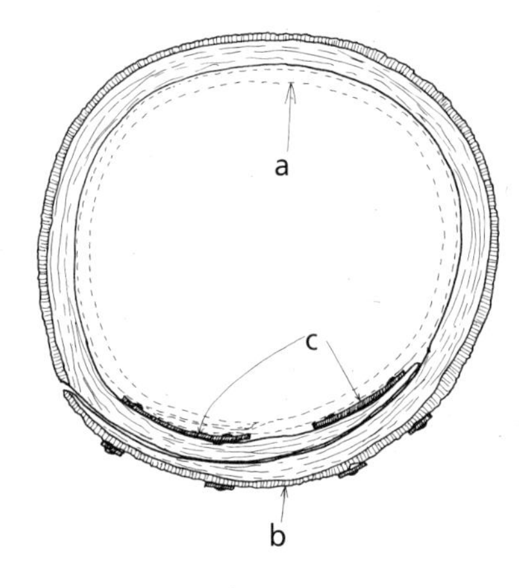

Fig. 18.4 Nailing a hoop: the green hoop (a) is coiled inside the strong truss hoop (b) and nailed in situ against a metal plate (c).

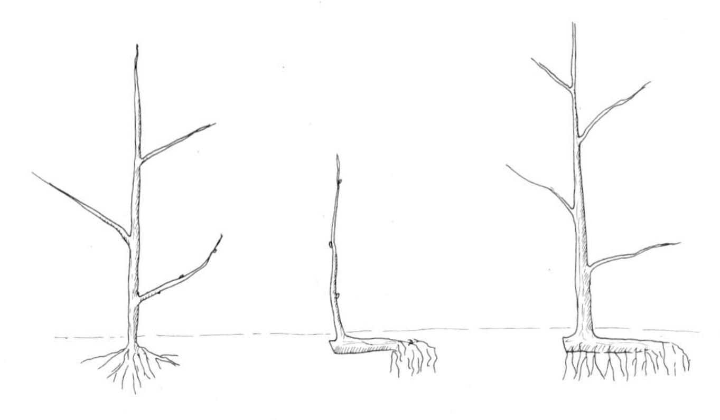

Fig. 18.6 Growing' a walking stick by cutting and turning a young sapling on its side to make a lateral shoot form the main stem.

Walking sticks

That traditional advice to 'cut a walking stick when you see it' is so right – I have lost countless promising sticks over the years.

Patterns: **(see fig. 18.5)** Straight ash plants between 19-25mm (3/4-1in) diameter provide the most basic sticks. They are better, however, with a knob, which may be cut from a part of the tree from which the stick grew, or which may be shaped separately and added later.

Sticks with a right angle handle are usually produced by pruning and growing saplings in a particular fashion (**fig. 18.6**). Other sticks have steamed and curved handles, essential for nutting or blackberrying.

Walking sticks are cut to the size of the user; for an average man approx. 915mm (36in). Thumb sticks are cut anywhere between 1.1m (45in) and shoulder height with a 'V' at the top, which should be shaped to comfortably fit a thumb (**fig. 18.7**). Shepherds' crooks are working tools, similar in length to a long thumb stick, but with a hook designed to catch sheep.

All sticks are better fitted with a ferrule to reduce wear at the base.

Tools: To make basic sticks you will need saw, chisel, carving knife, drills and bits, sanding boards, lathe if you want turned handles, bending jig and setting pins, and a hammer to pin the ferrules.

Materials: Almost any good straight stick with about 3 years growth will do, but ash, blackthorn, hazel, chestnut and hawthorn are the best. When cutting sticks, look for straightness, ends with potential to be shaped (**fig. 18.8**), spiral grooves caused by honeysuckle bines, and good thumb crotches. Cut them when the sap is down, season under cover and use between one and six months after cutting.

Method: The variety of sticks is enormous, so I shall describe only the key processes for the most basic types.

Preparing the stick:

- Do not cut your stick to size initially, leave spare wood to work with.
- Use a chisel to carefully remove knots flush to the stick without cutting into bark.
- Straighten the stick if necessary by steaming or heating over a blow torch, and then levering between setting pins.
- Form a curved handle by steaming or soaking the stick in hot water, then setting it in a jig (see Chapter 9).

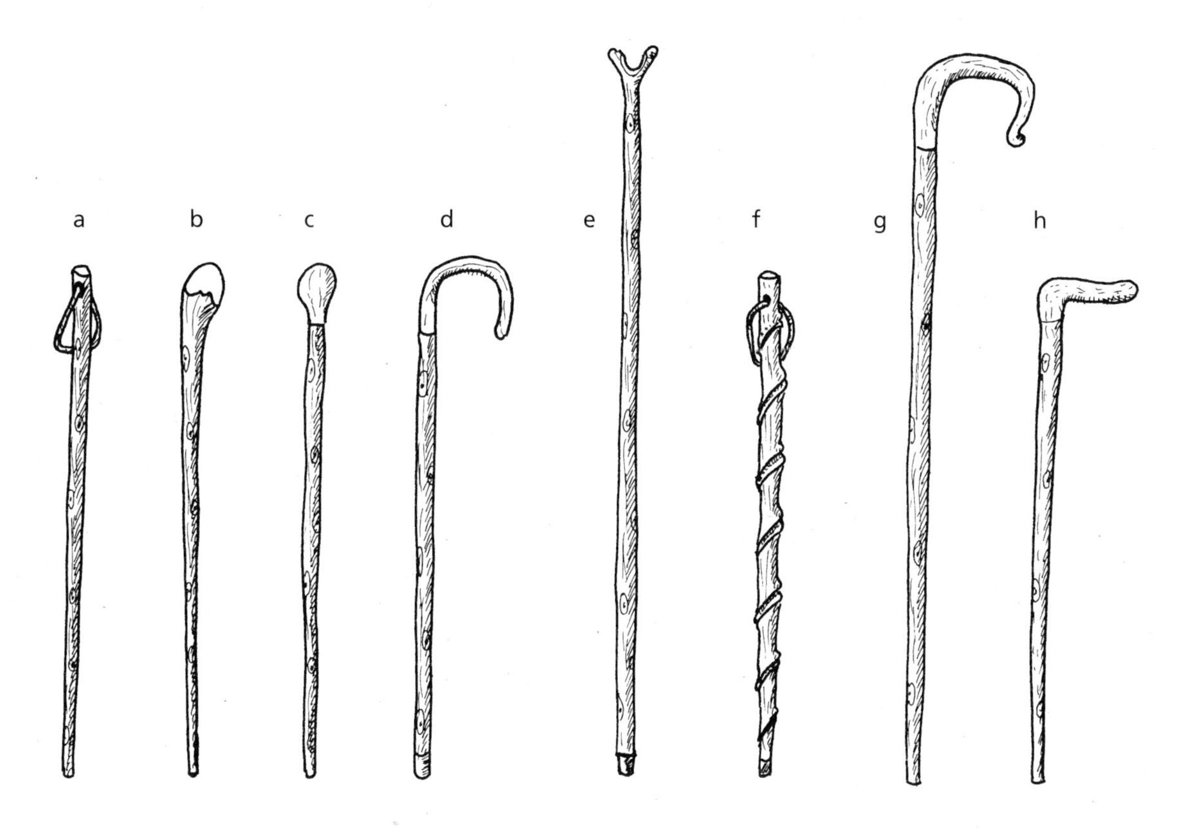

Fig. 18.5 A selection of sticks: e. is a thumbstick and g. a shepherd's stick.

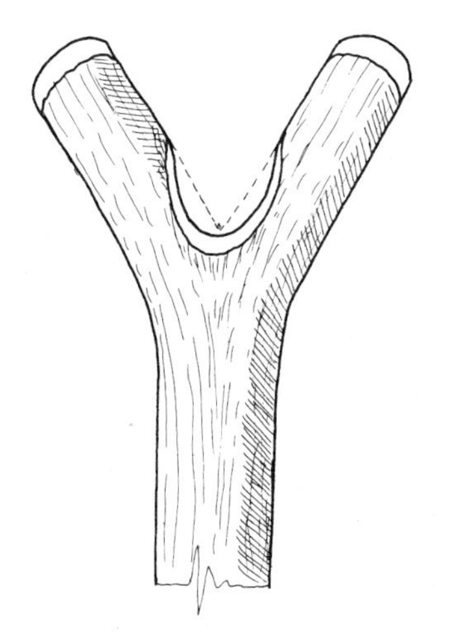

Fig. 18.7 Shape the crotch of a thumbstick so it smoothly fits the thumb.

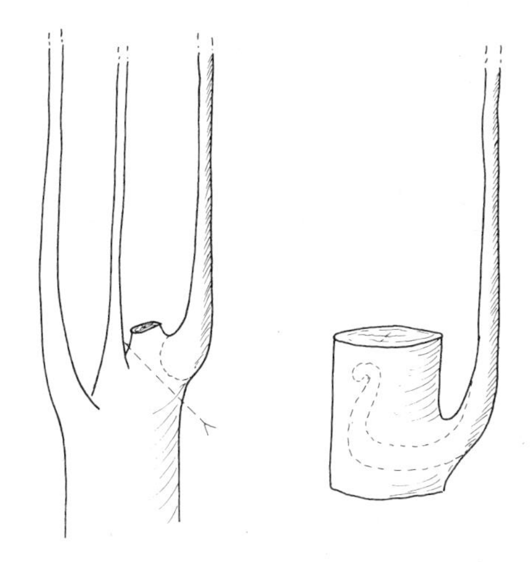

Fig. 18.8 When cutting sticks do so in a way that allows for a handle to be integrally shaped.

Shaping:

- Knobs can be turned on the lathe from suitable material.
- Carve or shape a head from the rough cut stick using saw, chisel, carving knife and sanding boards.
- When shaping always cut with the grain; produce a comfortable shape; do not raise the bark where it ends; draw the shape you want on the wood and cut to that.
- Fancy shaping will need carving tools – seek specialist advice on this.
- Shape inside the crotch of thumb sticks as shown.
- Sand to achieve a fine finish (see spoon making).

Fitting handles: **Figure 18.9** illustrates several ways in which a handle or knob can be fitted to a shaft.

- A round mortice and tenon, for which a hole approx. 13mm (1/2in) is drilled in the knob and

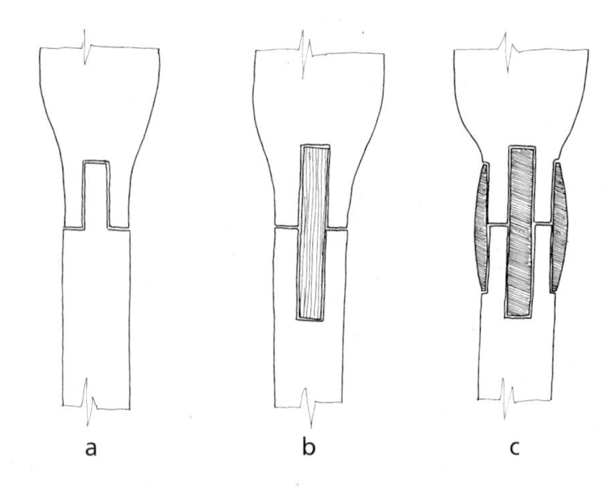

Fig. 18.9 Fixing the head to a handle: a. simple round mortice and tenon; b. a dowel; c. a dowel plus ferrule.

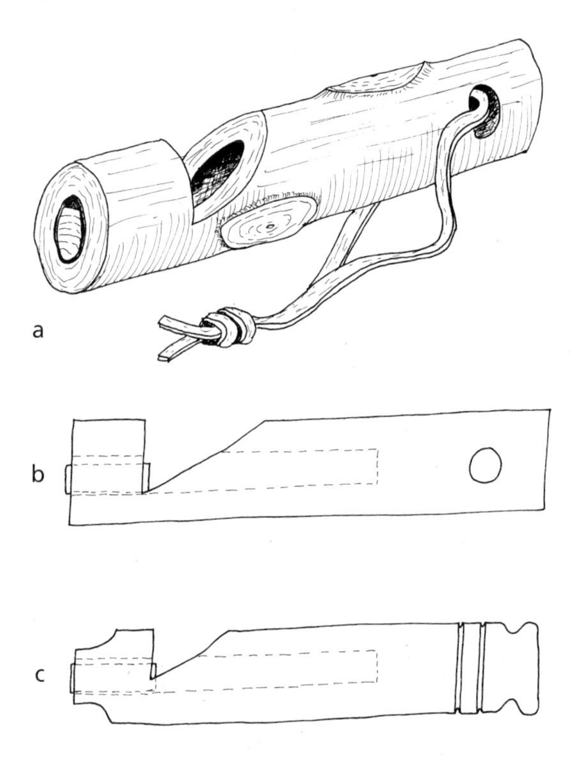

Fig. 18.10 Simple wooden whistles: a. and b. are hollowed round sticks; c. is turned from a cleft.

a round mortice of suitable size is created on the shaft. Use seasoned wood, and don't oversize the mortice lest the tenon splits. Glue two together.

- Alternatively drill a hole in both components and glue a wooden dowel into both to hold them together. Some makers use a steel pin to increase the strength of this joint.
- Joints can be further strengthened and made more attractive by the use of a ferrule. This can be of brass, copper, steel or horn. You should countersink the ferrule to give an even, smooth surface.

Finishing:

- Fit a ferrule to the point of the stick, countersinking it to give a smooth fit, and locate it using a pin.
- Smooth the surface of the stick using a fine glasspaper. Take care to only smooth the bark - do not remove it.
- Apply a coat of clear varnish. If you prefer a more natural appearance, polish with beeswax.

Whistles

Pattern: Simple wooden whistles are based on a blind hole with a notch cut part way along its length and a restricted orifice to blow into (**fig. 18.10**). This creates the air turbulence needed to make the whistling sound, although I have never made two that make the same note! They can be cut from simple rods, or turned on the lathe.

Tools and materials: A saw, drill and knife are all you need to make a whistle, and almost any small rod approx. 19mm (3/4in) diameter will serve. Yew clefts produce good turned whistles.

Method:

- Cut a suitable rod to approx. 100mm (4in) long.
- Drill a 10mm (3/8in) hole from one end approx. 64mm (2 1/2in) into the rod. Drill a hole transversely at the other end to hold a cord.
- Cut a wide 'V' 13mm (1/2in) from the drilled end 50-60% through the rod.
- Use a small seasoned hazel stick to make the fipple or plug. Shape it to fit the hole, then flatten one side to leave a 1.5mm (1/16in) hole after fitting.
- Push the fipple into place, then cut off surplus flush to the end of the whistle. Blow to test!

Sheep feeders

These are for feeding hay to sheep when other feeds are not available.

Patterns: There are two main styles of feeder.

Round woven type: These are approx. 1.0m (3 1/2ft) diameter, and the same height. They comprise 12 uprights that taper towards the top, held together by 2 bands of woven rods (**fig. 18.11**).

Cleft ash crib: These cribs are 2.4m (8ft) long by 0.6m (2ft) wide. A stout frame of four poles supports 11 curved hoops that are spaced and strengthened by clefts running the length of the crib (**fig. 18.12**).

Fig. 18.11 Round woven hazel sheep feeder: this one is shown still sitting in the round mould in which is was made.

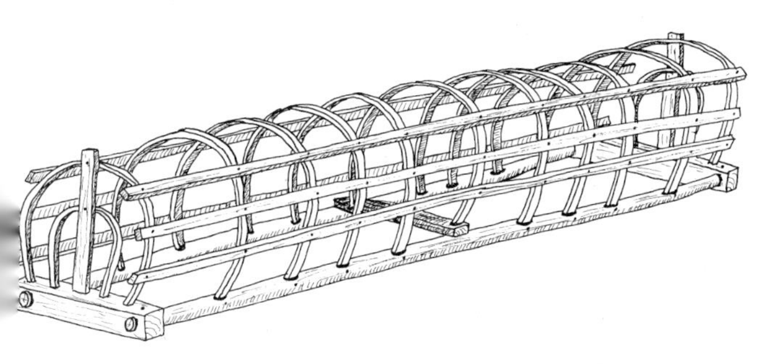

Fig. 18.12 A cleft ash sheep crib/feeder.

Tools: Woven feeders require a mould, billhook and nug axe to make them; ash cribs a saw, froe and brake, side axe, draw knife, brace and bit, steamer and hammer.

Materials: Woven feeders are all hazel or willow. Cleft cribs are ash or willow.

Methods:

Woven: (For this type you will need a wooden mould with 12 equally spaced holes at the right diameter. An old cartwheel was traditionally used, but a sheet of plywood will suffice if you drive the rods into the ground).

- For the verticals cut six rods of approx. 25mm (1in) diameter, 152mm (6in) longer than the finished height; rive them and gently sharpen one end.
- Erect vertical rods in mould.
- Use 13mm (1/2in) diameter rods to weave around the bottom. Pick up the weave in the same way as for a hurdle (Chapter 13) so that no rod end is unsupported and can drop out the bottom.
- Continue weave with cleft rods until approx. 10 layers high; tuck end of last rod into weave.
- If necessary, use a withe band to pull in the vertical rods to the desired shape, then, leaving a gap of approx. 46cm (18in) start another band of weaving, twillying the first rods to give a secure start.
- Progress until a similar thickness of weave as the base and secure the end of the last rod.
- Trim surplus ends of weavers and verticals to finish.

Cleft ash:

- Cut side poles approx. 50mm (2in) to length, remove bark, and shape ends to approx. 32mm (1 1/4in) diameter.
- Cut and shape two stouter ends, drill holes to take side poles and fit and nail both sets together.
- Rive 50mm (2in) poles 0.9m (3ft) long into 4 clefts, smooth edges, and shape ends to fit 25mm (1in) holes. Prepare 11, plus two shorter ones.
- Drill holes in base to take cleft hoops, steam or heat clefts, and insert one end of each cleft into base.
- Carefully bend clefts over and insert free end into other side of base (**fig. 18.13**). Nail into place. Note that centre hoop passes through an additional horizontal member.
- Take six 38mm (1 1/4in) diameter full length clefts shaved and smoothed; nail these to outside of hoops as shown.
- Nail two verticals at either end to complete.

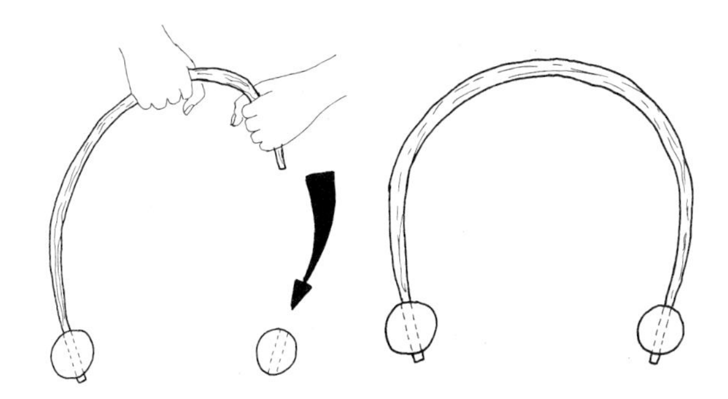

Fig. 18.13 Bending the hoops for the ash sheep crib.

Crates

The largest of these pottery packing crates, can hold almost one ton. They are a remarkable example of how a tough, resilient product can be made using round stick joinery.

Patterns: Crates are made to a standard pattern based on a combination of flat clefts (heads) with holes to accommodate round rods, together with smaller round rods wreathen to bind the sides (**fig. 18.14**).

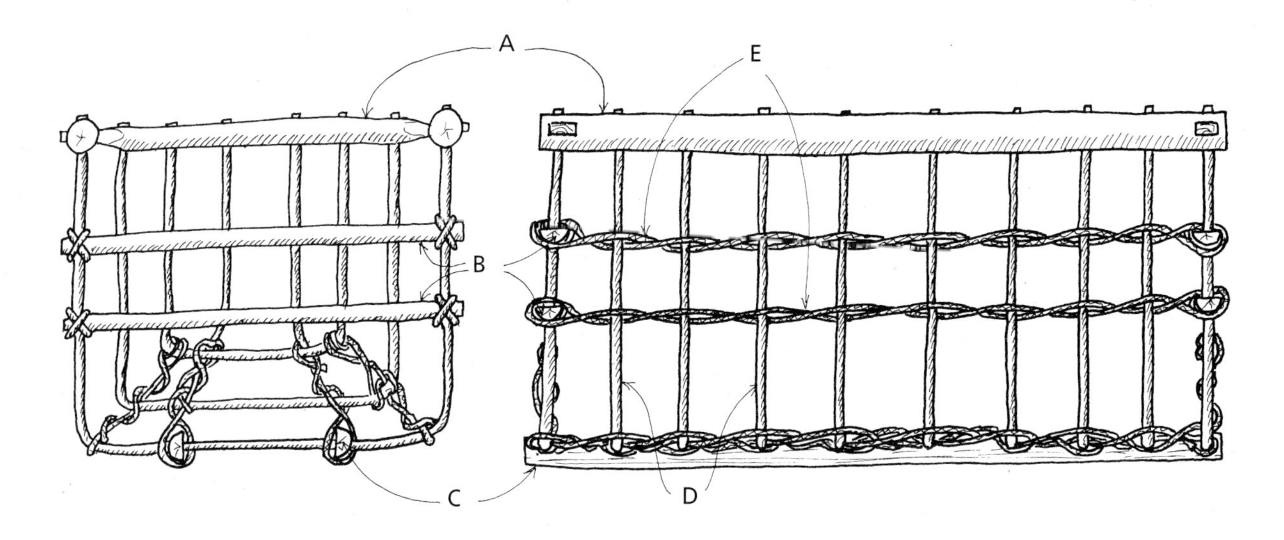

Fig. 18.14 The pottery crate: A. heads; B. end clefts; C. keel; D. bows; E. twilley rods.

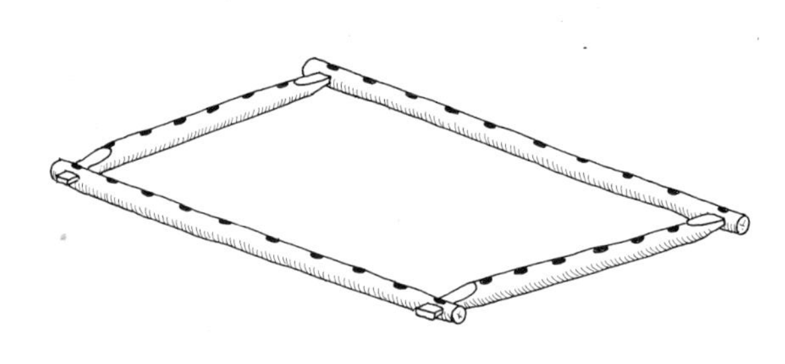

Fig. 18.15 Crate heads morticed and drilled.

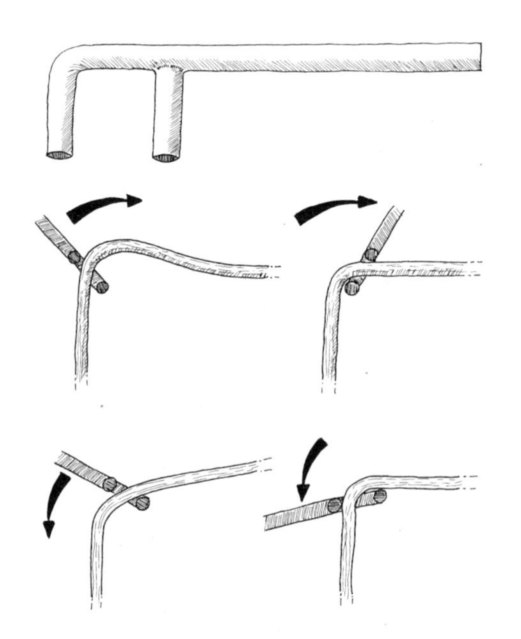

Fig. 18.16 The commander and how it is used to get the bend in a softened rod in exactly the right place.

Tools: Crate making needs a crate maker's horse, froe, side axe, brace and bit, twybil, billhook, hammer, commander and a means of heating small rods to render them supple.

Materials: Heads can be of hazel, chestnut, oak, birch or alder. The smaller rods are all of hazel.

Method:

- Cut four 76mm (3in) poles to length for the heads A; straighten (after heating) if required, and flatten on one side.
- Shape the ends of the short heads into tenons.
- Mark and drill the holes, required in all four heads.
- Cut mortices in the longer heads and fit the tennoned heads to them (**fig. 18.15**). Secure by drilling through the joints and pegging them. (Cut plenty of 9mm x 50mm (3/8 x 2in) pegs).
- Rive three poles into six clefts for the end clefts B and base (keel) C. Mark and drill holes in them as required.
- Now cut round rods for the end bows D, and after steaming, fit these into the end heads, remembering to incorporate the two end clefts. Use the commander to lever the rods to the correct shape (**fig. 18.16**).
- Remove one end of the outer bows, slide the keel clefts over, and replace the bows (**fig. 18.17**).
- Place two thin rods into the central holes at each end, using small wedges to secure them and the bow rods to the heads. Withe the fine rods to secure the keels as shown (**fig. 18.18**).
- Heat the rods that will form the base and sides D, pass them through the keels and locate their ends in heads (**fig. 18.18**).

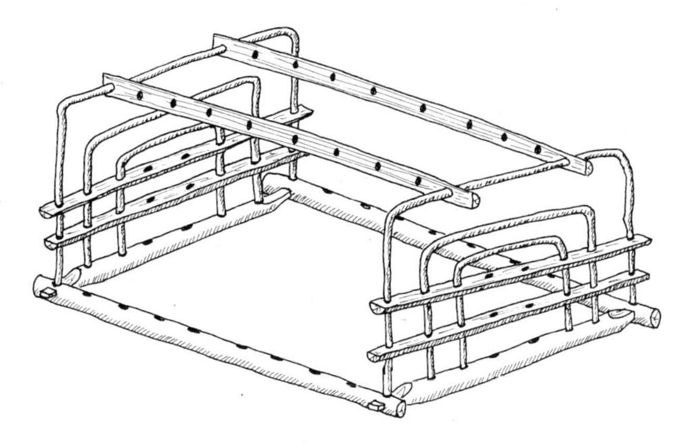

Fig. 18.17 Crate with the heads, ends and keels assembled.

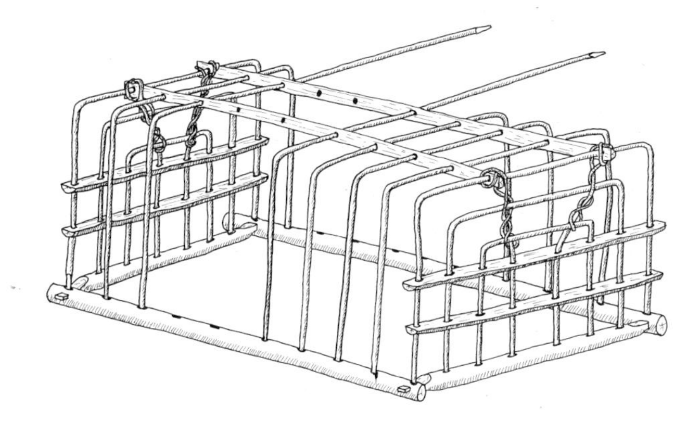

Fig. 18.18 Crate with keels fixed by wreathen rods and the bows being put in place.

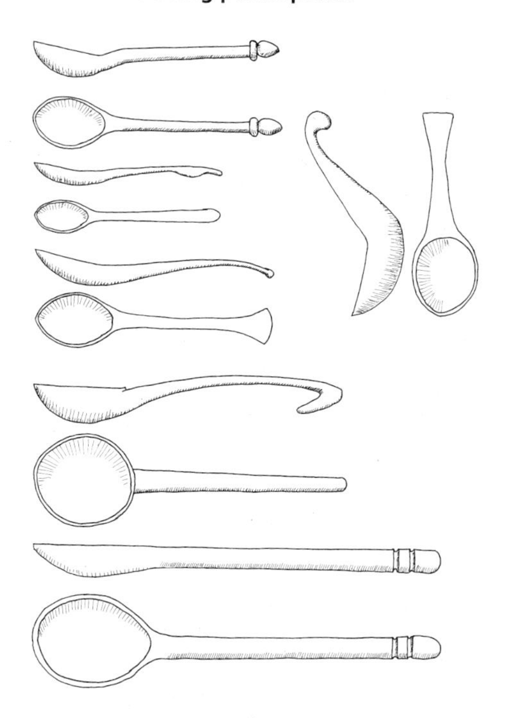

Fig. 18.19 A range of spoon patterns, some with turned handles.

- Twilley two rods along the bottom corner of the crate, and up to the end bow rods. Run two twilley rods E along each side between the end clefts, and one between the two keels.
- Secure rods into the heads by jamming wedges in the mortice holes; trim surplus ends.

Spoons

Sitting beside the woodstove creating a spoon both functional and beautiful from a branch is one of green woodworking's real pleasures.

Patterns: **(fig 18.19)** shows some different shapes. Simple spoons have bowl and handle in a straight line, and their handles may often be turned. The most useful spoons and ladles, however, are cranked – just try the difference to see how effective this is in use. The strongest spoons are made from branch wood in which the grain follows the shape of the spoon. The shape should also give strength where bowl and handle join. Beyond this, the design of a particular spoon is governed by its end use.

Tools: Saw, side axe or billhook together with pattern and file will be needed for rough shaping. Final shaping requires spoon knives and a spoon gouge. A mould for holding the spoon on a horse when using the chisel may help. Sanding boards and garnet paper will be needed for finishing.

Tool use: Only use proper spoon knives and keep them very sharp. When cutting with them, use the following methods (**fig. 18.20 a-e**):

- Hold the work piece in left hand and cut away from body.
- Holding the work piece against your chest, blade pointing upwards, cut with short strokes towards chest.
- Hold the work piece in left hand and cut away from body in short cuts using your left thumb to push back of blade.
- Hold work piece in left hand and rest right thumb behind it. Pull the knife, blade pointing up, towards body, but aiming to miss the ball of your thumb.
- When using the curved knife cut with and across the grain, never against it.

Material: Although you can make a spoon of any wood, maple, sycamore, birch, cherry, yew and spindle are excellent. Willow and poplars including aspen are too soft, and ash, hornbeam, hawthorn and chestnut tend to be too hard.

Cut suitable pieces from branch wood, but use them green for they work much more easily. If you cannot complete carving in one session, put spoon in a plastic bag in the fridge to retain its moisture.

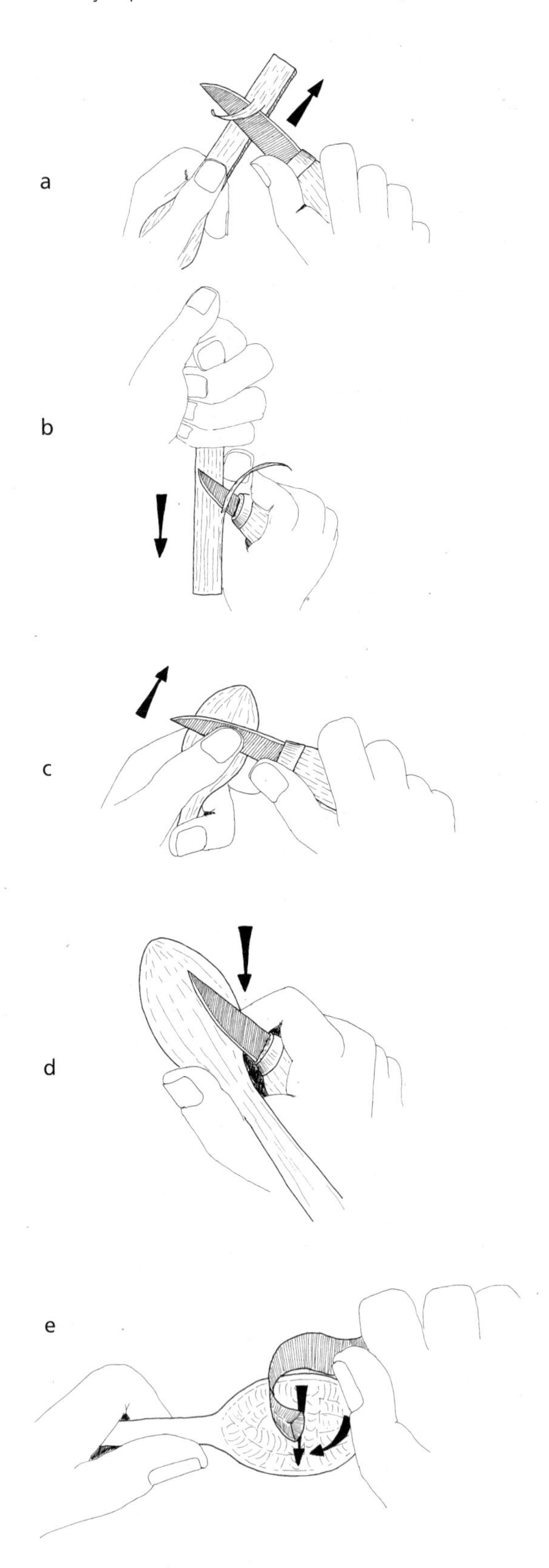

Fig. 18.20 Using spoon knives: a. powerful cuts away from the body; b. cutting towards body; c. using left thumb to push the blade; d. pulling the knife, thumb protected by spoon; e. using the curved knife.

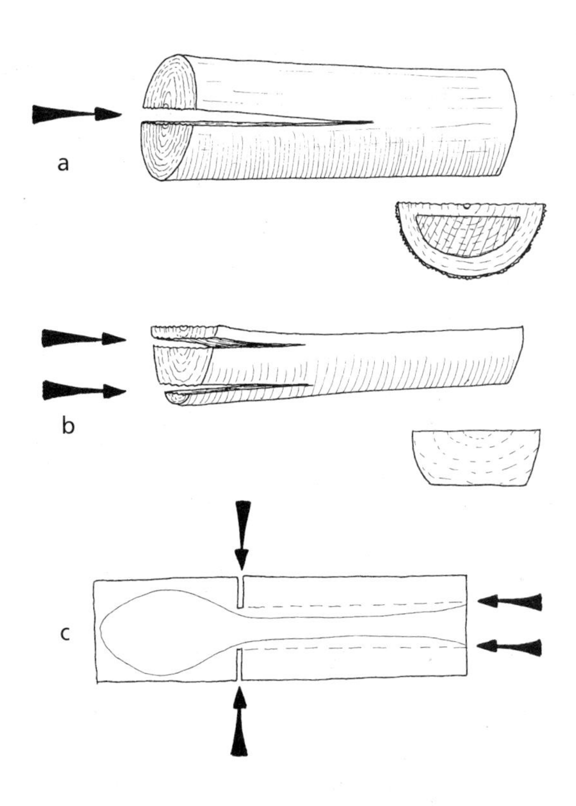

Fig. 18.21 Spoon making: a. split round stick; b. shave off inner and outer surfaces; c. cut away waste.

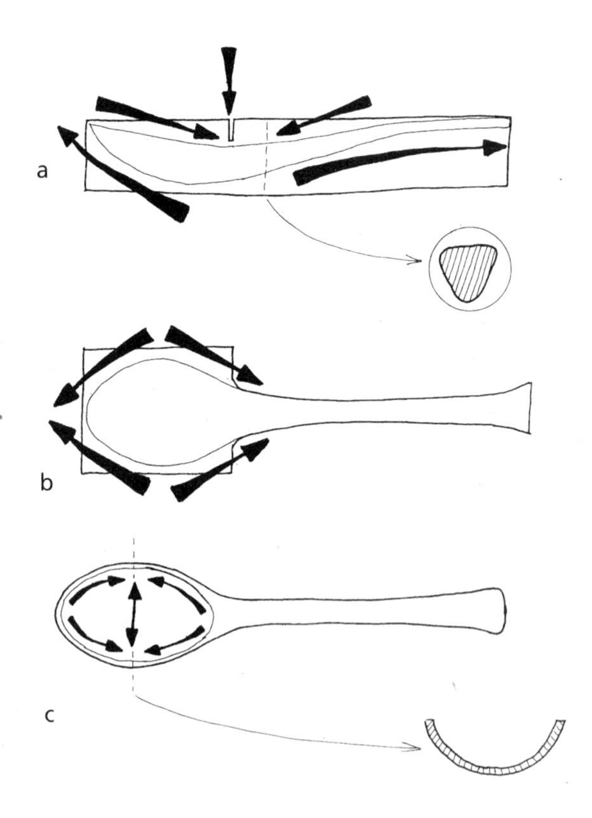

Fig. 18.22 Spoon making: a. and b. shaping the spoon – remove waste wood, always cutting with the grain; c. hollowing out the bowl – cut with or across the grain.

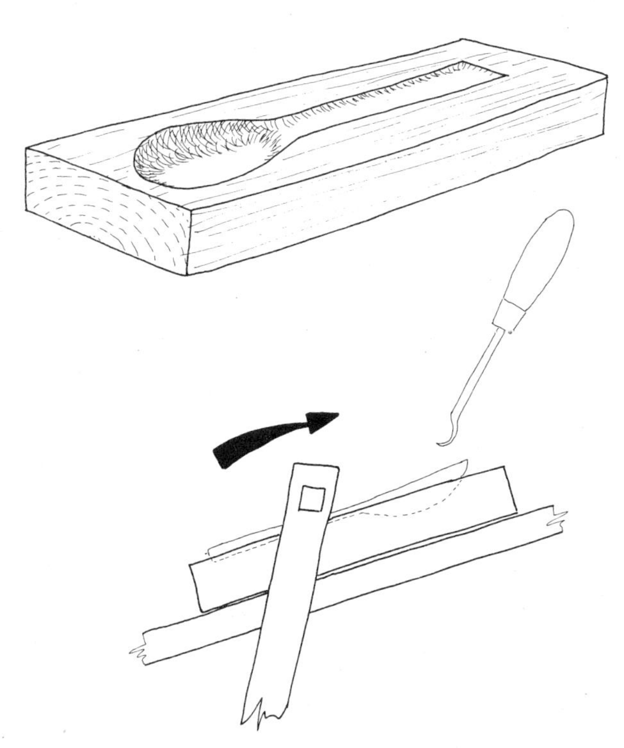

Fig. 18.23 A mould for holding the spoon is particularly useful when hollowing the bowl; it is best used on a horse with a spoon gouge to start the hollowing process.

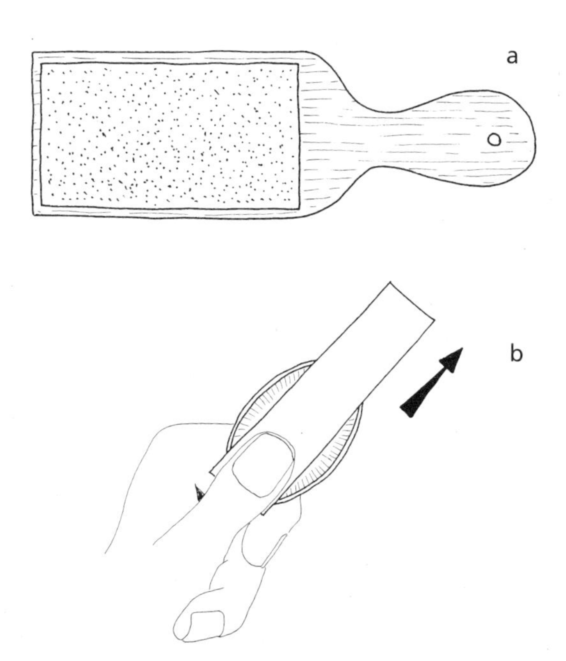

Fig. 18.24 Sanding spoons: a. fine paper glued to a board; b. pull a strip of garnet paper under the thumb in order to smooth the bowl.

Method: **(see figs. 18.21 and 18.22)**

- Cut branch to length and split it along the centre. Then remove bark, flatten the back and remove the pith.
- Draw the pattern of your spoon on cleft face. Then make saw cuts in waste wood at point where bowl and handle meet.
- Remove waste wood from around the handle.
- For a cranked spoon make a 6mm (1/4in) cut in top face where bowl and handle meet. Remove this waste wood with your billhook and then redraw top and side patterns of spoon.
- Remove the waste wood from the bottom and sides of the bowl using billhook or knife.
- Use your knife to improve and smooth this shape.
- Now remove the inside of the bowl using a hook knife. Try to keep it even and finally approx. 2.5mm (1/10in) thick except where it joins the handle. Curving cuts going with or across the grain give a smooth even finish.

If you have difficulty starting the hollow with a hooked knife, place your emerging spoon in a mould (**fig. 18.23**); this will allow you to hold it in a foot vice and use a spoon gouge to remove much of the waste wood. Then use the hook knife to obtain the finish and even thickness.

- When shaping is finished, allow the spoon to dry slowly for a couple of days, then smooth with a garnet paper either on a board or in strips you can pull under your thumb (**fig. 18.24**). Start with 180 grade paper, then wet the spoon to raise the grain, dry it again, then use 240 grade to finish.
- To seal for use, soak in an oil such as walnut (remember if selling the spoon to warn people who may have nut allergies) which is taken up faster if warm.

A final polish and your spoon is ready.

Further reading:

Fossel, T., ***Walking and Working Sticks,*** Apostle Press 1987
Langsner, D., ***Country Woodcraft,*** Rodale Press 1978
Ljunberg, ***Carving and Whittling: The Swedish Style***
Rodgers, E., ***Making Traditional English Wooden Eating Spoons,*** Woodland Craft Supplies, 1997
Underhill, R., ***The Woodwright's Shop,*** University. of North Carolina Press 1981

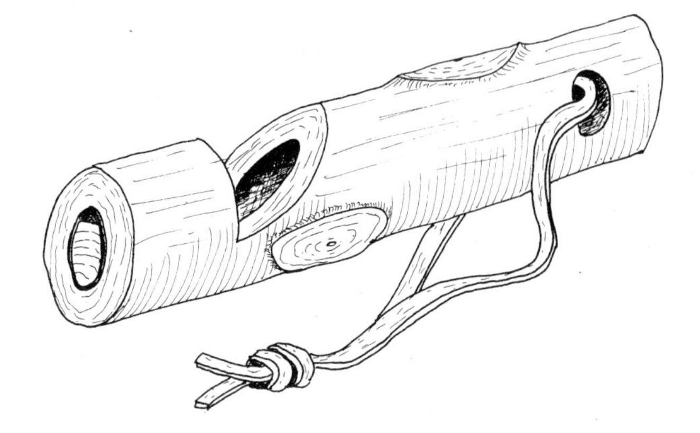

Appendices 1

Dimensions of Unusual Tools and Devices

Within the text various tools and devices are described that you will have to make or have made by a specialist. The following sketches include the crucial dimensions you will need in order to do this.

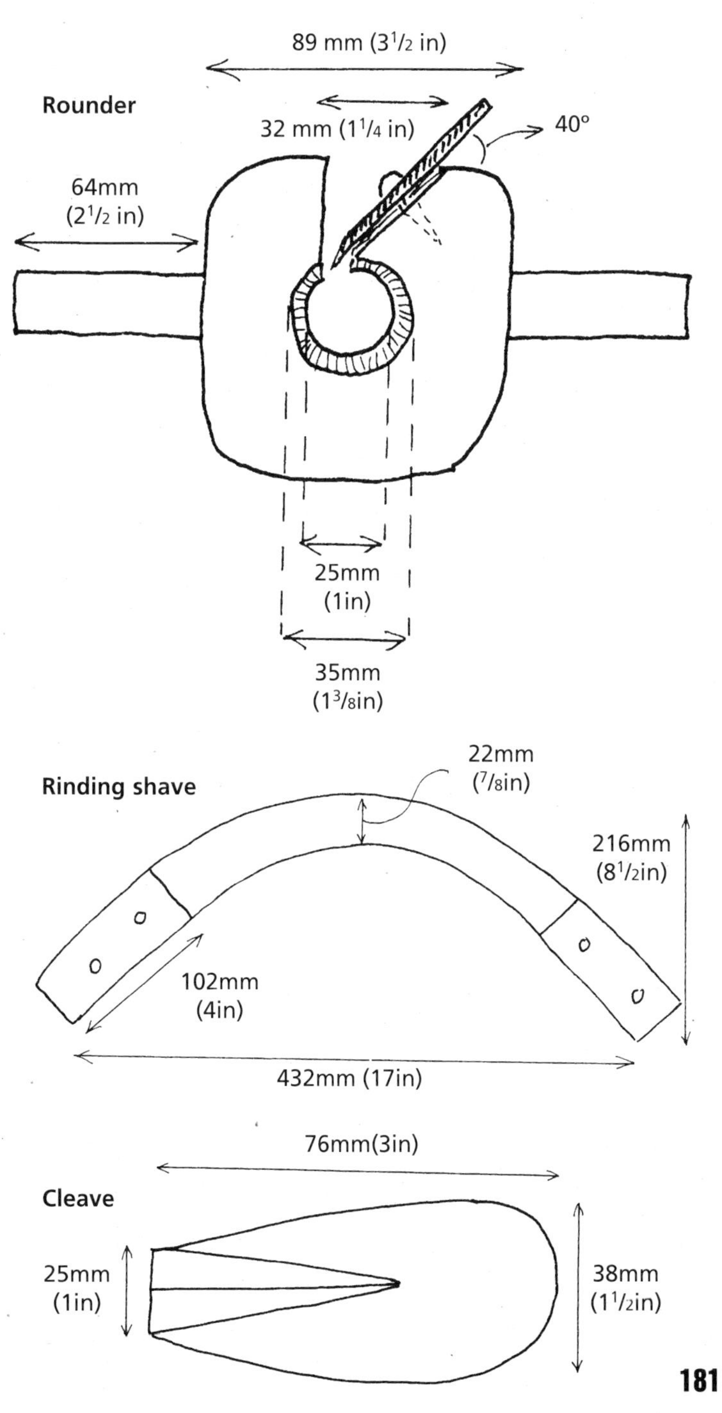

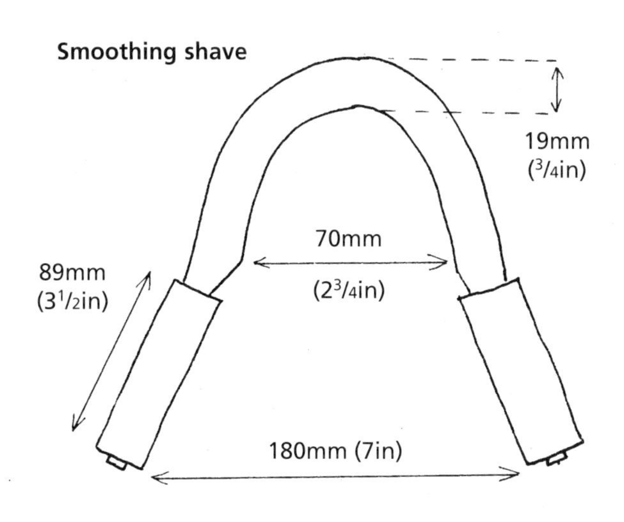

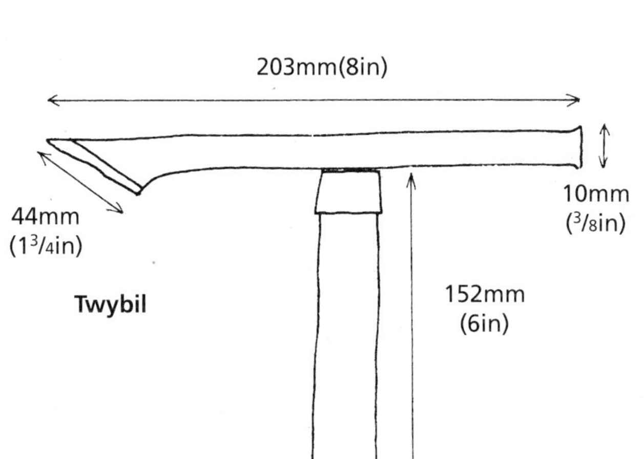

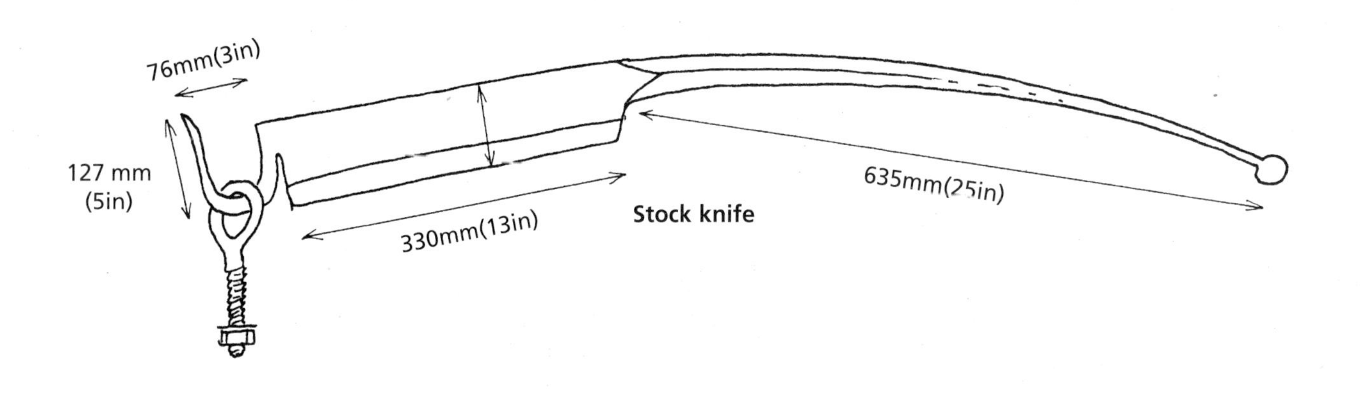
76mm(3in)
127 mm
(5in)
330mm(13in)
635mm(25in)
Stock knife

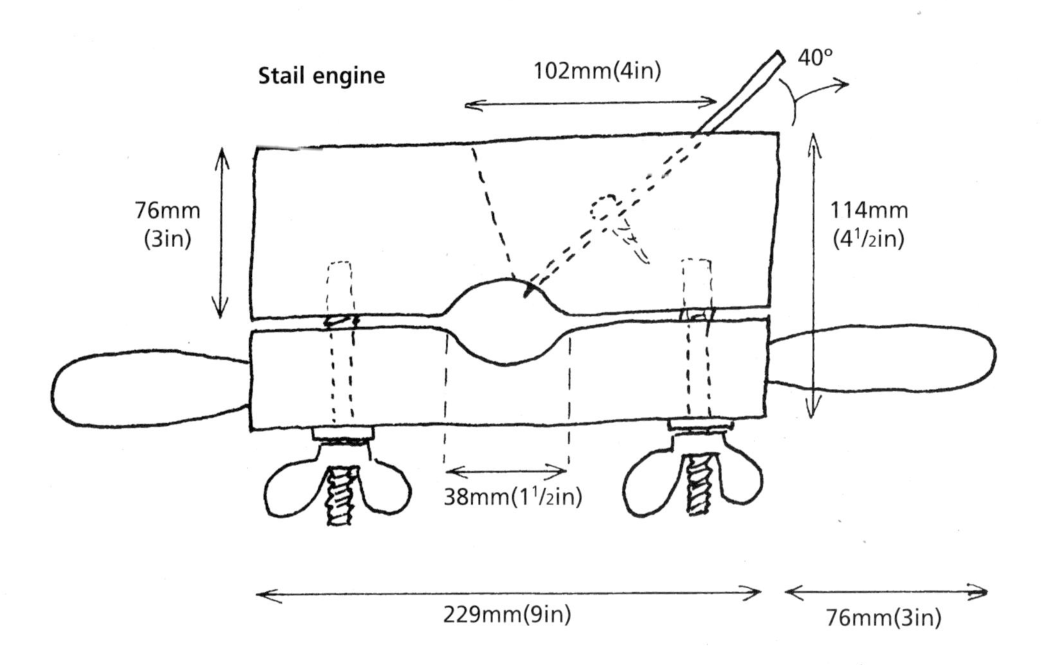
Stail engine
102mm(4in)
40°
76mm
(3in)
114mm
(4½in)
38mm(1½in)
229mm(9in)
76mm(3in)

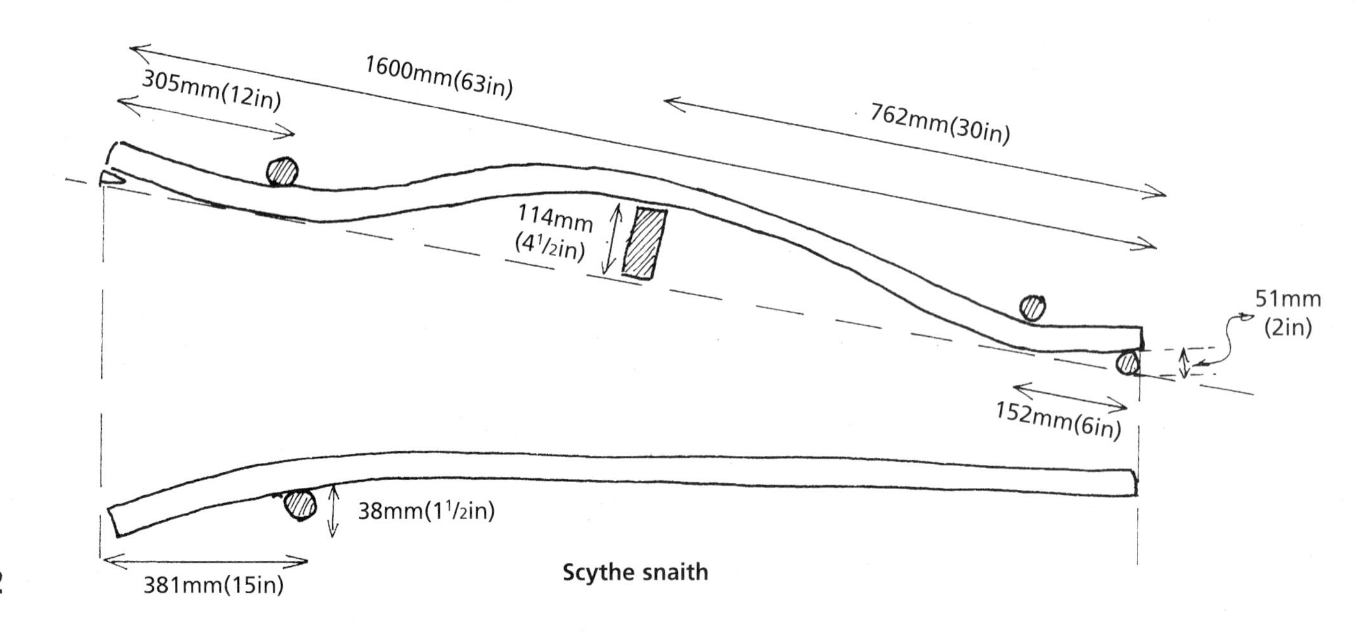
1600mm(63in)
305mm(12in)
762mm(30in)
114mm
(4½in)
51mm
(2in)
152mm(6in)
38mm(1½in)
381mm(15in)
Scythe snaith

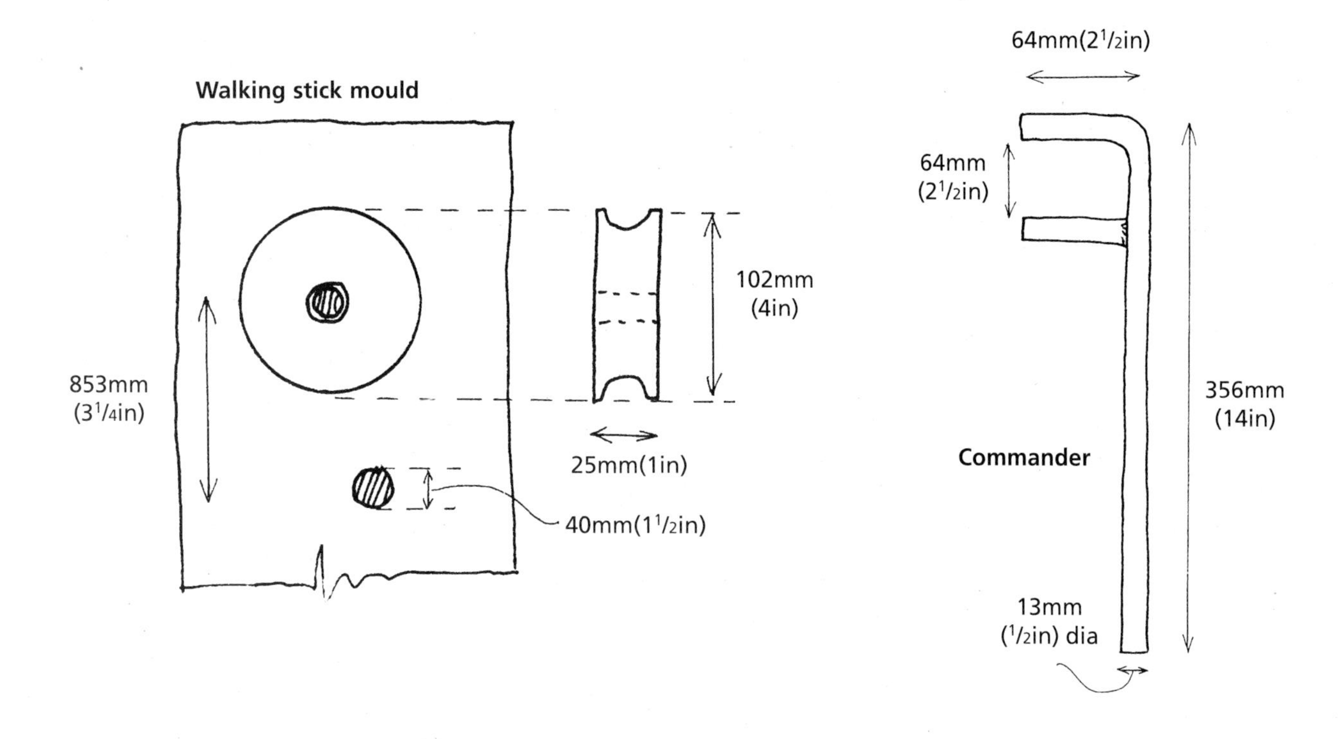
Walking stick mould
853mm
(3¼in)
102mm
(4in)
25mm(1in)
40mm(1½in)
64mm(2½in)
64mm
(2½in)
356mm
(14in)
Commander
13mm
(½in) dia

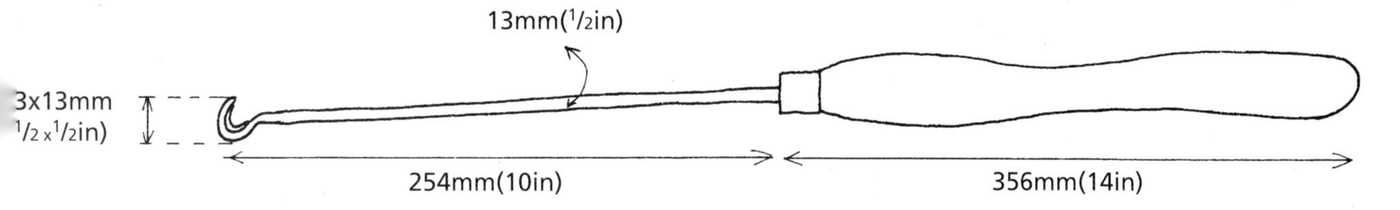
13mm(½in)
3x13mm
½x½in)
254mm(10in)
356mm(14in)
Hook chisel for bowl/platter turning

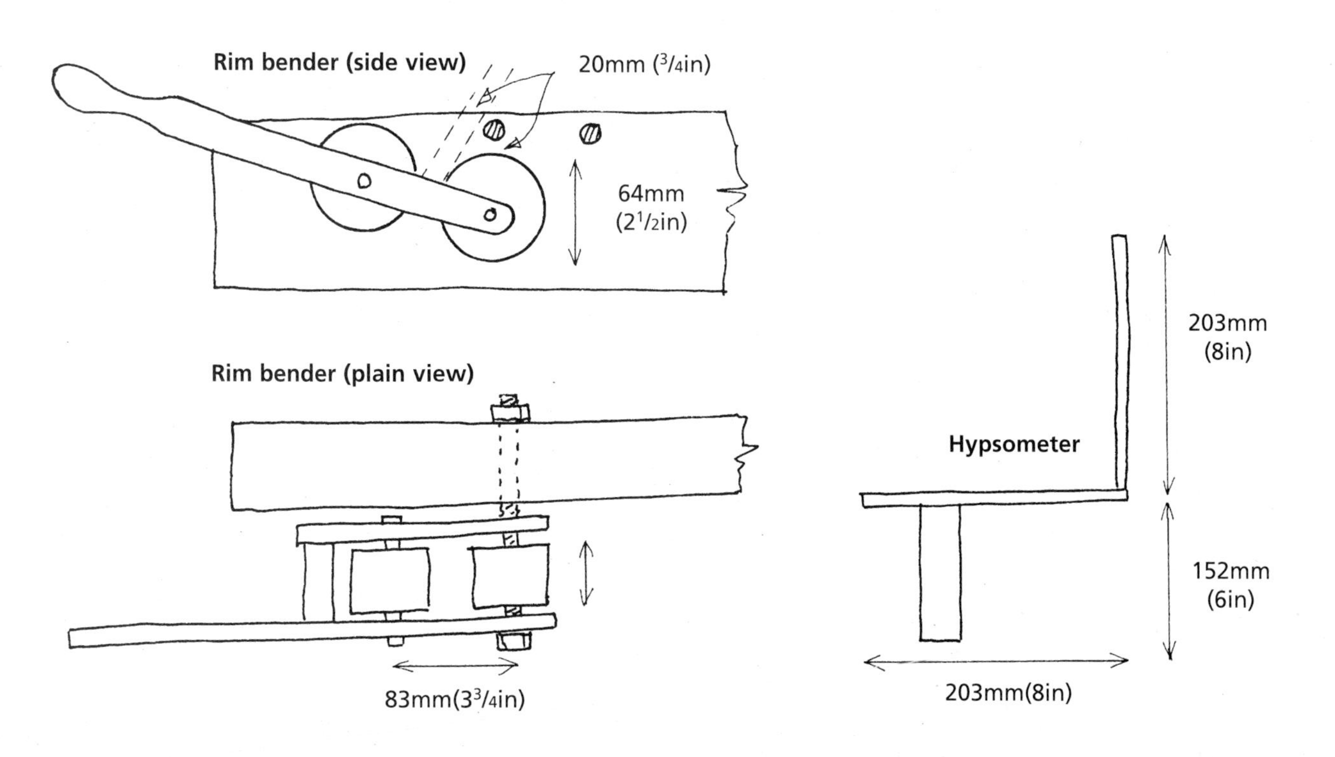
Rim bender (side view)
20mm (¾in)
64mm
(2½in)
Rim bender (plain view)
83mm(3¾in)
203mm
(8in)
Hypsometer
152mm
(6in)
203mm(8in)

Appendices 2

Marketing and Selling Your Produce

Instead of writing separately about selling each product, because there are so many local and regional variations it is better to deal with the topic generically. Every item described in this book can be sold, although some more profitably than others.

Make sure a market for traditional products exists in your area before you make any. Always keep an eye open for new ideas and use the techniques we have discussed to innovate; a really distinctive new idea will create its own market. Make sure your product quality meets your customer's expectations; you want repeat sales and the best advertising of all is recommendation. All of my biggest and best orders have come this way.

When you start selling there is an element of trial and error, but the latter can be reduced by judicious advertising. And I try never to refuse an order, even if I have to tell the customer it will be delayed or that I can only fulfil part of it immediately, or even if I have never made it before!

So here are some simple ideas that have worked for me:

Your Local Market: Traditionally most woodlands supplied their local village. This remains the best outlet for cheap products for you can sell direct to the user.

- Advertise in local village shops/post offices
- Contact local groups – scouts, guides, WI etc.
- Advertise in village/parish newsletters
- Sell at local fetes and markets
- Demonstrate at open days in local woodlands.

The Wider Market: Spread your wings by:

- Approaching garden centres and market gardens to stock or use your product
- Demonstrating and selling at regional craft fairs
- Selling to retailers (petrol stations often sell a lot of charcoal) and farm shops
- Approaching farmers and land owners direct
- Approaching local schools about product or demonstrations
- Approaching local newspapers or radio for a feature – this often works well
- Keeping in touch with potential big users – fascines for the Environment Agency for example
- Using the Internet. We may have a centuries-old craft but there is no harm in using modern technology. I have had enquiries from America about staves for Morris dancers!

Other Craftsmen: Another outlet for wood, if you have a surplus, is supplying other craftsmen. This can be done either directly via their Trade Association, or by advertising in a publication such as 'Woodlots'. I have sold material to

- Thatchers
- Furniture makers
- Willow craftsmen
- Wattle hurdle makers
- Rake makers
- Basket makers
- Firewood merchants
- Builders carrying out restoration

Above all keep your eye open for new outlets and new ideas – when it comes to selling, you can make your own luck.

Green Woodworking Glossary

Bagging hook: a sickle shaped hook, but thicker and stronger, for cutting undergrowth.
Bead: a raised decoration on a turned piece; usually curved.(*fig 15.1c*)
Beetle (Commander): a heavy wooden mallet or club.(*figs7.6b,7.7c*)
Besom: a broom consisting of a bundle of twigs tied to a wooden handle.(*fig 14.1*)
Blaze: mark made on a tree by removing a slice of bark.
Bodkin: a round tapered rod with a wooden handle used to open up a basket weave so a rod can be inserted.
Bole: the permanent trunk of a pollard or standard tree from ground to crown.
Bond (Lap): a very fine cleft of wood used to bind a bundle of twigs when making a besom. (*figs 11.30, 11.31, 14.4*)
Broche (Thatching spars, thatch peg): clefts of hazel or willow used by thatchers: to hold the thatch on a roof. (*fig 12.21*)
Bruzz: a 'V' shaped chisel; originally for cutting the corners of mortices, used by turners for some shaping.
Butt: the lowest portion (base) of a trunk or pole.
Cant: the area of a wood being felled in a particular year. (*fig 4.1*)
Caulked handle: a handle with a swelling at the end so the tool should not slip out of the hand. (*fig 6.1*)
Cleave (Bond splitter): an egg-shaped hard wood tool whose end is shaped to form three wedges and is used to make bonds (q.v.). (*figs 7.5, 11.15*)
Cleft: a segment of wood split from a round pole.(*fig 11.8*)
Commander: see Beetle. Also a metal tool for levering rods in order to bend them to shape. (*fig 18.16*)
Coppice: trees comprising a number of poles growing from a stool (q.v.) and which are cut close to ground level every few years; type of woodland managed to produce poles; the act of cutting poles from a stool.
Crate heads: stout clefts of wood that provide the rigid members in a crate. (*fig 18.14*)
Drifts: piles of rods from cut coppice laid in rows to be sorted. (*fig 4.2*)
Ethering rods (Binders): fine rods woven between stakes to hold the stems of a freshly laid hedge in place. (*fig 13.1*)
Fascine: a bundle of twigs c. 4m long mainly used to prevent coastal erosion. (*fig 12.17*)
Fipple (Nose bit): a shell (q.v.) bit (for a brace) which has a cutting lip which breaks up the core of wood produced by an ordinary shell bit; it is more efficient. Also used to describe the small piece of wood fitted into the end of a whistle to restrict the air flow. (*fig 18.10*)
Froe (Doll axe, riving iron, splitting knife): a tool with a wedge shaped blade and a handle at right angles to it used to split wood.(*fig 7.6*)
Glut: a wedge shaped from a round log. (*fig 7.4c*)
Harr: the strong vertical member of a field gate to which the hinges are fixed and from which the other members hang. (*figs 13.28, 13.30*)
Helve: an axe handle.
Kerf: the groove made by a saw.
Laps: see bonds.
Lug: a stout forked post used to support the boughs of fruit trees. (*fig 12.4*)
Motte peg: the central post around which the chimney of logs is formed in a charcoal clamp; it is removed before the burn commences. (*fig 12.20*)
Plashing: laying a young stem from a stool and pegging it to the ground to form a new tree. (*fig 4.8*)

Poll: the part of the head of an axe or adze opposite the cutting edge.
Pollard: a tree regularly cut back at c. 3m from the ground to produce a crop of poles out of reach of browsing animals. (*fig 4.4*)
Poppet: the tail stock of a lathe (or head and tail stock of a pole lathe) that carries the undriven centres on which the work piece rotates. (*fig 10.7*)
Prick up: using a knife to nick a rod so that it will bend to a right angle without breaking to produce the vertical side rods of a basket. (*fig 17.17*)
Progs: stout, forked stakes used for pushing and supporting jobs. (*fig 4.5*)
Rinding: to remove the bark from a pole.
Ringe (Slay): a stack of twiggy tops, such as pea sticks, often weighted down to keep it flat. (*fig 12.2*)
Rive: to split wood – afterwards called riven wood.
Riving brake: a device to assist in riving (splitting) poles. (*fig 8.19*)
Scarf: a long overlapping joint that does not increase the cross sectional area of the wood. (*figs 17.3, 17.6*)
Shingles: thin clefts of wood, like slates, used for roofing.(*figs 12.27, 12.28*)
Shrie: to remove the thorns from a bramble stem by pulling it through a gloved hand.
Slath: the base sticks of a basket opened out after being tied together by the first few rows of weaving. (*figs 17.31, 17.32*)
Slype: an angled cut at the end of a rod, or a curved cut thinning the middle of a rod in the slath (q.v.), both used during basket making.
Snaith: a scythe handle. (*fig 14.18*)
Sned: to trim the side branches from a pole.
Spalting: patterns created in dead wood by fungal invasion; often very attractive when turned.
Spelk (Spale, Swill): a spelk is a flat cleft of wood thin enough to be woven; spelk baskets are made from very thin sections of oak. (*fig 17.5*)
Spile: a name used in the southern counties for a cleft fencing stake.
Spoon (Shell) bit: a bit with a half cylindrical body with a sharpened nose. (*fig 7.8d*)
Spurtle: a short stick for stirring porridge. (*fig 15.20*)
Stail: a rake handle. (*fig 14.7*)
Stail engine: a rotary plane for shaping and smoothing rake handles. (*figs 6.13, 6.14*)
Stiles: the outer upright members of a piece of framing.
Stool: the base of a coppiced tree from which the shoots emerge.
Swayed: an axe handle shaped so the worker's hands are safely away from the trunk being shaped.
Sways and liggers: long clefts of small wood used by thatchers to decorate the ridges.
Swill: see spelk.
Taws: very thin cleft of oak used as weavers when making spelk baskets. (*fig 17.5*)
Tine: a wooden tooth for a hay rake.
Travisher: a chairmaker's shave. (*fig 6.12*)
Treen: a collection of domestic woodware, now replaced by metal or china.
Trenail: a corruption of tree-nail: a wooden pin, usually oak, used to secure joints in timber framing. (*fig 12.29b*)
Trug: a wooden basket made with thin strips of wood nailed to a frame. (*fig 17.1*)
Twilleying: a process where two round weavers (twilley rods) are woven at the same time between uprights to strengthen or straighten a basket or hurdle. (*fig 13.24a*)
Twybil (Morticing knife): corruption of two-bill: a tool with a cutting edge and a hooked arm used to make mortices. (*figs 6.15, 6.16*)
Upsett: the first few rows of weaving after the side rods of a basket are pricked up. (*fig 17.37*)
Waling: a basket weave using three or more weavers.(*figs 17.38, 17.39*)
Withe: a thin rod twisted and used for tying. (*figs 11.28, 11.29*)
Zales: the uprights in a wattle hurdle.

Useful Addresses

Tools and Books

Eco-logic Books – Mulberry House, 19 Maple Grove. Bath BA2 3AF. Telephone: 0117 942 0165

Ashem Crafts (Rounding tools) – 2 Oakleigh Avenue, Hallow, Worcs, WR2 6NG

Bryony Driver (Blacksmith) – 47 Kingston Road, Camberley, Surrey GU15 4AG

Woodland Craft Supplies (Books and tools) – Jon Warnes, Windsor's Cottage, Felixstowe Ferry, Felixstowe, Suffolk IP11 9RZ

Andrew Breese (Blacksmith) – Chalk Pits Forge, Chalk Pits Museum. Houghton Bridge, Amberley, West Sussex BN18 9LT

Alec Morris (Toolmakers) – The Iron Mills, Dunsford, Nr. Exeter, Devon.

Tool and Trade History Society – 60 Swanley Lane, Swanley, Kent BR8 7JG

The Tool Shop – Tony Murland. 78 High Street, Needham Market, Suffolk IP6 8AN

Roy Arnold (Books) – 77 High Street, Needham Market, Ipswich, Suffolk IP6 8AN

Craft Associations

Association of Pole Lathe Turners – Scullsgate Cottage, Benendon, Cranbrook, Kent TN17 ALE

Basket Makers Association – 37 Mendip Road, Cheltenham, Gloucestershire GL52 5EB

Coppice Association North West – c/o Cumbria Broadleaves, Rayrigg Meadow, Bowness on Windermere, Cumbria LA23 1BP

Sussex & Surrey Coppice Group – Robin Truscott, c/o Sussex Downs Conservation Board, Midhurst Depot, Bepton Road, Midhurst, W. Sussex GU29 9QX

British Stickmakers Guild – 104 Pakefield Street, Lowestoft, Suffolk NR33 OJS

British Charcoal Group – 72 Woodstock Road, Loxley, Sheffield S6 6TG

Kent Greenwood Directory Initiative – c/o Poulton Woodworks Greenwood Centre, Forge Hill, Aldington, Kent TN25 7DT

Berks, Bucks & Oxon Greenwood Network – c/o Graham McAll, 4 Warren Close, Langley, Slough, Berks SL3 7UA

Argyll Green Woodworkers – c/o Sean Trevarthen-Derby, 1 The Stables, Erines, By Tabert, Argyll PA29 6YL

Rural Development Commission – 141 Castle Street, Salisbury, Wiltshire SP1 3TP

Training

British Trust for Conservation Volunteers – 36 St. Mary's Street, Wallingford, Oxon OX19 OEU

Green Wood Trust – Station Road, Coalbrookdale, Telford, Shropshire TF8 7DR

Centre for Alternative Technology – Machynlleth, Powys SY20 9AZ

Mike Abbott – Greenwood Cottage, Bishops Frome, Herefordshire, via Worcester WR6 5AS

Gudrun Leitz – Hill Farm, Stanley Hill, Bosbury, Ledbury, Herefordshire HR8 1HE

Peter Lambert (Poulton Woodworks) – c/o Homelands, Forge Hill, Aldington, Kent TN25 7DT

School for Woodland Industries – Hooke Park, Parnham House, Beaminster, Dorset DT8 3NA

Woodland Organisations

National Small Wood Association – 3 Perkins Beach Dingle, Stiperstones, Shropshire SY5 OPF

Woodlots – Ecotech, Swaffham, Norfolk PE37 7HT

Woodland Trust – Autumn Park, Dysart Road, Grantham, Lincs NG31 6LL

Forestry Commission (also Forestry & Arboriculture Safety & Training Council) – 231 Corstorphine Road, Edinburgh EH12 7AT

National Trust – 36 Queen Anne's Gate, London SW1H 9AS

The Wildlife Trusts – The Kiln, Waterside, Mather Road, Newark NG24 1WT

Woodland Heritage – PO Box 2950, Epping CM16 7DG

Royal Forestry Society – 102 High Street, Tring, Hertfordshire HP23 4AF

Farming & Wildlife Advisory Group – National Agricultural Centre, Stoneleigh, Kenilworth, Warwickshire CV8 2RX

Index

eco-logic books is a small, ethically run company that specialises in publishing and distributing books and other material that promote practical solutions to environmental problems.

Those books that are still in print and mentioned in the Further Reading List plus many others are available from our comprehensive catalogue. Other topics covered in the catalogue include:

Gardening
Permaculture
Composting
Self Reliance
Food and related Issues
Keeping Hens and other Domestic Animals
Smallholding & Farming
Wildlife
Trees & Woodland Crafts
Forestry
Orchards and Fruit Growing
Community
Building & Construction
Alternative Energy
Urban Issues
Transport
Money and the Economy
Trade Skills
Sustainabilty
Radical Thinking
Managing for Change

To obtain a FREE mail order catalogue send a large s.a.e. or contact us at the address below :

eco-logic books
10 -12 Picton Street, Bristol BS6 5QA, England

Telephone: 0117 942 0165 Fax: 0117 942 0164 email: books@eco-logic.demon.co.uk